EAST WEST PERSPECTIVES ON 21ST CENTURY URBAN DEVELOPMENT

Details on the membership and activities of CIB are available from the following address:

CIB General Secretariat
Kruisplein 25-G
3014 DB Rotterdam
The Netherlands

Tel: +31 10 411 01 40
Fax: +31 10 433 43 72
e-mail: secretariat@cibworld.nl
http//www.cibworld.nl

East West Perspectives on 21st Century Urban Development

Sustainable Eastern and Western Cities in the New Millennium

Edited by

JOHN BROTCHIE
CSIRO
PETER NEWTON
CSIRO
PETER HALL
University of London
JOHN DICKEY
Virginia Polytechnic Institute

Ashgate

Aldershot • Brookfield USA • Singapore • Sydney

Published by
Ashgate Publishing Ltd
Gower House
Croft Road
Aldershot
Hants GU11 3HR
England

Ashgate Publishing Company
Old Post Road
Brookfield
Vermont 05036
USA

British Library Cataloguing in Publication Data
East West perspectives on 21st century urban development :
   sustainable eastern and western cities in the new
   Millennium
   1. Sociology, Urban 2. City planning 3. Cities and towns -
   Growth 4. East and West
   I. Brotchie, John
   307.7'6

Library of Congress Catalog Card Number: 98-74506

ISBN 1 84014 317 7

Printed in Great Britain

Contents

PART III: URBAN AND ENVIRONMENTAL AMENITY

PART IV: EAST WEST COMPARISONS

List of Contributors

Professor Sir Peter Hall, Bartlett School of Architecture and Planning, University College London, London, UK.

Professor Terry McGee, Director, Institute of Asian Research, Department of Geography, The University of British Columbia, Vancouver, Canada.

Professor Graeme Hugo, Department of Geography, University of Adelaide, Adelaide, South Australia.

Dr Michael Lindfield, Australian Housing and Urban Research Institute, Queensland University of Technology, Brisbane, Queensland, Australia.

Professor Robert Stimson, Australian Housing and Urban Research Institute, Department of Geographical Sciences and Planning, University of Queensland, Brisbane, Queensland, Australia.

Dr Ibu Budhy Tjahjati Soegijoko, Chair Urban and Regional Development Institute, Deputy Chair, Foreign Cooperation BAPPENAS, Jakarta Pusat, Indonesia.

Professor Kingsley Haynes, Institute of Public Policy, George Mason University, Fairfax, Virginia, USA.

Professor Roger Stough, Institute of Public Policy, George Mason University, Fairfax, Virginia, USA.

Professor Stephen Hamnett, School of Geoinformatics, Planning and Building, University of South Australia, Adelaide, South Australia.

Professor Michael Lennon, Regional and Urban Planning, University of Adelaide, South Australia.

Dr Reza Kazemian Department of Architecture And Town Planning, Royal Institute of Technology, Stockholm, Sweden, Waseda University, Graduate School of Social Sciences, Tokyo, Japan.

Professor Folke Snickars, Regional Planning Institute, Royal Institute of Technology, Stockholm, Sweden.

Professor Mamoru Taniguchi, Department of Environmental and Civil Engineering, Okayama University, Okayama, Japan.

Dr Peter Newton, Chief Research Scientist, CSIRO Building Construction and Engineering, Melbourne, and Associate Director, Australian Housing and Urban Research Institute, Melbourne, Australia.

Dr Peter Manins, CSIRO Division of Atmospheric Research, Aspendale, Victoria, Australia.

Dr Howard Dick, Department of Business Development and Corporate History, University of Melbourne, Parkville, Victoria, Australia.

Professor Peter Rimmer, Department of Human Geography, Research School of Pacific and Asian Studies, The Australian National University, Canberra, Australia.

Professor Peter Newman, Institute of Science and Technology Policy, Murdoch University, Murdoch, Western Australia.

Dr Jeff Kenworthy, Institute of Science and Technology Policy, Murdoch University, Murdoch, Western Australia.

Dr Felix Laube, Institute of Science and Technology Policy, Murdoch University, Murdoch, Western Australia.

Dr John Brotchie, CSIRO Building Construction and Engineering, Melbourne, Australia.

Dr Peter Gipps, CSIRO Building Construction and Engineering, Melbourne, Australia.

Dr David James, Director, Eco Services, Sydney, Australia.

Dr Don MacRae, Director, Plan Ecos, Canberra, Australia.

Mr Jeremy Morris, Director, Morris Consultants, Canberra, Australia.

Professor Gus Hooke, President, Australasian Institute, Sydney, Australia.

Professor John Dickey, Virginia Polytechnic Institute, Blacksburg, USA.

Preface

This is the fifth book in a series of international reports stemming from CIB W72, the Working Commission on Technological Change and Urban Form of the International Council for Building Research, CIB. The four earlier books—*The Future of Urban Form: The Impact of New Technology* (ed. Brotchie, Newton, Hall and Nijkamp, 1985); *The Spatial Impact of Technological Change* (ed. Brotchie, Hall and Newton, 1987); *Cities of the 21st Century: New Technologies and Spatial Systems* (eds Brotchie, Batty, Hall and Newton, 1991); and *Cities in Competition: Productive and Sustainable Cities for the 21st Century* (ed. Brotchie, Batty, Blakely, Hall and Newton, 1995)—all came out of meetings in the advanced western world—Canada, Australia, the UK and the USA. This fifth report marks a deliberate break: it results from a meeting held in Jakarta, Indonesia in June 1997, and it focuses on Pacific Asia, the most dynamic urban region in the world of the late 20th and early 21st centuries.

Established in the early 1980s, CIB W72 has had the opportunity of projecting and analysing the third great societal transition in the history of human settlement: the transition to an information-based economy—and its urban impacts—at a global, regional and city level. Each transition has had a major impact on human settlement.

The first, about five thousand years ago, was the shift from hunting and gathering to agriculture. It made possible permanent human settlements and the concentration of people into them for shelter and protection. Daily work was dispersed in the surrounding fields. Travel to work was largely by foot and the scale of settlements was contained accordingly.

The second transition, beginning just over two hundred years ago, was from agriculture to manufacturing. It resulted in a concentration of employment in the inner city, while the development of railways and tramways allowed the growth of the city in the form of suburbs along radial rail links; cities thus grew greatly in geographical scale. Later, the motor car allowed further expansion and infill between the rail lines. In particular, it allowed large-scale manufacturing industry to move to the urban fringe, where it could be serviced by road transport.

Our present transition, the third in human history, is proving to be the most profound of all. From the start of this transition, beginning some forty years ago, telecommunications and distributed commuting have allowed wider locational choice. Consumer services, including shopping, have moved to suburban centres and edge cities. Back offices of major companies have similarly moved to suburban centres with lower land prices and less congested roads and remain linked to their headquarters with new telecommunications systems. In consequence, cities again expanded, to begin to form vast metropolitan regions.

In the latest phase, a truly global information economy has begun to emerge, fuelled by:

- the growth of global telecommunications and fast transport networks;
- the convergence of previously—separate information and communication technologies;
- their further linking with transport and land use;
- the shift to information and knowledge as a resource base for new industries;
- the progressive breaking-down of national barriers to the movement of people and information;
- the emergence of cities as economic entities, network nodes, and centres for generating, exchanging and processing information;
- the growth of informational services, particularly finance and business services; and
- the competition among cities for these new key elements of the urban economy.

This last is particularly significant. As telecommunications converge with computing, there is an even wider spatial dispersal of activities, including globalisation of markets and of firms, the lowering of national barriers, and increasing competition between cities and regions for the production of goods and services. In advanced countries, there has been a shift of employment from manufacturing to services, as manufacturing has been outsourced in far-distant plants in emerging industrial nations—above all in Eastern Asia. Conversely, and by way of compensation, older-established cities in advanced countries have attracted new industries, particularly information-based activities. They act as a magnet for producer services—financial services, design services, media services—which not only serve local clients but increasingly act as footloose, export-oriented activities, operating from selected global cities which form the nodes of worldwide information networks. Acting as innovative milieux, and aided by the amenities and urban ambience, they attract a host of small, new, highly-innovative firms in a range of activities that span traditional manufacturing and producer services—particularly in the design and media-based industries, which increasingly depend on very sophisticated and specialised computer-based technologies.

These societal transitions have affected cities in very different ways, depending on their suitability—in terms of location and resources—to meet the needs of the new technologies. Many cities, which were once key regional centres in the agricultural economy, were bypassed in the industrial era by other centres closer to energy and material resources for manufacturing industry. But now many of them are experiencing a comeback, as their more pleasant environments have proven attractive to information and knowledge-based activities. Cambridge, Montpellier and Munich are examples. The major global cities—New York, Paris, London, Tokyo—have often suffered big losses in traditional manufacturing and goods-handling activities, but have continued to prosper through their key role as global network nodes and service and market cities.

Further changes are also underway. In western cities, information technology is continuing to replace labour through automation of routine and increasingly non-routine manufacturing tasks, allowing some manufacturing industries, such as motor car production, involving larger or heavier products, to be retained in western cities, with potential for new manufacturing industries to be established as automation capabilities increase. At the same time, the globalisation of markets, including finance and business services has seen the export of these services to major centres in the eastern world—and the creation of supplementary local services to support manufacturing and resource development. In this way, eastern cities are in rapid transition to industrial- and also information-based economies, while western cities are retaining some manufacturing as automation increasingly replaces expensive labour, with the prospect that this manufacturing also may increase with further advances and cost reductions in information technology and automation.

The present transition is by far the fastest and most comprehensive in world history, whether in spatial, technological, economic, social and urban development terms. And nowhere is its impact bigger and more momentous than in Pacific Asia. In particular, two aspects acting simultaneously—the outsourcing of large-scale high-technology manufacturing from the older industrial nations, and the development of new global information hubs—are creating a new urban phenomenon: the mega-city, a super-agglomeration numbering tens of millions of people and embracing between twenty and thirty separate cities and towns, sometimes indeed extending right across international frontiers but forming in effect a single functional city region. Such mega-cities pose acute problems of urban organization and planning; not least securing their development in ways that are sustainable and equitable. The present economic crisis in the east Asian region can only add to these problems in the short to medium term. Hopefully it will also provide the opportunity as well as the necessity to improve the transparency, efficiency and equity of the development process.

Acknowledgment

The workshop was sponsored by CSURD, the Joint Centre for Sustainable Urban and Regional Development, Jakarta, a partnership of the University of Indonesia, CSIRO and the University of Melbourne, with support from governments and industry—under a Memorandum of Understanding on Housing and Urban Development between the governments of Australia and Indonesia.

PART I

THE RISE OF

ASIAN MEGA-CITIES

1 Planning for the Mega-City: A New Eastern Asian Urban Form?

PETER HALL

There is, many observers believe, a new urban form appearing on the western side of the Pacific Rim: the mega-city, a vast urban agglomeration numbering perhaps 30 or 40 million people, living and working in a great variety of urban places ranging from giant cities down to semi-urban villages, but tied together by huge flows of people, goods and information. Writing about the Pearl River Delta, the journalist Dejan Sudjic describes it as '... the world's newest metropolis—a sprawling monster city still in the throes of a violent birth, that doesn't yet have a name' (Sudjic, 1995, 27). But he identifies it as the wave of the future:

> This nameless conurbation—its only close competitors are Shanghai and Jakarta—is exploding towards what has become the benchmark population for a new generation of turbo-charged metropolises. Within a decade—if it continues at its present rate—it will be home to 40 million people, leapfrogging Mexico City and Tokyo-Osaka to become the largest in the world (Sudjic, 1995, 30).

The Asia Pacific region is not, of course, alone in generating mega-metropolitan agglomerations. Indeed, the population of any mega-city very much depends on the precise definition used; difficult enough for the average monocentric city, it is almost impossibly difficult for such a complex phenomenon as this. What is certain is that the mega-city phenomenon is increasingly associated with the rapidly growing middle-income countries of Eastern Asia and Latin America. In the last two decades, less developed countries (LDC) have experienced an unprecedented growth of urbanisation: by 1990, 61 percent of the world urban population lived in these developing nations and it is projected that by 2025 this will rise to about 75 percent (Sit and Yang, 1997, 646-7). In 1950 Greater London numbered just over 10 million and New York 12

3

million. By 1994 the top cities were Tokyo with 27 million, New York and São Paulo with 16 million, Mexico City with 15 million, Shanghai with 14 million, and Bombay with 13 million. By 2015 the order is expected to be Tokyo 28 million, Bombay 27 million, Lagos 24 million, Shanghai 23 million, Jakarta 21 million, and São Paulo 20 million (Parker, 1995, 5).

The Asian Development Bank's annual report, published in April 1997, forecast that by the year 2025 Asia will have 20 cities with populations of more than 10 million; double the number in 1997. Currently there are nine 'mega-cities' with more than 10 million inhabitants in the region: Beijing, Bombay, Calcutta, Jakarta, Osaka, Seoul, Shanghai, Tianjin and Tokyo. They will shortly be joined by Bangkok, Dhaka, Karachi and Manila. By 2025 even Rangoon will be included, as well as Lahore, Hyderabad, Bangalore and Madras in India, and Shenyang in China (Montagnon, 1997, n.p.).

However, such comparisons are based exclusively on sheer population size. The critical consideration has to be the functional roles performed by these cities within an increasingly globalised economy. Much recent work on this topic suggests that a relatively few cities stand at the apex of the global economy, in the sense that they exercise a commanding and controlling function through their concentration of finance and specialised business services.

Table 1.1 The world's largest metropolitan areas

		1992	2000
1.	Tokyo	25.8	28.0
2.	São Paulo	19.2	22.6
3.	New York City	16.2	16.6
4.	Mexico City	15.3	16.2
5.	Shanghai	14.1	17.4
6.	Bombay	13.3	18.1
7.	Los Angeles	11.9	13.2
8.	Buenos Aires	11.8	12.8
9.	Seoul	11.6	13.0
10.	Beijing	11.4	14.4
11.	Rio de Janeiro	11.3	12.2
12.	Calcutta	11.1	12.7
13.	Jakarta	10.0	13.4

Source: Anon, 1993, 36, based on United Nations Population Division

A recent analysis by John Short and his colleagues shows the degree to which Tokyo, in particular, was tending to dominate these global command and control functions. It shows that in 1995, in terms of the head office location of the largest banks ranked by assets, the order was Tokyo 16, Paris 8, Frankfurt 6, New York 5 and London 5, and Osaka, Brussels and Beijing 4 each; in terms of market value of stock exchanges, the order in 1992 was New York $3888 bn., Tokyo $2321 bn., London $933 bn., Paris $328 bn., Frankfurt $321 bn.; in terms of headquarters of the top 50 foreign banks (in terms of assets in 1994) in the USA, the order was Tokyo 14, Paris 6, Osaka 4, Toronto and London 3; in terms of headquarters of the world's largest industrial corporations in 1993, the order was Tokyo 17, New York 6, London 5, Chicago and Seoul 4 and Osaka 4, Paris and San Francisco and Munich 3 (Short *et al.*, 1996, 701-5). Only in terms of international air passengers does the picture look different: in 1992, the order was London 1, Paris 2, Frankfurt 3, Hong Kong 4, New York 5, Tokyo 6 (Short *et al.*, 1996, 708).

Tokyo has 90 percent of foreign companies located in Japan, and between 70 and 80 percent of all financial transactions take place there; 60 percent of information workers—in television, newspapers, other media, computer specialists, major advertising agencies—work there. And 40 percent of Japanese university students are concentrated here, despite government efforts to decentralise higher education since the 1960s (Honjo, 1991, 6). Now, outer cities like Yokohama, are growing and are performing a wider range of functions, leading to a new division of labour (Honjo, 1991, 6).

Within Asia, Tokyo is the pre-eminent global city with 79 Fortune 500 headquarters, the second Stock Exchange in terms of market capitalisation, and a concentration of headquarters of foreign companies. Hong Kong and Singapore have grown as financial centres, transport nodes for air and sea, and providers of advanced services. Between 1969 and 1990 the balance sheet of Hong Kong banks rose 263 times and customer deposits soared 100 times (Yeung, 1996, 26).

Interestingly, the picture appears very different in terms of major public international government and non-government organisations (IGOs and NGOs). An analysis shows that Paris ranks highest with 866 entries, followed by Brussels 862, London 495, Rome 445 and Geneva 397. Eight of the top 10, 12 of the top 15 are in Europe. Tokyo comes at 20th position. The top 25 include 20 major international financial centres (Knight, 1989, 41). The picture is very similar for international conventions. In 1982-86, Paris and London retained first and second rank respectively; Geneva was at third place, Brussels 4th, Madrid 5th; 9 of the top 10 were European, with Singapore 8th (up from 14 in 1982); 14 of the top 20 are European (Gappert, 1989, 323). This rather powerfully supports the recent conclusion of a study comparing London, Paris, New York and Tokyo, which found that the concentration of high-level service functions in Tokyo reflected not so much an international orientation as the strength of the Japanese economy and Tokyo's dominant position within it (Government Office for London, 1996).

If Tokyo is marginal in this regard, other Asian cities like Beijing, Shanghai and Calcutta do not yet qualify as global cities. Yue-man Yeung concludes that Tokyo, Seoul, Taipei, Hong Kong, Manila, Bangkok, Kuala Lumpur, Singapore and Jakarta do qualify. They are networked in a functional system built around transportation, telecommunications, finance, production services and others; and they perform at least four global roles, personal services, goods and commodity transactions, information flows, and financial services. Their importance is measured by the functions they perform as control and management centres in the global economy: headquarters of transnational corporations and providers of advanced services such as banking, insurance, management consulting, engineering, advertising services, accounting and the like (Yeung, 1996, 25-6). But there is intense inter-city competition: three researchers—David Barkin, Garry Hack and Roger Simmonds—who studied 12 city regions in Europe, Asia and the Americas, all large but not necessarily mega-cities, showed that Bangkok, Taipei and Tokyo are working hard to become financial centres for Asia, betting on the demise of Hong Kong as a substantial competitor (Anon, 1996, 4).

Fu-Chen Lo finds the Eastern Asia cities constituting a distinct new development within the global economy and the accompanying world city system, which now has three elements: Group One, *debt and dependency*, characterises Latin American and African cities that have huge problems in financing structural adjustment and infrastructure provision, compounded by stagnation in basic commodity prices; Group Two, *blue collar and services*, represents Europe and North America, and is characterised by industrial decline and the growth of information processing and service industries; Group Three, *the World's New Growth Corridor*, comprises eastern and south-eastern Asian cities characterised by phenomenal expansion of their share in world trade and production: 'A network of Asian cities is expected to form a new growth corridor in the world city system', coinciding with a fifth Kondriatiff revolution (Lo, 1991, 11).

The Mega-City: A New Urban Form?

But what remains uncertain is precisely what form these vast agglomerations of people and activity are taking. The expression 'mega-city' recalls the earlier term coined by Jean Gottmann in his 1961 book, *Megalopolis*. But there is a rather subtle distinction. As defined by Gottmann in his celebrated 1961 study of the Boston-to-Washington corridor, Megalopolis was:

A remarkable development—an almost continuous stretch of urban and suburban areas from southern New Hampshire to northern Virginia and from the Atlantic shore to the Appalachian foothills ... No other section of the United States has such a large concentration of population, and such a high average density, spread over such a large area (Gottmann, 1961, 3).

That suggested a physical definition: Megalopolis was a continuously urbanised area, in the sense of continuous building. But later, Gottmann made it clear that he meant something different: Megalopolis was 'the cradle of a new order in the organisation of inhabited space', defined in terms of Standard Metropolitan Statistical Areas, in other words a *functional* definition; relatively little of the space may be developed physically. Thus, in an Anglo-American comparison of urbanisation patterns around 1970, only 17 percent of the Boston-Washington 'Megalopolis', and 26 percent of the corresponding 'Megalopolis England', had population densities characteristic of urban areas; in the British case, a few years earlier, less than 18 percent was physically developed (Clawson and Hall, 1973).

A better criterion is that the different parts of such vast and complex urban regions is a *functional* one: that they have common linkages with the nearest city, in terms of commuting to work, education, shopping, entertainment and culture, and services. On such criteria as these, urban geographers—first in the United States, later in Europe and Japan and elsewhere—have defined the notion of a Functional Urban Region, or Daily Urban System, or Metropolitan Statistical Area: the terminologies differ, but the organising principle is the same.

However, there is an increasing complication: that people appear indifferent as to which cities they relate to; and that the metropolitan cores lose their significance, as all kinds of activities relocate on the metropolitan periphery. As American geographers were the first to realise in the late 1960s, the regional shopping centre and the campus office park spell the death of the traditional concept of the Metropolitan Area, which was based on the notion of a single urban core. And if it is difficult enough to define a Metropolitan Area, it is even more difficult to grasp what meaning attaches to the term Megalopolis or Mega-City; we are talking not of the citizens that are thus linked to one city, but to a much larger number of people linked to many such cities, who may have little in common.

The study of major world urban regions by Barkin, Hack and Simmonds showed that all had decentralised radially under the influence of rising car ownership, most strikingly in Taipei where automobiles increased from 11,000 in 1960 to over one million in 1990 (Anon, 1996, 3). All are sprawling, but Tokyo and Taipei remain quite centralised, the first because of mountain barriers, the second because of the legendary rail system (Anon, 1996, 4). New towns or science cities are being developed on the edges of Taipei, Tokyo and Jakarta (Anon, 1996, 4).

However, Eastern Asian mega-cities seem to demonstrate at least four distinctive features.

1.   *Transnational   growth   triangles*   harnessing   different   factor endowments: Hong Kong-Southern China and Singapore-Johore-Riau Islands, a new mode of transnational development geared to the world market and global economic processes.   These global cities increasingly export capital and expertise—Goldstar, Samsung, Singapore Airlines, Hong Kong Bank (Yeung, 1996, 26-7). There has thus been a dramatic rise in *Foreign Direct Investment (FDI)*, from 30 to 75 percent of all capital inflows into less developed countries (LDCs), between 1980-85 and 1986-90; in this latter period the annual rate of FDI inflow was about twice as fast as their GDP growth rate. China has been exceptionally successful after its 1978 policy reversal: in 1993 it became the second-largest FDI recipient after the USA, and the largest among LDCs. By end-1995, foreign-invested enterprises numbered 120,000 and they employed 16 million people; of the world's 500 largest corporations, all 500 have invested in China (Sit and Yang, 1997, 648). In the Pearl River Delta, FDI share rose from 7 percent in 1979-80 to 35.5 percent 1990-93 (Sit and Yang, 1997, 648). 'Without doubt, China has become the most important FDI host among the LDCs, and, within it, the Delta is the region with the highest intensity of FDI' (Sit and Yang, 1997, 648).

2.   *Exo-urbanisation:* The effect has been a new form of urban development described for the Pearl River Delta by Victor Sit and Chun Yang:

In this most 'open' area of China a new pattern of exo(genous)-urbanisation has emerged, as distinct from the endo(genous)-urbanisation ((or urbanisation driven entirely by intra-national or regional forces) which existed in the pre-1978 period in the PRC and which is still prevalent in most parts of the country. This foreign-investment-induced exo(genous)-urbanisation is characterised by labour-intensive and assembly manufacturing types of export-oriented industrialisation based on the low-cost input of large quantities of labour and land (Sit and Yang, 1997, 649).

'Spatially', they write, 'it has promoted the growth of small places and rural areas whose economies are increasingly integrated with the world economic circuitry through the regional coordinating centre, Hong Kong' (Sit and Yang, 1997, 650).

3. *Desakota:* The third is in turn associated: as Terence McGee argues, the Asian mega-city constitutes a basically new urban form, without previous parallels. He writes that 'Very different sets of conditions are operating in Asia today than those which occurred in the Western industrialised societies in the 19th and 20th centuries' (McGee, 1991, 9). One feature is that about 20-30 percent of rural workers in Asia are non-farm in terms of income, and are essentially employed in manufacturing (McGee, 1991, 9). In the land stretching along the linear corridors between large city cores, there is an intense mixture of agricultural and non-agricultural activities, to which McGee gives the coined Indonesian term *desakota*, from *desa*, village, and *kota*, town. In them, cheap transport, especially two-stroke motorbikes, buses and trucks, make it easy to commute and move goods. So these zones 'tend to have an intense mixture of land-use with agriculture, cottage-industry, industrial estates, suburban development and other uses side by side' (McGee, 1991, 9). This is positive in providing jobs, especially for women, but negative in destroying agricultural land; they are, however, productive, catalytic regions for economic growth; 'The challenge to urban planners is how to take advantage of the positive aspects of these new sorts of urban rings, while controlling their negative ones' (McGee, 1991, 9). McGee may exaggerate the uniqueness of Asia here; some similar features were found in European countries, for instance in southern Germany, during the rapid industrialisation of the 1950s. But the pattern may be more pervasive in Asia in the 1990s.

4. *Urban Megaprojects:* Other cities of the world have urban mega-projects, and indeed the most characteristic and most famous are found in Europe and North America: La Défense (almost certainly the original

megaproject, dating from the late 1950s), London Docklands, the World Finance Centre and Toronto's Harbourplace.   But in the last ten years, a disproportionate number of them have been found around the Pacific Rim—to such a degree, that they emerge as a key feature of the new Eastern Asian urban form.

Urban Mega-projects (UMPs), as Kris Olds defines them, are

> ... large-scale (re-)development projects composed of a mix of commercial, residential, retail, industrial, leisure, and infrastructure uses.   They are developed primarily in the inner city, on large tracts of former port, railway, industrial, military, or racetrack lands, or on 'underutilized' suburban, agricultural, swamp, or island land within the extended metropolitan region (Olds, 1995, 1713).

Olds identified over three dozen UMPs in the course of development in Europe, North America, Asia and Australia.   They borrow heavily from each other, for they are invariably developed by professionals who have previous such experience, indeed often developed explicitly for internationalisation strategies, and are marketed to overseas firms and rich individuals for lease or purchase they are designed to symbolise a 21ˢᵗ century global 'utopia'.   They are particularly associated with the globalisation of property markets, as investors seek to diversify their holdings, and the rise of the transnational firms including professional organisations like chartered surveyors and architects (Olds, 1995, 1713, 1717).

UMPs are especially common in the Pacific Rim because of rapid urban growth and the increasing importance of cities in this region, coupled with rapid economic restructuring.   Here and in North America and Australia they include major development of seaports and airports;   high-technology office districts, including teleports, often acting as functional nodes in far-stretching development corridors which facilitate the movement of goods, people and information; and linked luxury residential districts for the capitalist elite (Olds, 1995, 1720-1).

Olds lists 18 Pacific Rim UMPs, two in Canada (Vancouver), one in the USA (Mission Bay), four in Australia (Sydney, two in Melbourne, one in Adelaide), one in Singapore, two in Malaysia (Johor Baru and KL), one in the Philippines (Manila), one in Thailand (Bangkok), one in China (Lujiazui), and five in Japan (Tokyo, Yokohama and three in Osaka) (Olds, 1995, 1721); oddly, she excludes the SEZs.

She studies three in detail.   One in Canada, Pacific Place in Vancouver, is interesting because the development company's shareholders are Hong Kong billionaires, notably Hong Kong's richest man, Li ka-Shing; a key role is played by his son Victor, a typical international figure who tells people his home is Cathay Pacific Seat 1A (Olds, 1995, 1723-5). Minato Mirai 21 in Yokohama, 'the new port city for the 21st century', results from a long process of restructuring of port activities that led to job losses, while city centre land values boomed due to speculation. The project is built on 110 ha of waterfront and 76 ha of landfill; it is based on an international cultural centre, active around the clock; an information city of the 21st century; and a human environment surrounded by water, greenery and history. Its heart is the Communications Centre, designed to give corporations and government access to international fibre-optic networks and ISDN, plus visual interaction. The aim is to provide 'centralised international market information services' appealing to global financial institutions, insurance companies, software development firms and the like; there is also the world's largest international convention centre and hotel. The daytime population will reach 190,000 by 2000, but only 10,000 people will live here, a matter of local concern because of the housing shortage (Olds, 1995, 1726-8).

Shanghai's Lujiazui Central Area was developed by 'developmentally oriented technocrats' in the Shanghai leadership, and it was an open coastal city from 1985. Mayor Zhu Ronji became the PRC's Vice Premier in 1991, which helped. The Pudong Development Area was launched in 1988 and officially designated in 1990; it is a 350 km² area to the east of the Huangpu River, comprising farmland, low-density industry and residential areas; it will be transformed in three stages to a free-trade zone, and export-processing zone and a financial services centre. The Lujiazui-Huamu District, opposite the CBD, will become the city's new business, trade and financial centre by the year 2000. Further out there will be high-technology districts. At least ten major infrastructure projects, including two bridges financed by the Asia Development Bank, a subway, rail lines and tunnels, are in various stages of construction. Even the first stage was estimated in 1991 to cost US $10 billion, and a minimum of US$70-80 billion is forecast for the whole project over 30-40 years. Money is coming from the Asia Development Bank, World Bank and Chinese government as well as from foreign investors, especially from Hong Kong, attracted by a package of incentives; VW and Hewlett-Packard are here, and dozens of Japanese missions have visited. The cental zone of 28 km² is being planned by the city, who were very influenced by a 1991 tour to La Défense; Zhu likes 'foreign monks'. Four foreign expert teams offered advice, but the Rogers-Arup partnership have been most influential, doubtless mainly because of their extensive international experience. The huge scheme includes over 2.65 m² of office space, 300,000 m² of luxury housing and 500,000 m² of hotel space. The decision processes proved very opaque to the foreigners, with plans constantly being changed. However, by 1994 virtually all the land in the core was leased, and speculative capital was financing 1.69 m² of space (Olds, 1995, 1729-34).

In summary, Olds notes that Vancouver's Pacific Place is financed by private equity generated by TNCs based in Hong Kong which benefited from the boom there, and have close links with Canada. Yokohama's MM21 is being built by a public-private partnership including some of Japan's largest TNCs. Shanghai's Lujiazui's Central Area project draws on the knowledge of a 'global intelligence corps' as the state seeks to create a functional and symbolic space for the international firms which are flooding into China in the 1990s; 90-storey buildings are financed by speculative capital, mainly from Hong Kong, supported at all levels of the state and by multilateral institutions like the Asia Development Bank. All three, developed on waterfront land in former industrial or port districts, 'are being structured by the agents of contemporary globalisation processes—a small epistemic community of professional elites with a comprehensive knowledge base and understanding of current and future trends in the design and commodification of built space for the global stage' (Olds, 1995, 1735).

There is a particular kind of planning behind this form of development, and it seems to be cultural in origin. The underlying belief is that developments in information technology require the restructuring of the city around intelligent building complexes connected by huge advanced telecommunications infrastructures. Japan was in the forefront here: its National Land Agency in 1985 foresaw using the NTT information network (INS) linking telecommunications and computers, which were expected to spread rapidly together with Community Antenna Television evolving into a pay-TV system. These ideas were incorporated into the Ministry of Posts and Telecommunications 1987 plan for 'Teletopias', which were to be further aided in 1995 by the introduction of ISDN (Rimmer, 1991, 245-6).

In the metropolitan area, a critical element would be the teleport, a ground base for handling expanding international and domestic satellite communications in an intelligent building, and also to LANs; it is expected to attract heavy users of telecommunications such as financial institutions, insurance companies, software development firms and information processing services. This teleport is associated with the large city's international information exchange centre. In turn, this is close to the heart of the city which has both office automation and LAN. It is connected by a trunk fibre-optic system to other metropolitan cores and to other parts of the city, containing residential areas with cable television, 'research and educational cities' with cable instruction, and new towns with a home cable television network and community information centre, and a satellite office (Rimmer, 1991, 251-2).

Mitsubishi in 1985 identified two major corridor areas where such information technologies might be created: Hong Kong-Guangzhou-Taipei-Seoul, and Chiang Mai-Bangkok-Penang-Kuala Lumpur-Singapore-Jakarta-Bali. The Chinese strategy developed by former general Secretary Zhao Ziyang was based on telecommunications galvanising small and dispersed enterprises into efficient production groups, with Guangzhou and Shanghai spearheading the process (Rimmer, 1991, 253-4). These ideas explain a great deal of what has actually been happening in eastern Asia mega-cities in the past decade.

Rimmer concluded that:

> Irrespective of the design chosen, the proposals on new hubs—technopolis or MFP—have driven home to people in eastern China, south-east Asia and Australia that urban and regional transport-telecommunications-land use developments within their major corridors must be seen in a western Pacific context. Above all, they must be aware of planning trends in Japan and the way in which cities are being packaged for export (Rimmer, 1991, 259).

A New Form of Economic Development?

All this suggests that the Asian mega-city is not only a new urban form but that it is the spatial expression of a new form of economic development on a transnational scale. Manuel Castells, in a penetrating comparison, argues that all four Asian Tigers are true developmental states in the classic sense originally coined by Chalmers Johnson, but that this is a state that 'establishes as its principle of legitimacy its ability to promote and sustain development, understanding by development the combination of steady high rates of economic growth and structural change in the productive system, both domestically and in its relationship to the international economy' (Castells, 1992, 56).

This specifically does not imply legitimacy to civil society in the western sense; these states are more like revolutionary states which represented avant-gardes of classes and nations not yet fully aware of their destiny and interests, but they are different in that they respect the broad parameters of social order while aiming at a fundamental transformation of the economic order. Generally such a project takes the form of building or rebuilding of national identity. Economic development was thus not a goal in itself but a means of surviving as a state and a society, and of breaking away from dependency. 'Survival came first' and this was in a situation when the outside world appeared threatening, as it did for all these countries at first (Castells, 1992, 57-8). They all starred in the Asian Cold War and were indirectly protected by the United States or Britain even while they sought independence (Castells, 1992, 63).

All these Tigers constructed an efficient, technocratic state apparatus—though this did not necessarily mean incorrupt, since corruption could be functional (Castells, 1992, 63-4). But 'the fundamental element in the ability of developmental states to fulfil their project was their political capacity to impose and internalise their logic on the civil societies' (Castells, 1992, 64). They did so both by repression and by making the dominant classes subservient, destroying them or making them subordinate, with the partial exception of Hong Kong (Castells, 1992, 65). However, in the process they transformed the society: 'The success of the developmental states in East Asia ultimately leads to the demise of their apparatuses and to the fading of their messianic dreams' (Castells, 1992, 66).

This explains what these states sought to achieve. However, the precise mode of operation was subtly different in each case. In some ways the exception was Korea, since growth was driven by the vast conglomerates or *chaebol*. In the other three cases, which all happened to be Chinese, there was a much greater reliance on intense networking of small (often very small) and medium enterprises, which was favoured by a metropolitan location and, in turn, favoured the growth of the metropolitan complex. And this, significantly, resembles the pattern in the original Asian mega-city, Tokyo.

Tokyo's Keihin Region : Prototype Asian Mega-City[1]

The Keihin region of Japan is the largest industrial region in Japan and one of the largest in the world (Itakura and Takeuchi, 1980, 47). In the mid-1980s it counted 68 percent of Japanese establishments in optical communication equipment; 62 percent in space apparatus; 58 percent in computers; and 47 percent in industrial robots. It had 50 percent of private R&D laboratories in engineering, and 37 percent of researchers working in national engineering institutes, and 30 percent of science and engineering university faculty. Most significant of all, 60 percent of Japanese information-processing engineers were found here (Murata and Takeuchi, 1987, 222-4, 228, 231, 237). Since World War II, especially after 1960, it has made an extremely successful

---

1 This section is largely based on Castells and Hall (1994), Chapter 7. A fuller account of the historical evolution is in Hall (1998).

transition from energy-intensive industries to knowledge-based ones, symbolised by the shift from electrical engineering to electronics.

The Networked Urban Region

As Kuniko Fujita argues, this enormous urban-industrial complex functions in a special way, representing the flexible Japanese production system. It does not fit a 'western' globalisation model characterised by a rigid division between high-level control and command/R&D workers and low-value low-pay production (Fujita, 1991, 269-70). The flexible production system, so characteristic of Japan, has a central characteristic: it has a network system of organisation. This is far more than just a production system: it involves

> ... a network of organized social relations (from the lower level of teams of multiskilled workers at the workplace to the middle level of maker-subcontractors, and to the higher level of business, government and community relations), which can coordinate and cooperate to quickly change from one product to another in response to changes in world or domestic markets... This system of organization interconnects R&D, production, distribution and marketing through intra- and inter-information networks between and among manufacturers, suppliers, government agencies, banks, trade associations and other service corporations (Fujita, 1991, 271).

A crucial feature of this industrial complex, since at least the 1930s, has been the intimate relationship between very large corporations—now household names across the world—and a host of small subcontractors. The assembly factories of the large corporations, which have moved to the region's outskirts, depend on the supply of sophisticated parts from those small- and medium-sized factories, still overwhelmingly located in Tokyo itself. Thus, Tokyo remains a seedbed for the entire Japanese engineering industry, including its high-technology leading edge; this small-scale activity is closely connected with the concentration of R&D and information functions there (Murata and Takeuchi, 1987, 232-5).

This industrial history goes back for well over a century—to the Meiji restoration of 1868, and indeed even before that (Ando, 1983, 16-8). The region's engineering industry was first established early in the Meiji Era in the Ginza-Kyobashi district, now the commercial centre of Tokyo, and then progressively expanded to the south and east through the reclamation of low-lying land, on the shores of minor rivers flowing into Tokyo Bay and the bay shore itself (Itakura and Takeuchi, 1980, 51-2, 59).

In doing so, its structure evolved. Before World War I the area was dominated by small workshops. But first in the period after the Sino-Japanese War of 1905, and then more sharply in the 1920s and 1930s, there was a growth of large companies, particularly in the electrical industry: Tokyo Shibaura Electric (Toshiba), Hitachi, Mitsubishi Electric, Nippon Electric Corporation, and Fujitsu (a subsidiary of Fuji Electric). Over fifty years later, these are the leaders of electronics-based industry in the world as well as in Japan, though their transformations have not always been smooth (Kanagawa, 1985, 271-2).

After the war, these companies would transform themselves into world leaders of the electronics industry. But their future success was underpinned by certain distinctive features of their industrial organisation, which began to emerge in the 1930s. One is cooperative subcontracting, which allows them to respond flexibly to rapidly changing markets, first developed by the Japanese the government's program for wartime production during 1931-1945. Even by the end of the 1950s, there was a clear distinction between Tokyo, where over 70 percent were in establishments with less than 300 workers, and the neighbouring Kanagawa prefecture to the south, where over 40 percent of employees were in giant establishments with more than 1,000 employees (Takanashi and Hyodo, 1963, 59-61). Even by the 1960s Tokyo, Kawasaki and Yokohama were recording declines in manufacturing employment Though engineering and electrical employment continued to grow in Tokyo, much of it still in small factories which subcontracted to the giant firms farther out; in the 1970s and 1980s, many subcontractors came to possess high levels of technology and skill, with cooperative subcontracting practices (Miyakawa, 1980, 270). Factories from Tokyo moved south into Kanagawa prefecture, outside its four cities of Yokohama, Kawasaki, Yokosuka, and Miura, causing the industrial belt to expand south-westwards into previously-rural areas (Takanashi and Hyodo, 1963, 106-7; Ando, 1983, 16). But most small- and medium-sized producers, who subcontract for the large companies, are still concentrated in the southern part of Greater Tokyo, particularly in the southern part of the city: 55 percent of the electrical sub-contractors and 85 percent of the machine tool sub-contractors are here (Itakura and Takeuchi, 1980, 60).

The industrial structure is thus characterised by a sharp contrast between the very large factories of the transnational corporations and the vast swarm of the subcontractors. The relationships are complex and multi-layered: an engineering firm will contract production of parts, even the same parts, to several producers to raise the quality of parts and lower the cost; the contractors in turn contract with as many makers as possible, to stabilise their business.

The resulting relationships are extremely complex; at least four types can be distinguished. First, the linkage between main producers and their parts producers; second, a diagonal linkage with another kind of machine producer, because of the technical features of the parts; third, sub-contracting of part of the output of completed products, as a form of benchmarking; fourth, second-level sub-contracting, where parts producers themselves employ sub-contractors. Given these complexities, it is logical that the entire complex is still locked into this region (Itakura and Takeuchi, 1980, 60-1).

The critical question is whether this region, and its network of relationships, constitute an innovative milieu. In a study of Toshiba, Fruin shows that its Yanagicho Works in Kawasaki Prefecture acts as a 'brain factory', producing a huge range of products with the aid of 164 supporting enterprises which supply two-thirds of the total value of output, many of them small family firms, more than half of them *gaichu-san*, key factories making special order goods to factory specifications, working with the Toshiba management to improve their own quality through complex performance specifications.

These contractors thus have acquired progressively greater autonomy in innovation, and their relationships are increasingly horizontal—with each other—as well as vertical; globalisation and offshoring have increased the scope and complexity of the system (Fujita, 1991, 271-2). Tokyo has thus become 'a special type of world city, a centre of manufacturing innovation ... Tokyo is still the place where new industries and hybrid industries originate, as used to occur in many other world cities' (Fujita, 1991, 272-3). The city's manufacturing output has declined since 1959, and employment has declined even faster; but most, notably the large plants, have remained in the Greater Tokyo region. Very small plants have increased in number, employing sophisticated equipment and moving up-market. They are clustered—machinery and metal products in the southern part; apparel, paper, leather and consumer industries and traditional crafts in the eastern or Shitamachi block; information—printing, publishing, informational services—in the northern Yamanote block (Fujita, 1991, 275).

> The planning and designing of new products occurs in central Tokyo, linking with R & D facilities in suburban Tokyo. Testing of products is also done in Tokyo's suburbs, with constant feedback to R & D and design functions. The actual production of new products is carried out in the neighbouring prefecture (Fujita, 1991, 275-6).

In electronics and machine tools the R&D has spread out towards Kawasaki and Yokohama, an area full of high-technology venture companies. As this has happened, HQs and banks, including foreign banks, have concentrated in the centre, but with routine functions decentralised to back offices in Tama new town. There is an increasing concentration of foreign companies (Fujita, 1991, 276-7).

But this is associated with another special feature: R&D, in sharp contrast to Silicon Valley, is concentrated within the large corporations, which transfer researchers and engineers between their research and manufacturing divisions. They reap pay rewards only if they stay with the company, thus guaranteeing intense loyalty. So a vital part of the Japanese innovative milieu is internalised within the big companies, which thus have gained the flexibility to enter new fields by moving human resources internally—as when they moved from electrical engineering into electronics in the 1960s and 1970s. They then cascade this innovative capacity down to their networks of small and medium-sized firms, forcing them to raise their own technological levels and to tighten their linkages to them. This system has progressively developed in this region over sixty years; it is thus both historically-specific but also spatially-specific to the Keihin region.

As said, this is a fundamentally different pattern from Silicon Valley, the world's other great innovative milieu. Makoto Kikuchi, a leading researcher in semiconductor physics and solid state electronics, suggests that the Japanese pattern is more suited to what he calls 'adaptive creativity': a succession of progressive improvements within an established technological framework. This worked at a time when electronics was technologically mature, its technological framework already set by American research. There is still an open question as to whether this region, and this system, could become the centre of future technological breakthroughs.

Problems of Urban Organisation

Nonetheless, this is an extraordinary example of a networked urban region on a huge scale—the largest the world has ever known. And it works—but only by extraordinary feats of urban organisation. The three central wards have a daytime population of 2.5 million; the region's railway system has proved able to cope with the commuter flows, but with very high peak flows; it carries 2 million passengers a day. The sub-centres on the Yamanote line have logically become major centres of activity (Honjo, 1991, 6). In 1985 Governor Shinjuchi Suzuki presented a plan to relocate the Tokyo Metropolitan Government (TMG) at the biggest of these sub-centres,

Shinjuku, and this was opened in April 1991 (Togo, 1991, 7). The 1986 second long-term plan of TMG stressed a multi-core metropolis around eight major centres: Ueno-Akasuka, Shinjuku, Ikebukuro, Shibuya and Kinshicho-Kameido. It has also sought to create a 'Teleport' on reclaimed land, which, when completed, should create 110,000 jobs—in telecommunications, business information, international companies, mass communications, advertising, printing and publishing, planning and business R&D—as well as an international exhibition centre and homes for 60,000 people (Fujita, 1991, 278-80; Togo, 1991, 7).

A major problem is the cost and shortage of housing (Fujita, 1991, 281). Many have been displaced up to two hours distant. The TMG have insisted that new office developments contain housing, as in ARK Hills in Roppongi, but this is ultra-luxury housing with gyms, restaurants and boutiques (Fujita, 1991, 282).

The Pearl River Delta: Emerging Asian Mega-City

The Pearl River Delta consists of the floodplain of the three rivers, Xi (West), North (Bei) and East (Dong), downstream of their convergence (Yeung, 1994, 3), together with their surrounding hills, with a total land area of 45,026 km². It is one of the most advanced regions of China, with Guangzhou (historically the only gateway into China), seven medium-sized cities and 13 *xians* or counties, plus two out of four of China's special zones, Shenzhen and Zhuhai. In 1993 its total population was 22.1 million, 34.2 percent of the provincial total, on only 25 percent of the land area. In turn, with a population of nearly 61.7 million and an area of 52.4 million acres, Guangdong is ranked fifth among Chinese provinces in population, with a mere two percent of its land area (Lin and Ma, 1994, 82; Sit and Yang, 1997, 651).

The Delta has many advantages: its subtropical climate, with relatively high winter temperatures of 13° to 16° which allow a long growing season; the fertility of its alluvial soils; a good irrigation and transport network; and nearness to Hong Kong and Macau (Xu and Li, 1990, 51; Yeung, 1994, 4). Topographically Guangdong province is separated from the rest of China by the east-west Na Ling range, and its long coastline gave it an early exposure to western culture plus a tradition of overseas emigration (Yeung, 1994, 3). Always open to the outside, the region has been regarded as a haven for risk-takers: 'East, South, West, North and Centre, go to Guangdong and you will be rich' (Chan R., 1995, 217).

But before the 1949 revolution there was little interaction among Guangdong's cities, and from the 1950s the Maoist developmental strategy emphasised self-sufficiency and self-reliance (Woo, 1994, 347). The change came with the historic Third Plenum of the Eleventh Party Conference, in 1978: collectivised land was divided among households which had to meet quotas but could then choose what they wanted to do; special economic zones, basically semi-capitalist, were also set up; these included the whole of the Pearl River Delta and the Yangtze Delta regions (Xu and Li, 1990, 51-2).

Six years later, in the Twelfth Central Committee of 1984, China started to give material incentives to managers, and set the authority of the manager separate from, and with priority over, the local party secretary; the decision gave the manager autonomy, separating this from ownership. Essentially, the reform was twofold: the production unit was removed from the direct control of the bureaucracy, and its management was turned toward a nascent market. But the new relationships would take time to learn. Despite another measure passed by the National People's Congress in 1988, managerial responsibility was not fully implemented until 1991 (Brosseau, 1994, 178-82, 189).

Nonetheless, the results have been spectacular. After the 1978 reform, GDP growth accelerated from a respectable 5.6 percent, achieved over the long period 1952-80, to 12.3 percent over the decade 1981-90. The non-state sector accelerated from 28.8 to 38.1 percent of the labour force (as against 78.5 percent in 1952) and from 27.8 to 58.1 percent of industrial production between 1978 and 1990 (Xu *et al.*, 1995, 136, 143). In the 1980s real economic growth averaged was nearly 50 percent more than in the country; between 1980 and 1991 GDP multiplied more than seven times. With lower than average GNP per capita in 1980, by 1991 it was 64 percent above it; seventh in its contribution to national GDP in 1978, it was first by 1989, and by the 1990s was top in foreign capital utilisation, exports, investment in fixed social assets and agricultural production (Yeung, 1994, 7).

In the core Delta region—the Pearl River Open Economic Area— growth was even more spectacular: during 1980-90 the annual GDP growth averaged 15.7 percent, far higher than the national figure and also higher than the 'Four Asian Little Dragons' during their take-off; in 1994 GDP per capita was 2.9 times the PRC. Many scholars consider it one of the most dynamic regions emerging on the Pacific Rim, with a growth pattern comparable to Japan, Taiwan and South Korea in their take-off stages (Lin and Ma, 1994, 83; Sit and Yang, 1997, 651). The 'four small tigers'—Shunde, Nanhai, Zhongshan and Dongguan—have averaged GNP growth above 20 percent (Brosseau, 1994, 186).

In 1992, Deng in his 'Speech on the Southern Tour' said that Guangdong must catch up with the Four Little Dragons (Maruya, 1994, 71). The plan was revised to give an annual average growth of 8.1 percent over the coming ten years, two percent higher than the national average; on this basis GDP would quadruple between 1980 and 1993 (Maruya, 1994, 71). In fact, in 1992 GDP rose by an incredible 19.5 percent, GDP per capita rose 16.9 percent, gross industrial output rose 31.5 percent, and exports rose 31.5 percent (Cheung, 1994, 46).

The key was an amazing rate of shift in economic structure: over the period 1978-93, agriculture's share of Guangdong's GDP decreased from 68.4 to 27.8 percent, manufacturing's share rose from 27.4 to 61.7 percent, tertiary production from 6.9 to 10.65 percent; in employment, primary production fell from 89.5 to 59.6 percent, manufacturing rose from 7.4 to 20 percent, tertiary from 3.1 to 20.4 percent; it is estimated that 70-80 percent of the rural labour force has been released from agriculture into non-agricultural activities (Sit and Yang, 1997, 653-4). Guangdong cameras rose from 10 to 80 percent of national production between 1978 and 1991; cassette recorders and electric fans rose to 60 percent; in refrigerators, washing machines, colour TV sets, Guangdong rose from virtually nothing to 25 percent (Maruya, 1994, 65; Yeung, 1994, 7).

The Role of Foreign Investment

The key to this growth was foreign investment, above all from Hong Kong, to some extent from Taiwan. Before 1978, the region was 'ready to fight'; investment was not emphasised, and during the entire 1949-78 period it got only 2.5 percent of state enterprise investment; but by the end of the 1980s, it had become a major production base for Hong Kong manufacturing enterprises which employed 3 million, five times the number in Hong Kong itself. Accumulated foreign investment 1991-93 was US$13.4bn., over twice the total of the previous decade. During 1980-93, 73.9 percent of FDI came from Hong Kong and Macao and 82 percent from Asia. Hong Kong's share is especially predominant in smaller cities like Dongguan, Zhongshan, Jiangmen and Zhaoqing, where it amounts to 90 percent of FDI. Manufacturing accounted for nearly two-thirds of all foreign investment into the Delta. Within this sector, over 70 percent of foreign-invested enterprises are in electronics, wearing apparel, toys, metal products, and plastic, rubber and leather products—all labour-intensive, light manufacturing branches which characterised Hong Kong's original manufacturing phase. Again, this investment goes into small and medium cities, where it constitutes over 90 percent of the total (Sit and Yang, 1997, 651-3).

FDI enterprises account for one quarter of gross output value in the Delta, rising to half and more in some cities (Sit and Yang, 1997, 654). 'While TNCs or large firms from the US, Europe and Japan come to LDCs mainly for trade in capital goods and raw materials and occupying the Chinese market for consumer goods, the objective of most Hong Kong-based firms investing in the Delta is the maximisation of short-term profits in lower-level, labour-intensive, industrial processing through exploiting the local labour and land factors'. Equipment and materials come from outside, and the markets are in Hong Kong and the developed countries. It is mainly this activity that has promoted exports, which increased from US$0.63bn. in 1980 to US$199.6bn. in 1993, an average annual growth rate of 30.3 percent. FDI enterprises accounted for over half the export value of the delta in 1993 (Sit and Yang, 1997, 654-5).

Within the Pearl River Delta region, Guangdong would specialise in heavy industry and R&D, Hong Kong-Shenzhen would be a 'window' to the outside world for the latest developments in technology, design and world market trends, and Hong Kong would remain the predominant hub for finance, insurance and shipping, while the intervening areas would become a manufacturing base (Guldin, 1995, 113-4). This reflected the realities that emerged during the 1980s, as an internal spatial division of labour appeared between the Delta and Hong Kong, whereby the new industrial economy of the former has been integrated with the world economy (Sit and Yang, 1997, 655). Basically, the Hong Kong economy has been rapidly restructured out of export-oriented industrialisation based on exporting traditional, light, labour-intensive products to capital- and technology-intensive manufactured products and international business service, while traditional labour-intensive, low-value-added manufacturing has relocated into the Delta. Some 75 percent of the goods made under the name of Hong Kong enterprises are currently made in the Delta; for toys the figure is 92.8 percent, for electrical and optical appliances 84.1 percent and for electronics 78.9 percent (Sit and Yang, 1997, 655-6). The model is 'front shop, back factory' (Sit and Yang, 1997, 656).

More than three million Guangdong workers are thus employed in Hong Kong owned and managed enterprises, much larger than the total manufacturing workforce in Hong Kong which numbered about 0.74 million in 1991 (So and Kwok, 1995a, 252). 'As a result, the colony has upgraded itself to be the financier, investor, supplier, designer, promoter, exporter, middleman and technical consultant of the Peal River Delta economy' while 'Guangdong is turning into the periphery of the Pearl River delta economy'

(So and Kwok, 1995a, 252). Hong Kong instigates the mixed economy, provides economic stability, acts as agent for industrialisation, opens the economy, helps transform the metropolis into a service centre, makes Hong Kong the apex of the urban hierarchy, and makes Hong Kong the intermediary for Guangdong-Taiwan trade (Xu *et al.*, 1995, 148-51).

The process continued unabated, and it was estimated that toward the mid-1990s no less than five million people in the Pearl River Delta were employed in factories controlled by Hong Kong interests. By 1993, manufacturing accounted for only 17.7 percent of the Hong Kong workforce, services accounted for 60 percent (So and Kwok, 1995b, 259).

Despite the role of foreign investment, there is one aspect that has not been well understood: in Shenzhen more domestic enterprises have registered than foreign ones, and they have contributed 53.5 percent of funds for urban physical construction in the 1980s, while foreign capital contributed 24.1 percent (Zhu, 1996b, 200). Privately owned enterprises were playing a steadily increasing role (Zhu, 1996b, 200).

The result was equally rapid urbanisation. Extraordinarily, the Chinese urban population increased only from 10.6 to 12.8 percent of the total between 1949 and 1978, and there was very little urban investment. In contrast, between 1978 and 1985 the proportion in cities increased to 19.7 percent (Zhu, 1996a, 188). But in Guangdong it took an extreme form. In 15 years, the Pearl River Open Economic Area—comprising the SEZs of Shenzhen and Zhuhai, the Open Coastal City of Guangzhou, the Economic and Technological development Zones in Guangzhou, and the Open Coastal Economic Area, comprising the 28 cities and counties of the Delta—changed from a rural area with only 13.2 percent urban population to over 40 percent, one of the five most urbanised regions of China together with the Yangtze River delta, the Beijing-Tianjin-Tangshan area, the Shenyang-Dalian region and the Eastern Shangdong Peninsula Area; it is the most advanced and intensive area of the PRC with respect to foreign investment, economic development and urban growth (Sit and Yang, 1997, 650-1).

The agent, of course, was migration from the countryside. Between 1985 and 1990, migrants to Guangdong came mainly from the areas located on the mountainous periphery of the province. The majority ended in the Pearl River Delta, especially Shenzhen, Guangzhou, Dongguan, Foshan, Zhuhai, Huizhou and Shaoguan—all except the last in the delta. Data for Guangzhou show that the migrants were overwhelmingly young: 24.1 percent were 10-19 and 50.7 percent 20-29 (Si-Ming and Yat-Ming, 1994, 383, 385, 388). So urban population grew—by 7.7 percent per annum between 1978 and 1986—but with a significant variation: a much faster growth of smaller places than of larger cities, resulting in a marked loss of primacy and clear signs of emergence of a rank-size or Pareto distribution and an integrated system of cities (Xu and Li, 1990, 53). There was a major growth of rural industrial enterprises: they numbered 32,400 by 1984 with 60 percent of total provincial sales; these small places offered low wage and land costs, but had close family ties to Hong Kong (Xu and Li, 1990, 60-1).

A New Urban Region

What began to emerge here, at extraordinary speed, was a new urban region *(Figure 1.1)*.

> The outlines of a highly urbanized zone, a megalopolitan triangle, stretching from Hong Kong and Shenzhen in the southeast of the delta to Guangdong and Foshan in the north and then to Macao and Zhuhai Special Economic zone in the southwest, have already appeared. What seems to be emerging is a classic megalopolitan cluster, for the physical distance between Hong Kong and Guangdong, 130 kilometres, fits the pattern for other megalopolises: New York and Philadelphia are 150 kilometers apart, while Beijing-Tianjin, Osaka-Hiroshima, Tokyo-Nagoya, Taibei-Taizhong, Milan-Turin, and Amsterdam-Antwerp are all about 130 kilometers distant from each other. The Pearl River Delta would thus form a distinct urban area in southern China, while both Guangdong and Hong Kong would retain their separate identities and political-economic functions as the twin poles of a common sociocultural entity (Guldin, 1995, 113).

Within the Delta, there has been a distinct spatial bias in the process of investment-related linkage, and it resulted in differential urbanisation: foreign direct investment has mainly flowed into cities and counties around the mouth of the Delta, next to the cities of Hong Kong and Macao, thus forming an inverted 'U'-shaped belt Hong Kong-Shenzhen-Baoan-Dongguan – Guangzhou - Panyu-Foshan – Nanhai – Shunde – Jiangmen – Zinhui – Zhongshan - Zuhai, which takes 70 percent of FDI in the entire Delta, and especially in the Shenzhen-Dongguan which took 47.7 and 20.3 percent of FDI in 1993. But this obscures the fact that there is increasing FDI activity at lower levels in the hierarchy: over 1980-93 Guangzhou had a relatively modest share; the medium-sized cities—Zhuhai, Foshan, Jiangmen, Zhaoqing and Huizhou—took over one-fifth of the total, but small cities and counties took no less than 34.7 percent, rising to 46.5 percent in 1993 (Sit and Yang, 1997, 657-9). These small places tend to be more flexible and less bureaucratic (Sit and Yang, 1997, 661). Significantly, the larger towns (state capitals) had an economy largely based on state enterprises while that of smaller market towns depended mainly on collectively owned enterprises, not included in state planning. They have received more of the immigrants from the countryside, though ironically they lack the resources to cope with them (Lin and Ma, 1994, 92-3).

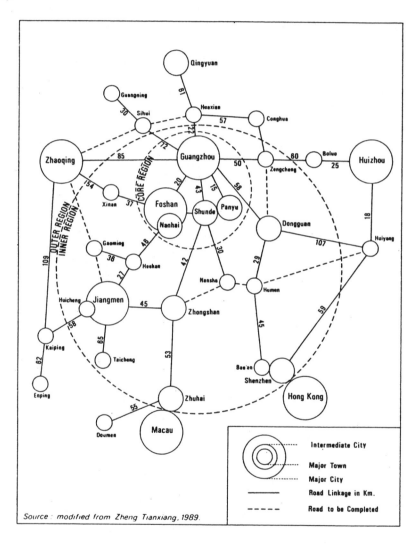

Figure 1.1 Pearl River Delta: major links and nodes
Source: Woo, 1994

Xu and Li have used population potential analysis to study the changing pattern of population distribution in the Delta. In 1978 the area was dominated by Guangzhou, but by 2000 there will be two major nodes, Guangzhou and Hong Kong-Shenzhen, with Zuhai-Macau forming a rather small but fast-growing third zone. Such rapid diffusion is contrary to much conventional regional development theory, which suggests that rapid development leads to spatial polarisation (Xu and Li, 1990, 62-8). Indeed, the increase in the number of smaller urban places, and their higher growth rates, indicate that a process of 'reverse polarisation' may be under way, but this was not a regular downward shift, rather an outward movement from Hong Kong and Macao. The process is one of 'relatively concentrated dispersal' or 'triangularised urbanisation', a process locally concentrated first in the border zones of Shenzhen and Zhuhai and then in the 'four little tigers' of Dongguan, Zhoingshan, Nanhai and Shunde. All this is associated with vertical disintegration of production and external economies of agglomeration (Sit and Yang, 1997, 668-70).

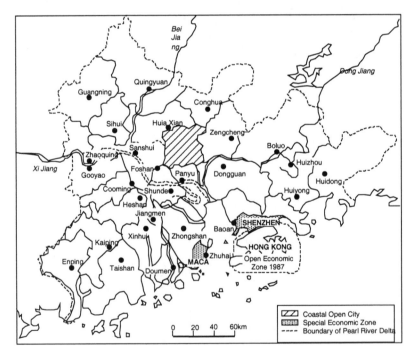

Figure 1.2   Pearl River Delta: types of open area
Source: Sit and Yang, 1997

In the early years, 1978-85, the growth of industrial output disproportionately came from the Shenzhen and Zuhai SEZs: 22.4 and 20.7 percent respectively (Xu and Li, 1990, 58). The Shenzhen Special Economic Zone, SSEZ, was established in 1980 to experiment with a form of the free-market system and to assist with the integration of Hong Kong (Zhu, 1996a, 189). This and the other two SEZs initiated in 1979 were to perform three objectives: observe and understand capitalism at work and follow the trend of modern economic development in the capitalist world; test different policies, especially those connected with different economic systems; and acquire modern technology and management methods (Chu, 1994, 450).

These special arrangements for Guangdong served not only the interests of the province but also those of reformers in Beijing (Cheung, 1994, 30). The SEZs were Deng's pet project and their special status was protected in the Central Document (1981) No. 27, passed in July 1981 to consolidate the initiative (Cheung, 1994, 31).

Initially, a set of preferential tax incentives was offered, including a 15 percent corporate tax rate and 1-3 years of tax holidays but 5 years for investments of over US $5 million. In fact, these have proved to be a necessary but not sufficient condition (Chu, 1994, 455). Further, the SEZs were planned from the start to be under separate administrative and political tutelage, to reduce red tape to the minimum; a SEZ office was created under the Ministry of Foreign Economic Relations and Trade (Chu, 1994, 455). The key organisation in each zone was the SEZ Development Company, a government planning and development enterprise but at the same time an official bureau to negotiate with foreign investors, responsible also for all infrastructure and land allocations; they pioneered the separation of ownership and land-use rights, soon applied to the rest of Guangdong and then to other parts of China (Chu, 1994, 457). The enormous capital construction costs have not come from the centre but are generated locally through land sales and retained profits (Chu, 1994, 462).

Critical in these arrangements was the role of land. And here, it seems, the Chinese borrowed directly from the Hong Kong colonial experience. Between 1954 and 1984, urban land had been effectively free in China, and no price signals were given, leading to serious economic inefficiency. But in 1982, the SSEZ Land Management Regulation declared the end of free land use, and five joint-venture companies were developed in 1982 and 1983, with Hong Kong capital and leases on the land; by the end of 1987 there were 24 such schemes with a total inflow of HK$1.4 billion. Problems inevitably arose with the scale and complexity of the developments, especially when they started displacing people. Private development began in the mid-1980s and no-state sectors placed 55.8 percent of the total 12.7 billion yuan in fixed asset investment between 1983 and 1988. The first sale of a plot on a 50-year lease was in September 1987. In 1988, the Provisional Ordinances on Land Management in the Shenzhen Special Economic Zone formally provided that land use could be leased. The effect was odd: since much of the land was leased to the existing occupiers, it remained idle, substantially reducing the gains to the local authorities, and thus their ability to provide services. Even in 1990, more than 80 percent of land was exempt from fees or rents (Zhu, 1994, 1612-9). Nonetheless, by 1992, 109 development companies were registered, and non-state sectors were playing a significant role in shaping the city. This has provided a model for other coastal cities such as Shanghai, Guangzhou and Xiamen (Zhu, 1996a, 190-4).

Such arrangements gave direct incentives to local governments to become pro-development: revenue-sharing schemes encouraged them to collect taxes and engage directly in profit-making activities, such as retaining 80 percent of commercial and industrial tax revenues originating in their areas, and collecting additional funds such as profits and depreciation funds. Throughout Guangdong, township enterprises, many joint venturers with Taiwanese and Hong Kong companies, contributed 70-75 percent of the revenues of a typical small town in 1992; land sales have become one of the main sources of revenue, and one of the main ways of attracting foreign investment, contributing about 35 percent of total annual revenues in southern China generally and rising to 50 percent in the cities of Shenzhen and Zhuhai (Hsing, 1996, 2246-7).

Between 1979 and 1990, GDP in the Shenzhen SEZ increased from 0.27 to 23.1 billion yuan and its employment from 26,500 to 485,100 (Zhu, 1996a, 189). With a territory of 327.5 km², Shenzhen had a population of 71,400 before 1979, which rose to 1,198,000 (432,100 permanent) in 1991; in Zhuhai SEZ population increased from nothing to 278,600 (all permanent) and in Shantou SEZ from nothing to 91,000, all permanent (Chu, 1994, 463; Zhu, 1994, 1611). Industrial firms grew 24 times between 1979 and 1990, and industrial employment nearly 21 times.

The Delta as Economic Network

Guangdong is hailed in the PRC as the province that moves 'one step ahead' (Chan R., 1995, 214). In the 1980s Hong Kong and China became the biggest mutual trade partners, and over 80 percent of trade through

Hong Kong was coming from, or going to, China (Chan, 1995, 214). More than 17 million trips were made from Hong Kong to China in 1990 (Chan, 1995, 214). Possibly the Hong Kong-Guangdong link will even become the nucleus of a new China Economic Community in the south, extending to cover Taiwan, Hainan and Fujian as a highly dynamic part of the Pacific Rim (Chan, 1995, 58-9).

What emerged during the 1980s in the Delta was an extraordinary system of interdependent relationships between Hong Kong and Taiwan entrepreneurs and local officials. For export-oriented manufacturing, the main business of these overseas Chinese investors, speed is of the essence; lower-level officials at city and country levels are more willing to be flexible than higher officials, offering more favourable tax policies, cheaper land and utilities in the initial stage, simplified (even bypassed!) customs procedures, apathetic execution of environmental and labour regulations, and so on. You-Tien Hsing interviewed a Taiwanese electronics company owner about the nationwide three-year tax holidays for foreign investors; she was told that these policies were 'made for fools', since the real breaks were obtained through individual arrangements with local officials. These officials get big salary rises through bonuses on joint ventures (Hsing, 1996, 2248-9).

By taking advantage of their linguistic and cultural affinity, Taiwanese investors could successfully cultivate interpersonal relationships with officials and build social networks with governmental agencies in the region. This can become corrupt, as when customs are bypassed or the books not properly audited: they would 'open one eye, with the other closed' when visiting the factory. Many Taiwanese investors said that China was more attractive to them than other overseas sites because of the cultural and linguistic affinity. There is thus a 'gift relationship', as Smart and Smart have defined it; Japanese investors were frustrated by their lack of *guanxi* (Hsing, 1996, 2248-51).

All this reflects the fact that in China there has been a long history of tension between the centre and the local state, so that Chinese bureaucrats have developed a skill in making decisions based on what higher officials would not oppose rather than what they would allow; this is called 'looking for holes' (*zuan kong-zi*). There is a Chinese idiom, 'policies from the top, counter strategies at the bottom' (*shangyou zhengce xiayou duece*). Central south China has a special advantage because of its remoteness from the central government. And Guangdong officials have been faster-moving and more flexible than Fujian ones in this regard (Hsing, 1996, 2251, 2256). One Taiwanese investor said, 'No favourable investment policies issued by the government can be as favourable as the special deals I made with local officials' (Hsing, 1996, 2252). Thus, as Hsing found, 'The increasing economic autonomy of Chinese local governments, combined with the culture of Chinese local bureaucracy in their flexible interpretation and implementation of centrally imposed laws, has provided an institutional framework in which the actual practice of gift exchange is carried out' (Hsing, 1996, 2252).

This is embedded in ongoing personal relations; the value of the gift is not always measurable in monetary terms, and gifts have a utility independent of monetary value; nor need gifts be returned immediately (Hsing, 1996, 2252). '... the art of gift exchange is to maintain the balance between offering the material favours and expressing friendship and loyalty to each other as the basis of mutual trust, which goes beyond immediate material benefits' (Hsing, 1996, 2253). Often, the non-material gift is more valuable than the material one, especially if it involves a degree of risk. It cannot take place between strangers; they must be linked, if only through mutual acquaintances, and this takes time. It is also a continuous practice, and must never be stopped. A good example is taking managers of state-owned factories on 'trips to look at equipment' which are in fact pleasure trips to the USA. (Hsing, 1996, 2253-5).

In Guangdong, Taiwanese and locals converse in Mandarin, the 'official' language. Sharing a common language is not the only way to establish and keep relationships, but it is very effective because it allows understanding of hidden meanings (Hsing, 1996, 2255). For instance, an official will say 'let me yanjiu about it'; this means 'think, research' but also means 'liquor and cigarettes' (Hsing, 1996, 2256).

This is almost bound to lead to corruption (Zhu, 1994, 1622). On 28 December 1995, Chinese officials executed Wang Jianye. A senior official in Guangdong province, with responsibility for the planning bureau of the Shenzhen Special Economic Zone, he had been charged with taking bribes, corruption, bigamy and illegally crossing the border; some $2 million of embezzled funds were said to be involved. He was executed by firing squad (Kirby, 1996, iii).

The question is what kind of city is emerging here. And here Manuel Castells' analysis is significant: like Greater Tokyo, this is a new kind of metropolitan form defined not in terms of physical urbanisation (though that is spectacular enough) but essentially in terms of a *network of linkages* stemming from the 'Front Shop, Back Factory' model (Figure 1.3):

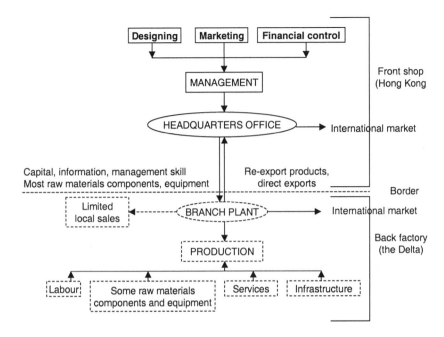

Figure 1.3   Pearl River Delta: the 'front shop, back factory' model
Source: Sit and Yang, 1997

The Southern China Metropolis, still in the making but a sure reality, is a new spatial form. It is not the traditional Megalopolis identified by Gottman (sic) in the 1960s on the north-eastern seaboard of the United States. Unlike this classical case, the Hong Kong-Guangdong metropolitan region is not made up of the physical conurbation of successive urban/suburban units with relative functional autonomy in each of them. It is rapidly becoming an interdependent unit, economically, functionally, and socially, and it will be even more so after Hong Kong becomes functionally part of China in 1997, with Macau joining the flag in 1999 ... The internal linkages of the area and the indispensable connection of the whole system to the global economy via multiple connection links are the real backbone of this new spatial unit. Flows define the spatial form and processes ... The Southern China Metropolis, only vaguely perceived in most of the world at this time, is likely to become the most representative urban face of the twenty-first century (Castells, 1996, 409).

It will be parallelled by another, even larger, Asian mega-city when Tokyo-Yokohama-Nagoya—already, as seen, a functional unit—links up with Osaka-Kobe-Kyoto, 'creating the largest metropolitan agglomeration in human history, not only in terms of population, but in economic and technological power' (Castells, 1996, 409). But by that time, the Pearl River Delta may have merged into an even larger Southern China metropolis, extending to cover Taiwan, Hainan and Fujian as a highly dynamic part of the Pacific Rim (Chan, 1995, 58-9).

Sit and Yang agree with Castells that this is no Megalopolis: the term suggests flows of people, goods and financial instruments, yet here barriers exist and will continue to exist; migration does not take place out of the metropolitan centres, but rather between the periphery and an even more extended periphery in China itself; further, the intricate specialisation characteristic of such regions is not found here. The pattern is more that of McGee's 'desakota' areas, corridors of urbanisation with intervening agriculture; but this area lacks the mixture of activities, often within the same households, that McGee describes (Sit and Yang, 1997, 672-3). 'In the Delta, the core city suffers from relative decline, whereas growth in the small centres and rural areas is unrelated to the dispersal or spread effect of the core' (Sit and Yang, 1997, 673). So this region is different, they think. But they think it is a 'volatile creature', subject to competition from other emerging areas like the Yangtze delta, Vietnam, Indonesia and Malaysia (Sit and Yang, 1997, 673).

Emerging Problems of Urban Organisation

Growth at this speed could not come entirely without problems, even if it were extraordinarily well organised. And evidently, problems are emerging on a huge scale. There has been a dramatic 32 percent loss of cultivated land in the Delta between 1980 and 1993, due both to urban construction and a shift to more profitable crops (Sit and Yang, 1997, 663-4). There are ecological impacts in the north-west part of the Hong Kong New Territories, where farms and fish ponds have been replaced by parking lots, and these effects spread across the border, as the disastrous summer flood of 1994 showed (Chan, 1995, 218-9) (Figure 1.4).

Some of the biggest problems concern the lack of infrastructure. There has been a huge infrastructure investment programme including the Guangzhou-Shenzhen super-highway, completed in 1994, doubling and electrification of the parallel railway, and improvement of telecommunications (Chan R., 1995, 215-7). Again, this has required foreign investment. In 1987 Gordon Wu of Hopewell Holdings in Hong Kong reached an agreement with Guangdong to construct a super-highway connecting the two SEZs of Shenzhen and Zhuhai with Guangzhou, the first phase of which between Shenzhen and Guangzhou was to have been completed in 1990; it was actually finished in 1994 apparently, because of problems with land purchase. But in the not-too-distant future highways should fully integrate the province in both north-south and east-west directions (Chiu-Ming, 1994, 305-6, 322).

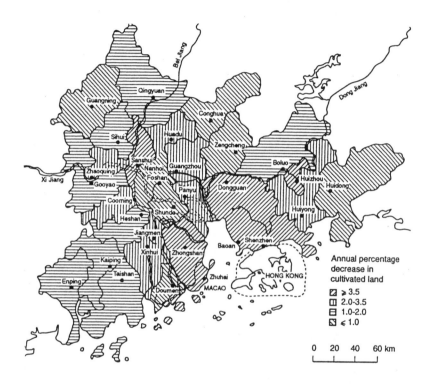

Figure 1.4   Pearl River Delta: cultivated land loss, 1980-93
Source: Sit and Yang, 1997

There are also social problems in the huge flood of labour moving from the poor inland provinces, and the desperate attempts of China to counter the 'decadent' and 'materialistic' Hong Kong influences, extending to fining people for tuning their TVs to Hong Kong commercial channels. The floating population is regarded as the harbinger of urban crisis (Chan, 1995, 221, 224); there are allegations of rising crime rates; during the Lunar New Year of 1989, an estimated 1.5 million flooded the railway station, many stranded without a job or money; similar events have occurred subsequently, though the authorities are now more prepared for them (Si-Ming and Yat-Ming, 1994, 396-7).

And, underlying this, there is the most basic problem of all for the Beijing government: the importation of alien western values. In the 1980s the government deliberately encouraged the overturning of the old People's Republic orthodoxies: 'Serve the People!', the Maoist slogan, became 'Getting Rich is Glorious!'. Hong Kong, unlike the PRC or Taiwan, never had any real ideology except business and the pursuit of wealth, save perhaps for some residual British values which began to be eroded in the run-up to 1997. Hong Kong's mass communications media thus became the vehicles for the penetration of Hong Kong values into the Delta; though officials try to keep papers out, videos are smuggled in and radio and TV are received. This only became significant with the growth of ownership in the 1980s, when colour TV ownership was running at 64-73 percent for Delta counties by 1988. This has fostered a strong demand for the consumer goods seen on TV. English loan words common in Hong Kong Cantonese—*bye-bye*, *dik-see* (taxi) and *ah Sir*—have become common in the delta. So a composite culture is emerging; and it is extending beyond the metropolitan zone (Guldin, 1995, 94-9, 112). An unkind comment has it that the SEZs are getting assimilated by Hong Kong, Guangdong is getting assimilated by the SEZs and China is getting assimilated by Hong Kong. What is less clear, however, is whether they are becoming truly innovative in their own right (Chu, 1994, 466).

Postscript: Problems for Tomorrow?

What is happening in the Delta is being repeated across all the emerging mega-city regions of Eastern Asia, as foreign capital and rural people pour into them. The benefits are evident, for cities are more productive—Shanghai's GDP per capita is 3.7 times the Chinese average in 1990. They benefit from a large labour market, a hub role and a concentration of services. But, as the Asian Development Bank's 1997 report reminds us:

> Without better intervention to address these problems, mega-cities will become even more congested, polluted, unhealthy, expensive and socially divided. A downward spiral will follow if inward investment is deterred: the mega-city's comparative disadvantage will diminish, with correspondingly fewer resources to manage the growing problems (Montagnon, 1997, n.p.).

Governments can help, the ADB suggests, by shifting from providing services to facilitating provision by others, including services such as water and public transport by public-private partnerships, and phased provision of infrastructure with well-conceived strategic plans. But inadequate sewage treatment is creating widespread risk of epidemics. Between $20 bn. and $40 bn. would be needed annually to provide services sufficient to sustain productivity and achieve improvements in the quality of life, the Bank believes (Montagnon, 1997, n.p.).

The pace of growth in these cities brings huge pressures for change, as the increase in global advanced-service functions leads to escalating rent levels, in turn squeezing out other activities. This is shown in Tokyo, Hong Kong and Singapore, where manufacturing has declined in importance in the 1980s and 1990s. But, accompanied by relentless in-migration of people, they also put pressure on housing land, pushing new housing construction in two directions: higher and higher, denser and denser near the centre, as in Hong Kong and to some degree in Singapore; and further and further out, even 100 km. away in the case of Tokyo, where the city government has passed an ordinance requiring new office buildings to have residential accommodation. The resulting long commuting times—up to two hours each way each day in the case of Tokyo—are a classic case of negative urban externalities. Another result is growing and generalised traffic congestion across the entire metropolitan region, only partially countered by mass transit construction and traffic restraint (Yeung, 1996, 27-30).

Asian cities have some advantages here. Perhaps because some of them are colonial and post-colonial regimes, perhaps because of a great sense of collective welfare, their administrations have often been in the world forefront in developing solutions such as traffic restraint; Singapore's electronic road pricing system, scheduled for introduction in 1998, will be the world's first. But these solutions work better in closely-bounded high-density cities, like Singapore and Hong Kong, than in sprawling polycentric edge cities; the outer prefectures of the Keihin region offer object lessons here, for even though they have dense and far-reaching rail systems they have become highly car-dependent, with generalised congestion stretching over vast areas.

The danger on the one hand is that in the scramble for growth at all costs, these newest of the world's great city regions will forget the need to protect and enhance the quality of life. If so, they will surely come to regret it. For, faced with rising costs, not least the costs of land, investors could all too easily pick up sticks for less-developed areas just down the road (Yeung, 1994, 14). They will not be willing to pick up the bill for the social costs they have imposed. And, particularly in the early stages of development—as in the Pearl River Delta at the present time—local governments have neither the resources nor the professional competence to do much about the problem. This is the central dilemma for the new mega-cities of Asia.

2 Urbanisation in an Era of Volatile Globalisation: Policy Problematiques for the 21st Century

TERRY McGEE

Introduction

It is probably overdramatic to suggest that the fiscal crisis which began in the second half of 1997 in several Asian countries has increased doubts concerning the general assumptions on ongoing global economic growth. But when these events are associated with the economic stagnation of much of Africa in the last decades; persistent dualism with continuing poverty in many Latin American countries; the difficulties that OECD countries are experiencing in developing social policies for problems of unemployment and the more global problems of environmental deterioration and persistent poverty, they do reinforce these doubts.

There are no doubts, however, about the overall global increase in urbanisation. It is variously estimated that somewhere between 2010 and 2020, the world will become 50 percent urbanised and that the level of urbanisation will increase over the next 30 years to almost 60 percent by 2050. As with all estimates, this urbanised world of the future assumes a continuation of present trends, a somewhat tenuous relationship between economic growth, technological change and sectoral shifts at a global level from agricultural to non-agricultural employment. While there are reasons to believe that these assumptions will be mediated at the national and sub-global level by what may be sub-global forces, there is no persuasive argument that can be presented against the inevitable urbanisation of the world.[1]

---

[1] I am only too well aware of the popularity of various doomsday scenarios which envisage a future world in which urban centres have collapsed to be replaced by a disintegrating tribal society. Kevin Costner's two films, 'Waterworld' and 'The Postman', while panned by critics, present interesting views of this future.

I realise that this assertion may be contested and this is one reason why I take up so strong a position. We need to force the issue of urbanisation into a central position in the policy problematiques of the twenty first century. There is one more fact that needs to be inserted in this blatant plea: this is the demographic fact that almost 80 percent of the urban increase in the next two decades will occur in developing countries, of which almost two-thirds will occur in Asia, including the population giants of the South Asian countries, and the People's Republic of China.

I would therefore ask you to bear with me as I focus my arguments concerning urbanisation and the development problematique on Asia in the ensuing sections.[2]   My essay is divided into four parts. First, the demographic components of the urbanisation process and the emergence of mega-cities; secondly, a discussion of the current era of globalisation and its relationship to urbanisation; thirdly, the challenges of urbanisation and; fourthly, a discussion of policy problematiques.

A Definitional Aside

Before that, a brief aside on terminology. Like virtually everyone else who studies the development process, I realise that the term, '*developing countries*' has lost its conceptual usefulness except in so far as it carries the idea of *path followed* by previously underdeveloped countries to reach a level of economic growth similar to those of the so-called developed countries. But if we except the *path* idea, then by whatever measure we choose to use, a major part of the world's population located in Africa, Latin America, and Asia still live in developing countries. This claim does not even attempt to address the issue of those people who live below variously defined national poverty lines.

Secondly, it is well known that the urbanisation process is multi-faceted and diverse in its impact from country to country. This makes the task of cross-country comparison difficult. However, the general dimensions of the urban transition; the increase in the number of people living in places defined as urban; the growth in the proportion of the working population in non-agricultural employment and the growing contribution of the non-agricultural sector to GDP are all accepted as part

---

[2] I do not feel any guilt about this focus. I have spent the last 40 years doing research on Asian urban problems at many levels from squatter settlements to National Planning Agencies.

of the urbanisation process, although the relationship between urbanisation and economic growth or decline still remains the subject of much debate. Finally, there is the use of the term *mega-city*. Like my colleague, Alan Gilbert, I am sceptical from years of scrubbing through national statistics of a definition based upon a *threshold size*, for example, eight million used by the United Nations. But I remained convinced the urbanisation process in most developing and developed countries is characterised by the emergence of large urban-based regions often centred on a mega-city core of eight million or more. I am equally convinced that most national data systems are ill-organised to record the statistical dimensions of the emergence of these urban regions.

Urbanisation Trends and the Inevitability of the Urban Transition

Long-term United Nations projections estimate that the world's population will grow from 5.3 billion in 1990 and stabilise at about nine billion people by 2050 (United Nations, Department of Economic and Social Information and Policy Analysis, 1993). The single component of this projection which excites the most attention is that this increase will occur mostly in urban areas which will grow from two billion to six billion with nearly all of this increase occurring in the developing world. The crucial excitement that this figure of 'urban six billion' evokes is what challenges this unprecedented global urbanisation poses to the broad nexus made up by population, resource demands and environmental impacts which is often assumed within the idea of a sustainable world society. Creating livable cities is obviously an important goal of this process.

In the shorter term, it is estimated that by 2020, the world's population will reach a 50 percent urbanisation level of which almost 80 percent of the urban increase in the next two decades will occur in developing countries. However, these overall trends mask substantial differences between the world major regions, particularly between more and less developed regions. By 1990, the world's population stood at an estimated 5.3 billion persons with 4.1 billion living in developing countries. Approximately 45 percent (2.6 billion) of the total population of the world lived in urban areas and of this urban population, almost 41 percent lived in Asia. Accepting the overall trends, this means that by 2020, there will be an addition of 1.5 billion people to the urban centres of Asia. Thus, looming over all current discussion of world urbanisation trends is the great volume of population that resides in, and will move to, the urban areas of Asia.

There are dangers in using statistics such as these at the macro-level for they fuel the ideology of anti-urbanists who see this demographic explosion of cities as the cause of innumerable problems of management, environmental deterioration, energy consumption and social crisis. This view is also fed by the persistence of the ideas that rural society (as opposed to urban society) should be reinforced and conserved as a type of spatial block of societal good as opposed to the evil of urbanisation. For any number of reasons ranging from political gerrymandering and food self-sufficiency to a belief in the morality of rural society, the state is often the supporter of these ideologies.

But while these may be excellent reasons, they do not suggest that urbanisation can be prevented or even put on hold. They also represent a collapsing of the concept of urbanisation into a single factorial process; namely the growth of urban places. The definition of the urbanisation process is much more complex. Most authorities agree that it consists of at least four components: first, the formulation of territorial definitions of urban areas; secondly, the growth or decline of populations in these urban areas which is generally attributable to the movement of population between urban and non-urban areas, natural increase and boundary expansion; thirdly, an increase in people engaged in non-agricultural occupations; finally the argument is often presented that the existence of a distinctive built environment and organisation of cities encourages ways of life, which are often different from the life in rural areas (although access to education, mass media and consumption are making this distinction less relevant).

Ultimately, then, much of the description and analysis of urbanisation depends upon definitions of urban places made by various countries and these vary dramatically (see McGee and Griffiths, 1995). A major problem here is presented by the changes in the territorial configuration of urban places. In many cases, the failure of data gatherers to incorporate urban expansion may result in the under-estimation of urban population. For a variety of reasons, including lifestyles, modes of transportation and the changing structure of employment, the outward expansion of urban places is a more or less universal feature of the growth of urban places. The continued spread of residential areas and dispersion of employment have created polynucleated urban centres linked by transportation corridors (see McGee and Robinson, 1995). This has led to an argument that some form of counter urbanisation which involves a shift from larger cities down the urban hierarchy is occurring (see Champion, 1989).

While I appreciate that these trends represent accurate statistical analysis, I think they represent some form of 'statistical smokescreen' that covers up the real dimensions of the urbanisation. If more generous interpretations of urbanisation are created to include the concept of large mega-urban regions based upon large core urban places such as London, New York, Tokyo, Sydney, Taipei and so on, there is increasing evidence of a high proportion of population increase occurring in large mega-urban regions (see Vining, 1986).

Volatile Globalisation and its Relationship to Urbanisation

I have reviewed the reasons for these growth of mega-urban regions elsewhere (see McGee, 1985, 1991a). Briefly summarised, the two main processes are the transactional revolution and globalisation. The transactional revolution involves fundamental changes in the means of communications, exchange and interaction between and within countries. The transactions involve people, commodities, capital and information. Commuting is a form of geographic transaction involving people; the shipping of automobile parts from Nagoya to Malaysia represents commodity transaction; the transfer of funds from New York to Singapore is a capital transaction and CNN transmissions to all parts of the world are information transfers. A major recent development is that the constraints of time and space are no longer so important for the transmission of capital and information through space. However, the flows of people and commodities, though becoming faster, are still subject to constraints, including those related to time and distance.

Most planners realise that the transactional revolution is strengthening the processes leading to the greater centralisation of the urban system, to the extent that urban development is increasingly concentrated in a few urban regions within a country. However, the current process of urban concentration involves the creation not only of mega-cities or primate cities, but rather of extended metropolitan regions that can take the form of corridors, as in the case of Jakarta-Bandung or Rio De Janeiro-Sao Paulo, or of sprawling urban regions, as in the case of the Bangkok Metropolitan Region (see Ginsburg *et al.,* 1991, Fuchs *et al.,* 1994 and particularly Hamer, pp. 172-91 in the same publication; see also Lo and Yeung, 1996).

Centralisation stems from the importance of transaction nodes whose existence permits the minimisation of transaction costs. Therefore, the new extended metropolitan regions are characterised by including international container ports, international airports, industrial estates and free export zones, as well as international hotels close to multi-nodal offices, and retailing complexes scattered throughout urban space.

Globalisation defined as an increasing integration of global economic activity reinforces this form of urbanisation that, at the level of individual regions, can create discontinuous patterns of land use which are generally most marked in the urban periphery where agriculture, industry, leisure activities and residential developments are juxtaposed. In the peripheral areas of the extended metropolitan regions there are often major environmental and administrative problems as well as conflicts regarding land use (see McGee, 1991b). Despite these difficulties, it is the emerging extended metropolitan regions in the developing world that evince the most rapid economic growth.

Another facet of globalisation is the considerable increase in capital flows at a global level. Data reported by Truman (1996) in the Federal Reserve Bulletin shows total net capital inflows to developing countries increased from 54.1 billion US dollars in the period 1973-1989 to 104.8 billion US dollars in 1990-1994 of which 50 percent was directed to Asia. There were also considerable increases in FDI and portfolio investment. There is ample evidence that many of these flows were directed to the stock exchanges, fiscal institutions and property speculation in the mega-urban regions of Asia. The collapse of these markets precipitated by the withdrawal of some of this foreign investment indicates the volatile nature of fiscal globalisation and its relationship to urbanisation.

Globalisation processes are also affecting the global and regional mode of economic operations. At the global level, the emergence of the new international division of labour has involved the relocation of industrial activity to developing countries where labour costs are low. Such relocation has been made possible by improvements in transport and communication, as well as in production technologies. The major international investors (often in joint ventures with local entrepreneurs) have identified production niches in various locations. The industries created are producing both goods for export and for local consumption, especially if the local population is generating enough surplus capital to buy those products. The decentralisation of production at the global level has been made possible by new forms of organisation and marketing. During the 1980s, order cycle times in developed countries were reduced by 400 percent and the use of just-in-time production and delivery systems expanded. Clearly, better logistical management depends on improvements in telecommunications and information systems. To become part of the global market and maintain competitiveness, developing countries have to provide access to those systems. That is the reason for the continued success of the semi-conductor assembly zone in Bayan Lepas, Penang, Malaysia, which remains globally competitive even though wages have risen.

Another facet of accelerating globalisation is the emergence of global cities serving as major nodal points in the movement of capital, people and commodities. Within the ASEAN region, for instance, there has been considerable competition between Bangkok and Singapore to become the major air transportation node in the region. Singapore has several advantages, being a stable city state without a large rural population. Indonesia, because of its proximity with Singapore, stands to benefit from the global expansion of Singapore in transactional terms.

Developing countries are currently competing to develop a 'niche' in the global market. Virtually no major city lacks today a world trade centre or first class convention facilities. Joining the global market entails important changes in cities, not only to the built environment but also in terms of establishing and expanding telecommunication networks, improving airports, and expanding the road system, especially in areas linked to the global market.

If these assertions concerning the inevitability of mega-urbanisation are accurate, they need to be evaluated critically. A major complication in the evaluation is the fact that the process of global economic growth is highly uneven which is reflected in sharp differences in the economies and wealth of different states in the global system. This also informs the theoretical arguments of convergence and divergence which, for example, see a convergence of urban features in global cities such as Tokyo, New York and London (see Sassen, 1991) which play a major role as financial centres of global centres of financial transactions and a range of cities below them in the global economy which are characterised by immense economic difference.

The central component of this 'convergence' argument is, of course, the view that the 'transactional revolution' discussed in the preceding section is creating regularities in the 'transactional space' of cities and that these regularities are occurring in virtually all urban spaces. Far more acceptable is the view that these 'networks' are less regular and show considerable variation from city to city. Certainly this view is central to my own perception of how many city regions are developing in Asia.

In addition, although this convergence argument appears very plausible, it does not appear to pay sufficient attention to the immense historical, cultural and political differences that characterise the conditions of countries undergoing urbanisation. One group of writers has argued that, 'Our thinking about the city in the twenty-first century must begin to be as differentiated as the discreet realities reflected by urban communities and regions. We have organised these distinct realities that cities bring to the emerging era of globalism into five distinct paths based on historical and cultural conditions.' (see Ruble *et al.*, 1996, p. 5). These five different types of cities are:

1.   *the post-industrial city* located primarily around the North Atlantic Rim, but including Tokyo and Los Angeles characterised by a dominance of the service sector and a major emphasis upon 'consumption';

2.   *new age boom towns* located within or in close proximity to emerging markets of the Pacific Rim such as Singapore, Taipei and Hong Kong;

3.   *the post-socialist cities* which are located in the formerly socialist states of East Central Europe and Asia still struggling to manage the transition to market economies;

4.   *the partially-marketed city* which is characteristic of the urban communities of the developing world, particularly in Latin America, with statist regime that have protected the capital and property of the elites; these policies have created 'dualistic cities' characterised by sharp differences between the rich and the poor; and

5.   *the marginalised city* located primarily in Africa and some other parts of the developing world which have been bypassed by global growth and technology (see Ruble *et al.*, 1996. pp. 1-22 for a more lengthy discussion of these city types).

The Major Challenges of Mega-Urbanisation

These are powerful arguments that assert that there are uniform globalising processes of which telemediated urban processes, restructuring and the public culture of mass consumption, together with the need to reorientate urban regions to be globally competitive, are forcing global convergence in large mega-urban regions. At the same time, these processes appear to be resulting in developing countries in the emergence of disarticulated urban regions in which the lower income populations suffer serious problems of access to services. These are important challenges to 'urban planning' paradigms at both a theoretical and empirical level (see Castells, 1996).

In a recent paper, Graham (1997) lists several theoretical challenges which these processes present. Undoubtedly, the most intriguing is the fact that the paradigms that inform urban planning '...are rooted in the development and management of the *industrial* city...at the core of their analysis were the social, economic, spatial, and environmental aspects of cities dominated by manufacturing and the physical distribution of goods, services, and people' (Graham, 1997, p. 111). Crucial to this paradigm was the treatment of space and time in which both were considered to be passive objects in which the major planning concern was the friction caused by distance and the need to mediate incompatible land-uses that exacerbated this friction (see Friedmann, 1993). The advent of telecommunications provides opportunities to overcome space and time constraints but also to create networks '...*within which* new forms of human interaction, control and organisation can be *constructed in real time*' (Ibid, p. 112). The effect of these processes is not just to create 'electronic spaces' but they facilitate a reconfiguration of urban space. For example, the advent of just-in-time distribution systems which involves electronic ordering of goods direct from factories reduces the need for warehouses formerly located in the central city close to transportation breakpoints. Another example is the way advanced telecommunications and fast transport infrastructures link nodes and city centres into networks whilst excluding much of the intervening or peripheral spaces from accessing networks, because the networks pass through these spaces without allowing local access' (Ibid, p. 112). This concept is crucial for understanding the idea of a connected and disconnected mega-urban region which is typical of Jabotabek in Indonesia. Thus, the major challenge for policy is to identify the ways and means whereby this 'disarticulated' urban place may become more effectively integrated, which centres on the issues of management and local participation.

In a recent keynote address to a Conference on Urban Planning in Asia, John Friedmann identified three major challenges posed to the management of the urban transition in Asia (see Friedmann, 1997).

First, the need to develop effective systems of governance for the growing urban regions that can legally, fiscally, and technically provide the institutional frameworks to manage the urban transition. Secondly, the need to take account of sustainability in the management of this transition. Thirdly, that '...planning should become a more open and participatory process than it is at present capable of harnessing the energies of organised civil societies, particularly of excluded sectors of the population...' (Ibid, p. 4).

Dealing with the issue of urban governance in the Asian context is in some ways the most complex of these three challenges. First, because it is deeply embedded in the political economy of the majority of Asian states. In a very real sense, this issue is also deeply integrated with the globalisation processes we have explained earlier. The vision of the BMW City (see Leaf, 1996) as a globally competitive urban place is central to this vision. Whereas research on governance issues in the developed countries has focused on the emergence of the mega-urban region as the predominant urban form in the late 20th century, political power still rests at the national, provincial and state level in most developing nations, and the issue of mega-urban governance has not received high priority in Asia.

Given the fact that the majority of large mega-urban regions in Asia are the major islands of wealth generation as well as being the capitals of their countries, it is obvious that political elite who rule their countries are unwilling to share political control. They are concerned with maintaining both political and economic control and promoting a 'growth' strategy designed to make their cities more competitive regionally. However, there are growing pressures for devolution of this power through local elections. Opposition parties have been successful in local elections in Seoul, Tokyo and Taipei and have opposed aspects of national policies designed to position their cities more advantageously in the Pacific Rim system of cities.

This issue of devolution is of crucial importance to the success of urban governance for it ultimately depends upon the willingness of national governments to permit local city governments to assume greater responsibilities for taxation, land management, urban infrastructure and transportation. There is a paradox here, for while national governments want to retain political control of their largest cities, the current policy framework of deregulation, privatisation and government budgetary restraints, which are part of the developmental package promoted by the international funding agencies such as the IMF, requires that they devolve this power to a variety of governmental, quasi-governmental and private agencies at the city level. Within the Asian context, the pace of this devolution is very uneven.

A second challenge posed by the growth of mega-urban regions is the problem of making cities more livable. This seems to me to be a much more acceptable term than sustainable since it is clear that urban places rely at least in part on resources which they do not supply themselves. In general, the issue of sustainability is focused upon environmental deterioration in these regions (see Yok Shui Lee, 1997, pp. 140-60 for a useful summary): atmospheric and marine pollution, waste removal problems and land removal are presented as problems for the sustainability of the mega-urban regions. Often these environmental problems are presented as the consequence of the growth of cities rather than the failure of management. I agree with John Friedmann that this approach to sustainability is inadequate, and that more emphasis should be placed upon sustainable human development. Ultimately, the creation of sustainable environments will not depend only upon a technological fix but upon adopting policies of human development. The recent thrust in development studies to incorporate the concept of 'social capital' as one of the major elements needed for development accepts the fact that human and institutional capital are a central requirement for development. Nations that fail to develop this 'social capital' are faced with major developmental problems. Moving to the level of the mega-urban regions, it can be argued that generally they possess higher levels of 'social capital' than the nation, particularly as reflected by human capital. The major requirement, however, is to develop institutional capital which enables more effective management of mega-urban regions.

Part of this requirement could be satisfied by John Friedmann's third challenge which is to make systems of city governance more responsive to the people's needs and desires. In some contexts, this is presented as an 'enabling strategy' which offers people at local levels (neighbourhoods, districts) to have more say in the planning of their local areas. Such enabling strategies can only be effective if local communities are empowered by fiscal devolution, etc., to ensure that local decisions are carried out. In the next section, we will discuss the policy implications of these challenges.

Policy Implications of the Emergence of Mega-Urban Regions

The argument of this piece is comparatively simple, namely that the urban systems of most developing countries will be dominated by the large mega-urban regions. This can be seen as very challenging to governments of developing countries because the macrocephalic process of urbanisation raises a central question: how are governments going to reconcile national goals of spatial equity with the unequal distribution of wealth that mega-urban regions appear to cause?

This important strategic issue is further clouded by the popular view that large cities are a drag on development. Five important myths have contributed to this attitude. They need to be defused if mega-urbanisation is to be managed effectively (see Hamer, 1990).

Myth One is that the large size of cities, or urban regions, is a problem. Undoubtedly their size in terms of population is a major problem for decision makers. The thought of having to provide services to populations that will, for the most part, be in excess of 20 million by 2020 is indisputably alarming. These are aggregated numbers for large urban regions, however, and they are made up of a very large number of subregions with different responses to needs. The subregions could utilise their own revenue-generating capacity in conjunction with national and provincial governments to provide services and infrastructure.

Myth Two, often supported by some international agencies, is that large cities cannot be sustained. It is often argued that the high rates of energy consumption and large volume of non-recyclable waste of developing countries render the large urban regions very difficult to sustain. But such practices impose challenges to develop systems that make use of recycling and that use renewable sources of power such as hydro-electric power. If urban regions were not sustainable, we would have witnessed large-scale economic collapse already, and this has not occurred.

Myth Three is that large cities are economically parasitic. Implicit in this viewpoint, most provocatively developed by Lipton (1977), is the argument that urban regions are unfairly favoured by terms of trade at the national level. Put simply, regulatory intervention by national government (i.e., food and transportation controls) favours urban regions over rural regions and the former therefore benefit at the expense of rural regions.

While this is certainly true in some cases, it is also correct that the agglomeration economies of urban areas reduce transportation costs, and the greater productivity of the urban regions is far more important in explaining their greater wealth than the transfer of surplus income from rural to urban areas. Certainly the fact that the urban areas of, for example, Indonesia, generate between 50 and 60 percent of the non-gas and oil GCP cannot be explained in terms of rural-urban transfer alone. Indeed, there is an increasing amount of evidence that urban-rural transfers (remittances, government transfers) are well in excess of any surplus transfer developed out of rural-urban transfer. This is particularly the case in Java, where high rates of mobility (circulatory migration)—greatly facilitated by intermediate transportation—permit the transfer to be carried out very regularly.

Myth Four is that large cities are characterised by excessive problems of poverty. It cannot be denied that urban regions have ongoing problems of poverty, but it is also true that the household income in these regions is, on average, four times that of the nation at large. More personal income (admittedly unevenly distributed) can therefore flow over into opportunities for the poor in the informal sector. In fact, the whole issue of urban poverty, including its measurement, needs to be carefully evaluated as part of programmes of welfare transfer and so on.

Myth Five is that large cities are places of disharmony and poor quality of life. This is a very arguable assertion. Most evidence supports the view that cultural life of nations is primarily articulated in the large cities. They have the major concentration of institutions of higher learning, national theatres, museums, and art galleries. The quality of life is primarily developed at the household level, however, and for most urban dwellers (apart from the hard-core poor) this, too, is superior to that of rural areas.

It is therefore important to spell out the implications of these extended metropolitan regions for the future of global urbanisation. It can be argued that such zones are catalytic regions for economic growth and that economic growth should be encouraged. It has been suggested, however, that such regions are extraordinarily difficult for planners to handle. The mixture of activities often creates serious environmental, transportation, and infrastructural problems, particularly if such regions are treated with conventional city planning. In a conventional approach, the capital requirements for infrastructure alone seem totally out of reach to most national governments in the developing world, even more so in Asia with its present fiscal problems and huge population. On the other hand, the very mixed, decentralised, intermediate, and small scale of economic organisation and the persistence of agriculture in these mega-urban regions offer exciting prospects for recycling, use of alternative energy sources, and so on, which are difficult to introduce into conventional city space. The challenge to planners is to take advantage of the growth feature of these regions, while ameliorating the costly side-effects of growth and the problems of regional inequality that will emerge as the areas grow. As we have shown, the problems of management are made even more difficult by the prevailing belief that all solutions can be provided by physical improvements in cities.

The livability of these regions is even more important if one accepts the rather gloomy predictions based on the unilinear model of Western urbanisation. As many writers have often observed, if the cities of China and Indonesia alone were to reach the level of energy consumption of New York or London, the demand on world fossil energy sources would be impossible to fulfil. Similar arguments can be presented with respect to food supplies. Many writers have commented on the likely food demands of large Asian cities and the problem that future growth poses to national food supplies. Increasing food imports is a viable option, but the opportunity to maintain a high level of national food self-sufficiency through increasingly intensive agricultural production in the desakota regions is very attractive.

It is, of course, a legitimate question to ask how persistent these mega-urban regions will be? Will the processes of concentration ultimately triumph and lead to a reassertion of the conventional city? For the reasons already cited, particularly those relating to the collapse of time-distance and the mix of transportation technology available, I believe that such regions will be remarkably persistent. Indeed, data becoming available from the 1990 round of census support this claim.

This assertion has important implications for planning and policy formation for the regions. There appear to be six priorities for most developing countries, and these I group under the term 'metrofitting'.

First, policy makers will have to decide the policy priorities to be given to the urban regions. Careful analysis of the geographical extent of the regions and collection of data on population, employment, economic growth, and infrastructure and welfare needs of their populations are necessary. If the regions are as important to economic growth as has been suggested here, then governments will have hard decisions to make about their explicit spatial policies, such as industrial dispersal or regional development. This does not mean that governments should discontinue policies designed to improve the quality of life and economic growth of less-developed regions. Rather, they should carefully reconsider explicit policies designed to force economic activities away from centralising mega-urban regions.

Second, policy planners will need to develop an integrated approach to the management of these urban regions. At present, they are administered by a plethora of administrative units and sectorally responsible departments. As a consequence, the possibility of developing an integrated response to, for example, waste management, is very difficult. This is where the package of policies that is part of metrofitting comes into play. These include the following:

- integrated national, regional, and local strategies for national development;
- institutional changes including a shift from sectoral management to metropolitan management, involving decentralisation of decision making and contra;
- increased capacity to generate income, particularly from land and property tax;
- human resources at all levels capable of managing urban regions; and
- adequate policies to deal with environmental problems.

Only by developing the institutional, management and human resource capacity to manage urban regions can governments respond to the many challenges they face in the coming years. In this respect, recent experiments with 'strategic coalitions' of stakeholders are of considerable interest (see Newman and Thornley, 1997). However, the establishment of such alliances in many developing urban regions is difficult because of the power of the central state.

Third, policy planners will need to improve access in these zones of intense interaction which make up these mega-urban regions. The important issue here will be the mix of private and public transportation. It is very clear that public transport systems (privately or publicly owned) are crucial to the effective functioning of these regions. The largest mega-urban region globally, Tokyo, relies primarily on public transportation for most commuting. Governments should also take every advantage of pre-existing systems such as water routes and encourage flexibility in transportation modes.

Fourth, policy makers will have to monitor environmental and land-use problems carefully to keep conflict to a minimum. There must also be policy developed to prevent the deterioration of the urban environments. The development of fast systems of data collection is crucial to this activity, as are responsive, decentralised implementing agencies.

Fifth, policies will have to be developed for welfare of the inhabitants of the region. By 2020, almost 80 percent of the world's urban poor will be in developing countries. They remain extremely vulnerable to the volatile nature of globalisation. A recent field visit to Indonesia (December 1997) indicated to me that the fiscal crisis was leading to increased food prices, unemployment and serious problems for the urban poor. There are grave consequences to the social stability of these mega-urban regions in such situations. On the other hand, some writers have argued that the fiscal crisis will force governments into decentralisation, local empowerment and greater democratisation because of their fiscal inability to increase social transfers (see Gilbert, 1996).

Finally, it will be necessary to address the activities of the private sector and its role in these regions. It must be clear from the previous discussion that private capital pursuing labour has stimulated developments within an envelope of state and international policy decisions. From the point of view of private capital, the regions are attractive because of cheaper labour, cheaper land, and a more flexible work environment. Here, capital is deployed in an extraordinary diverse set of ways: capital intensification in chicken rearing; subcontracting of production processes; industrial estates and upper-income housing estates; and so on. The 'planning trick' will be to make these regions continue to attract capital and still avoid the grave social, economic, and environmental problems of rapid growth and volatile globalisation. But what seems important is that the fundamental features of the regions—flexibility in economic and political organisation, facilitative transactive networks, and a constant acceptance of change—be incorporated into the planning process.

Conclusion

To conclude, the challenge of urbanisation in the twenty first century forces a reconfiguration of the developmental problematique. In simple terms, the ultimate challenge of development will be to develop the capacity for urban populations to negotiate with volatile globalisation. While I am not over-optimistic that this challenge can be overcome in the short term, if the various coalitions of interests who want to create livable urban regions (government, business and non-government organisations) can be convinced that they are engaged in a massive social transition which involves flexibility and, above all, the realisation that constant experimentation is needed with new institutional, technological and social mechanisms, then the 21ˢᵗ century may see the creation of livable urban regions.

3 Demographic Perspectives on Urban Development in Asia at the Turn of the Century

GRAEME HUGO

Introduction

Of all transformations sweeping across Asia in the post war period none has been so striking and significant as the urban transition, which has seen the proportions of Asians living in urban areas double from 17.4 percent in 1950 to 34.7 percent in 1995. Moreover, the latest United Nations projections (UN Secretariat, 1997a) anticipate that within three decades more than half of the region's population will live in urban areas. Also, rural dwellers are now much more likely than ever before to have direct contact with urban areas through regular visiting and indirect contact through the penetration of mass media. In Indonesia for example, the number of persons per vehicle has decreased from 1,507 in 1950 to six in 1995, while in 1996, 69.3 percent of Indonesians regularly watched television (Biro Pusat Statistik, 1997, 160). Asia's urban transition has been, and will continue to be, rapid. It is indicative of other profound changes in such fundamental areas as the economy, the family, the role of women and in the way people live their daily lives. Moreover, it raises a range of policy challenges which are not only different to those of the past in nature, but also in scale and pace of change. The present chapter seeks to provide one perspective on the nature and implications of the urban transformation occurring in the region. This perspective is not comprehensive, but it is argued that demography provides a window through which we can view some aspects of the urban transition and thereby understand it better.

The present chapter will first chart the dimensions of recent and likely future patterns of urbanisation and urban growth in Asia, making considerable use of the United Nations 1996 revision of their population projections (UN Secretariat, 1997a). We will then move to a consideration of the demographic processes involved in the urban transition and the effect of these processes on the changing characteristics of the people living in Asian cities. Some implications of these demographic processes are then traced for the planning and management of those cities. Finally, some policy issues relating to urbanisation and urban growth in Asia are considered.

Patterns of Urbanisation and Urban Growth in Asia

The problems associated with defining urban areas and urban populations have long been recognised and differences in the criteria adopted by countries have bedevilled attempts at comparing levels and patterns of urbanisation. These problems have been exacerbated in Asia and elsewhere in recent decades by an increased blurring of the boundaries between urban and rural areas, which has been a consequence of reductions in the time and cost of travelling. Increasingly, people who work and spend much of their lives in built up metropolitan areas have their home place in non-metropolitan areas and circulate between them on a daily or less frequent basis. Long distance commuting is not the preserve of cities in MDCs, but is equally significant around Asia's major cities. Moreover, in many Asian cities there are even larger numbers of non-permanent migrants who leave their families at home in the village or small town and work in a large city, returning home for visits on a regular basis. Hence, there are many people who are counted as rural dwellers in official population counts but spend much of their lives in large urban areas. In such a context it is difficult to differentiate urban and rural populations and be able to compare between countries adopting different approaches to urban definition. Nevertheless, bearing these limitations in mind, it is useful to examine the official data relating to urban growth and urbanisation in the Asian region.

The rapid pace of urban growth and urbanisation is evident in Table 3.1. Over the 1950-95 period urban growth was fastest in South East Asia where the numbers of urban dwellers increased sixfold, compared with 4.34 times in East Asia and 4.37 times in South Central Asia.

This pattern is expected to continue over the next quarter century with South East Asia's urban population being expected to double to 326.4 million and those of East Asia and South Central Asia to increase 1.7 and 2.3 times respectively, to number 892.9 and 837.9 million respectively in

2020. These rates of growth are considerably faster than those of national populations as a whole so that rates of urbanisation have also increased significantly. Hence, the proportions of national populations living in urban areas increased 2.26 times between 1950 and 1995 in South East Asia, 1.99 times in East Asia and 1.73 times in South Central Asia. The differences between the regions in the degree of urbanisation ranging between 28.7 percent in South Central Asia to 35.9 percent in East Asia in 1995 are likely to be maintained so that in 2020 more than half (53.7 percent) of East Asians will be urbanites as will 49.4 percent of South East Asians and 42.1 percent of people in South Central Asia.

Table 3.1   Asia: urban population change 1950-1995 and projected change 1995-2020

	South East Asia		East Asia		South Central Asia		Total	
	No. (000)	%	No. (000)	%	No. (000)	%	No. (000)	% (000)
1950	26,915	14.8	120,839	18.0	82,917	16.6	230,671	17.1
1975	72,213	22.3	276,011	25.2	196,543	22.2	544,767	23.6
1995	161,678	33.5	524,107	35.9	362,642	28.7	1,048,427	32.1
2000	192,674	36.9	601,582	40.6	458,539	30.7	1,252,795	35.8
2010	258,791	43.5	752,821	47.7	628,234	35.8	1,639,846	41.7
2020	326,354	49.4	892,874	53.7	837,864	42.1	2,057,092	47.7
% Growth								
1950-75		4.03		3.36		3.51		3.50
1975-95		4.11		3.26		3.11		3.33
1995-2020		2.85		2.15		3.41		2.73

Source: UN Secretariat, 1997a

On the other hand, there has been a significant reduction in the rates of growth of population in rural areas of Asia. In 1950 there were 1.12 billion rural dwellers in Asia, by 1995 this had almost doubled to 2.19 billion, but increased at a rate less than half that of the urban population. However, the outlook for the next quarter century shown in Table 3.2 is one of overall stability with the rural population of the region in 2020 expected to number around 2.26 billion. Moreover, the rural population increases will mostly occur in South Central Asia. In East Asia the rural population is anticipated to begin declining in absolute numbers in the late 1990s and in South East Asia twenty years later. However, absolute declines in rural population have already begun in parts of South East Asia as well as over much of East Asia. In Indonesia for example, the rural population of Java declined from 64.3 percent in 1990 to 58.3 percent in 1995.

Table 3.2   Asia: rural population change 1950-1995 and projected change 1995-2020

	South East Asia ('000)	East Asia ('000)	South Central Asia ('000)	Total ('000)
1950	155,120	550,317	415,665	1,121,102
1975	251,768	820,999	689,170	1,761,937
1995	320,242	897,208	974,225	2,191,675
2000	329,310	881,429	1,037,439	2,248,178
2010	336,120	826,118	1,128,607	2,290,845
2020	334,373	771,370	1,152,806	2,258,549
Percent Growth Per Annum				
1950-75	1.96	1.61	2.04	1.82
1975-95	1.21	0.44	1.75	1.10
1995-2020	0.17	-0.60	0.68	0.12

Source: UN Secretariat, 1997a

Urban populations in the less developed parts of Asia grew at 3.5 percent per annum between 1990-95. However, Figure 3.1 shows that rates of urban population growth in Asia have begun to decline in the 1990s and are anticipated to continue to decline in the early decades of the next century. It is expected to fall below two percent in East Asia in 2015-2020 and in South East Asia in 2020-2025.

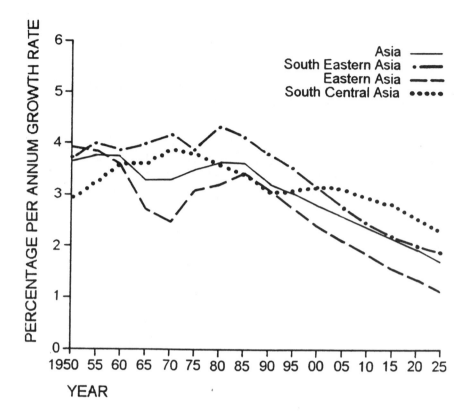

**Figure 3.1 Asia: urban population growth rate 1950 to 1995 and
projected change 1995-2025**

Source: UN Secretariat, 1997a

This decline in urban population growth rates is associated with the
overall decline in population growth rates in the region. The 1996 revision
of the United Nations population projections for Asia have been revised
downward to see the population increase from 3.4 billion in 1995 to 5.4
billion in 2050 (Haub, 1997, 2) and the overall growth rate will fall from
around 1.6 percent per annum in the mid 1990s to 0.4 percent per annum in
the middle of the next century. This is a function of the massive declines in
fertility from a total fertility rate of 5.06 in the early 1970s to 2.9 in the
mid-1990s.

One of the most distinctive features of Asian urbanisation has been
the emergence of mega-cities (defined by the United Nations as cities with

10 million residents or more).   Figure 3.2 shows that Asia's share of the world's 30 largest cities has increased from around a quarter in 1950 to almost half at the turn of the century.   If Japan is excluded, the number of mega-cities located in Asia has increased from one in 1975 to five in 1995 and by 2015 as Table 3.3 shows, Asia will have 16 of the 22 mega-cities in LDCs and 18 of the 26 world wide.

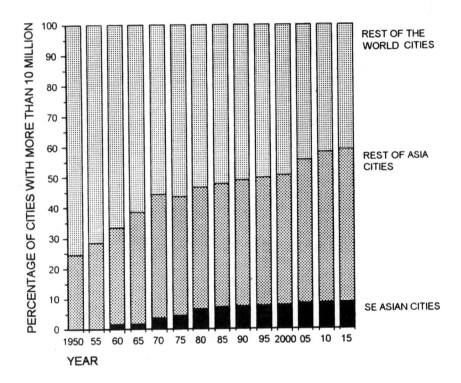

Figure 3.2   Proportion of the world's largest cities located in Asia, 1950-1995 and projected population in 1995-2025

Source: UN Secretariat, 1997a

Table 3.3   **Number of mega-cities in 1975 and 1995 and projected in 2015**

Region	1975	1995	2015
World	5	14	26
Less Developed Regions	3	10	22
Africa	0	1	2
Asia*	1	5	16
Latin America and the Caribbean	2	4	4
More Developed Regions**	2	4	4
Northern America	1	2	2
Japan	1	2	

*   Excluding Japan
** Including Japan

Source: UN Secretariat, 1997a, 22

Hence, Asian countries will increasingly dominate among the world's largest cities over the next two decades. As Table 3.4 indicates the Asian mega-cities have experienced rapid growth over the last two decades. This was especially marked in the mega-cities of South East Asia. United Nations projections show that most mega-cities in Asia will continue to have high but reduced growth rates over the next two decades. It is interesting to note that in Latin America mega-cities have experienced substantial slowdowns in their population growth, and their dominance of national population distributions is being reduced (United Nations Secretariat, 1997a, 26). It will be interesting to observe whether or not Asian mega-cities follow this pattern.

It is important to recognise that while most Asian nations have experienced rapid urban growth and urbanisation over the last two decades, there are wide variations between countries in their urban situation. Hence, Table 3.5 shows that in 1996 urban populations in Asian nations ranged between 71,000 in the Maldives to 382 million in China. Similarly, degrees of urbanisation vary between the virtual city state of Singapore to 11 percent in Nepal.

Table 3.4   **Average annual rate of change in the population during 1975-1995 and projected change 1995-2015 for urban agglomerations ranked as mega-cities in 2015 (percentage)**

Urban Agglomeration and Country	1975-95	1995-2015
A. Less Developed Regions		
Beijing, China	1.40	1.60
Bombay, India	3.96	2.74
Buenos Aires, Argentina	1.27	0.80
Cairo, Egypt	2.33	1.99
Calcutta, India	2.06	1.86
Delhi, India	4.05	2.64
Dhaka, Bangladesh	7.45	4.12
Hangzhou, China	6.72	4.99
Hyderabad, India	4.83	3.25
Istanbul, Turkey	3.94	3.22
Jakarta, Indonesia	2.91	2.40
Karachi, Pakistan	4.47	3.44
Lagos, Nigeria	5.68	4.37
Lahore, Pakistan	3.68	3.48
Metro Manila, Philippines	3.10	2.28
Mexico City, Mexico	1.94	0.73
Rio de Janeiro, Brazil	1.30	0.76
Sao Paulo, Brazil	2.49	1.03
Seoul, Republic of Korea	2.67	0.56
Shanghai, China	0.86	1.40
Teheran, Iran (Islamic Rep. of)	2.35	2.05
Tianjin, China	2.12	1.81
B. More Developed Regions		
Los Angeles, United State of America	1.65	0.68
New York, United States of America	0.14	0.37
Osaka, Japan	0.37	0.00
Tokyo, Japan	1.55	0.34

Source: UN Secretariat, 1997a, 23

Table 3.5 Population in the Asia-Pacific Region, 1970-1996 and percent urban

	1970		1980		1990		1996	
	Total in '000	% Urban	Total in '000	% Urban	Total in '000	% Urban	Total in '000	% Urban
World Total	3,697,849	36.6	4,448,037	39.5	5,292,195	45.2	5,767,774	46
ESCAP Region Total	2,029,106	12.3	2,484,720	14.2	2,979,676	18.7	3,603,753	37
NIES*								
Hong Kong[a]	3,959	89.7	5,039	91.6	5,705	94.1	6,191	95
Republic of Korea	31,466	50.1	37,436	68.8	43,411	79.8	45,314	83
Singapore	2,075	100.0	2,414	100.0	2,723	100.0	3,384	100
Other South East Asian Countries								
Brunei Darussalum	130	61.7	185	59.9	266	57.7	300	70
Indonesia	120,280	17.1	146,776[a]	22.4[a]	179,321[a]	30.9[a]	200,453	36
Malaysia	10,852	27.0	13,763	34.6	17,567[a]	43.0	20,581	54
Philippines	37,540	33.0	48,317	37.4	62,413	42.6	69,282	55
Thailand	35,745	13.3	46,718	17.3	55,702	22.6	58,703	20
Myanmar	27,102	22.8	33,821	24.0	41,675	24.8	45,922	26
Cambodia	6,938	11.7	6,400	10.3	8,246	11.6	10,273	21
Lao People's Democratic Republic	2,713	9.6	3,205	13.4	4,139	18.6	5,035	21
Viet Nam	42,729	18.3	53,700	19.3	66,693	21.9	75,181	19

Table 3.1 (Contd.)

	1970		1980		1990		1996	
	Total in '000	% Urban	Total in '000	% Urban	Total in '000	% Urban	Total in '000	% Urban
South Asia								
Afghanistan	13,623	11.0	16,063	15.6	16,557	18.2	20,883	20
Bangladesh	66,671	7.6	88,219	11.3	115,593	16.4	120,073	19
India	554,911	19.8	688,856	23.1	853,094	27.0	944,580	27
Nepal	11,488	3.9	14,857	6.1	19,143	9.6	22,021	11
Maldives[a]	114	14.0	158	21.5	213	25.8	263	27
Pakistan	65,706	24.9	85,299	28.1	122,626	32.0	139,973	35
Sri Lanka	12,514	21.9	14,819	21.6	17,217	21.4	18,100	22
China[b]	830,675	17.4	996,134	19.6	1,139,060	33.4	1,232,084	31
Iran (Islamic Republic of)	28,429	41.0	38,900	49.6	54,607	56.7	69,975	60
Pacific Island Countries								
Fiji	520	34.8	634	37.8	764	39.3	797	41
Papua New Guinea	2,422	9.8	3,086	13.0	3,874	15.8	4,400	16
Samoa	143	20.3	155	21.2	168	22.0	166	21

Table 3.5 (Contd.)

	1970		1980		1990		1996	
	Total in '000	% Urban	Total in '000	% Urban	Total in '000	% Urban	Total in '000	% Urban
Solomon Islands	164	8.9	225	9.2	320	10.6	390	18
Tonga	85	21.4	97	19.7	95	20.5	98	42
Vanuatu	83	13.1	117	18.7	158	25.8	173	19
Developed Countries								
Australia	12,552	85.2	14,695	85.8	16,873	85.5	18,057	85
Japan	104,331	71.2	116,807	76.2	123,460	77.0	125,351	78
New Zealand	2,820	81.1	3,113	83.3	3,392	84.0	3,602	86

* NIES: Newly Industrialising Economies.

a: Government data.

b: The Government of China has recently provided the following data for total population and percent non-agricultural urban population: 1970: 825,420–12.2; 1980: 982,550–13.6; 1990: 1,129,542–18.98; 1992: 1,152,428–20.4

Source: UN ESCA, 1993; UN Secretariat, 1997b

Of course, differing variations in definition of urban areas make comparisons difficult but it is apparent that a wide variety of levels of urbanisation and urban growth are evident in the Asian region. There is less variation, however, in the rate of growth of urban populations as depicted in Table 3.6. It is notable that some of the most rapid rates of growth have occurred in the largest countries of the region, especially China (five percent per annum), Indonesia (5.2 percent), Pakistan (4.5 percent) and Bangladesh (6.8 percent).

There is clearly a relationship between urbanisation and economic development. Figure 3.3 shows that although the relationship is by no means a perfect one, there is a correlation between the level of urbanisation in Asian countries and the level of development as indicated by GNP per capita. In fact, a correlation coefficient of 0.6995 was found to apply, indicating a quite strong association between average incomes and levels of urbanisation among nations in the region.

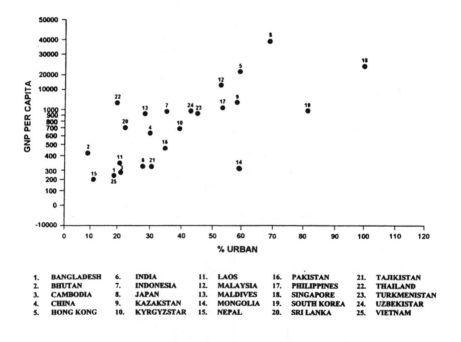

1.	BANGLADESH	6.	INDIA	11.	LAOS	16.	PAKISTAN	21.	TAJIKISTAN
2.	BHUTAN	7.	INDONESIA	12.	MALAYSIA	17.	PHILIPPINES	22.	THAILAND
3.	CAMBODIA	8.	JAPAN	13.	MALDIVES	18.	SINGAPORE	23.	TURKMENISTAN
4.	CHINA	9.	KAZAKSTAN	14.	MONGOLIA	19.	SOUTH KOREA	24.	UZBEKISTAR
5.	HONG KONG	10.	KYRGYZSTAR	15.	NEPAL	20.	SRI LANKA	25.	VIETNAM

Figure 3.3   Asian countries: relationship between level of urbanisation and GNP per capita, 1995

Source: UN Secretariat, 1997a; Population Reference Bureau, 1997; World Bank, 1997

Table 3.6 Average annual population growth rate 1970-1995

	1970-75 Total	1970-75 Urban	1975-80 Total	1975-80 Urban	1980-85 Total	1980-85 Urban	1970-90 Total	1970-90 Urban	1990-95 Total	1990-95 Urban
World Total	1.96	2.61	1.73	2.63	1.74	3.06	1.81	2.89	1.48	2.43
ESCAP Region Total NIES*	**2.26**	**3.65**	**1.83**	**3.31**	**1.83**	**3.46**	**1.94**	**3.98**	**1.73**	**3.79**
Hong Kong^a	2.11	2.40	2.77	2.96	1.60	1.90	1.84	2.09	1.42	1.60
Republic of Korea	1.80	5.40	1.55	4.70	1.36	3.20	1.48	4.00	0.93	2.85
Singapore	1.73	1.73	1.30	1.30	1.15	1.15	1.37	1.37	1.96	1.96
ASEAN 5										
Brunei Darussalam	3.65	3.73	3.41	2.72	3.80	3.07	3.65	3.30	2.64	3.65
Indonesia	2.41	4.92	2.14	4.88	2.06	5.37	2.16	5.17	1.54	4.48
Malaysia^a	2.59	4.70	2.17	4.58	2.61	4.87	2.48	4.79	2.37	3.87
Philippines	2.51	4.02	2.53	3.54	2.63	3.97	2.57	3.90	2.20	4.24
Thailand	2.92	5.59	2.44	5.05	1.99	4.66	2.24	5.00	0.94	2.20
Other South East Asian Countries										
Myanmar	2.32	3.25	2.11	2.15	2.09	2.13	2.19	2.59	1.74	2.69
Cambodia	0.46	2.09	2.07	2.07	2.59	3.54	0.87	0.84	2.84	5.93

Table 3.6 (Contd.)

	1970-75		1975-80		1980-85		1970-90		1990-95	
	Total	Urban	Total	Urban	Total	Urban	Total	Urban	Total	Urban
Lao People's Democratic Republic	2.18	5.52	1.16	4.50	2.29	5.58	2.13	5.56	3.0	5.73
Viet Nam	2.34	2.86	2.23	2.75	2.19	3.22	2.25	3.17	2.02	1.73
South Asia										
Afghanistan	2.42	6.11	0.87	4.17	2.02	0.47	0.98	3.55	5.74	7.47
Bangladesh	2.77	6.74	2.83	6.76	2.73	6.57	2.79	6.83	1.49	4.58
India	2.24	3.76	2.08	3.66	2.21	3.80	2.17	3.78	1.76	2.72
Nepal	2.47	6.72	2.67	7.35	2.59	7.21	2.59	7.29	2.67	5.50
Pakistan	2.57	3.76	2.64	3.87	3.82	5.01	3.17	4.47	2.68	4.15
Sri Lanka	1.67	1.83	1.71	1.28	1.67	1.23	1.61	1.49	1.00	1.74
China	2.20	2.09	1.43	3.94	1.23	6.72	1.59	4.96	1.09	3.95
Iran (Islamic Republic of)	3.19	5.35	3.08	4.71	4.05	5.43	3.32	5.00	2.87	3.79
Pacific Island Countries										
Fiji	2.03	3.13	1.91	2.47	1.97	2.36	1.94	2.56	1.53	2.17
Papua New Guinea	2.38	6.32	2.46	4.25	2.29	4.06	2.38	4.87	2.27	3.63
Samoa	0.75	1.41	0.81	1.01	0.91	1.01	0.81	1.23	0.57	0.57
Solomon Islands	3.36	3.73	3.01	3.38	3.77	4.82	3.40	4.18	3.32	6.39
Tonga	0.58	0.22	2.10	1.29	0.27	0.27	0.56	0.27	0.36	3.46

Table 3.6 (Contd.)

	1970-75		1975-80		1980-85		1970-90		1990-95	
	Total	Urban	Total	Urban	Total	Urban	Total	Urban	Total	Urban
Vanuatu	2.89	6.51	3.89	7.39	3.07	6.38	3.27	6.80	2.49	3.20
Developed Countries										
Australia	1.64	1.82	1.51	1.47	1.40	1.33	1.49	1.51	1.13	1.03
Japan	1.33	2.55	0.93	1.06	0.68	0.81	0.85	1.24	0.25	0.42
New Zealand	1.79	2.19	0.19	0.33	0.84	0.92	0.93	1.10	1.16	1.43

* NIES: Newly Industrialising Economies. a: Government data.

Source: UN ESCAP, 1993; United Nations Secretariat, 1997b

One of the most distinctive features of urbanisation in the Asian region is the high incidence of primacy in the distribution of national urban systems. Table 3.7 shows that in more than half the countries of the region more than a fifth of the national urban population lives in the largest city. These major cities are overspilling their boundaries and forming huge and complex urban regions, which are poly-centred and present new challenges to policy makers and planners.

The case of Jakarta in Indonesia is illustrative. The extent of overspill from the Special Capital City District of Jakarta into the surrounding province of West Java is shown in Figure 3.4. Whereas at the 1980 census there were 456,625 residents of West Java who gave their previous province of residence as Jakarta, this had more than trebled to 1,558,641 in 1990 and 2,239,821 in 1995 as Table 3.8 shows. Of course, many settling in the overspill areas are migrants from elsewhere in Indonesia. Some indication of the growth of Jakarta as a 'mega-city' and the overspill into the adjoining *kabupaten* in the province of West Java can be gained by examining some trends in those adjoining areas. Table 3.9 shows growth in the Jakarta metropolitan region over the last two decades and indicates how unrealistic 'official' data on the population of the city are. The first part of the table shows growth in the administrative region of Jakarta giving a population of 9.1 million in 1995 and 1990-95 population gains of around 10 percent. The second part shows growth in those parts of the adjoining three overspill *kabupaten* defined as urban at the three censuses. This gives a metropolitan region population of 15.4 million in 1995 and very rapid growth rates between 1980 and 1990 partly because of reclassification of formerly rural areas as urban between censuses. The final part of the table includes the fixed boundaries of the entire Jabotabek region and shows a more than doubling of the population between 1971 and 1990 (while the national population increased at less than half this rate) and gives a metropolitan region population of 20.16 million in 1995. In functional terms the latter figure is certainly more realistic than that for DKI Jakarta.

Table 3.7   Percentages of urban population in the largest city and an index of primacy, 1970-1990

	% of Urban Population in Largest City				Index of Primacy***
	1970	1980	1990	2000**	(most recent census)
NIES*					
Hong Kong[a]	96	97	99	100	+
Republic of Korea	41	38	35	33	2.74
Singapore	75	100	100	100	+
Other South East Asian Countries					
Brunei Darussalam	-	42	39	-	2.17
Indonesia	19	18	16	16	5.00
Malaysia[a]	16	20	13	-	1.99
Philippines	29	33	32	31	5.00
Thailand	65	59	57	55	33.79
Cambodia	100	100	100	100	+
Lao People's Democra Republic	-	53	66	-	5.39
Myanmar	23	27	32	32	4.71
Viet Nam	26	26	22	18	2.91
South Asia					
Afghanistan	34	39	52	44	5.42
Bangladesh	30	33	35	35	2.59
India	6	6	5	5	1.60
Nepal	-	20	26	-	2.53
Pakistan	19	21	20	19	1.75
Sri Lanka	-	17	16	-	3.21
China	8	6	4	3	1.06
Japan	20	19	19	19	2.61

*   **NIES**: Newly Industrialised Economies; ** Year 2000 predicted; +only 1 urban area identified; ***Ratio of largest city's population to the second largest city.
a: Government data.

Source: UN ESCAP, 1995

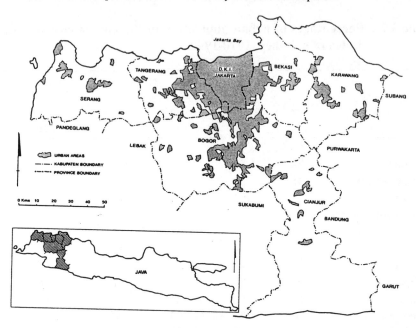

Figure 3.4   The functioning urban region of Greater Jakarta, 1990
Source: BPS 1990 Census and 1995 SUPAS, Unpublished data

The transformation of the population of the areas adjoining DKI Jakarta reflected in the fact that the number of residents in these areas who were employed in non-agricultural occupations increased from 583,450 in 1971 to 3,357,819 in 1995. It should be noted that there was already substantial commuting out of the region to Jakarta in 1971 but the growth of non-agricultural employment in the next two and a half decades was 475.5 percent compared with an increase in total population of 140.7 percent. The massive change occurring in the Botabek area can be appreciated from the fact that the numbers working in agriculture fell from 720,666 in 1971 to 36,3791 in 1995 but those working in manufacturing increased from 98,405 in 1971 to 954,757 in 1995. Between 1990 and 1995 alone the numbers working in manufacturing increased by 42.4 percent from 670,279 to 954,717.

Table 3.8 Bogor, Bekasi and Tanggerang: birthplace of population, 1990

Birthplace/Origin	Males 1990	Females 1990	Sex Ratio 1990	Total 1990	Percent of Population 1990
Jakarta	11,249	10,992	102.3	22,241	7.41
Central Java	7,869	7,849	100.3	15,718	5.23
Yogyakarta	898	884	101.6	1,782	0.59
East Java	2,256	2,071	108.9	4,327	1.44
West Java	123,932	123,041	100.7	246,973	82.24
Other Indonesia	5.148	4.127	124.7	9,275	3.09
Total	151,352	148,964	101.6	300,316	100.00

Source: BPS, 1990 Census and, 1995 SUPAS, Unpublished Data

Table 3.9   Population in Jakarta metropolitan area according to different definitions, 1971-1995

	Population				Increase (%)		
	1971	1980	1990	1995	1971-80	1980-90	1990-95
Special Capital City District of (DKI) Jakarta	4,546,492	6,071,748	8,227,766	9,112,652	33.5	35.5	10.8
DKI Jakarta and Urban Bogor, Bekasi and Tanggerang Kabupaten	4,838,221	7,373,563	13,096,693	15,397,091	52.4	77.6	17.6
DKI Jakarta, Kotamadya Bogor and Tanggerang and Kabupaten Bogor Bekasi and Tanggerang (Jabotabek)	8,374,243	11,485,019	17,105,357	20,159,655	37.1	48.9	17.9

Source: 1971, 1980 and 1990 Censuses and 1995 Intercensal Population Survey of Indonesia

The Changing Dynamics of Population Growth in Asian Cities

The higher rates of growth of urban compared to rural populations which have been experienced by each of the Asian nations over the last quarter century can potentially be the result of any or all of the following

- areas formerly classified as rural being reclassified as urban;
- fertility of urban-based women being higher than their rural based counterparts;
- mortality of urban-based people being lower than their rural-based counterparts;
- a net redistribution of people from rural to urban areas through migration; and
- a net gain of migrants from overseas greater than in rural areas.

Dealing firstly with the issue of natural increase, it is clear that throughout Asia fertility levels in urban areas are, in fact, *lower* than those among rural populations. To take a particular example, Figure 3.5 shows that in Indonesia there is a difference of almost one child (0.85) in the average number of children borne by urban and rural women. Moreover, this difference has widened over time as overall fertility has declined (in 1967 the difference was 0.56). Hence, the fertility decline which has seen the average number of children which Indonesian women halved between 1967 and 1994 has been more intensive in urban areas which experienced a 54.7 percent decline in fertility compared to 44.3 percent in rural areas. Figure 3.5 also shows the transition in fertility in Jakarta. Whereas pre-transition fertility levels in the mega-city in the late 1960s were similar to those in other Indonesian urban areas, the subsequent decline in fertility has been more substantial in Jakarta than in other cities. In fact, fertility declined by 62.9 percent over the 1967-94 period, to such an extent that fertility levels reached replacement level around 1990 and fertility is now below replacement level (Total Fertility Rate of 1.9) in Jakarta. This massive fertility decline is an important but neglected characteristic of Asia's mega-cities and needs closer study.

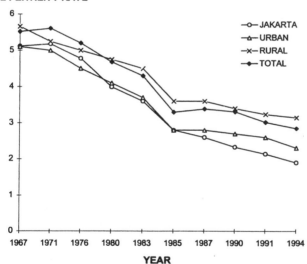

Figure 3.5 Indonesia: trends in total fertility rate in urban and rural areas and in Jakarta 1967-1994

Source: IDHS, 1987, 1991,1994; BPS, 1994

Hence, fertility levels do not provide the explanation for Asia's urban populations growing faster than their rural counterparts. In fact, if other things were equal the rural populations would be growing faster than urban populations.   Turning to mortality, Figure 3.6 shows trends in infant mortality between urban and rural areas in Indonesia.   The country has experienced a huge improvement in mortality with the infant mortality rate being halved from 140 infants out of every 1,000 born dying before their first birthday in 1969 to 66.4 in 1994. There has been a slight lowering of the gap between urban and rural infant mortality rates from 36 to 32.1 deaths per thousand births between 1969 and 1994.   Nevertheless, there are very large mortality differentials between urban and rural areas in Indonesia with levels in urban areas being 43 percent lower in urban areas than in villages.   Moreover, the mortality decline has been greater (61.9 percent) in urban areas than in rural areas (49.5 percent) over the last quarter century. Again, it is interesting to consider the experience of the mega-city of Jakarta separately.   Figure 3.6 shows that in 1969 Jakarta had infant mortality a little higher than the average for urban areas, although lower than that occurring nationally and in rural areas.   However, the decline in mortality has been greater than elsewhere in Jakarta, with a 76.1 percent decrease in the infant mortality rate from 125 per 1,000 in 1969 to 29.8 in 1994.   In 1994 infant mortality levels were less than half the national average in Jakarta.   This is typical of the mega-cities of the region and needs to be set against the stereotypes of mega-cities as unhealthy sinks of poverty and massive loss of life.

Clearly mortality differentials in Asia are favouring a more rapid growth of urban population than rural populations.   However, this differential is probably only sufficient to counterbalance the effect in the opposite direction caused by lower fertility levels prevailing in urban than in rural areas.   Hence, overall national increase (i.e., births minus deaths) is not contributing significantly to *urbanisation*, i.e., the increasing *proportions* of national populations living in urban areas.   On the other hand, natural increase is contributing significantly to *urban growth* in Asia since fertility levels are still high relative to MDCs and the populations of such cities are quite young, with large proportions in the childbearing age groups.   Hence Table 3.10 shows that over the entire Asian region natural increase contributed 37.8 percent of urban growth in the 1980s and 40.7 percent in the 1990s.   There is considerable variation between countries in the extent to which natural increase is contributing to urban population growth as Table 3.10 indicates.   The highest levels of natural increase contribution tend to be in the higher fertility area of South Asia and lowest in the low fertility countries.

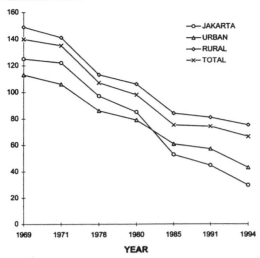

INFANT MORTALITY RATE

Figure 3.6   Indonesia: trends in infant mortality rates in urban and rural areas and in Jakarta 1969-1994

Source: IDHS, 1987, 1991, 1994; BPS, 1994

It is clear from Table 3.10 that net migration gains and reclassification of areas as urban account not only for virtually all of the increases in levels of urbanisation but also provide more than half of urban population growth. Unfortunately it is very difficult to separate these two components in the data that are available for many Asian countries. It is apparent that reclassification has been significant in many countries. For example, it was reported in Indonesia (Gardiner and Oey-Gardiner, 1991; Gardiner, 1997) that the number of *desa* (the basic building block area units for urban and rural classification) which were classified as urban doubled between the 1980 and 1990 Censuses from 3,500 to around 6,700. While in such cases many people will have been classified as rural in 1980 and urban in 1990 without having changed their place of residence, it must be remembered that the reclassification has almost certainly been triggered by a substantial in-movement of population and increase in population density. Hence, reclassification itself often involves significant rural-urban migration.

Table 3.10   Components of urban growth, by country or area (percentage of urban growth)

Subregion Country or Area	1980-85 Natural Increase	1980-85 Migration and Reclassi-fication	1990-95 Natural Increase	1990-95 Migration and Reclassi-fication	2000-05 Natural Increase	2000-05 Migration and Reclassi-fication
Asia	**37.8**	**62.2**	**40.7**	**59.3**	**42.6**	**57.4**
East Asia	**21.9**	**78.1**	**28.0**	**72.0**	**30.3**	**69.7**
China	15.9	84.1	23.7	76.3	27.2	72.8
Hong Kong	61.0	39.0	58.2	41.8	75.3	24.7
Japan	81.5	18.5	78.5	21.5	70.3	29.7
Mongolia	93.6	6.4	85.6	14.4	73.4	26.6
Rep. of Korea	35.5	64.5	38.8	61.2	50.7	49.3
South East Asia	**49.1**	**50.9**	**44.9**	**55.1**	**41.7**	**58.3**
Cambodia	70.9	29.1	49.5	50.5	30.6	69.4
Indonesia	35.2	64.8	37.0	63.0	36.7	63.3
Lao, People's Democratic Rep.	43.8	56.2	44.7	55.3	43.8	56.2
Malaysiaᵃ	22.0	78.0	38.0	62.0	40.0	60.0
Myanmar	110.0	-10.0	63.2	36.8	44.5	55.5
Philippines	66.0	34.0	62.4	37.6	57.0	43.0
Singapore	100.1	-0.1	100.1	-0.1	98.9	1.1
Thailand	39.6	60.4	31.4	68.6	31.2	68.8
Viet Nam	1.7	28.3	50.5	49.5	38.1	61.9
South Asia	**56.0**	**44.0**	**54.4**	**45.6**	**47.0**	**53.0**
Afghanistan	-589.1	689.1	30.4	69.6	46.1	53.9
Bangladesh	37.6	62.4	39.9	60.1	41.9	58.1
Bhutan	41.5	58.5	34.8	65.2	34.1	65.9
India	55.6	44.4	52.1	47.9	44.8	55.2
Iran(Islamic Rep	56.0	44.0	81.4	18.6	71.0	29.0
Nepal	31.9	68.1	32.5	67.5	32.6	67.4
Pakistan	69.0	31.0	67.8	32.2	54.9	45.1
Sri Lanka	170.8	-70.8	66.8	33.2	33.6	66.4

Note: The contribution of natural increase is calculated by assuming that the urban population has the same rate of natural increase as the national or regional population. The category or migration and reclassification is calculated as a residual. a: Government data.

Source: UN ESCAP, 1995

Although the data we have available are very limited, it can be concluded that rural to urban migration has played a major role in both the rapid urbanisation and urban growth in Asian countries over the last two decades. Again, to take Indonesia as an example, Table 3.11 shows that urban Indonesians are close to their rural migrant origins. For example, in 1995 the 17.7 percent of urban dwellers in Indonesian cities were migrants from another province. Since intra-provincial migrants outnumber their inter-provincial counterparts by up to five to one (Hugo, 1975), it is apparent that migrants or their offspring make up the majority of Indonesian urban dwellers. This is apparent in the data for DKI Jakarta which is a totally urban area. Moreover, field surveys have indicated that not only has migration to cities increased in tempo in Indonesia, but rural-urban interaction has become more complex with greater incidence of commuting and other forms of circulation between urban and rural areas. At least 25 percent of rural households on Java in the early 1980s had one or more family members working for part of the year in urban areas (Hugo, 1991). This implies that at least 3.75 million people are involved in this form of migration on Java, equivalent to 16.5 percent of the reported 1980 urban population. The effect on the urban labour force is much greater since virtually all such movers are either employed, or looking for work—the figure of 3.75 million is equivalent to just over half of recorded urban employment in Java at the 1980 census. Of course, since migrants are only working in the cities for part of the year the average effect is less than this, but quite likely about one-sixth of the average daily urban workforce consists of temporary migrants.

Table 3.11   Indonesia, Indonesia urban and Jakarta: percent of population ever lived in another province

| | Percent Born in Another Province | | |
Year	Indonesia	Indonesia Urban	Jakarta
1961	n.a.	n.a.	48.4
1971	6.1	n.a.	41.1
1980	7.3	17.2	40.7
1990	9.1	17.3	39.0
1995	10.6	17.7	37.8

An increasing feature of mega-cities in Asia is the significance of international migration in their growth. In this sense they are similar to Global Cities in MDCs (Sassen, 1991; Freedman, 1986). These international migrations tend to be of two kinds. Firstly in some nations, developed (e.g. Australia, Japan), NICs (e.g. Taiwan, South Korea, Singapore) and near NICs (e.g. Malaysia, Thailand) the cities are experiencing the influx of relatively unskilled workers. This occurs largely through the process of labour market segmentation (Piore, 1978). This occurs because the local workforce is unwilling to go into dirty, dangerous, difficult, low status, low paid jobs such as in the construction sector and domestic service. Accordingly low skilled migrants from labour surplus nations such as the Philippines, Indonesia and the South Asian countries supply increasing numbers of low skilled workers to the mega-cities of Asia. In Kuala Lumpur, for example, several hundred thousand Indonesians have been working on major construction projects such as the Commonwealth games stadium and the new international airport. The second type of international migrants tend to be highly skilled persons, often from MDCs, who are either transferred by multinational companies or fill gaps in fast expanding economies where the education system has been unable to provide sufficient locally trained persons in areas such as management, engineering, architecture, computing, accountancy, banking and a range of technical areas. Again, if we take Jakarta as an example, more than 90 percent of foreigners in Indonesia live in and around the mega-city of Jakarta. The influx of legal foreign workers to Indonesia, a labour surplus nation, increased from 20,781 new workers in 1990 to 57,159 in 1995. These foreigners are significant not just in MDCs, NICs and near NICs but also in LDCs like Indonesia where there is a mismatch in the education system and the needs of a rapidly expanding and restructuring urban economy. Hence Asia's mega-cities are becoming more heterogeneous ethnically and also more linked into the world economy.

Characteristics of Population in Asian Cities

The influx of people from other parts of the country and from other countries into large Asian urban areas over recent years have given them a distinctive population composition. One of the major characteristics relates to ethnic heterogeneity compared to the total national population. Many of these cities in South East Asia have a large Chinese population which has its origins in precolonial Chinese Trade and colonial migration policies. These groups often have a disproportionately large significance in the South East Asian mega-cities because of their control over the economy. During the 1997-98 economic crisis in Indonesia this has seen the Chinese becoming the target of a great deal of protest. In recent times the mega-cities have drawn people from the full range of areas within the national space and this has resulted in a wide range of ethnic groups. Similarly, international migration has resulted in increasing numbers of people from a range of ethno linguistic groups settling in Asia's mega-cities. Hence, while Thais make up the majority in Bangkok, Burmese, Cambodians and Bangladeshis makes up significant minorities. While these cities are often characterised by ethnic quarters where there are spatial concentrations of the various ethno-linguistic groups, they are also characterised by a high degree of inter-marriage between ethnic groups. Hence, the mega-cities have the most emphatic demographic expression of national unity in countries like Indonesia, the Philippines, etc., where there is a high level of inter-marriage between the various ethnic groups making up the nation. In some countries the ethnic mixture in mega-cities has resulted in conflict between groups. In Karachi, for example, substantial ethnic conflict has resulted from migration. One of the crucial issues in mega-cities is the extent to which the migrants from overseas and within the country intend to settle permanently in the mega-cities. In many cases of both international and internal migration migrants intend their stay in the mega-city to be a temporary one but issues of social cohesion loom large in many such cities.

Another dimension of urban areas in Asia's large cities relates to the age structure of those areas. While LDCs generally have very young age structures it is true that there are disproportionate numbers of young adults in the mega-cities of the Asian region. Hence, Figure 3.7 shows that in Indonesia, whereas 35.9 percent of the total population live in urban areas, some 41 percent of those aged 15-29 live in urban areas. It will be noted in the diagram that it is only in the young adult years that there is an above average representation of an age group. Both dependent children and elderly persons are significantly under-represented in urban areas. This is the result of migration, both national and international, being highly selective of young adults but also due to significant retirement migration of older people out of urban areas into villages. In Indonesia 6.1 percent of the population aged 15-29 live in Jakarta compared with only 4.7 among the total of the population. This high representation of young adults in mega-cities is of particular significance. It is this group which experiences the highest levels of open unemployment. Moreover, they are the most educated among the working age generation and there has been a selective in-migration of young educated persons into mega-cities in search of high paying urban based jobs. The educated in LCDs tend to eschew agricultural occupations and with the spread of universal education the proportion of rural based young people being 'educated to migrate' is increasing. This conjunction of a disproportionately large representation of young adults with high levels of unemployment and high levels of education in mega-cities may represent a recipe for civil discontent based in urban areas. In Indonesia, for example, this has been noted as a potential negative impact of urbanisation by the ruling elite.

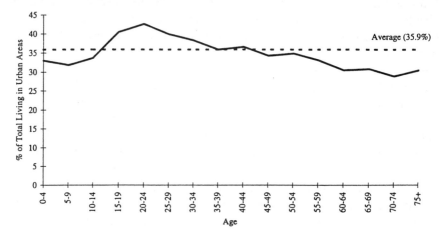

Figure 3.7   Indonesia: proportion of total population living in urban areas, 1995

Source: 1995 Intercensal Population Survey of Indonesia

Another major dimension of change in major urban areas of Asia is the increasing feminisation of those cities due to increasing dominance of females in the movement to some of those cities, both in internal and international migration. This is especially the case in the cities at South East Asia. Table 3.12, for example, shows the increasing significance of women among all interprovincial migrants and in Jakarta toward women increasing in significance. Moreover, in Indonesia the migration data understate the involvement of women in rural to urban migration since migration of women tends to be over a shorter distance than that of men. Hence, the 1985 intercensal survey which collected data on inter-*kabupaten* as well as interprovincial mobility found that women outnumbered men among inter-*kabupaten* migrants living in urban areas (Hugo, 1992, 51).

There are a number of processes operating to increase female migration to mega-cities in South East Asia. Firstly in the formal sector the growth of off-shore manufacturing industries in low labour cost situations in South East Asian countries has greatly created job opportunities for young women in the huge factories established to manufacture clothing, toys, shoes, electronics and other intricate goods. Women are preferred in many areas because of their greater docility, more industriousness, more nimbleness and lower wages. Young educated women are travelling in their hundreds of thousands from rural parts of Asia into the large cities to work in factories and work under often exploitative conditions.

Table 3.12   Indonesia and Jakarta: change in sex ratios of interprovincial migrants 1961-1995

Year	Indonesia		Jakarta	
	Urban Population	All Migrants	Total DKI Population	Interprovincial Migrants
1961	n.a.	n.a.	103.9	108.9
1971	n.a.	122.1	102.1	104.6
1980	n.a.	n.a.	102.6	n.a.
1990	111.2	116.8	102.0	99.0
1995	105.1	110.8	100.6	96.7

Source: Indonesian Censuses and Intercensal Surveys

The second major type of female migration involves largely lesser educated women moving to work in the domestic sector and in the informal sector of the urban economy. Again these young women are subject to exploitation, especially those working in the informal and so-called sex sectors. However, it is apparent that women are increasingly moving toward urban areas in the Asian region as independent migrants and this process is increasing in significance.

To give some idea of the scale and rapidity of change it is useful to take the three kabupaten and two kotamodya surrounding Jakarta. The overspill of Jakarta in these areas has been characterised by the development of large factories, many employing young women. In 1980 there were 312,186 women working in the region—more than half of them in agriculture. However, by 1992 the number of females working in the region had increased by 127.4 percent to 709,968 and in 1996 there were 990,938 who were employed in the BOTABEK region—more than half of them in manufacturing.

A crucial factor relates to the incidence of poverty in the mega-cities of Asia. It is clear that it is extremely difficult to measure poverty in different cultural contexts. For example, there is great debate about what constitutes poverty in particular contexts. Table 3.13 shows trends in government measured poverty in Indonesia over the last two decades. It will be noticed that there has been a substantial decline in both the numbers in poverty in urban areas and the proportions. The Indonesian poverty line is fixed by the cost of a particular basket of goods and on this basis the proportion of urban Indonesians living in poverty decreased from 38.8 to 9.7 percent between 1976 and 1996 and the numbers from 10.0 to 7.2 million. However, this severely understates the numbers living near poverty. Moreover, it is clear that the currency crisis of 1997-98 has greatly increased the numbers living in poverty in Indonesian urban and rural areas.

Table 3.13   Percentage of population in poverty in urban and rural areas

Year	Poverty Line		Percentage Population Poor			Total Population Poor (m)		
	Urban	Rural	Urban	Rural	Total	Urban	Rural	Total
1976	4,522	2,849	38.79	40.37	40.08	10.0	44.2	54.2
1978	4,969	2,981	30.84	33.38	33.31	8.3	38.9	47.2
1980	6,831	4,449	29.04	28.42	28.56	9.5	32.8	42.3
1981	9,777	5,877	28.06	26.49	26.85	9.3	31.3	40.6
1984	13,731	7,746	23.14	21.18	21.64	9.3	25.7	35.0
1987	17,381	10,294	20.14	16.14	17.42	9.7	20.3	30.0
1990	20,614	13,295	16.75	14.33	15.08	9.4	17.8	27.2
1993	27,905	18,244	13.45	13.79	13.67	8.7	17.2	25.9
1996	38,426	27,413	9.71	12.30	11.34	7.2	15.3	22.5

Source: BPS and UNDP, 1997, p.111

Another of the particular features of the mega-cities of Asia is the high levels of participation of the workforce in the informal sector. The informal sector is the unregulated part of the economy in which workers do not usually receive a monthly or fortnightly wage, pay income tax or work for a large scale enterprise. In Indonesia the proportion of the workforce in the informal sector declined from 73.2 percent in 1986 to 64.8 percent in 1996. In 1996 in Jakarta around one-third of the workforce were in the informal sector (BPS and UNDP, 1997, p.88). Nevertheless, until the 1997-98 economic crisis the economies of Asian nations were undergoing significant structural economic change. This is readily apparent in Table 3.14 which shows that in recent years there has been a decline in agricultural employment but manufacturing employment growth has increased at over 6.3 percent over the last eleven years.

Table 3.14 Indonesia: growth of sectoral division of gross domestic product and employment 1980-1996 (percent per annum)

Year	Agriculture	Manufacturing	Services	Total
Growth of Output				
1980-85	3.4	4.2	6.9	5.0
1985-90	3.0	7.0	7.3	6.3
1990-93	3.2	7.7	7.0	6.6
1993-96	2.6	11.6	7.4	7.9
Growth of Employment				
1980-85	4.0	5.3	3.8	4.1
1985-90	0.8	7.0	3.2	2.5
1990-93	-1.8	6.3	4.9	1.5
1993-96	-2.0	7.7	6.7	2.7

Source: BPS and UNDP, 1997, p.80

Policy Considerations

The rapid growth of urbanisation and the development of mega-cities have presented policy makers and planners in Asia with new sets of issues and challenges to confront. In this section we will briefly summarise some of the major policy implications of contemporary and likely forthcoming trends in the demography of Asia's urban areas.

One of the major concerns of governments in the region relates to urbanisation and urban growth. In the most recent United Nations survey of government's population policies of the 23 nations that responded, 20 indicated that they considered their national spatial distribution was unsatisfactory. In almost all cases this was a function of them considering the rate of urban growth, especially of the largest cities, to be too rapid. Moreover, only five of the countries of Asia feel that their patterns of internal migration need to be changed. Hence, there is a great deal of concern about rural-urban migration, especially that directed toward mega-urban centres. Nevertheless, the fact remains that massive structural change is occurring in most Asian countries which is displacing labour from agriculture and creating opportunities in non-agricultural activities. There is still significant scope for labour displacement from agriculture in the region as commercialisation has increased and increased scientific inputs and modernisation have displaced more workers. Many Asian policy makers and planners still maintain an anti-urban position and seek to develop plans and policies which attempt to stop people migrating to large cities either before they leave their village or turning them back after arrival in the city. The latest example of this occurred in Jakarta in early 1998 when buses and trains arriving in Jakarta in the days following Lebaran or the feast following the celebration at the end of the Muslim fasting month were being met by city officials and anyone who couldn't prove they had a job were returned to their village (*Republika*, 17 February 1998). This type of activity is bound to fail, as have earlier attempts, to close the cities of Jakarta and Bandung. Such policing activities will not have an effect if government policy favours investment in major metropolitan areas. For example, investment data shows the lion's share of the massive foreign investment in Indonesia has concentrated in and around Jakarta.

Hence, it is crucial that policy makers and planners in Asia adopt accommodating rather than anti-urban policies in confronting urban problems in the early twenty first century. This, however, must be undertaken in the knowledge that urban growth rates universally are going to substantially reduce in the next few decades in Asian urban areas. This will be a function firstly of a massive fall in fertility in the Asian region as a whole but also the fall has been especially notable in Asia's mega-cities with cities like Shanghai—not only recording substantially below replacement fertility but some of the lowest fertility levels around the world. Hence, although the very young age structure of mega-cities and the disproportionately large representation of young adult women will ensure significant natural increase, the extremely low levels of fertility will dampen this growth. The high costs of housing, and living more generally, the importance of multiple income families, older ages at marriage, enhanced levels of education, high levels of contraceptive provision and government policy have combined to make fertility in mega-cities extremely low. There is potential for substantial rural to urban migration in the largest countries of the region. In China there are estimates of 150 to 200 million rural workers surplus to needs; and Indonesia, Vietnam and the South Asian nations have a potential for producing large numbers of rural to urban migrants. Nevertheless, as is shown earlier in this chapter, the still rapid growth of Asian urban areas in the early decades of the next century will be significantly lower than that of the 1980s and 1990s. Moreover, the impact of the 1997-98 currency crisis on urbanisation in the region is yet to be assessed. Moreover, it is apparent that one of the effects has been a substantial return to the village of displaced workers. The extent of the crisis and its longer term effects are yet to become clear in countries like Indonesia, Korea, Thailand and Malaysia but it may be to reduce the extent and rate of urban growth.

One of the major policy implications of recent demographic change in mega-cities in Asia relates to human resources. The over-representation of young adults, unemployment, educated unemployment and youth unemployment in large cities in Asia is an issue of considerable concern which needs to be addressed. There are significant mismatches in many countries between the types of highly skilled jobs becoming available in a rapidly restructuring and growing economy and the types of education and training being provided for young people. Moreover, there is a clear need for work creation programmes in large urban areas. These are being undertaken as an emergency measure in Indonesia in response to the increased unemployment created by the crisis. Even before the crisis, Table 3.15 shows that in urban areas there is a virtual negative correlation between the level of unemployment and education. This clearly not only represents a significant waste of resources but also provides the seeds of political unrest in the mega-cities.

Table 3.15 Indonesia: level of unemployment according to education 1996

Level of Education	Urban	Rural	Total
No Schooling	1.2	0.4	0.5
Didn't Complete Primary	2.2	0.9	1.1
Primary	3.8	2.4	2.7
General Lower Secondary	7.6	6.1	6.8
Technical Lower Secondary	7.1	6.8	6.9
General Upper Secondary	14.9	14.8	14.9
Technical Upper Secondary	13.0	8.7	11.3
Diploma I/II	8.9	8.0	8.5
Diploma III	10.8	8.0	10.2
University	13.2	16.8	13.9
Total	8.3	3.2	4.9

Source: BPS and UNDP, 1997

Another significant area of policy intervention relates to non-permanent migration to the urban areas of Asia. Again anti-migration policies appear to be dominant. Yet circular migration would appear to have significant advantages for major cities. While there are disadvantages to individual migrants and their families caused by separation, they experience gains through spreading the risk of family income earning between urban and rural locations and the cheapness of living in the village. The cities gain advantages since the costs of bringing up children are borne by the village and reduce pressures on health, education and housing services, etc. There may be advantages of encouraging non-permanent migration through such programmes as the construction of barracks, etc., since this is one way how the economic benefits of urbanisation are spread more widely.

It is clear that there is a need for a close examination of national economic, social and political policies to establish the extent to which they create an unlevel playing field for economic forces in favour of mega-cities. Clearly in such cases there may be possibilities of legislative change to favour development outside of the mega-cities. Nevertheless, there are clear economic and social advantages to the development of such cities and the benefits of these have to be maximised to the benefit of the entire nation. This may mean the development of a more accommodationist than anti-urban strategy in dealing with mega-cities. This means the development of realistic and workable policies and programmes to improve the life of residents rather than the adoption of anti-urban, anti-migrant policing tactics. It means the adoption of more user-pays principles, especially when industry entrepreneurs and the wealthy are made to pay realistic rates for the use of services. It also means greater site and service programmes, adoption of realistic housing regulations and policies which differ from those in MDCs, encouragement of the informal sector, increasing local autonomy and financial power, etc.

The informal sector is virtually ignored in urban economic planning in Asian cities yet it employs more than the formal sector which is the focus of the attention of planners. The informal sector is and can be not only highly productive but an excellent absorber of unemployed and under-employed workers. Loan programmes, training, reduction of regulation, etc., can be used to encourage the expansion of a vibrant informal sector. Instead the informal sector is too often seen as an unproductive involuntary sink for people who can't get a job in the formal sector.

International migration issues will figure more in Asian metropolitan urban areas of the future. Greater personal mobility, globalisation, the development of regional blocs into ASEAN and APEC, the expansion of social networks and the development of an immigration industry (Hugo, 1996) have greatly expanded international migration of workers in the region. Moreover, illegal migration is growing apace where governments have attempted to stem the flow of migrants. City governments in Asia will increasingly be confronted with issues relating to undocumented migrant workers, both men and women. Increasing segmentation of urban labour markets, the eschewing of dirty, dangerous and difficult jobs by natives, the establishment of enclaves of foreigners in mega-cities and greater economic and social linkages between nations all have encouraged greater movement of workers between countries in the region. This raises issues of social conflict where migrants come into direct competition with natives and this is most likely to occur in the largest cities.

The rapid expansion of cities in the Asian region has led in many cases to cities, especially mega-cities, overlapping their political boundaries. In many cases the political boundaries have not been adapted to take account of these changes so that functioning cities have a number of regional and local governments. This makes cohesive planning of these cities extremely difficult and leads to lack of coordination, increased costs and duplication. Moreover, powerful multinational companies can often take advantage of low levels of administrative, management and political expertise in localities on the fringes of large cities. The rapid growth of these cities can over tax the city's ability to provide basic services and carry out effective planning. It means that even where there are substantial environmental contrasts and labour force legislation, these can be easily avoided by unscrupulous entrepreneurs.

Conclusion

There can be no doubt that the future of Asia is an increasingly urban one. Within a quarter century the majority of Asians will live in urban centres. This represents a profound change from an absolutely dominantly rural-based population—which characterised the bulk of Asian countries as colonisation came to an end. The urbanisation of Asia in the 1990s is not only unprecedented in rapidity and scale but also in some of the spatial forms that urbanisation is taking. The rate of growth of cities has outpaced the development of structures and institutions to direct this growth to the benefit of the maximum number of Asians. While the outlook is for a continuation of rapid urban growth in the region in spite of massive national declines in fertility in Asia the rate of growth will decline in the early years of the twenty first century. This reduction in population growth rates represents a significant opportunity for the institutions and structures in these cities to catch up and consolidate in their planning and management of these cities.

4 Urban Economic Development and Globalisation Linkages in the Pacific Rim

MICHAEL LINDFIELD and ROBERT STIMSON

Introduction

Increasingly it is city regions that are the 'nexus of the new global economy and society' (Knight, 1989: 327) as the barriers between nations are being eroded and the control of governments over the flow of capital, technology and innovation is reduced. Nowhere are the dynamics of the interplay of the forces of globalisation and the roles of cities as engines of economic growth more dramatic than in the Pacific Rim region and its rapidly emerging mega-cities and extended metropolitan regions (EMRs) (McGee, 1995; Stimson, 1996, 1997).

For city regions to be competitive in the new global economy, it is imperative that they develop effective policies for economic development by identifying a 'trajectory' by which a city can integrate within the global economy, with the objective being the generation of employment and wealth and the achievement of sustainable development.

Traditionally, the competitiveness of nations was measured by the ability of companies to access the lowest cost inputs—capital, labour, energy and raw materials (Porter and van der Linde, 1996). But in recent times, globalisation has changed the perception of competitive advantage, as companies source low cost inputs anywhere in the world, and as new rapidly emerging technologies offset many cost disadvantages of 'high cost' labour. Today it is not simply having resources that matters; rather it is using resources productively that constitutes competitiveness. Consequently, to be globally competitive is to be able to innovate rapidly and to provide the right conditions to attract or sustain individual business activities. For example, the recent economic boom in many south-east and east Asian urban economies has made it harder for them to compete on price alone, as it is increasingly necessary to compete on the basis of knowledge at relatively low costs—that is, relative to OECD countries (Knowledge in Action, 1996)—while high cost urban economies, as in the United States, are nonetheless competitive because of the innovative milieux they have developed.

This chapter overviews the implications of processes of globalisation for major city regions in the Pacific Rim. It provides a descriptive framework by which city regions might assess their competitiveness and pursue strategic directions for economic development in the context of their existing and potential factor endowment, including labour, capital, land and infrastructure, producer services and innovation networks.

Globalisation Forces and Urban Regions

The changes in the global economy that occurred in the wake of the breakup in the mid-1970s of the Bretton Woods Agreement (the system of regulation of the international economy that was established at the end of World War Two) and the progressive deregulation of trade, along with technological advances in transport, communications and manufacturing materials and processes, have combined to result in a closer global web of economic linkages which, in turn, have created global production systems with significant spatial consequences. Castells (1989: 348) provides a summary of these processes as creating 'a veritable geometry of production and consumption, labour and capital management and information—a geometry that defies the specific meaning of place outside its position in a network whose shape changes relentlessly in response to messages of unseen signals and unknown codes'.

Over the last decade or so, there has been a plethora of literature dealing with globalisation and the new global economy (e.g. Knight, 1989; Castells, 1989; Dicken, 1992). This global economy is a highly urbanised phenomenon. The 1994 Joint OECD/Australian Government conference on *Cities and the New Global Economy* (1995) highlighted from a policy perspective the importance of the linkage between rapid economic growth and urbanisation occurring in Asian-Pacific cities. It emphasised how the capacity of these cities to grow and change will be critical to the ongoing expansion of the global economy. Already major urban corridors stand astride the rapidly developing economies of the Pacific Rim, as outlined by researchers including Rimmer (1989), McGee (1995), and Stimson (1995). The importance of these mega-cities and EMRs is illustrated dramatically by Prud'homme (1995), who notes, for example, how the gross domestic product (GDP) of Tokyo, Osaka, Los Angeles, Paris and New York exceeds that of the 16 smallest OECD nations; how the GDP of Osaka exceeds that of Australia by 10 percent and of India by 25 percent; the GDP of Seoul exceeds the entire GDP of Indonesia, and Yokohama's that of Bangladesh; how the Tokyo region contributes over 30 percent of the GDP of Japan; and how many of the primate 'mega-cities' of the Pacific Rim region have a significant role in the economic development of the region, and will have an even more significant role in the future. This has changed dramatically down for many of these since the 1997-98 Asian currency crisis.

Globalising Forces Described

To provide a context for this chapter, we provide a brief overview of some of the significant forces of globalisation that are redefining the roles of EMRs and impacting their competitive positions.

The first is the increasing centrality of the financial structure through which money is created, allocated and put to use, which has increased the power of finance over production. Harvey (1989) emphasises the degree to which finance has become an independent force in the modern world, while Strange (1991) tells of the increased 'structural power' exercised by whoever or whatever determines the financial structure, especially the relations between creditors and debtors, savers and investors. The global reach of finance is particularly striking, as global financial institutions, in a variety of forms, influence and discipline the world's national economies and many businesses, and as characterised by the rise of world capital markets in 'world cities' such as New York, London, Tokyo, Hong Kong and Sydney, and as evidenced by the incredibly rapid increase since the 1970s in the volumes of foreign direct investment (FDI) in both developed and developing nations across a wide range of economic activity sectors encompassing manufacturing, property, business services, retailing, tourism, transport and telecommunications and media. Supra-national institutions have emerged that spread way beyond the old manufacturing trans-national corporations.

The second is the increasing importance of the 'knowledge structure' (Strange, 1988) or 'expert systems' (Giddens, 1990) in production and, later, the distribution and exchange of knowledge as a crucial element of global and local economic systems on a scale not previously known and which is facilitated through strategic alliances and networks developed by corporations, business, professional groups, institutions, organisations and community movements.   The overwhelming dominance of technology-based solutions, the acceptance of a scientific ethos, and a common cultural context of shared products, entertainment and symbols of status, provides a 'common language' among professionals.   This, combined with the ubiquity of enabling communications media and technologies, means that the 'knowledge structure' is becoming less and less tied to particular national or local business cultures, although some 'technopoles' continue to thrive. The term 'technopole' is used to describe deliberate attempts to plan and promote within one location technically innovative, industrial-related production.   But most successful examples of technopoles have emerged as a result of synergistic collaboration bridging private and public sectors. They include industrial complexes of high technology firms that eventuated in the absence of deliberate planning, although government and universities had a significant role in their development (e.g. Silicon Valley in California and Boston's Route 128).   Technopoles include 'science cities' or scientific research complexes that are spatially separated from manufacturing (e.g. Tsukuba in Japan and Taedok in the Republic of Korea).   Many attempts to generate technopoles have failed to achieve the 'innovative milieu' necessary to drive the synergy between different firms and R&D institutions, that allows a technopole to achieve self-generating development.   There are also old metropolises which retain their leading role as centres of high technology firms and research (e.g. Paris and Tokyo), and newer metropolitan centres that developed as centres of high technology production (e.g. Los Angeles and Munich) (UNCHS, 1996).

These trends have resulted in a need for both firms and localities to 'go global'.   There is a sense in much recent writing that corporations have no choice but to 'go global' very early on in their development, for at least two reasons (Strange, 1991).   First, new methods of production with different patterns of returns to scale have resulted in a need to market globally to take advantage of these changes.   Second, greater trans-national mobility of capital has made investing abroad easier, quicker and cheaper, resulting in corporations being open to competition at an early time and major changes have occurred in the ease of transport and communication. The result is that national measures of concentration and market share have become less relevant as corporations manoeuvre in global markets, with obvious consequences for the balance of economic power.

A third phenomenon is globalisation of organisations, as seen in both the growing power of global corporations and the rise of trans-national economic diplomacy.   Governments and firms bargain with themselves and one another on the world stage.   In addition, trans-national 'plural authority' structures, such as the World Trade Organisation (WTO), the UN, G7, the European Community (EC), the North American Free Trade Association (NAFTA), and the Asia Pacific Economic Cooperation (APEC) forum, have become increasingly powerful (Held, 1991). The result appears to be an increasing use of members of 'plural authority' structures (Gilpin, 1987).

New Global Geographies

An outcome of the processes described above is the rise of 'new global geographies' (Amin and Thrift, 1995), of borderless geographies with quite different breaks and boundaries from the past. This is of specific relevance to urban regions. Whether the global economy is seen in terms of a 'space of flows' (Castells, 1989), or as almost without a border (Ohmae, 1990) or as localised production districts strung out round the world (Storper, 1991), or as the centralisation of economic power and control within a very small number of global cities (Sassen, 1991), or as something in between these extremes, it is nonetheless clear that it is now an important factor in local geography.

Impact on Cities in the Pacific Rim

The key elements of the impact of globalisation on urban areas around the Pacific Rim region has been addressed by the Asian Development Bank (Stubbs and Clarke, 1996: 66) as well as by academic researchers (e.g. Blakely and Stimson, 1992; McGee, 1995; McGee and Robinson, 1995). Some of the implications are outlined below.

Investment Decisions

The development of international markets for goods and services is encouraged by large free trade zones, such as ASEAN and, more recently, NAFTA and APEC, and the establishment of new industrial core areas, such as the Special Economic Zones (SEZs) in the People's Republic of China, which support the development of industrial companies with access to air transportation and business services. The Pacific Rim nations are now dominating the global economy in both labour-intensive and high technology manufacturing, and these activities are overwhelmingly based in cities within EMRs.

Increasingly, decisions on manufacturing location by multi-national firms are based on comparison of labour costs and other key factors of production across a range of potential host countries. Such decisions are strongly influenced by the qualitative attractions of alternative locations, as well as by financial cost considerations, by long-term economic prospects for a potential nation, and by sector-specific conditions concerning such items as investment incentives and regulations.

Cities in the Pacific Rim region, and particularly the mega-cities and the EMRs, are competing among each other for inward FDI that originates from OECD nations as well as from Asian regional investors in such countries as Japan, Korea, Hong Kong, Singapore, Taiwan and China. For example, at one level the massive commercial development of Pudong in Shanghai competes with the fast growing Eastern Seaboard development in Thailand. At another level financial service conglomerates in Europe may be trying to choose between Bangkok, Jakarta, Kuala Lumpur and Singapore for a new regional base for their operations. For example, an OECD-based textile conglomerate may compare labour costs, textile quotas and many other factors in a decision whether to locate in Dhaka, Calcutta, Manila or Shenzhen.

Knowledge-Based Activity Agglomeration in Poly-Centric Metro Regions

In parallel with the above, there is an emergence of high concentrations of knowledge-based, information intensive producer services and communication industries—such as financial services, advertising, legal services, research and development, and media—in 'world cities' which attract the headquarters of large corporations. This trend goes hand-in-hand with new technologies for the faster diffusion of information. Cities are the natural base for information-based industries. Sassen (1995) notes how the increasing inter-relationship of services and the increased importance of time is leading to the formulation of a producer services complex in all major cities. It might be expected, given advances in communications, that such services could be located in more dispersed patterns but, in fact, the advantages of agglomeration economies and the economies of scope, and highly innovative environments of these cities, are major forces favouring their competition advantage.

This agglomeration trend is, however, taking new spatial forms. While the information-based services might prefer a central location, particularly those with a strong international orientation, other more traditional service industries may prefer cheaper locations in the suburbs or outer metropolitan area, giving rise to what Garreau (1991) has termed the 'edge city' phenomenon. Sassen (1995) envisages a new geography of the city, one that could involve a metropolitan grid of networks connected through advanced telematics. These are not suburbs in the way we conceived of them 20 years ago, but a new form or space of centrality. These newly structured poly-centric mega-metro regional forms are common to both Western and Asian cities (Blakely and Stimson, 1992) and to cities in developed and developing nations, as seen in cities as diverse as Los Angles, San Francisco, Tokyo, Bangkok, Singapore, Jakarta and Sydney. The archetypical poly-centric metropolitan region is Los Angeles, a sprawling EMR of 'cultural innovation and entrepreneurial dynamism, with a history of rejecting the past and realising its own dreams of the future' (Castells and Hall, 1994: 182).

Smart Infrastructure

The link between infrastructure and productivity in cities has long been established, but in the contemporary era infrastructure has taken on a perspective much wider than traditional physical and social infrastructure. The above pressures mean that there is not only an increasing need for cities to promote themselves in terms of their traditional comparative advantages of transport links, communications, and infrastructure related to this production base, but also there is in addition a need for cities to provide innovative milieu and quality lifestyles, including good housing, cultural attributes, and tourism opportunities.

Thus, the concepts 'smart infrastructure' and 'strategic infrastructure' become crucial (Smilor and Wakelin, 1990). Typically today key strategic and smart infrastructure includes international airports and sea ports, telecommunications, education and R&D facilities, and cultural facilities and services. It involves integrated road, rail and air network linkages with other 'world cities' and with other cities within the nation, minimisation of energy and utility service costs, access to capital market institutions, and flexible and responsive institutional arrangements to enhance a competitive business culture and innovation.

Human resource development is a fundamental component of urban infrastructure. Smilor and Wakelin (1990) refer to smart infrastructure as comprising talent, technology, capital and know-how, with public policy being influential in determining how these key factors are harnessed in promoting technological activities, innovation, and value added production.

Institutions, both public and private, are crucial in creating the smart infrastructure for generating an innovative milieu, including business angels networks, venture capital pools, consortia, and professional support organisations. And regulatory environments need to facilitate enlightened but quality-oriented planning and development controls, business incubators, technical support programmes, competitive taxation arrangements, intellectual property protection, quality indicators, and advanced transportation and telecommunications systems access.

Many cities are using professional marketing companies to promote their infrastructure attractions, and their quality of life and business environments. It goes without saying that government incentives for such footloose manufacturing or service employment are common, and include tax-free holidays for an initial period, enterprise zones and export processing zones (EPZ), subsidised housing, and training facilities. Increasingly, Asian cities are likely to benefit from trends to specialisation among inward investments, as they do from specialisation trends in the domestic economy.

Environmental Quality and Equity Issues

Globalisation has both positive and negative impacts, the latter in particular being environmental and social. Cohen (1995) notes how 'the natural and physical environments in cities and towns, and particularly the largest cities, have deteriorated to a degree which is now imposing heavy economic, financial and social costs on urban residents'. Congestion, pollution of air and water, noise and other environmental impacts of large scale urbanisation are affecting human health and quality of urban life as well as imposing costs. In efforts to hold down costs in order to compete in the global economy on product price, many countries and cities are tempted to 'go easy' on enforcement of environmental standards.

But globalisation also spreads environmental awareness and forces for compliance to standards. For example, multi-nationals are lobbied to apply the same standards abroad as at home and international non-governmental organisations (NGOs) monitor activity throughout the world and the multi-lateral banks and official development assistance (ODA) agencies often enforce environmental screening in their projects.

Significant social problems arise from urbanisation and globalisation through the concentration of wealth and the growing disparities between the rich and the poor. Cohen (1995) cites the paradox identified by the World Bank that cities have become both the engines of growth and the locus of impoverishment of millions and millions of people. Richardson (1989) has shown how there has emerged within cities the

> ...bifurcation of the labour market; the development of 'citadels' and 'ghettos', the widening fluctuations in metropolitan economies in response to the 'hypermobility' of capital, exchange rates and resources price changes; erosion of the metropolitan tax base as a result of competitive subsidies to attract and retain internationally mobile economic activities; a shift from investment in social overhead capital to economic overhead capital; a rise in CBD land and property values attracted by the internationalisation of Pacific Rim metropolitan economies.

The urban poor lack access to infrastructure, housing and many types of jobs, and they are most severely affected by urban environmental degradation (Poungsomlee, 1995). Low investment in human capital in many developing nations perpetuates the inability of vast numbers of poor people, including rural to urban immigrants, to take advantage of urban employment opportunities in expanding areas of the economy. There is intense competition for formal sector jobs, and more and more people in mega-cities of the developing world are locked into the informal sector.

City Response

The global economy thus has, and will continue to have, a major impact on urban regions and has implications for urban management objectives and policies.

The Agendas

Globalisation forces generate a series of challenges for governments in addressing the structural and sectoral reforms that need to be put in place in cities if parallel improvements in productivity and in urban amenity and quality of life are to be achieved. Cohen (1995) cites the 'four P's' for which there is a need for a stronger national government presence to deal with: 'population growth' and its consequent resource demands; 'poverty' and the need for assistance programmes to be directed to its alleviation through training, employment and enhancement, and housing; 'pollution' and the emerging brown agenda; and 'political changes' to strengthen institutions and improve governance. Within this context are a complex range of issues requiring innovative and concerted public policy and governance responses.

Transportation and urban development planning are particularly important areas for public policy. Increasingly it is crucial that transport decisions are not made in isolation. 'Urban planning and development must integrate transport with decisions issues, such as land use and economic development' (AHURI, 1995: 19). But Hall (1994) questions the degree to which the transport issues and solutions in cities of the developed world, with their decentralised urban populations and jobs in wide suburban belts crossed by freeway systems, are applicable to the traffic and transport issues facing cities like Bangkok, Manila and Jakarta.

Water pollution and wetlands management are further major environmental issues resulting from urban, population and economic growth, as are waste generation and management. However, despite the urban environmental problems, the mega-cities and EMRs continue to grow, and in fact the problems they create represent considerable opportunities for environmental technologies and urban management, and government regulation and economic incentives can be used to hasten the search for solutions to improve environmental management.

Governance and Institutional Reform

Perhaps the greatest challenge for cities in the new global economy is to evolve more appropriate government structures to deal with issues of land, infrastructure, services, housing environment, and economic development bearing in mind that 'to keep a competitive edge, cities must provide the right environments that will attract entrepreneurs, financiers, managers and the workforce' (Abaya, 1996).

Within the Pacific Rim region are located most of the world's highest performing economies in the decade to 1996. According to the World Bank (1993: 3-6) many of these nations had 'got the basics right' by encouraging domestic investment and facilitating rapid growth in human capital. Governments have intervened through multiple channels to foster development of targeted industries, provide public investment in key infrastructure, facilitate and encourage firm establishment, specify export targets, and share information between public and private institutions. Government policies sought to achieve macro-economic stability and export growth; to provide friendly environments; to build an institutional basis for shared growth; and to keep external debt under control and minimise exchange rate fluctuations. However, the events of late 1997 have raised questions about the stability of financial institutions and the sustainability of growth in many of the economies of south-east and east Asia as currencies went into a downward spin and levels of indebtedness blew out.

Through the 1980s and into the 1990s many of the national governments of East and South East Asian countries have recognised the benefits to be gained from linking national economic policy with city and regional policy. For example, Indonesia's national economic development plan gave explicit recognition to the role of cities, and in particular the provision of infrastructure necessary to attract investment in economic activities in an increasingly competitive global capital market (Moochtar, 1995). Parkinson (1995) stresses how national urban strategies need to focus on 'how governments can help cities to help themselves to flourish', but that there remain major institutional impediments in governance because it is common for cities to be characterised by fragmented governmental responsibilities and funding arrangements, as evident in cities like Bangkok. Helping city leaders to make strategic choices is critical, particularly in being flexible and responsive to change. Singapore has been hailed as a shining example of how an urban economic development strategy has worked to transform that city-state into a global metropolis through the 'intelligent island' and 'global hub' strategy (Lim and Malone-Lee, 1994).

But it is clear that the complexity and extent of the issues facing cities are such that they cannot be addressed by any single organisation or group of organisations alone, nor by any single level of government (AHURI, 1995). Coordinated action, involving public-private partnerships and collaboration across the various levels of government are pressing areas of institutional reform to ensure that the development and planning of cities and the provision of infrastructure and services, enhances the international competitiveness of nations as well as achieving more sustainable urban growth. Sustained strategic leadership is an essential catalytic factor towards these ends. The issue of managing sustainable urban systems and societies ultimately depends on the 'ability of local societies to negotiate solutions for the places in which they live' (McGee, 1995: 14). The globalisation process in which cities get bigger presents a planning and management imperative the magnitude of which cannot be underestimated.

Some Approaches to Stimulating Economic Development and Urbanisation

As discussed earlier, as a response to the dynamics of the global economy, many countries in South East Asia have created EPZs mostly near established urban areas and have, at a macro-level, linked nearby areas of complimentary economic structure (Yeung, 1990). EPZs include those in Baguio and Bataan in the Philippines, Bayan Lepas in Penang and several others on the west coast of peninsular Malaysia, and Lat Krebang outside Bangkok in Thailand, which were mostly formed in the late 1960s or early 1970s. A variant of the EPZ is China's SEZs, the first of which was created in 1979 at Shenzhen. Other SEZs include Zhuhai and Shantou, located in Guangdong Provence because of their proximity to Hong Kong and Macau, and Xiamen in Fujian Provence with the geographical advantage of being close to Taiwan on the western side of the Taiwan Strait. The latest creation of EPZs is in Vietnam which, with its recent re-entry into the world community, has been active in promoting FDI inflows and market-based economic development. The commonality of all these zones is that, to a large extent, their establishment was predicated upon job creation through manufacturing production, primarily for the world market. Another innovative economic device to access the world market is the emergence of sub-regional economic cooperative zones, called 'growth triangles', to date a uniquely Asian phenomenon. Such sub-regional economic entities, crossing national boarders, came into being to maximise the efficiency of utilisation of the factors of production, which single country development would not permit (Thant *et al.*, 1994). For this reason, Singapore, Malaysia (Johore) and Indonesia (Riau Islands) have been actively pursuing cooperative development in the State of Johore and Batam Island, in an area that has been called the SIJORI Growth Triangle. Here excellent economic complementarities exist where Singapore as a world city has been providing capital, technology and entrepreneurship, while the other parts of the neighbouring countries provide land and labour at cheaper costs. One impact, from a spatial viewpoint, is the acceleration of ribbon-type urban and industrial development in western Johore.

Other growth triangles exist or are at the planning stage in the Pacific Asia. The Southern China Growth Triangle, centred on Hong Kong (often described on the Pearl River Delta region), involves the participation of Hong Kong with Taiwan and China's southern provinces of Guangdong and Fujian. In addition to economic complementarities that exist in abundance, there are cultural and linguistic affinities which further facilitate cooperative development. Growth triangles have also been proposed at the mouth of Tumen River in North Asia and several others in South East Asia, such as one linking Myanmar, Laos, Thailand and China's Yunnan (called the Golden Quadrangle); the Northern Growth Triangle involving northern Malaysia, southern Thailand and northern Sumatra (Indonesia); and the Eastern Growth Triangle covering Mindanao (Philippines), Sulawesi (Indonesia), Sabah and Sarawak (Malaysia) and Brunei (Yeung, 1990). There is some potential benefit in this form of economic cooperation for countries in the Asia-Pacific region, as it provides impetus for its current emphasis on free trade and open regionalism.

Related to the above processes of cooperative regional development focused on sub-regions and EPZs, has been the emergence of EMRs in Pacific Asia. The process has been documented by Ginsburg *et al.* (1991), and has been referred to earlier. In the context of globalisation, even more complex issues of policy are raised for concerned countries and planning authorities in the areas of land use, population migration, FDI flow and pollution control, to name just a few important areas.

Implications for Urban Regional Economic Development

The implications of the preceding discussions for the formulation of urban economic development policy are important. A nation and its cities seeking to adapt to take advantage of the challenge of the international economy, need to address several issues. These are six fold.

First, strengthening financial systems in view of the primacy of finance is essential, with the challenge being to ensure the poor have access to appropriate services from the financial system in order to finance income generation/poverty alleviation activity.

Second, strengthening the knowledge structure and technological development is crucial. For the urban poor it is important that a broad educational base be provided which links through to the 'higher tech' sectors of the economy, thereby avoiding a dualism in the structure of human capital development.

Third, it is necessary to ensure competitive forces are at work to achieve efficient outcomes and regulatory processes are not co-opted by vested interests. This also means selective 'pork barrelling' of the poor will be more difficult, and thus the process is controversial even among the poor as it will usually involve the application of 'user pays' principles.

Fourth, it is important to strengthen the city's bargaining and promotion skills in respect of FDI providers to attract appropriate higher value-added industry and to create employment. The challenge here is to adequately protect workers whose low cost is the key motivation for their employment.

Fifth, it might be appropriate to look at strengthening regional trans-border urban systems through growth triangles and corridors.

Finally, supporting network integration is vital, both in terms of technology (especially communications) and in terms of including representatives of cities in regional and global networks for sharing of information, through formal government forums such as APEC, and through informal organisations and networks, such as the Pacific Rim Council for Urban Development (PRCUD), business networks, and NGO collaboration and through effective city twinning arrangements.

The question is, however, in what economic industry sectors should these activities be focused?

A Framework for Focusing Policy: Competition Versus Complementarity

In the context of the global economy, the competitiveness of a city region presents a difficult concept, because unlike a firm, whose competitiveness might be with respect to its cost structure and its market success for one or a limited range of products or services, the economic competitiveness of a region represents the sum of all the firms in all the industry sectors that constitute the regional economy, the totality of the regulatory arrangements across all levels of government that impact on the region, and the region's total infrastructure. Thus, when we talk about regional competitiveness, we need to be clear about on what, and with what we are competing, and we need to be clear about what it is that we wish to be competing on. For as Porter (1990) points out, there is no accepted definition of competitiveness, and it needs to be considered from the viewpoint of the goals of those competing. In the global economy, competition is a race without a finishing line; it is ongoing and never-ending (Roberts, 1996).

However, it is possible to develop a framework—or a set of frameworks—by which a city region can assess its competitiveness, by which it might identify those industry sectors for which it already has developed, or for which it potentially might develop a competitive advantage. In addition, it is necessary to identify the complementarities which might be enhanced across industry sectors, for example, and through inter-regional linkages in production processes and by trade ties.

The Competitive Paradigm

For convenience, 'competitiveness' might be viewed at two distinct levels: at the industry level; and at the national or regional level. Traditional analysis at the industry level views international competitiveness as being achieved and maintained by meeting market demand more efficiently and effectively than competitors, with firms making decision about price, quality, marketing, reliability of products and services, and so on, with the firm that best meets market demand being considered the most competitive, measured against standard indicators of success such as capture of market share and relative profitability. At the national or regional level, competitiveness can be seen as referring to 'the degree to which a nation [or region] can, under free and fair market conditions, produce goods and services that meet the test of international markets, while simultaneously maintaining and expanding the real income of its citizens' (Bureau of Industry Economics, 1994: 30). This approach is one of 'Pareto optimality', where a nation or region is not considered competitive if its citizens suffer a decline in standards of living as a result of the striving for greater industry competitiveness.

The competitiveness of nations has been assessed for some time by the IMD-WEF multi-variate index developed by the Swiss-based World Competitiveness Project. In this approach, competitiveness is defined as follows:

> Competitiveness is the ability of a country to create added value and thus increase national wealth by managing assets and processes, attractiveness and aggressiveness, globality and proximity, and by integrating these relationships into an economic and social model (Garelli, 1996:6).

The IMD-WEF proposes that at the heart of a nation's competitiveness will be six inter-related concepts: 'assets' and 'processes'; 'globality' and 'proximity'; and 'attractiveness' and 'aggressiveness'.

'Assets' refer to 'inherited assets' which generally create competitive advantage and these include natural resources, land and population size. However, it is important to note that increased levels of productivity means that fewer national resources are required to meet demand. Thus, we find increasingly that nations that are asset rich (e.g. Australia) nowadays have a lesser comparative advantage as commodity prices have fallen, while the prices for higher-value manufacturers and advanced producer services have risen or remained stable, benefiting places like Japan and Singapore.

In contrast, 'processes' increasingly are defining competitive advantage, as they are the processes of creating value-added rather than relying on the intrinsic value of assets. New production techniques reduce unit costs, increase productivity, improve quality, and maximise value, and the drivers of these processes are knowledge-based and information-intensive inputs. Thus, we have seen the rise, for example, of the 'asset poor' but 'process efficient' economies of Japan and the 'Asian tigers', and the dominance by Japan of consumer electronics and semi-conductor industries, both of which were created by the United States (Thurow, 1992: 177-86).

'Globality' refers to the trend toward integration of some nations and some regions within them into the global economy, which assumes that factors related to production need not belong to the end user. Singapore is a perfect example of this trend, as the more a place integrates the greater is its benefit from the competitive advantage of other countries which can produce certain products cheaper and better than they can themselves, with the local emphasis being devoted to improving their own competitive advantage, through harnessing information technology and logistics.

In contrast, 'proximity' is about the traditional activities which provided added value close to the end user, as seen in the rise and later fall, as a result of 'globality', of the manufacturing cities of the developed world.

The difference between 'attractiveness' and 'aggressiveness' is basically that between an exported and an investment-led form of economic growth; thus, 'attractiveness' refers to the efforts of a nation or region to attract inward FDI to create jobs and wealth within its borders (as evidenced by the emerging new tiger economies of Thailand and Indonesia), while 'aggressiveness' involves encouraging local firms to export and invest overseas to create export-led growth.

Overall, the IMD-WEF identifies a commonly used single indicator to measure the competitive progress of a nation, this being the 'ability of a country to achieve sustained high rates of growth in GDP per capita'. But it sees competitiveness in a wider context, defining it as follows:

> ...competitiveness refers to the fitness of a country's economic institutions and structure to produce growth, in view of the overall structure of the world economy. In this meaning, an economy is internationally competitive if its institutions and policies will support sustained and rapid economic growth. The competitive nations [regions] are the ones that have chosen the institutions and policies that promote long-term growth (Sachs *et al.*, 1996: 12).

This can also be applied to regions, such as a major city, although the range of data sources to develop indicators might be more limited than at the national level.

Applying the IMD-WEF Competitiveness Concept in Regional Development Analysis

It is possible to benchmark nations against nations and regions against nations and regions on any indicator or on synthetic dimensions or factors derived from sets of these indicators. For example, the IMD-WEF uses a set of some 400 qualitative and quantitative indicators of competitiveness but Figure 4.1 shows, for a selection of nations, including many from the Pacific Rim region, how on a dynamic measure of real GDP growth per capita 1990-94, there is a number of orders of magnitude of variation in performance of national economies. For example, China records a rate over double that of Hong Kong, which is about double that of Australia and over double that of the United States, which is about three times that of Portugal, with some nations (especially those of the former European communist bloc) having significant negative growth.

Kasper *et al.* (1992) provide an interesting and innovative regional application of the IMD-WEF approach to study the internationally benchmarked regional competitiveness of the Gladstone-Fitzroy region in Queensland, Australia. More recently the Queensland Department of Tourism, Small Business and Industry (Howard, 1996) has replicated and extended this approach to benchmark the competitiveness of the Queensland state economy.

Howard (1996) outlines the components which constitute the development of a 'regional competitiveness evaluation framework'. It begins with a 'macro-level location analysis' of general investment environment issues employing the IMD-WEF indicators weighted into 55 indices called 'aspects of competitiveness', which in turn are weighted into eight primary indices called 'factors of competitiveness'. These are listed in Table 4.1. For space reasons the full list of IMD-WEF indicators used as the basis for deriving these indices is not reproduced here. However, this approach enables a region (or a nation) to be ranked based on their comparative performance measured in all indicators, aspects and factors.

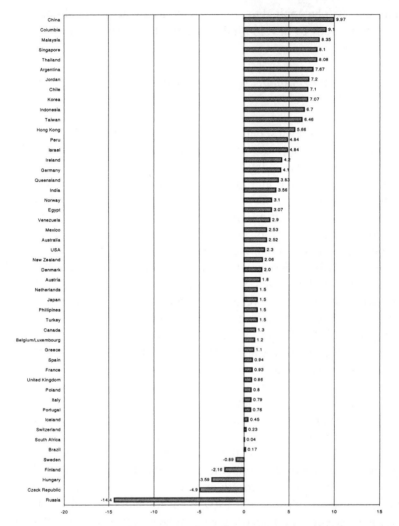

Figure 4.1   The performance of nations and a case study region, Queensland on an overall competitiveness indicator, real GDP compound annual growth, 1990-1994

Source: Compiled from IMD-WEF reports, Barelli, 1995, and as cited in Howard, 1996

In the Queensland study, two weighting regimes were used: a 'general industry weighting' where all indicators are essentially equally weighted or comparable to the IMD-WEF weightings; and 'specific

Table 4.1 Factors, aspects and indicators of national and regional competitiveness derived from the IMD-WEF world competitiveness report and applied to Queensland: eight factors and 57 aspects

	No. of IMD-WEF Indicators used to Derive Aspects	No. Of Indicators used for Queensland Study
Factor 1: Domestic Economic Strength		
Aspects		
1.1 Value added	18	9
1.2 Capital formation	6	1
1.3 Inflation	3	2
1.4 Cost of living	4	2
1.5 Private fund consumption	3	3
1.6 Economic forecast	7	2
1.7 Industrial production	8	6
1.8 Services sector	4	3
1.9 Agriculture	6	6
Factor 2: Internationalisation		
Aspects		
2.1 Trade performance	13	10
2.2 Exchange rates	3	2
2.3 Export of goods & services	23	22
2.4 Import of goods & services	14	13
2.5 National protectionism	5	2
2.6 Partnerships with foreign firms	4	0
2.7 Foreign direct investment abroad	3	0
2.8 Foreign direct investment inward	3	0
2.9 Cultural openness	6	2
Factor 3: Government		
Aspects:		
3.1 National debt	9	4
3.2 Official reserves	2	0
3.3 Government expenditure	4	3
3.4 State control of industry	9	3
3.5 Government efficiency & transparency	8	4
3.6Nature of competitive environment	3	0
3.7 Fiscal policies	12	2
3.8 Social & political stability	6	0
Factor 4: Finance		
Aspects:		
4.1 Cost of capital & rate of return	4	1
4.2 Availability of finance	7	0
4.3 Stock markets	8	2
4.4 Financial services	9	3
Factor 5: Infrastructure		
Aspects:		
5.1 Energy production	7	6
5.2 Energy consumption	5	4
5.3 Energy self-sufficiency	4	2
5.4 Environment	12	2
5.5 Transport infrastructure	7	2
5.6 Information technology	11	3
5.7 Technological infrastructure	5	1
Factor 6: Management		
Aspects:		
6.1 Productivity	8	8
6.2 Labour costs & compensation levels	5	4

Table 4.1 (Contd.)

	No. of IMD-WEF Indicators used to Derive Aspects	No. Of Indicators used for Queensland Study
6.3 Remuneration of top management	2	2
6.4 Corporate performance	8	1
	No. of IMD-WEF Indicators used to Derive Aspects	No. Of Indicators used for Queensland Study
6.5 Entrepreneurship	4	0
6.6 Management efficiency	9	2
Factor 7: Science and Technology Aspects:		
7.1 Research & development expenditure	9	8
7.2 Research & development personnel	9	0
7.3 Scientific research	3	0
7.4 Patents	10	0
7.5 Technology management	8	5
Factor 8: People Aspects:		
8.1 Population characteristics	10	9
8.2 Labour force characteristics	10	9
8.3 Employment	10	9
8.4 Unemployment	2	2
8.5 Educational structure	12	3
8.6 Quality of life	10	7
8.7 Attitude of workforce	6	3

Source: Derived from Howard, 1996

industry weighting', where the needs and preferences of particular industries or firms in location decisions decide the weight applied to each indicator. 'These weightings are important given the influence of varying coast structures and market conditions within an industry or competitiveness' (Howard, 1996: 16-7). The Queensland study analysed 39 industry sectors at the four digit ASIC level, and from this, 10 sectors were identified as 'priority' sectors for development at a State level— namely, pharmaceuticals and veterinary products, scientific and medical equipment, fabricated metal products, electronic equipment, red meat, vegetable products, clothing, packaging, construction machining, and material handling equipment (DBIRD, 1994: 11).

The next step in the Queensland competitiveness study was to conduct a SWOT analysis on the most significant industry sectors in terms of the 12 characteristics listed in Table 4.2. This approach provides a structured basis for determining specific industry weights on the industries of the multi-variate competitiveness analysis, thereby permitting a competitiveness analysis on the basis of the competitive needs of a specific industry (Howard, 1996: 10).

Table 4.2   Twelve characteristics for conducting SWOT analysis for most significant industry sectors

1	Industry growth and growth trends
2	Industry structure and major players
3	Major markets and market share
4	Future market potential
5	Level of value-added in production
6	Labour and capital productivity
7	Exports and export growth
8	Imports and import growth
9	Import coverage
10	Investment levels
11	Capacity utilisation
12	Labour and capital intensities and a host of other information relating to the competitiveness and future growth prospects of specified industries in the region

Source: Howard 1996:10

However, it is as well to recognise that competitiveness is not simply dependent on supply-side factors (i.e., factor costs per unit), but also on market demand (i.e., market size and pricing range acceptable to the market. Thus, the fourth stage of the process involves 'strategic market analysis' to ascertain the 'location, size, structure and complexity of the major markets for each industry or firm as well as the cost and logistic problems which limit a firm's capacity to service that market from particular locations' (Howard, 1996: 11). This also provides information on the growth prospects for identified key industries for a region and the likely changes in strategy which might be required to remain competitive. The Queensland case study identified competitive strengths and weaknesses across the factors and aspects derived from a selection of the IMD-WEF indicators, giving its overall rating against the nations (as identified in Figure 4.1). Table 4.3 reproduces those outcomes.

Finally, 'micro-level location analysis' can be undertaken to conclude the regional competitiveness evaluation process. This should relate to industry specific locations for a plant or facility siting. It might involve specific comparative cost and returns on investment analyses for particular investment projects relative to the most competitive regions for such activities. The Queensland case study has not yet proceeded to this stage.

In proposing the above framework a relatively comprehensive overview of regional competitiveness is provided through key industry identification, strategic market analysis, and site selection for activities. This could be developed and applied to any region, allowing for the inevitable variations in data availability between developed and developing nations, and the ease with which primary data can be collected, bearing in mind that the IMD-WEF indicators are a mixture of secondary data and primary survey data. What is important is the notion that competitiveness is a dynamic concept, that the conditions for regional competitiveness change as the nature of the global economy changes, and that the competitiveness evaluation process must be flexible (Howard 1996: 11).

A City Benchmarking Exercise: Melbourne, Australia

A benchmarking exercise using a wide range of indicators, not dissimilar in general terms to some of the IMD-WEF indicators, has been undertaken by Melbourne City Council, located at the heart of Australia's second largest city. Called the 'Capital City Index', it provides key statistical indicators of the level of performance across key indicators including property, employment, investment, retail confidence and cultural amenity, derived from a benchmarking study, *Advantage Melbourne*, completed in September 1994 by the KPMG Management Consulting group.

Table 4.3   The balance of competitive strengths and weaknesses of Queensland on the IMD-WEF derived competitiveness factors and aspects ranked relative to a selection of 48 nations

Competitive Strengths	*Rank Against Benchmark Nations*
DOMESTIC ECONOMIC STRENGTH	
Real GDP Compound Annual Growth 1990-94	17
Real GDP per Capita Growth 1990-94	19
Total Gross Domestic Investment 1994	10
Consumer Price Inflation 1994	10
Average Monthly Rent 1994	2
Chemicals as % Manufacturing Output 1991	13
Retail Sales per Capita 1992-93	17
Agricultural Productivity 1992	3
INTERNATIONALISATION	
Trade to GDP Ratio 1993	15

Table 4.3 (Contd.)

Competitive Strengths	Rank Against Benchmark Nations
Terms of Trade Index 1990-93	11
Balance of Commercial Services 1993	12
Exports of Goods and Services 1993	18
Marginal Propensity to Import 1989-93	4
Tourism Receipts 1994	10
GOVERNMENT	
Central Government Total Debt 1993	5
Central Government Budget Surplus/Deficit 1993	13
INFRASTRUCTURE	
Coal Production 1991-93	4
Electricity Generation 1993	7
Total Indigenous Energy Production 1992	2
Arable Land Area per Capita 1992	5
International Telephone Costs 1994	10
Electricity Cost to Industrial Clients 1994	13
MANAGEMENT	
Productivity in Manufacturing 1992	9
SCIENCE & TECHNOLOGY	
Private Funding of Business R&D 1993	4
Research Cooperation (Survey)	16
PEOPLE	
Population Density 1994	1
Population Growth 1986-94	5
Dependency Ratio 1994	18
Life Expectancy at Birth 1990-95	10
Labour Force 1994	13
Growth of Labour Force 1986-93	9
Working Hours 1994	7
Higher Education Enrolment 1991	14
Population per Physician 1988-93	12
Population per Nurse 1988-93	4
DOMESTIC ECONOMIC STRENGTH	
Gross Domestic Product 1994	42
Gross Domestic Product (1990 Constant) 1994	41
Capital Goods Production 1991	40
INTERNATIONALISATION	
Balance of Trade 1994	38
Coverage of Imports by Exports 1993	36
Growth in Exports of Goods & Services 1991-93	34
Exports of Manufactured Products 1993	37
Export Credit and Insurance (Survey)	39
Access to International Distribution (Survey)	43

Table 4.3 (Contd.)

Competitive Strengths	Rank Against Benchmark Nations
GOVERNMENT	
Government Subsidies (Survey)	42
FINANCE	
Bank Savings per Capital 1993	20
Banking Sector (Survey)	37
INFRASTRUCTURE	
Energy Intensity 1992	30
MANAGEMENT	
Overall Productivity 1994	23
Change in Overall Productivity 1988-94	33
Labour Productivity 1992	26
SCIENCE & TECHNOLOGY	
Total Expenditure on R&D 1993	24
Business Expenditure on R&D 1993	29
R&D in Key Industries	23
Anticipated R&D Spending by Firms (Survey)	44
Financial Resources (Survey)	41
PEOPLE	
Skilled Labour (Survey)	48
Competent Senior Managers (Survey)	45
Industrial Disputes 1991-93	36
Brain Drain (Survey)	35
Public Expenditure on Education 1992	20
Central Government Expenditure on Health 1993	20

Source: Howard 1996: 27-8

The cities against which Melbourne is benchmarked are Auckland, Bangkok, Brisbane, Guangzhou, Jakarta, Kuala Lumpur, Los Angeles, Osaka, Singapore, Stuttgart and Sydney. It used a series of cost indices identified through interviews with 26 CEOs of exporting, trader-exposed companies operating in the city to reflect the choice of Melbourne as an investment location with respect to construction costs, office rental, labour, utilities, telecommunications, professional services, and freight. These were compared to the 11 benchmarked cities.

Key positive findings were that Melbourne, and the wider State of Victoria, was a low cost location relative to much of Asia, and important parts of the region's industry considered themselves to be part of Asia in relation to their plans for expansion. In addition, the benchmarking exercise showed that the region provides an environment in which companies generally may achieve and retain world cost competitiveness. In particular, Melbourne was cost competitive as a location in the areas of industrial land and factory construction, factory and warehouse rental, office rentals, professional services, air and sea freight, telecommunications, high-voltage electricity, and gas and water. Melbourne was identified as having a highly trained and educated labour force in services.

The development of a strategic directions plan for Melbourne, under the *Victoria's Capital City Policy* (1994)—a joint exercise conducted by the Victorian State Government and Melbourne City Council, and involving a business and community reference group—drew heavily on data collected in this benchmarking exercise, using the banner 'Creating Prosperity'.

The Reality of Global Production

The nature of global production processes also needs to act as a basis for any serious attempt to understand how a city or region might 'attract' and 'retain' investment in a significant industry sector. The key issue is to ascertain how a firm in an industry in the context of that particular region might best fit into what stage or stages in the production process, and what competitive advantages the region has vis a vis the production elements required for a firm to perform a specific task in the production process, as depicted in conceptual terms in Figure 4.2.

The global production process proceeds from R&D, through 'detail development' (which, in respect of manufactured goods, is product development but this stage applies also to service products), to component manufacture (in which a destination between high and low value added is important), to assembly, and thence to marketing and distribution. Each of the steps in the production process uses different proportions of factor inputs. The traditional economics-based categorisation of factors of production—land, labour and capital—does not capture the detail of productivity and determining impacts to the production process. In an attempt to be more specific in relation to such impacts, Figure 4.2 lists a set of 'production elements' which are relevant to determining productivity, expanding the set of traditional factors of production to capture the production cost categories on which some degree of influence can be exerted by public policy. Broadly defined, these might include, for example, transportation and telecommunications infrastructure, which will influence logistics, a crucial facilitating component of 'just-in-time' inventory requirements in global production processes. Thus, the production elements which might be considered in terms of cost and access efficiency and effectiveness are: land and infrastructure; human capital (labour costs and skills base); the cost of efficiency of delivery inputs; the cost and availability of service inputs, in particular for finance and logistics; and the existence of 'innovation networks' for the part of the process concerned. Innovation networks are an essential input to production, especially for high value added parts of the production process.

Each of the steps in the production process uses different proportions of production elements. Thus the competitive advantage of a region for a firm will vary according to what part of the production process it performs. The IMD-WEF derived indices of competitiveness discussed earlier could provide a basis for such consideration, as might data relating to the other components of the regional competitiveness process. For example, if a city is trying to attract a high value added R&D activity, characterised by small inputs of land and physical resources, a policy of low property taxation to hold down land prices and low energy taxes to hold down import prices would have little if any effect on investment decisions as those measures have little impact on productivity. Rather, such an activity would be attracted by a high quality skilled labour force, advanced business services, access to world class research institutions, access to an international airport, and the type of attractions enhancing quality of life of professionals, including high quality schools, a sophisticated cultural environment, and high amenity housing areas.

The multi-faceted nature of the global production process provides a multiplicity of other opportunities for a city or region to 'capture' parts of that process. A city does not have to capture an entire industry or even the whole of one part of that process. It is not, therefore, in a 'zero sum game'. Complementary activity among cities may be possible, such as supplementing production process constrained by resource shortages in a particular city. As with the regional benchmarking approach derived from the IMD-WEF indicators, it is possible to identify key indicators for a given region that are apposite for the production elements shown in Figure 4.2 when considering a specific industry or firm activity for any stage in the production process. This enables the design of a framework for comparative analysis of the capacity of a given city region and its economy to support a particular part of a global production process. The intensity of usage of elements by that part of a production process can be established through a mixture of secondary data sources and primary data collection through survey techniques, including case studies. The 'fit' between a

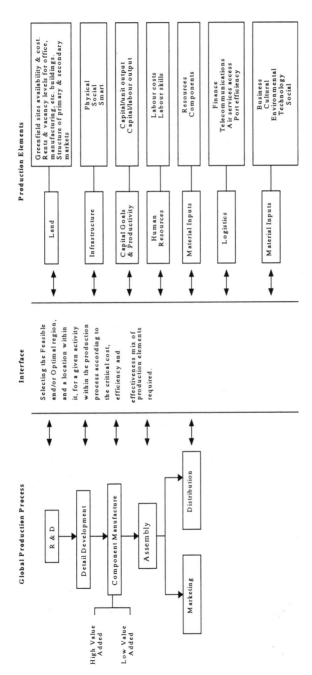

Figure 4.2 The global production process and production elements interface

given city region and the part of the production process under analysis can thus be empirically analysed.

In qualitative terms, it is a relatively simple task to develop a matrix of scores rating a given region's known or potential capacity to be competitive, vis a vis other regions, across the key production elements required at any stage in the global production process for a particular industry. Where possible, quantification should be undertaken.

In policy terms, the objective of urban managers would then be to implement mechanisms to adjust production element process to have the most impact on productivity, and such activity can be guided by the 'fit' established through the above process. The cost of establishing 'fit' would determine the cost-effectiveness of intervention.

Policy Responses for the Emerging Metroplex

As engines of economic growth, the major cities of the Pacific Rim region play increasingly important roles in their national economies, and as such their competitiveness in the global economy is a crucial strategic issue. Roberts (1996), in a paper to the ESCAP Second Urban Forum, outlines how cities are becoming increasingly diverse centres of market exchange; how as centres of technology and innovation they are the 'crucibles of culture and knowledge'; and how the city is also 'the place where our expectations and hopes for a better future are being realised'. The striving for economic efficiency and the achievement of greater social equity prove a series of difficult issues and, according to Roberts, we must address two fundamental questions: first, 'how can we create a new path for the future based on a partnership of equity and efficiency?'; and second, 'how can we leverage the benefits of economic efficiency and social equity to enhance economic performance and quality of life in cities?' (Roberts, 1996). This poses a significant challenge for city regions, for their leaders and managers, and for their businesses and communities, to look for new strategic frameworks for regional economic development.

The Need for a New Approach to Strategic Regional Economic Development

Current thinking is diverse on how to plan and facilitate regional economic development in an environment of global competition and rapid change. For example, Imbroscio (1995) advocates strategies of greater self-reliance;

Park (1995), McGee (1995) and Ohmae (1993, 1996) advocate strategies based on strategic alliances and inter- and intra-regional network structures; Henton (1994) and the Silicon Valley Joint Venture Network (SVJVN, 1995, 1996) promote economic development based on strategic collaboration and networked partnerships; and Held (1996), Waits (1995), Sternburg (1991), and Stough *et al.* (1995) argue the need to base economic development on the growth of cluster industries. The strategic planning approach, derived largely from the Harvard Business School-developed SWOT analytic methodology, and so widely applied since the late 1970s in urban and regional planning and economic development studies (e.g. Bryson and Einsweiler, 1988; Blakely, 1994), provides a sound basis for analysing regional performance, identifying strengths and weaknesses, and identifying potential opportunities and threats. But it does have limitations.

Rosebury (1994) talks of the need for regions to 'create a path for the future' by laying down the 'strategic architecture' to support a range of economic possibilities, based on the competitiveness of resources, infrastructure, governance, and core competencies. Guided by the work of Hamel and Prahalad (1994), Roberts (1997) proposes a new framework for regional economic development (Figure 4.3), the intent being to establish a 'platform for change'. The process uses regional audit and benchmarking techniques (such as those discussed earlier), and embraces input from the facilitators and agents of change within, and central to, the region, to evaluate economic possibilities through multi-sectoral analysis and industry cluster analysis. It sets 'strategic intent' for the region, and develops alternative futures for testing against external and internal stakeholders and decision makers (especially investors).

'Strategic intent' outlines the vision for a region, and 'describes the path for creating its economic future, based on a sound, comprehensive and realistic appraisal of the ability of the region to capitalise upon its resources, and to create new possibilities for the future' (Roberts, 1997: 15). This might involve directing a region towards greater self-reliance; identifying collaboration, networks and partnership to achieve 'resource stretch and leverage'; enhancing regional competitiveness through civic engagement; and developing cluster industries as the engines of economic growth and expansion (Roberts, 1997: 16). But to realise the strategic intent it is necessary for a region to build 'core competencies'; to develop 'strategic leadership'; to enhance its infrastructure, resources and governance; and to provide marketing information systems as support mechanisms to enable development to happen.

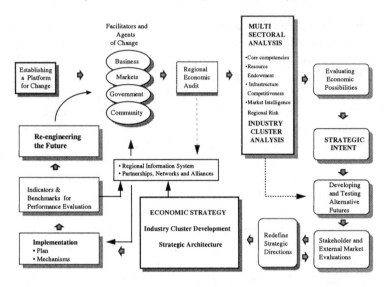

Figure 4.3   New framework for regional economic development

Source: Roberts, 1997

The way these strategic elements operate together to drive the economic development process in a region is referred to as 'strategic architecture', which Roberts (1997: 16-7) identifies as the 'game plan' or 'blue print' for realising strategic intent.   It will define what core competencies are needed to build or maintain an industry sector; it will identify what sector markets need to be developed and maintained; it will identify the strategic and smart infrastructure required to be developed; it will identify what competitive resources need to be protected or managed more efficiently; it will outline what approach is needed to develop appropriate marketing intelligence; and will identify and appraise what risks need to be managed to enhance existing and new cluster industry development.

'Governance' issues are of crucial importance for strategic plan implementation by facilitating the institutional arrangements most appropriate in the local circumstances to 're-engineer' the region for the future to realise its 'strategic intent'.   Herein lies possibly the greatest challenge for a city region, as it has been very common for the best of strategic intents in regional economic development plans to fail at the implementation stage because of the institutional inertia which characterises government in particular.

In this context, it is as well to reiterate the advocacy of the World Bank (1992: 3) that the role of governance is fundamentally changing: it is no longer an exercise of authority, control, management, and power of government; rather it is the manner in which power is exercised in the management of economies and social resources for development. The traditional role and lines of accountability of government, business, and countries are no longer as clearly defined as they might have been in the past, and will become ever less so in future. New approaches are needed that will be more flexible, open, transparent and accountable, and they need to foster ownership through community empowerment and devolution to local institutions of society (World Bank, 1994). Thus, governance in strategic planning and development processes is 'no longer a public function; it is a community function' (Roberts, 1997: 19). The importance of partnerships between community organisations, business and government functionaries increasingly is recognised as a mechanism for driving regional economic development (e.g. OECD, 1993; Coburn, 1995). As an example of the institutional issues that need to be addressed to enhance regional competitiveness, Garelli (1995) provides the list of 10 shown in Table 4.4.

Table 4.4   Key features of competitive places and societies

1	Create a stable and predictable legislative environment
2	Work on a flexible and resilient economic structure
3	Invest in traditional and technological infrastructure
4	Promote private savings and domestic investment
5	Develop aggressiveness on international markets (exports, etc.) as well as attractiveness for foreign value added industries
6	Focus on quality and speed in the conduct of administration and reforms
7	Maintain a relationship between wage levels, productivity and taxation
8	Preserve the social fabric by reducing wage disparity and strengthening the middle class
9	Invest massively in education, especially at secondary level, and in life-long training and improvement of the workforce
10	Balance the economy of globality and the economy of proximity to ensure wealth creation, maintain social cohesion and preserve the value system citizens desire.

Source: Garelli 1995:11

Obviously regions would be expected to vary in the ways they implement such policies depending on their competitive starting point and their socio-political and cultural characters. As Garelli (1995: 17) states, 'the critical element in competitiveness is not found by designing competitive policies but, rather, by determining the social costs acceptable'.

Abaya (1996) reinforces this view in the context of cities in the developing world, saying that:

> ...to keep a competitive edge, cities must provide the right environments that will attract the entrepreneurs, financiers, managers and the workforce. This means provision of schools, power plants, telecommunications, seaports and airports. Public health must also be a primary concern, which means efficient collection of garbage and control of air and water pollution. There must be adequate transport for the movement of goods and people and efficient traffic management. To attract people there must be a humanised environment of clean and safe neighbourhoods, parks, and amusement areas, and the implicit promise that things will get better for this and the next generation.

Creating the Metroplex for the 21ˢᵗ Century

The evolution of urban landscapes in the mega-cities and the EMRs of the Pacific Rim region as we move into the 21ˢᵗ century will see a change from the 'pyramidal power structure' that has characterised most of the post World War Two era, during which time 'cities centralised their power and traded their citizens like political pawns, the poor and minorities were disenfranchised, and corporate leaders and politicians typically controlled the distribution of information, jobs and services' (Tatsuno, 1992: 18). This is being rapidly eroded. Now it is common in poly-centric urban forms that typify mega-cities and EMRs around the Pacific Rim for medium and high tech industries to be dispersed, and for jobs and political power to be in the suburbs. Downtown areas are often impoverished and multi-culturally diverse as new immigrants replace the departing middle class. Cities are suffering from 'political gridlock' because of the unwillingness of local authorities and various levels of government to work together to resolve overlapping problems.

Over time, the evolution of urban landscapes in these city regions has tended to reflect the evolution of technologies, as illustrated in Table 4.5. In the contemporary era of knowledge-based and information-intensive development in the global economy, a new paradigm has emerged for city structure and form, which starts with human resources rather than with the needs of industry for material inputs, and which places emphasis on choice for community often related to low density life styles, and for more opportunities to exercise social and institutional choice. Blakely and Stimson (1992) see this as producing an urban pattern reflecting 'preferred' rather than 'required' locational decisions, as proposed in Figure 4.4.

In the emerging poly-centric city, new synergies evolve through economic systems that are redefining the evolution of urban functions and forms through what might be termed a 'metroplex' of places and spaces, of functions and people, operating in a global as well as in a regional and local environmental context. The synergies have core activities facilitated through education, telecommunications, transportation, and services, residential and recreational infrastructure, facilitated through networks and strategic alliances. 'The overlapping reaches of environment, humanity and technology focus attention on environmental management, the development of renaissance community pursuits, and the formation of technopole agglomerations of R&D, advanced products and services. This is the 'fifth sphere' city of the 21st century in which work, home, recreation and life style diversity are transformed into a single living organism where built form of the city accommodates the socio-economic system that is evolving through the globalisation processes (Blakely and Stimson, 1992).

Table 4.5   Technology and the evolving urban landscape

Pre-1950	1960-90	1990 and beyond
Seaports and railports	Airports and technopoles	Teleports and mediaports
Heavy industries	High-tech industries	'Humanware' industries
Low-value-added services	Medium-value-added services	High-value-added services
Central city	Suburbanisation	Multinodal networked cities
Company towns	High-tech suburbs	Global villages
Centralised power	Dispersed power	Interactive power
Monocultural	Multicultural	Cultural fusion

Source: Tatsuno, 1992

The synergies of this metroplex are conceptualised in Figure 4.5. For urban planning and management, it will be a fundamental requirement to redirect attention away from traditional modes of operating through 'vertical' or 'siloed' administrative departments—such as planning and land

use, transport, industry, health, social services, environment, and finance—
to integrated approaches of governance if a city region is to facilitate the
operation and interplay of these synergies.

Emerging new technologies will require the successful cities of the
21ˢᵗ century to be 'highly interactive, flexible and rapid' clusters of
dispersed economic nodes linked by massive networks of airports,
highways and communications, no longer dependent on central cities, but
on global networks of cities. They will be characterised by networking,
power sharing, information exchange, and decentralised management, not
centralised control. Their competitive edge comes from focusing on high-
value-added industries, such as design services, genetic engineering, super
conducting, and new materials research, which are increasingly being
pursued by entrepreneurs and start-up companies' (Tatsuno, 1992: 199).
The challenge will be how urban policy makers can harness critical new
technologies to solve the problems of poverty, unemployment, traffic
congestion, pollution and crime, while creating economically competitive
and sustainable cities with quality life style.

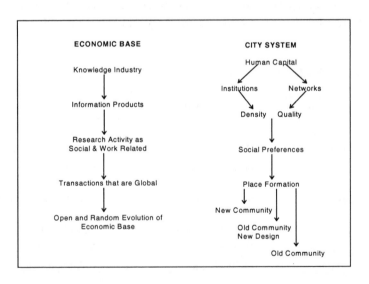

Figure 4.4   The basis for the new city form

Source: Blakely and Stimson, 1992

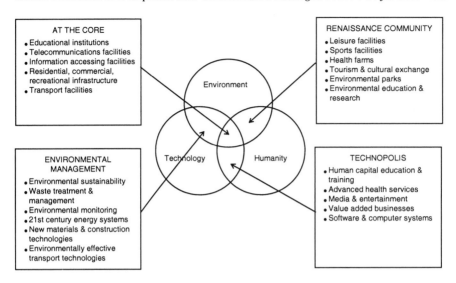

Figure 4.5   Synergies for the new metroplex

Source: Blakely and Stimson, 1992

5 National Urban Development Strategy in Indonesia— Case Study: Jabotabek

IBU BUDHY TJAHJATI SOEGIJOKO

Introduction

Prior to the recent economic problems, Indonesia had experienced rapid economic growth and changing economic structure during the last two decades. Per capita income had increased from US$50 in 1967 to US$650 at 1994 (World Bank, 1994). The economic growth which was initially driven by import-substitution and oil-based industries had been increasingly promoted by export-oriented manufacturing industry. The economy had become more market-oriented, opened, to and interlinked with, the world economy through trade and flows of foreign direct investment. This was assisted by the deregulation of fiscal, trade and investment procedures to accelerate the flows of foreign investment and to increase the involvement of the private sector in economic and infrastructure development. The changes of the Indonesian economy are expected to continue, in the longer term, resulting in the acceleration of the transformation from a rural-based economy to an urban-based economy. These have affected the urban development processes and their roles in national economic development. In this process, the roles of the private sector in directing urban development have increased, whereas the roles of government tend to shift towards enabling the development. However, the urban poor and other disadvantaged groups have persisted as the other side of the success story of urban development. Despite government efforts to alleviate urban poverty, the urban poor are still large in absolute numbers creating masses that may have significant political power in the urban development process.

Indonesia has been undergoing a major demographic and economic transformation. The average urban population growth rate was 5.5 percent during the last decade which is higher than the average of national population growth of 1.9 percent and rural population growth of 0.8 percent during the same period. As a result, the urban proportion of population which was 32.8 million or 22 percent of total population in 1980 increased to 55.4 million or 31 percent of the total population in 1990. Although the 1990 urbanisation level was below the levels of low and middle income countries, which was 38 percent and 60 percent respectively, the growth rate during the last decade was among the highest in Asia (World Bank, 1993: 3). In the future, Indonesia's urbanisation level might become higher than that of other developing countries. The urban population will grow from 65 million (35 percent of the total population) in 1992 to about 155 million or around 60 percent of the total by the end of the second long-term development plan (PJP II). Indonesia has one of the highest urban growth rates in the world.

In addition to the high urban population growth rate, urbanisation in Indonesia is characterised by some peculiar features. First, there is an unequal distribution of urban population between Java and outer islands as a reflection of the concentration of economic development in Java. In 1990, the urbanisation level of Java was 36 percent, whereas the level for Sumatra was only 26 percent. Other islands had even lower urbanisation levels (World Bank, 1993: 3). Second, most of the population growth has taken place in urban areas, particularly cities in Java. The World Bank estimates that about 70 percent of total population growth takes place in urban areas, yet 70 percent of this occurs in the cities located in Java. In contrast to two decades ago, when urban growth was, by and large, due to natural growth, evidence shows that during the last decade, two-thirds of urban population growth was contributed by migration or expansion of urbanised rural areas. Furthermore, it is estimated that in the 1990s, urban areas may absorb as much as 95 percent of the total population increase (World Bank, 1993: 18).

Third, although the growth rate of small and medium cities was higher than that of large cities, the number of large cities with population above one million has doubled from five to ten during 1980-90. Seven of them are located in Java. In addition, large cities, particularly in Java, have expanded into their surrounding areas as far as a hundred kilometres, forming what McGee called region-based urbanisation or mega-urban regions (see Dharmapatni and Firman, 1992). This phenomena is not only reflected by the expansion of industrial and commercial activities intermingled with agricultural activities but also by the faster population growth of the surroundings compared to the main cities. The population growth rate in Jakarta city for instance, was 3.1 percent during the 1980s, whereas the surrounding areas (Botabek region) grew at a rate of 13.3 percent (World Bank, 1994: 68). Surabaya and Bandung metropolitan areas experienced the same growth path. Fourth, at the beginning of the sixth five-year plan (Repelita VI) 11 urban centres (some of which consist of more than one local administrative unit) had populations of one million or more. Eight of them were on Java. By the end of PJP II, there are likely to be about 25 urban centres with populations of one million or more, yet, about 44 percent of them (11) were off Java. Four centres are likely to have populations of over five million. Jabotabek, the greater metropolitan area of Jakarta, has already 15 million population which is likely to grow to 30-35 million in this period.

These demographic changes are occurring in conjunction with major economic changes. Per capita GDP is likely to have increased almost fourfold by the end of PJP II (from about US$670 in 1989-90 at constant price at the end of Repelita V to about US$2,600 in the year 2018-19). These changes will have profound implications for lifestyles and for demands on public services in both urban and rural areas.

Literature points out that one of the major factors contributing to rapid urbanisation and urban development in Indonesia is the accelerated economic development. There is no doubt that cities have become the engine and centre of national economic activities.

National Urban Development Policies and Strategies

Indonesia's Development Objectives and Themes for the Sixth Five-Year Plan

The basic objectives being pursued in the sixth five-year plan, include: greater equity and the elimination of poverty; human resource development; improved environmental quality; fuller opportunities for participation in development decisions; and cultural enhancement. There are a number of necessary conditions for the achievement of these objectives. These include sustained economic growth, with an efficient use of resources, security, and stability.

These objectives and the conditions necessary for their achievement have direct, and perhaps obvious, implication for decisions on the kinds of investment to be made in individual regions and cities, the kinds of social services to be given priority in individual areas, programmes to increase the geographic mobility of workers and their households and the structure of government.

The goals of urban policy are to support a national development process that promotes economic development with equity, poverty alleviation, environmental sustainability, and cultural enhancement. Five themes will guide urban policy toward these goals:

1. To develop policies in a manner that assists in decentralising decision-making in urban planning and management and builds local capacities. The regional governments at the second level of governance (Dati II) will have to strengthen their capacity for urban management to enable them to contribute to development.
2. To enhance community and private sector participation in urban development. The participation of communities and private interests in all urban development endeavours is to be enhanced. It includes the shift of government's role from initiator or regulator to enabler of development.
3. To increase and improve access to the need for physical, social, economic, and culture facilities and services, and establish a more coordinated system of law, regulations, processes, and procedures to support urban development and management, especially in land development.
4. To enhance the role of cities in promoting national and regional development. Urban development should be within the context of the national urban system, as should urban-rural linkages, because by the end of PJP II, about 40 percent of the rural population will still live in rural areas. The cities are expected to play an important role in promoting regional and national development.
5. To secure an environmentally sustainable process of urban development. The expected urban management of the future should be integrative, efficient, and effective, not only by government but in partnership with the community and the private sector.

The Strategies and Programmes for Urban Development

Because of the interdependence of urban and rural development, the rapid transitions from rural to urban that are taking place, and the increasing importance of integrated 'agro-urban' development, the strategy for urban development is being conceived and implemented in Indonesia in the context of the regional development strategy.

Regional Development. The regional economic strategy is designed to strike a reasonable balance between sustained economic growth, with increased efficiency and a reduction in provincial disparities. In arriving at this strategy two major options were considered—one continuing with an allocation of governmental investment similar to recent allocations, and the other, which was finally chosen, with greater priority given to investment in less-developed regions.

The adopted strategy promotes continuing diversification in the economy. Geographically, it promotes growth outside Java, to the extent that this is consistent with the real economic potential of each province. At the same time, advantage will be taken of the productivity of Java itself.

Consistent with the principle of focusing resources strategically and integrating rural and urban development, approximately 111 regions have been identified as strategic and potential regions for national development that is called kawasan andalan. Each region consists of a system of cities and townships and their rural (in some cases coastal) hinterlands in which there are various combinations of manufacturing, service, agricultural, fishing, forestry, mining or other activities. The criteria used to define regions as 'strategic' include their economic potential, the severity of the social problems found in them, their natural resource endowments, their importance for environmental management, their historic and/or cultural importance, and, in some cases, their importance for national security or stability.

These are within the overall spatial development framework spelled out in the National Spatial Development Plan (RTRWN). RTRWN strengths are in its integration of national, inter-regional, and intra-regional perspectives. Its intention of spatially organising the future of Indonesia's development is important for national integration in that it seeks to heighten the potential for economic growth and development across the archipelago. In addition, the Spatial Development Plan is also a template for prioritising the development expenditure.

In the lower order, there are Provincial Spatial Development Plans (RTRWProp). For example, RTRWProp for Jakarta, West Java and East Java, is a spatial development plan that coordinates and integrates development activities using areas within provincial boundaries. The Provincial Plan integrates and coordinates the Kabupaten/Kotamadya Spatial Development Plan (RTRWKab/Kodya).

Urban Development. In urban development, given the concern with efficiency, there will be further growth in strategic locations on Java, subject to constraints imposed by the need to preserve high-productivity agricultural areas there.   But there will also be substantial urban development in Sumatra, Kalimantan and Sulawesi.   There is to be a large number of productive and well-serviced small urban settlements on all of the principal islands, and some of the smaller ones, linked with mining, forestry, agriculture, the fishing industry, and tourism.   Quasi-urban development in agro-urban corridors between cities, or dispersed through the overall structure of the larger urban areas (which is taking place already, especially on Java) will become an even more important part of the regional landscape.

The urban strategy for the PJP II (together with the programme for Repelita VI) is articulated in several parts—for Jabotabek (which already has an urban population of over 15 million and is the fifth largest metropolitan area in the world), for strategic metropolitan centres, for other strategic cities, for strategic townships, and for other urban settlements. This recognises the different roles and needs of these distinct types of urban area.

Accelerating and Improving Urban Infrastructure Facilities and Services. A general strategy for accelerating and improving infrastructure, facilities, and services is developed by combining two perspectives. The first is to differentiate priorities in each sub-area of infrastructure facilities and services—energy, transportation, environment, communication, and social services. The second is to link these priorities to on-going and proposed programmatic approaches to integrate infrastructure planning and management at the national and local levels and to develop the role of government as facilitator. In response to the need for a more integrated approach, Indonesia has developed, since 1984, the Integrated Urban Infrastructure Development Program, which is a tool for managing urban infrastructure facilities and services. It relies upon the enhancement of the institutional and financial capacity of local governments (Dati II). Thus, decentralisation is a key aspect of implementing this integrated plan, in which the overall project cycle, starting from the planning stage and including implementation, operations, and maintenance, as well as the subsequent monitoring stages, is the responsibility of local governments. Indonesia has tried to evolve the concept of this Plan further to the new Integrated Urban Development Program. This will involve extending the number of activities to be covered, more genuine involvement of local government, and human resource development in infrastructure facilities and services, planning, and management.   It includes integrating infrastructure with comprehensive spatial planning, land management, and transportation planning as tools for implementation of spatial plans. Institutional development and financial management are required to make cities operate effectively.

Another important policy for improving urban infrastructure facilities and services is to promote the expansion of infrastructure facilities and services in order to strengthen economic development within the national system of cities and regions. Infrastructure investments will be allocated to conform with the role and functional system of cities by using the National Spatial Development Plan as a basis for allocating the investments for infrastructure facilities and services and the integrated Plan scheme to accelerate the information of urban functions in economic development.

Strengthening Urban Finance System. There are two basic policies for strengthening Indonesia's urban finance system. The first is to enhance the opportunities to decentralise authority and responsibility to local government (Dati II). Decentralisation of planning and management depends on increasing financial resources and strengthening the financial capacity of local governments. Despite past efforts, local units in Indonesia are still heavily dependent on central government finances (85 percent of local government spending in the region originated from the central government). Reforms are therefore needed to increase their own source revenue through: (1) improving the grants/transfer system; (2) increasing local revenue generating authority; and (3) improving efficiency in tax collection, administration of user charges, and improving the profitability of local enterprises. There is a need to transfer more resources from the centre to local governments and to increase the proportion of discretionary block grants in such transfers.

The second is to enhance the role of the private sector in providing services, infrastructure and entrepreneurial abilities. Urban policy has been focused primarily on the role of government. Experience has shown, however, that urban planning and management can profit tremendously from greater involvement of the private sector. Many urban services can benefit from the effectiveness and efficiency of private enterprises, including water supply systems, transport, markets, solid waste collection and disposal, energy, mail systems, and telecommunications. The private sector, through taxes, fees, and other charges, strengthens the financial position of local governments. It may also participate actively, through the commercial banking system, in improving the credit worthiness of municipal governments.

Improving Urban Environment Management.   Indonesia's cities are experiencing serious environmental deterioration.   Urban development efforts are to be used to minimise the negative environmental impact of economic growth on cities and improve the monitoring of urban and regional ecological carrying capacities for an environmentally sustainable process of economic development.   There are several policies for improving urban environment management:

1. To ensure equity by accelerating progress toward achieving basic standards in environmental quality in all cities and urban settlements through reduction in pollution levees and prevention from further pollution.
2. To improve the quality of air, water, and the living environment to enhance urban development.
3. To promote sustainable land use and utilisation of natural resources for urban development through effective use of structural plans, improved spatial coordination in land use development, advanced training, and human resource development in environment and land use planning and management, expeditious processing of land development permits with clear environmental guidelines and enforcement, greater efficiency in natural resources use, and reliance on more participatory mechanisms, including indigenous culture practice in resource management.   The objective of achieving long-term environmental sustainability through improving land use and natural resources management is as important as meeting basic environmental standards and supporting economic growth through environmental planning.
4. To alleviate urban poverty by improving the accessibility of low income populations to good environmental quality in places of residence, work, and daily travel in the effort to increase their health, productivity and general well-being.
5. To utilise and enhance community participation in urban environmental management to better use local knowledge, skills, and resources, and to support an urban development process that respects cultural value.
6. To improve urban environmental management processes and capacity in an efficient and transparent manner to reduce costs to the private sector, create a positive atmosphere for private sector compliance with

environmental standards, and promote enterprise-initiated adoption of pollution-reducing technologies and production processes.

Development and Critical Problems of Jabotabek Metropolitan Area

The Development of Jabotabek Metropolitan Area

The internationalisation of the economy and the government's macro-economic policy, attempting to increase the country's competitiveness in the world economy, have had large impacts on cities in the country, particularly large cities. Since the early 1980s large cities in Indonesia, including DKI Jakarta, have grown very rapidly. In the case of DKI Jakarta, rapid development has not only occurred in terms of population growth but has also been characterised by the very dynamics of social, economic and physical development. Originated as a small harbour city of Sunda Kelapa, the city has developed as far as Tangerang in the west, Bogor in the south and Bekasi in the east, forming a united economic region, Jabotabek. Recently, the development of DKI Jakarta has spilled over as far as Serang in the west and Karawang in the east.

As a national capital and the main gateway to the international economy, and as a 'service city', it is most likely that the increasing linkages of the Indonesian economy with the global economic system will accelerate the transformation of DKI Jakarta's as well as Botabek's social, economic and physical conditions. On the one hand, such a transformation is an inevitable consequence of rapid economic growth, but on the other hand, it should be anticipated to minimise negative impacts and to harness the opportunities of economic development offered by the economic internationalisation.

As mentioned before, the population of Jabotabek has increased rapidly during the last thirty years. With an average annual growth rate of 3.9 percent, its population tripled from 5.9 million in 1961 to 17.1 million in 1990. The region, which accommodates about 8 percent of the total country's population, has always had higher population growth rates than that of the country. It can be seen from the annual growth rate of Jabotabek during 1980-90 which was 3.7 percent whereas the country's was only 1.98 percent.

Urban population in Jabotabek increased at an average annual growth rate of 5.3 percent (almost the same as that of the national urban figure, which was 5.37 percent for the last decade) which tripled its number from 4.8 million in 1971 to 13.1 million in 1990. For such a small area compared to the whole area of the country, Jabotabek has seen the concentration of urban population. In 1980, the urban population in the region was 7.8 million or 22.45 percent of the national urban population. By 1990, the urban population in Jabotabek had almost doubled, that is, to 13.1 million, or 23.62 percent of the national urban population.

Jabotabek is the most urbanised region in the country. In fact, the urbanisation level of the region has always been higher than that of the country during 1970-90. While the level of urbanisation of the country (using the criteria of Central Bureau of Statistic Office) was 17.1 percent in 1971, the figure for Jabotabek was 58.2 percent. The level of urbanisation in Jabotabek in 1990 was 76.6 percent or more than twice that of the country which was only 30.9 percent. The urban population growth in Botabek has accelerated its urbanisation level from only 7.8 percent in 1971 to 55 percent in 1990.

The urbanisation process in Jabotabek is also characterised by the transformation of economic activities from the primary sector to the secondary and tertiary sectors. With regard to employment, the share of the primary sector in Jabotabek has decreased from 19.9 percent in 1971 to 15.8 percent in 1990, while at the same time, the contribution of the secondary sector increased from 16.2 percent in 1971 to 26.4 percent in 1990. Although it decreased from 63.9 percent in 1971 to 57.8 percent in 1990, the share of the tertiary sector was quite high during 1971-90, that is, more than half of the total employment.

The urbanisation process in Jabotabek is also reflected in the expansion of the built-up areas where non-urban uses have been transformed into urban uses. With an average annual growth rate of 4.9 percent during 1971-94, DKI Jakarta had a built-up area of 54,506 hectares or 82 percent of the total city administrative area in 1994. In contrast to DKI Jakarta, the built up area in the Botabek region has been much lower, but its expansion rate is much higher. The encroachment of built-up areas from DKI Jakarta to the Botabek areas increased its urbanised areas, that is, a number of localities which were previously considered 'rural' have been transformed into 'urban'.

The direction of the expansion of built-up areas has changed during 1970-90. Since the late 1970s, rapid expansion has been to the southern part of the city. But since the early 1980s the expansion has been largely following the east-west axis. The spillover development along the east west and the north south axis of DKI Jakarta and Botabek region has created an urban ribbon development which has blurred the distinction between urban and rural areas in Jabotabek. This pattern of development, which McGee (1987) called mega-urban development, is a region-based urbanisation.

Development Constraints of Jabotabek

Jabotabek has faced several major problems which need serious attention if the country wants to continue its national economic growth and wants to compete with large cities in other developing countries in the globalising world. Some of the constraints are, among others:

The Lack of Housing in DKI Jakarta. Rapid population growth of DKI Jakarta (the population growth rate for 1980-90 was 2.4 percent, much higher than the national population growth rate that is, 1.98 percent) has increased the demand for housing. It is estimated that in 1995 about 500,000 units of housing were needed. This includes new houses, dilapidated houses that need to be rehabilitated and the lag in needed houses that had not been provided in the previous year. With the present annual population growth rate of 2.4 percent, it is estimated that 70,000 units of housing will be needed each year. About half of this number is needed by the low-income urban population. It is important to note here that only one-fourth of the total number of houses needed each year is built by the formal sector, that is, private developers and government enterprises, whereas the rest are built by non-formal developers or individuals. The lack of housing is indicated by the mushrooming of slum areas along the riverside, railways, and in unoccupied state and private lands. Statistical data show that 217 'kelurahan' (urban villages) or 82 percent of the total kelurahan in Jakarta have slums with a total area of 2,855.2 hectares or 4.8 percent of the total area of DKI Jakarta. This area contains 891,880 people or 9.72 percent of the total population of DKI Jakarta. Most of them are seasonal migrants.

The Relatively Low Quality of Human Resources. Most of the population of age over 10 years, which is the potential labour force, have only received primary education. This condition has not changed during the last twenty years, although the proportion of potential labour force who have succeeded in completing their higher education and university degrees increased (see Table 5.1 below). This implies that economic activities in Jabotabek would only be supported by a low skill labour force if the government is unable to accelerate the higher-level education programme to most of the population. In other words, Jabotabek would lose its competitive power in attracting international investment as, in the future, foreign direct investment would choose higher technology and knowledge-based skills and industries in other cities with these capacities.

The Increase of the Informal Sector and Employment Problems. The high and increasing numbers of seasonal migrants have exacerbated the unemployment problem in DKI Jakarta. The informal sector has flourished and occupied all corners of roads in the city. Statistical data show that the number of registered seasonal migrants has increased from 238,034 persons in 1990 to 414,234 persons in 1995. It is estimated that the actual number of seasonal migrants is much higher than the recorded one, at 1,265,051 persons in 1995. Most of them came from the nearby provinces, with 48 percent from Central Java and 34 percent from West Java in 1994. The 1994 census recorded that there were 301 legal sites of 'kaki lima' or sidewalk vendors in DKI Jakarta, comprising 14,453 businesses. This type of business generates transactions of Rp 1.87 billion every day. Besides these legal sites, there are many more illegal sidewalk sites in DKI Jakarta. Survey data show that on the average there are 75 businesses at each illegal sidewalk site, with daily transactions of Rp 65,000-125,000 per unit of business. Although the informal sector provides employment for the many unemployed and contributes significantly to the city's overall economy as well as to the local government income, on the other hand, it also creates problems for the city. Its large and increasing numbers have caused traffic problems and reduced orderliness as well as cleanliness of many parts in the city.

Table 5.1   Distribution of population 10 years of age and over by educational attainment (%), by time

	No Schooling	Elementary School	Junior High School		Senior High School		Academy	University	Total
			General	Vocational	General	Vocational			
1971									
DKI Jakarta	22.56	55.14	9.15	6.03	2.26	2.52	1.15	1.19	100.00
Bogor Reg.	48.52	40.50	9.10	0.50	0.82	0.42	0.07	0.06	100.00
Bekasi Reg.	63.51	34.51	1.09	0.32	0.30	0.22	0.01	0.06	100.00
Tangerang Reg.	51.98	44.46	2.00	0.64	0.41	0.37	0.09	0.05	100.00
Bogor Mun.	21.59	58.64	7.67	5.46	2.58	2.34	0.81	0.91	100.00
1981									
DKI Jakarta	34.06	29.45	14.44	1.82	11.48	5.70	1.58	1.46	100.00
Bogor Reg.	46.75	25.65	13.19	1.96	6.29	4.98	0.68	0.47	100.00
Bekasi Reg.	44.64	28.13	9.95	1.80	7.65	6.12	0.81	0.83	100.00
Tangerang Reg.	39.60	25.77	15.23	2.23	8.56	6.49	0.76	1.16	100.00
Bogor Mun.	33.93	28.95	13.28	3.56	9.46	7.12	1.60	1.58	100.00
1991									
DKI Jakarta	5.01	46.91	18.06	0.78	16.58	7.37	2.51	2.77	100.00
Bogor Reg.	13.83	63.93	9.56	0.75	6.25	4.09	0.89	0.69	100.00
Bekasi Reg.	20.61	52.33	10.51	0.78	8.33	4.77	1.56	1.12	100.00
Tangerang Reg.	16.21	55.42	12.27	0.67	8.19	4.85	1.21	1.18	100.00
Bogor Mun.	4.97	47.12	16.73	1.58	18.21	6.97	1.78	2.64	100.00

Source: Population Census for DKI Jakarta and Jawa Barat

The Limitation of Land Availability. Population growth and economic development have increased the land demand despite its constant availability. As a consequence, land prices in Jakarta city have increased dramatically and the competition for land uses via high increases and conflicts amongst government, developers, and communities has become intensified. In turn, urban development activities encroach on the areas surrounding Jakarta city which have vast undeveloped and relatively cheap land, mostly agricultural. Encouraged by the regional policies that promote the east-west axis of development towards Tangerang (West) and Bekasi (East), particularly through the toll road construction, increasing industrial and housing estate development has occurred in the Botabek region. Despite these encouraging facts, as a reflection of the ability of Jabotabek in positioning itself as part of global city networks, this trend of development has created another problem. The urbanisation of the surrounding areas of Jakarta, that is, the Botabek region, has reduced its prime, irrigated agricultural land from the total area of 39.4 percent in 1980 to 34.1 percent in 1990. As a result, in 1990, the irrigated agricultural land in Bekasi, Tangerang and Bogor was only 50.7 percent, 52.2 percent and 20.1 percent of its respective total areas. It is anticipated that areas of prime agricultural land would decrease over time as the pressures of the accelerated urbanisation continue in Jabotabek. This creates a dilemma where, on the one hand, government tries to sustain the national self-sufficiency in rice, but on the other hand, would like to increase national and regional economic development through increasing the attractiveness of Jabotabek to FDIs.

The Limited Availability of Water. The availability of water has become more limited, reducing its capacity to sustain the increasing needs of Jabotabek's population and economic activities. Since the early 1970s, the water needs of Jakarta have been fulfilled by sources that are located far from the city, that is, from Bogor and Purwakarta. Until now, only one-third of the raw water needs of Jakarta could be fulfilled by the two main water resources, that is Citarum River and the Jatiluhur Dam. Therefore, most of the water needs in Jabotabek, particularly in Jakarta city, are obtained from groundwater. Studies indicate that the extraction of the groundwater in Jakarta has exceeded its renewable rate so that land has subsided at a rate as much as 34 cm per year in the northern part of the city and the sea water intrusion has reached as far as the central part of the city. In addition, most of the surface water, particularly rivers that flow through the city, have been highly polluted and some officials anticipate their water will become 'dead water resources' which ultimately can no longer be used for any kind of activity. Shallow groundwater has also been polluted by bacteria E. Coli which affects about nine-tenths of the people's wells.

Environmental Degradation. The relocation of 'sunset industries' from developed countries and NICs to a country such as Indonesia, particularly to the Jabotabek region, has no doubt made substantial contribution to our national economic growth. Unfortunately, however, most of these industries are highly polluting and one reason for their relocation is seeking countries that have lower environmental awareness and more flexible environmental regulation. This, in fact, has been indicated by the accelerated degradation of the environmental quality in Jabotabek in the last two decades. Rivers that flow through Jakarta, particularly those located in the eastern part of the city, have high concentrations of BOD and COD. The Jakarta Bay has also degraded as it receive all of the water of the rivers that flow through Jakarta. Based on records from local government of West Java, the concentration of BOD in the Citarum River fluctuated from 5.2-31 mg/l and the concentration of COD from 233-267 mg/l. In terms of air pollution, Jakarta is recorded as one of the ten most polluted cities in the world. In 1992, the concentrations of NOx in the central city of Jakarta had reached 4.051 ppb and 1.271 ppb, whereas, based on the DKI Jakarta Governor's Decree number 587/1980, the ideal limit for air pollution in this area was 200 ppb and the maximum limit (threshold) was 500 ppb.

Lack of Management Coordination Amongst All Levels of Government. As a region where the national capital is located and as the most fast-growing region in the country, there is no doubt that Jabotabek accommodates the national interests, as well as provincial and kabupatens (districts) interest. This needs a coordination and integration of planning and implementation of development policies as well as management of development. The BKSP of Jabotabek (Coordination Development Board of Jabotabek) has so far had insufficient power to coordinate and integrate the rapid development. Although it was promulgated by a Presidential decree, the rapid and dynamic patterns of development, lack of political will amongst all levels of government, as well as lack of human resources and institutional capacities, have hindered the effectiveness of the coordination power of BKSP Jabotabek. As a consequence, one might see the private sector as the most progressive agent of development take advantage of a situation where government lacks the capacity to manage development. In this situation, the involvement of the private sector and community in decision making in the whole process of development should be encouraged and incorporated in the daily management practices at all levels of government bureaucracies.

Limited Infrastructure and Transportation Facilities. As is obvious in many large cities in developing countries, Jabotabek has also experienced a lack of infrastructure and transportation facilities. The limited availability and quality of roads, telecommunication facilities, electricity, water, drainage and sewerage as well as treatment plants and facilities have inevitably forced the economic activities to operate in a high-cost economy. For illustration, the road ratio of DKI Jakarta is about five percent, whereas in the developed countries the road ratio is about 15 percent. For electrification, Jabotabek region has a ratio of electrification of about 54 percent. There is almost 50 percent of households in Jabotabek that have not been electrified. Beside that, the Jabotabek region still lacks water supply. Moreover, the leakage of water distribution has reached about 30 percent. Backlogs of these infrastructure and transportation facilities have therefore resulted in the lessening capacity of the region to compete with other global cities in attracting FDIs which need to operate efficiently in a pleasant environment.

Development Strategy for Jabotabek Region

Not only for the Jabotabek metropolitan region, the development strategy of all metropolitan regions in Indonesia, including metropolitan Bandung, Medan, Surabaya, Semarang and Ujung Pandang, should be put in the context of national economic development in the attempt to obtain a balanced and optimal growth of economic development. In other words, the national development strategy should look at policies at the macro as well as the micro levels. The National Spatial Development Plan underscores that firstly, the development of metropolitan cities will be directed so that their growth will not exceed their carrying capacities. Secondly, the plan will develop priority areas as well as medium and small cities to create counter magnets for metropolitan cities to become less primate growth centres.

There are four aspects of current changes that have particularly important implications for the development of the Jabotabek regions. These are: (1) the globalisation of the world's economy—global cooperation or multinational corporation—due to decreases in the relative cost of transportation, information technology and international communication; (2) the increasingly important role of Jakarta as a capital city with a mission to improve national and regional economic development; (3) the increasing role of the private sector in overall urban development and housing investments; and (4) the increasing importance of mobilising community resources for full participation in the planning and management of development. In this context, the development strategy for the Metropolitan Urban Region (MUR) of Jabotabek has three dimensions, as follows:

1. Support and enhancement of its roles in the global region by improving infrastructure facilities and services, environmental quality, and management. In line with the view of government as facilitator rather than the provider of urban services, urban management must be focused on intervention that harnesses private sector initiatives.
2. Support and enhancement of its roles in the national context as a centre of regional and national development. Spatially, the strategy emphasises paying greater attention to its economic linkages with other urban centres within a national hierarchical system of cities. It should be able to utilise the potentials of its hinterland regions and should be competent to provide services to these regions.
3. Support and enhancement of its roles as Metropolitan Urban Region (MUR) of Jabotabek in that it should be able to provide services to its population by constantly considering the efficiency and effectiveness of utilisation of natural and human resources, fulfilling the needs of its population and maintaining environmental sustainability. The strategy emphasises greater attention to improving human resource development and strengthening of financial capacity building. In other words, the strategy must give greater attention to empowering the urban poor to achieve a better life through collective and individual efforts.

In the context of these main policies, the principal strategies of development of MUR Jabotabek are outlined as follows:

1. Specify in more detail and clarify the development objectives of Jabotabek as the national centre of growth and increase its roles in international and national trade and as a financial centre. To enhance

the competitiveness and the role of Jabotabek within the international urban system needs, among others, the following efforts:

- to develop an efficient and effective infrastructure and services of international standard, particularly roads, railway and train system, airport and seaport, electricity and water supply as well as export processing zone;
- to promote and develop good quality government services, including the reduction of bureaucratic processes of obtaining permits for internationally-related economic activities. This needs capacity building of the government apparatus not only in their knowledge and management skills but also in their perception and practice in managing an internationalising region such as Jabotabek. This also needs a review and improvement of existing laws and regulations;
- to develop human resources which are not limited to government apparatus, but also include the community in general, and the labour force in particular, as the intensifying linkages between Jabotabek and investing countries through Foreign Direct Investment (FDI) will need a highly-skilled labour force;
- to create a transparent and participatory urban governance involving all actors in urban development which would allow efficient allocation of resources and better management of the infrastructure and services as well as reduce the 'high cost' economy. Private sector, government and community should work together in the spirit of partnership to produce synergic efforts in urban development. Local government and the community should improve their awareness and ability to deal with the private sector. Mechanisms for this partnership should be created;
- to promote good quality social and cultural environments, including security and safety from criminals which, as indicated by some newspapers recently, has resulted in high transport cost for goods within Jabotabek. This should be overcome not only by providing more social and cultural facilities, but also by creating employment opportunities and reducing the income gaps between groups. In addition, Jabotabek should maintain and promote a healthy physical environment to have good quality water, air and urban landscape through better environmental management; and
- to promote the development of service facilities and amenities with international quality and standards. This could be another factor that will attract foreign investors to Jabotabek so that they do not have to go to Singapore or other cities to obtain services.

2. Increase and promote job opportunities in the small and medium cities in Jabotabek so that all of them can function as self-sufficient cities. This could be done by providing infrastructure that can stimulate and attract investments that create jobs in these cities.

3. Strengthen institutional capacity, include the following efforts:
   - define more clearly the spatial jurisdiction of the Jabotabek region for regional planning, infrastructure investments, and service provision proposed;
   - strengthen the governmental, administrative apparatus for urban planning, management of municipal affairs, and governance;
   - enhance the institutional aspect of development management in Jabotabek which can be in the form of a collaborative forum among the kabupatens (local government districts) in planning, implementation and monitoring, including in financing urban infrastructure development;
   - modernise the urban development management and improve the capability of the government apparatus in development; and
   - increase and enhance the functions and roles of institutional bodies so that coordination of development programmes could be carried out in a more effective and efficient way. This can be done through: (a) the establishment of 'Jabotabek Forum' consisting of government, private sector and community to obtain an increasing awareness and congruous perceptions on many development issues and opportunities; (b) the augmentation of participation of private sector and community in the urban development programmes in Botabek region; (c) the enhancement of the collaboration among governments in planning, implementation, evaluation and in financing infrastructure development, land and environmental management in Botabek region; and (d) the establishment and enhancement of training programmes for urban managers to improve their capability, particularly in promoting the involvement of private sector and community in infrastructure development.

4. Provide and improve infrastructure facilities and services through involving the private sector and the community:
   - increase private sector and community participation in the provision of public infrastructure, facilities, and services. Many urban services can benefit from the effectiveness and efficiency of private enterprises, including waterworks systems, transport, markets, solid

waste collection and disposal, energy, post offices, and telecommunication;

- provide adequate infrastructure facilities and services for low income urban communities by incorporating low income settlement with urban development and other local government programmes, and by empowering people to provide self-help infrastructure facilities and services; and

- improve the integration of transportation services among cities through the development of a multi-modal system with increased participation of the private sector. The development of transportation in the Jabotabek region aims to create an integrated transportation system including various modes of land, sea, and air transportation.

5. Law and regulation enforcement:
   - establish a more coordinated system of laws, regulations, processes, and procedures to support urban planning and management, especially in the following areas: land development, procurement, administrative adjudication and appeals, and issuance of official permits and licenses;
   - strengthen the regulatory basis for water and air pollution control by determining the desired functions and passing the appropriate standards as the regulatory tools to achieve those functions;
   - increase the potential project planning process as an effective tool to prevent pollution, by improving project screening and scoping, and the assessment of regional and cross-sectoral impacts; and
   - reduce the utilisation of groundwater to avoid the expansion of seawater intrusion through the increased provision of urban water supply and public hydrants. In addition, improve the services of garbage collection and waste water to reduce pollution, and increase control on automobile and industrial emissions in order to reduce air pollution.

These are some guiding principles for planning for urban development in Indonesia in the medium-term, especially for Jabotabek metropolitan region. Maybe they can be used in a comparative study for other countries.

PART II

CHANGING

WESTERN CITIES

6 Space, Technology and the Edge City: Patterns of Service and Infrastructure Investments—The US National Capital Region

KINGSLEY HAYNES and ROGER STOUGH

Introduction

The development of a metropolitan region, which is also a national capital region and has a technology base supported in part by government policy funding is outlined. The link between government technology policy spending, research and development, infrastructure development and growth of a range of private sector, innovative, high technology industries and services is considered. The US National Capital Region, along with its major subports (Northern Virginia, Suburban Maryland and the District of Columbia (see Figure 6.5)) is treated in particular. It is a possible model for a broader range of multi-nodal, multi-jurisdictional, high tech-based, metropolitan developments occurring both win the USA and elsewhere in the world.

The low density, decentralised, multi-nodal metropolitan region is moving quickly from an American to a wider pattern of urban organisation. Despite resistance from city and regional planners and extremely powerful state and provincial regulation, the pattern continues to proliferate, particularly in developed economies. Further predictions of disastrously long commuting times and mass return to the inner city appear to be over drawn. This is a pattern of urban spatial organisation that is not likely to go away in high income automobile oriented democratic societies. Policies may modify this pattern at the margins but are not likely to create wholesale restructuring. Such systems of edge cities have patterns of organisation, public service delivery and infrastructure investment that are intriguing in their own right—whether viewed as desirable or not.

Regional Organisation

The emergence of the new urban regions raises a number of important policy questions. Many of these focus on the changing role of actors such as the nation state, the state/province, local government and business and community organisations in the economic development process. Others focus on the fact that these are high cost regional economies and need access to low cost inputs such as back office production operations. As these new regional economies emerged their role expanded and in many cases now supersede that of local and state/provincial governments in providing leadership and steering for economic development. The steering of development activities and policies has been largely organised in the form of a partnership between the public and private sectors. Universities and other research organisations (e.g. national research laboratories) also figure prominently in these partnerships. Today, one finds formal but not necessarily governmental organisations representing the interests of regions and taking responsibility for steering their development as, for example, in Baltimore, Cascadia (Vancouver, BC, in Canada to Portland Ore in the US and incorporating the Seattle region) and the Ruhrgebiet (a region that overlaps with parts of France, Germany and the Netherlands).

This leadership/steering process has not been widely institutionalised in formal government bodies although much experimentation is underway in Europe (e.g. formation of autonomic regions in Spain, Portugal and Italy; and, regional decentralisation in France). Experience in the US is that the development and steering of economic development strategy comes initially from the non-government sector where longer range objectives can be considered in a non-partisan and non-political context since in the political context short-term objectives tend to dominate. The partnership later broadens to include government representatives (political partners are important but not dominant) and other grass roots and special interest groups.

The highly fragmented jurisdictional complex of the US National Capital Region has retarded the development of organisations that can lead or steer economic development at the metropolitan level. Yet other new urban technology regions have highly sophisticated and well developed organisations that maintain economic development strategies. These strategies have targeted product and service niches along with associated markets; have advanced regional production and marketing network cultures that includes regionally coordinated and integrated technology development; and have relatively smooth interaction among public and private sector components, and among research and educational components.

The National Capital Region is a complex of, at best, loosely confederated counties that belong to the Washington Metropolitan Region which is composed of a federal district and several other suburban counties located in the states of Maryland, Virginia and West Virginia. Most other metropolitan regions are located in one or two states and as a consequence have developed richer region-wide institutional infrastructures including region-wide community foundations; transportation, housing, social services, etc., planning and management bodies, development policies and institutions to implement them; and in some cases region-wide governments. Because of the high level of jurisdictional fragmentation in the larger functional region and the Federal district versus the rest of region (inside/outside beltway) mentality, these institutions have developed in only the most rudimentary fashion for the National Capital Region. However important, building regional cohesion at the National Capital Region level may be an activity that will most likely evolve slowly and, more importantly, will evolve even more slowly as long as the level of cohesion in its sub-regional components remains low. Northern Virginia's relatively high placement in the regional value-added chain places it in a position to provide leadership for cohesive planning and development of the National Capital Region. However, it must become more cohesive itself before it can exercise this leadership potential.

The Northern Virginia sub-region, for example, was, for the most part, dominated by a rural orientation as recently as twenty years ago, Life among its residents was relatively uncomplicated and predictable and for the most part county level institutions and government were sufficient to address all but a few issues (for example, waste water treatment became a regional issue in the early 1970s). Consequently, few regional institutions were needed and only a few such institutions existed (for example, the Northern Virginia Planning District Council was formed in the late 1960s but even today its role is primarily information provision and advisory in nature). With the increased growth of the 1970s and 1980s, issues and problems spilled across local jurisdictional boundaries. Yet the development of institutions to deal with these new region-wide issues (e.g. transportation, development, housing, human services, health—AIDS) have been slow to develop and to the extent that they have they may for the most part be viewed as being in a nascent stage of development. Even the business community which operates across jurisdictional boundaries has been slow to develop representative bodies that cross jurisdictional boundaries, e.g. each jurisdiction has its own chamber of commerce, economic development agency or authority, and the Northern Virginia Technology Council which is a region-wide organisation is still almost totally dominated by participation from one jurisdiction, Fairfax County,

There is a need for much more robust and more rapid development of institutions that can address the regional manifestations of problems and opportunities. Some of the key issues that need to be effectively managed by such regional institutions include the cost of congestion and high cost of business operations in such an environment as Northern Virginia as well as barriers to entry for individuals (affordable housing) and to firms. A first step that would be helpful in this would be the formation of a regional organisation for strategic regional economic development.

This does not speak to the patterns of growth of shadow governments (e.g. TYTRANS—Tyson's Corner's Business Transportation Organisation or local housing owners associations that manage private streets and garbage disposal) or privately delivered 'public' services (e.g. multi-purpose mall and commercial centre private security services). There are patterns of developing new organisations to meet rapidly expanding local needs in locations where previous systems for meeting those needs were not in place.

Infrastructure

Infrastructure policy is driven by many considerations—public interest, institutional dynamics, political assessment, ideology, and knowledge or perception of how a process works. Historically, infrastructure investment has been seen as an acceptable point for public policy intervention in the national and regional economy. In fact, traditionally, infrastructure investment has been the pivotal point of partnership between the private and public sector in pursuit of economic transformation. The use of infrastructure by the private sector to assemble inputs and distribute outputs has been widely appreciated. Further, the ability of private sector organisations to benefit from shared use of infrastructure investments is also well recognised. Similarly the role of the public sector in directing large, risky investments and allocating their use among competitors may be a contentious issue but certainly is not new. What is less appreciated is the changing meaning of infrastructure and its many roles in regional system dynamics.

A new conceptualisation of infrastructure is central to the development of strategies for infrastructure investment in the restructured economies of the 21ˢᵗ century. It is also central to our appreciation of the comparative advantages of regions. Most recently we have seen new attempts to link change in national and regional productivity to patterns and levels of infrastructure investments (Reich, 1991; Munnel, 1990). In the US, Senator Moynihan's proposal for a national infrastructure policy and a federally backed infrastructure investment fund is another manifestation of the recognition of linkage between infrastructure, economic development and the role of public policy in stimulating or providing an underpinning for private sector expansion. However, before policies are enunciated it is important that we recognise some central concerns in infrastructure definition and in its changing role in regional economies.

The division of infrastructure into social and economic components is a place to begin. The concept of social overhead capital or simply soft infrastructure has been linked to education, health, social and recreational support, and partially to environmental concerns. This human capital/quality of life perspective is augmented by a direct orientation to the welfare of human resources and its consequences which is assumed to be increased labour productivity. Economic or 'hard' infrastructure in the form of roads, harbours, airports, and utilities is also seen as a complement to productivity. In this case it is recognised as a complement to producer capital in the form of making factories, machinery, equipment, and production technology more efficient. Finally, consumer capital is also made more efficient through the volume and quality of housing and the distribution structure produced (Chatterjee and Hasnath, 1990). In such cases the purpose of public infrastructure investment is to lower relative prices, increase access to labour, raw materials and technology and to reduce the costs of production and hence the cost of final products. Theoretically at least this moves us from one equilibrium level to another with lower prices and higher consumption resulting in better incomes and higher levels of employment (Lakshmanan, 1989).

The long-time horizon of the productive life of infrastructure facilities, their large scale, and the all or nothing nature of the investments, make them very sensitive to the costs of capital, and inherently risky. This, it has been suggested, requires a public sector role for such investments. Further, the fact that infrastructure is shared both by public and private sector users and across alternative private sector users with no industry or firm specific characteristics, and often has natural monopoly elements to it, suggests that the public sector has an appropriate production, allocation and distributional responsibility. Hence, although it is assumed that private sector benefits flow from infrastructure investment the public sector has traditionally played a central role.

There has been much discussion of the crucial role of infrastructure and the temporal order in which infrastructure and other forms of capital should be provided so as to stimulate economic development. However, what infrastructure consists of is rarely reviewed, and its characteristics and composition are often defined ad-hoc. In spite of speculation about the causes and the patterns of economic change, there is no coherent theory of economic development into which infrastructure has been incorporated. This makes the attempts to describe the role of infrastructure difficult, since countries or regions in different stages of technological evolution are usually interested in incorporating infrastructure investment into policies for expanding economic development.

In developed economies, on the other hand, especially those undergoing structural transformation from an emphasis on manufacturing and goods production to services and information management, infrastructure investment is still a central concern. The change from a goods producing economy towards a service economy relates to both what is produced, how it is produced and where (Gershuny, 1978; Stanbeck *et al.*, 1981). Not only is there a trend toward a greater variety of services but increasingly services are produced jointly with goods. Further, goods are produced that incorporate a demand for services for effective utilisation. There is a significant growth in producer services and producer service like functions and an expanding emphasis on investments in human capital. Change in the organisation of production reflects the shifts in technology, in labour and consumer markets, and in the organisational system as a whole, including the process of service delivery itself which has become increasingly routinised, standardised and 'industrialised' (Levitt, 1976; Gershuny, 1978). As a consequence of the above changes, different types of services appear to be locating at different levels in the urban hierarchy thus transforming the urban system (Daniels, 1985).

Information utilisation is the differentiating characteristic of the expanding service sector industries. Telecommunications systems are central not only to solicit business, to deliver products but to design products that fit specific consumer wishes. To quote Lakshmanan (1989):

> Communication systems are to service industries what road, railways and canals are to (goods-producing) manufacturing. A major effect of the emerging innovations in telecommunications, electronics and computing is to increase the sizes of the service markets by breaking down the market barriers, integrating dispersed markets and facilitating the creation of new markets. These innovations increase the speed, density, and quality of information flows, which in turn augment the potential pace of

technological change and the diffusion of innovations. Further, since these developments in the telecommunications sector are taking place in a period of increasing internationalisation of the service sector, the facilities and networks extend beyond national boundaries (undersea Cable, Geostationary Satellites, etc.). Currently the impacts of these telecommunications developments are keenly felt in many information-rich producer services, whose range and quality are being transformed. When the potential of these developments is realised by consumer services as well, major impacts on the range and quality of services, on labour utilisation, and work organisation are likely. The key analytical questions here are: What role does this increase in capacity and lowered unit cost in telecommunications and information technology have on future economic growth and in facilitating the transition to a dominant service economy? Given the rapid technological innovation and the growing deregulation of the telecommunications industry, public policy choices on types, sizes and locations of communications infrastructure investments become important to future economic growth in an increasingly international production system.

Infrastructure Content

In order to clarify the use of the infrastructure concept, Youngson (1967) concluded that infrastructure is not a set of things but a set of characteristics. Two such characteristics are recognised. Capital is infrastructure if (a) it is a source of external economies; and (b) it has to be provided in large units 'ahead of demand'. If capital expenditures satisfy either of these characteristics, Youngson suggests they should be viewed as infrastructure. Both imply the desirability of a certain amount of public investment since, due to positive, external economies, the pattern of investment in a private enterprise economy would be below that which is socially optimal. The second characteristic of provision ahead of demand indicates an expectation about the future and this is an important consideration. Error uncertainty and imperfect knowledge about that future will play a central role in an infrastructure investment whose purpose is to serve the cause of regional economic change.

The argument for such infrastructure is particularly strong in the case of those investments which may be thought of as somewhat non-specific in character—that is, those which can be utilised in the production of a wide variety of final outputs such as social overhead capital investment in education. The ultimate return to society for education may be out of all proportion to the costs. The indirect benefits which are derived from public and private spending in education extend far beyond the direct benefits (e.g.

the economic returns from a major new idea or the effective incorporation of such an idea into existing technology). It is indeed a matter of facilitating the evolution of new ideas, of new combinations of the factors of production, and generally promoting the Schumpeterian notion of innovation. In that context innovation is the key to economic advancement. Infrastructure facilitates investment that promotes innovation (Suarez-Villa and Hasnath, 1993). As appreciation of the role of infrastructure in facilitating the emergence of new combinations of factors of production it is recognised that the analysis of infrastructure inevitably includes the study of economic transformation and system dynamics.

Infrastructure and Regional Dynamics

Many regions that directly provide capital goods—designed both to supplement and to induce a favourable response from productive enterprises—take advantage of the beneficial effects of infrastructure. It would appear that the stock of infrastructure has several effects on the level and mix of directly productive activities. First, investments in physical and social overhead capital will increase the efficiency and reduce the prices of production inputs. Not only do costs such as those of material assembly and skilled labour become lower, but increases in the capacity of infrastructure very often lead to an improved quality of service. A multi-lane limited-access highway has a greater capacity than a single-lane road. However, it is also faster and safer. Further, it also generates new demands in terms of labour and capital.

Although the improvement of transportation infrastructure will result in production expansion in some regions and production reduction in other regions as inter-regional trade is facilitated and competition intensified, relocation of capital and labour will also take place (Rietveld, 1990). For example, even though infrastructure construction is locally produced, the locality may not reap the final benefit of development, as a new transportation line may create a 'corridor' effect by channelling economic activities through or around the locality to both ends of a distribution with direct origin and destination linkage bypassing intermediate nodes.

These cost reduction and output expansion effects of infrastructure investments are empirically captured through the formulation and estimations of cost functions and production functions. Since social overhead capital is available to all firms in a region, it is viewed as entering the production functions of regional firms. However, while available to all, total use must be equal to or less than the physical capacity (e.g. traffic lane capacity, sewage pipe diameter, etc.) in order to maximise benefits (i.e., at an efficient level of congestion). In this way infrastructure is viewed as a stock variable at least in the intermediate term.

Further, inadequate supply of certain infrastructure elements will produce bottlenecks hinderous to the full utilisation of other production factors. According to Rietveld (1990), two approaches are found in relation to bottleneck phenomena: (1) a bottleneck exists when actual production costs are far above potential production costs as predicted by the production function (Biehl, 1986); and (2) a bottleneck exists when the mutual relationships between inputs as represented by marginal rates of substitution are out of balance (Blum, 1982).

Infrastructure investments are viewed as facilitating economic change and rationalising regional production distribution, in other words as a mechanism of system dynamics. Public infrastructure investment affects private investment in two ways. On the one hand, public capital appears to enhance the productivity of private capital, thereby raising the rate of return and encouraging more private sector investment. On the other hand, public capital may serve as a substitute for private capital—to the extent this occurs, more public capital will result in less private investment (Munnel, 1990). This is a critical balance and must be disaggregated by infrastructure type to be fully appreciated. In particular it appears that transportation and telecommunication infrastructure generate the highest regional output elasticities, followed by water investments, with the lowest contributions from public building investments in public operations (Munnel, 1990).

Future Infrastructure

Much of our focus up to this point has been a review of the general thinking and analytic procedure we use in evaluating infrastructure investments for regional systems. However, much of this has been limited to historically important fixed infrastructure mostly for the support of traditional manufacturing capital. Lakshmanan (1989) has suggested movement of information is to the service sector what goods movement is to the manufacturing sector. With the rapid expansion of the service sector in general and its information management subcomponent, communications will be the 21st century's substitution for highways. In Batten and Thord's (1989) book on *Transportation for the Future* the issue of substitutability between communications and mobility is a constant theme. Anderson, Anderstiz, and Härsman (1989) develop the argument that knowledge and communications infrastructure will be the backbone for a global system of interactions. This integration plays a central role in bringing together the demand and supply side of a complex global economy. It is the attempt to reduce the costs of interaction (transaction costs) that is the driving force in the new infrastructure patterns and technology choices.

Smilor and Wakelin (1990) divide future infrastructure into the same hard and soft categories we have already seen but the content of their lists change. Hard infrastructure includes transportation, telecommunication, research parks and support facilities, quality of life facilities and utilities; soft infrastructure includes human resources, financing, business services, technology transfer, leisure activities, legal and institutional services. They argued that it is this soft category of infrastructure which will grow at a much accelerated rate and will be essential to future economic growth and technology development and applications.

As noted above, communication infrastructure includes a variety of information capital (e.g. telephones, satellite communications, integrated digital networks, etc.) and information labour. Such capital reduces the temporal and spatial costs of coordination and over time increases the division of labour productivity. All of this, in turn, increases the output of goods and services, income, assets, reinvestment in infrastructure, and institutional complexity. Thus, the information communication infrastructure is viewed as a key sector, receiving resource inputs and imposing transaction costs and making claims on production output as well as providing production inputs. This sector influences the nature and level of social of political participation and the structure of incentives and organisations in society.

In the competitive game of international economic growth, societies that have vigour and adaptability in their social and political institutional structure incur adjustment costs more effectively and hence speed up their technical change and development. The private and public organisations in such societies adopt a dynamic strategic perspective (in addition to their ongoing system maintenance) and engage in future scanning, goal setting, strategic decision making and programming, that lead, in turn, to modification of the incentive and organisation structures. In such adjustment activities the communication infrastructure plays a key role.

Northern Virginia Infrastructure

What we have outlined here is a highly abbreviated version of a future model of infrastructure and many more linkages need to be identified. However, it gives an idea of future infrastructure development trends and of the need to integrate our current investment patterns so as to be responsive to these future needs.

Transportation Capital Costs[1]

Highways. Through 1995, funds committed to highway projects total $912.6 million. This figure includes $209.9 million for freeways—$546.9 million for arterial roads; and $155.8 million for other roads, including local collector roads and miscellaneous projects.

Planning documents adopted by individual local governments for the year 2010 include $1,104.8 million for freeway improvements—$1,162.4 million for arterial highways; and $165.4 million for other roads. Total locally planned expenditures are $2,432.6 million.

The 2010 Virginia Department of Transportation (VDOT) recommended plan for the Northern Virginia region projects $1,684.3 million needed for freeways; $1,407.4 million needed for arterial highways, and the same $1,65.4 million for other projects. Total highway expenditures recommended by VDOT are $3,257.1 million through 2010.

HOV. HOV lanes are designated as 'separate' express lanes and 'diamond' lanes. Through 1995, $168.8 million has been committed for constructing separate HOV lanes, and $15 million for designating and constructing diamond lanes. Total committed funds are $183.8 million.

Local plans through 2010 call for spending $672.8 million on separate lanes, and an additional $15 million for diamond lanes. Locally adopted plans call for total HOV spending of $687.8 million.

VDOT's recommended plan encourages major expansion of the region's HOV lane designations. It calls for $753.3 million for separate lanes, and $563.8 million for diamond lanes. The total recommended by the state for HOV is $1,317.1 through 2010.

Transit. Public transit plans designate four categories: commuter rail, other rail (including rehabilitation of Metrorail rolling stock and facilities), bus on HOV, and Metrobus and local bus (including rehabilitation of Metrobus stock and facilities). The total committed for spending through 1995 includes $59 million for commuter rail; $171 million for other rail; zero for bus on HOV; and $93.7 million for Metrobus and local bus.

Plans adopted independently by local governments through 2010 include $59 million for commuter rail; $734 million for other rail; zero for

---

[1] Transportation cost data are taken from the *Northern Virginia 2010 Transportation Plan*, produced by the Virginia Department of Transportation.

bus on HOV; and $283.4 million for Metrobus and local bus. Total local public transit spending is planned at $1,076.4 million.

The VDOT 2010 plan is more strongly supportive of public transit than the local governments, calling for a total of $2,687.9 million. It recommends spending $118 million for commuter rail; $2,090 million for other rail; $189.7 million for buses on HOV; and $290.2 for Metrobus and local buses.

All Surface Modes Combined.   Committed spending for capital costs through 1995 for all modes is $1,420.1 million. Locally adopted plans call for spending $4,196.8 million through 2010, compared to VDOT recommendations of $7,262.1 million for the long-run period.

Airports.   Both Washington National and Dulles airports are in the midst of major capital improvements.   The Metropolitan Washington Airports Authority Capital Development Program is divided in two components, one for each airport. Total capital improvements for Washington National will cost $933 million. Of that, $165 million is already completed; $186 million is in the construction phase now; $478 million are in various stages of design and procurement; and future improvements total $104 million. The FY 1994 budget is $205 million.

Capital improvements for Dulles International Airport will cost $985 million; of that total, $119 million is already completed; $320 million is currently in construction; $61 million is in design and procurement; and $485 million is required for future improvements. The capital budget for Dulles for FY 1994 is $199 million.

Information Technology Infrastructure

Significant deregulation in the telecommunications industry began in the late 1970s, followed by a trend toward privatising the provision of many public services, including information and   communications.   One important result of these policies has been a blurring of the distinction between the public and private sectors, a fact made clear by ubiquitous calls for public-private partnerships.   The outcome of these twin trends of deregulation and privatisation has been the emergence of what Fortune magazine has called The Netplex, more than 1,200 telecommunications and information technology firms in the National Capital region—most in Northern Virginia—that have formed the foundation of the nation's information infrastructure.

At the core of the new information infrastructure is the Internet, the network of more than 25,000 computer networks and systems around the globe originally pioneered by the Pentagon about 20 years ago to allow communications to continue in any event, without relying on centralised computer systems. The investment in this new infrastructure must be measured largely in financial capital spent for services and data. Depending on what yardstick one uses, current annual expenditures range from $1 billion to $2.8 billion. However, MCI, one of the most aggressive providers of telecommunications and information services, estimates that figure will rise to as much as $40 billion a year by 1998.

Sewer and Water

Fairfax County. Fairfax County provides sewer service to its citizens through a system that includes its own sewer lines and pumping stations, one county-owned treatment plant, and contractual agreements in the District of Columbia, the Alexandria Sanitation Authority, and the Upper Occoquan Sewage Authority. Fairfax County has a capital improvement programme that includes support for 19 facilities expansions or upgrades. Expenditures through FY 1994 for these projects were $293.5 million. Proposed expenditures for FY 1995-99 are: FY95, 30.1 million; FY96, $96.43 million; FY97, $105.2 million; FY98, $105.2 million; and FY99, $483.8 million. Total costs planned for current capital improvement projects from FY 1994-99 are $820.8 million.

Fairfax County water services are provided in a manner similar to sewer services, including a county water authority and agreements with neighbouring jurisdictions. Projects are financed with revenue bonds and net operating revenues. Revenue bond financed projects include $116 million through FY 1994; FY95, $26.2 million; FY96, $10.15 million; FY97, $4 million; FY98, $2 million; and FY99, $1.2 million. Total revenue bond project costs FY 1994-99 are $161.453 million. Additional projects paid for with net revenues bring the total capital improvement programme for water to $249.175 through FY 1999.

Loudoun County. The Loudoun County Sanitation Authority Capital Improvements Program (CIP) for water and wastewater systems for the 1994-98 period is projected at a cost of approximately $60.6 million. The 1994 CIP is budgeted at $13.9 million; for 1995, $13.7 million; for 1996, $12.2 million; for 1997, $10.8 million; and for 1998, $9.9 million.

Educational infrastructure is another key element in fostering and maintaining economic growth. The continuing knowledge explosion makes information obsolete at an accelerated rate.   Universities and other educational channels (ranging from local level training centres to inter-regional satellite teaching systems) will be an important part of the future infrastructure package, which will be important not only for human resources producers but also for incubators of new business and technology.

Implications

Clearly the Northern Virginia infrastructure is continuing to expand at a rapid pace fuelled by a modestly strong regional economy that, even during the recent recession, had resilience and job generating capability.   The result is a strong tax and user fee base for support of infrastructure growth. Incomes remain high with the result that the demands for high quality infrastructure also remains strong.   Further, the rapid expansion of infrastructure in the 1980s means that age and technological obsolescence has not caught up with the infrastructure that has been put in place.   Hence, maintenance costs have not been impacted by large scale replacement requirements.

With respect to a regional perspective the three major transportation corridors—l-95, I-66 and the Dulles corridor—still dominate as radial arteries from the Washington-Arlington-Alexandria core.   The beltway's partial circumference is now complemented by the cross Fairfax Parkway and what soon will be the western bypass.   Except for the two major environment zones residential in-full is marked by a few dominant employment centres—Garreau's Edge Cities—Crystal and Pentagon City, Fair Oaks, Tyson's Corner, and the Dulles Complex.   The air interface to other regions and the rest of the world is dominated by the expanding airports of National and Dulles.

The northern Dulles Corridor has the largest concentration of vacant commercial space in the region which can be viewed as a problem or an opportunity depending on your perspective.   However, significant vacant commercial space still exists throughout the region, particularly on the periphery, although residential space has been rapidly absorbed.   The cost of support of the underlying infrastructure in these peripheral areas will remain significant for some time to come.

All in all the infrastructure growth pattern is still built on an optimistic growth perspective and except for ground transportation still leads development.

Institutional Infrastructure

The development of institutional infrastructure has, in part, been dealt with above. However, there are other institutional issues including education. Here the problem is not so much with the provision of quality education services in the region but rather with the provision of educational services in the future that are integrated directly into and targeted to the needs of the regional economy, i.e., worker retraining and life long learning. Only when a long-term strategic plan for the development of the region is adopted and executed will it be possible to accurately identify many of the areas of retraining that will be needed. Thus, the efficient design and delivery of practical education services will depend on the formation of the regional steering organisation described above. Further, it will depend on the development of a much more advanced intra-regional communications infrastructure to support new forms for delivering educational services and learning, e.g. distance learning. Being able to target educational services in this more precise way is important given the significance of a highly skilled and adaptable work force to the continued competitiveness of the high technology region. Some estimates of the contribution of education (training and knowledge production) to regional product are as high as 60 percent of the total and more than twice as much as the contribution of traditional capital.

Currently regional analysis for the Northern Virginia Region is fragmented. There is a need to make data on the region available through a centralised or decentralised clearinghouse mechanism and to add value to this data through analysis that is readily available. Such a process could be enhanced by a regional communication and data network with open access to public and private users. Today, research of this nature is provided in part by the Northern Virginia Planning District Commission, local governments, the Washington Council of Governments, the Greater Washington Research Center as well as some private research firms in the area. The region-wide organisations tend not to take a specifically Northern Virginia orientation while the Northern Virginia groups tend to focus on providing information more than to adding value to the information through analysis (there are some exceptions, some of the work by the NVPDC is quite good with respect to this larger perspective). The Center for Regional Analysis in the Institute of Public Policy at the region's higher education centre—George Mason University—is building the capacity to fill some of this gap.

Patterns of Technology Investments

Below we provide a summary of an analysis of the technology sector of the Greater Washington regional economy. It is based upon original data collected from a data base of technology firms in the region developed for this project. The study was motivated by the recognition that much of the rapid economic growth experienced during the last twenty years was driven by the development of a large cluster of technology-intensive companies. The report describes and analyses the size, distribution of companies by type of technology, geographic distribution within the region, economic effects, occupational structure, and educational needs, as well as some of the barriers and opportunities facing the technology sector.

The Greater Washington region, in addition to being one of the nation's fastest growing regions, also has the highest average family income and the highest educational attainment of any metropolitan area in the United States. This occurs partly because the region is the seat of the federal government and, therefore, attracts highly educated people. It has also been accentuated by growth of the technology business sector which now forms the core of the region's economic base, despite a continued high level of dependence on the federal sector. The study aims to learn more about the technology sector in order to help sustain economic development in the region.

Technology firms produce technology, produce products that are technologically intensive, or use technology to address complex problems. This definition is consistent with prevailing views of technology as described in the scholarly literature on the subject.

Characteristics of the Firms in the Data Base

- There are 2,331 technology firms in the Greater Washington region: three percent in the District of Columbia, 41.6 percent in Maryland; and 55.4 percent in Virginia;
- technology sector employment is 262,337: 1.5 percent in the District of Columbia; 39.1 percent in Maryland; and 59.4 percent in Virginia;
- the region's technology firms are most heavily concentrated in computer software and hardware; technical and management consulting and professional services; systems integration; information services and communications; engineering services; defence/aerospace; and bio-technology/bio-medicine. There are small but significant clusters of firms in the critical technological areas of energy, environment and transportation;

• the large majority of companies have fewer than 100 employees, illustrating that the technology sector is composed of many small- and medium-sized businesses. Yet the 29 firms that employ 1000 or more account for 42 percent of all technology employment. There are significant differences in the presence of large and dominant companies among the different technology subsectors, with technical and professional services, telecommunications, defence and aerospace, and energy technology groups having more large companies. Computer software and hardware, information services and other communications, engineering services, manufacturing, biotechnology and biomedicine, environment, and transportation are dominated by small- and medium-sized businesses; and

• technology firms are located in clusters along major transportation corridors. These are the Capital Beltway; Interstate 66, Route 28 and the Dulles Toll Road in Virginia; and I-270 and 1-95 in Maryland. This pattern is characteristic of all technology subgroupings except defence/aerospace and bio-technology/bio-medicine which are located primarily in Virginia and Maryland respectively. It is important to re-emphasise that only three percent of the firms and 1.5 percent of the employment in the technology sector are located in the District of Columbia. Thus, most technology activity is clustered in the outer geographic part of the region.

The Economic Effects of the Technology Sector

The technology sector of the Greater Washington region plays an important role in the formation and dynamics of the region's economic base. Directly employing 262,337, the technology sector ranks second in size behind retail trade among all sources of private employment. The sector is characterised by above average earnings and directly generates approximately $21 billion in total industry output—10 percent of the region's total. It also contributes significantly to state and local government finances. It is the fastest growing large technology region in the United States, outpacing, for example, the employment growth in the Silicon Valley and the Boston 128 regions by 30 percent or more between 1988 and 1992. Major findings of the study include:

• Northern Virginia, with 155,675 technology employees, accounts for almost 60 percent of the region's technology work force, while suburban Maryland's technology sector employs an additional 102,654. Although the sector is relatively small in Washington, DC, (4,008 employees) it ranks 23rd among the 54 metropolitan areas that were considered;

• total earnings in the technology sector amount to $9.3 billion and are distributed across the region in a manner similar to employment. Although the sector accounts for only 1.7 percent of all private sector firms, it directly generates 16 percent of all private sector earnings;

• economic impact analysis shows that the 262,337 jobs in the technology sector indirectly support an additional 234,733 jobs in other sectors of the regional economy;

• earnings associated with employment indirectly linked to the technology sector are approximately $5.5 billion. Direct, indirect, and induced earnings of the technology sector account for 24 percent of all private sector earnings;

• the fiscal impact is significant, with technology directly generating $2.3 billion of own-source revenue to state and local governments, and indirectly generating an additional $1.5 billion annually;

• local governments in Northern Virginia receive $546 million annually from direct technology-related activity, while local governments in suburban Maryland receive $440 million. In the District of Columbia, $14 million in own-source revenue are generated by this technology sector;

• the total own-source revenue impact to local governments is $1.67 billion annually, $912 million in Northern Virginia, $741 million in suburban Maryland, and $19 million in Washington, DC;

• in total, this sector accounts for nearly 16 percent of local government own-source revenue region-wide. In Northern Virginia, over 33 percent of this revenue source is linked to the technology sector; and

• own-source revenue accruing to the state governments of Virginia and Maryland total $1.2 billion and $988 million, respectively.

Labor Force and Training Requirements

Analysis of the labour market implications of the technology sector focused on occupational utilisation of the sector and the educational requirements associated with this set of occupations. While some occupational segments of the technology sector resemble those of other sectors, there are also some distinct differences.

• like other sectors of the economy, the technology sector utilises a large proportion of executive, administrative, and managerial personnel.

Together, these occupation classes account for 55,178, or 21 percent of the technology labour force;

- administrative support occupations make up an additional 68,128 positions while marketing, production, maintenance, and other support occupations contribute 51,061 positions;

- the technology sector also utilises a large proportion of skilled and technically trained personnel belonging to the broad classification of professional specialties and technologists;

- among the utilised occupations belonging to this class are (16,807) engineers, (8,132) surveyors and architects, (7,302) computer, math, and operations researchers, and (27,117) a variety of technicians and technologists. These workers, combined with executive and managerial positions, account for 50 percent of the technology labour force;

- the educational profile of the industry reflects its occupational composition. On average, technology firms utilise proportionately more labour with at least some college training than the rest of the economy. In addition, the education and training utilisation rates increase with higher levels of education;

- proportionately, the technology sector uses approximately half as many workers with less than a high school education, 10 percent more labour with some college training, 19 percent more labour with four years of college, and 23 percent more with at least some graduate level training than the total economy; and

- it is suggested that the ability of the region to attract, train, and produce a quality work force could prove to be one of the most critical factors to the continued vitality of the technology sector.

Barriers and Opportunities

The technology services that characterise much of the technology businesses in the region in many cases, (1) are in the early part of development cycles, (2) have limited traditional assets given that they are human capital intensive, and (3) tend to be small- and medium-sized. These attributes, when combined with rapid innovation and change, pose a number of barriers and opportunities. Several of the more important ones are considered in the report and the related findings are summarised below.

- the region's traditional asset poor, small- and medium-sized technology firms have difficulty obtaining financing, especially for growth. This problem is accentuated by the limited availability of capital in the region. More and expanded capital formation programmes like those in suburban Maryland and planned for Virginia are needed.   Further, public and private programmes are needed to market the technology sector because its scale and nature are not well known and not well understood by investors outside of the region. More information is needed to better understand the amount and the nature of the need among the different technology firm groups;

- neither the size nor the nature of the education demand of the technology sector is well understood. Clearly there is more demand for advanced and graduate level training than for most other sectors. However, because of the rapid pace of innovation and change in many parts of the technology sector, traditional 'talking head' type training programmes will not be as effective. New approaches to education and training, emphasising continuous and process specific interaction among the firm, the student/trainee, and the education provided are needed.   An analysis and forecast of the education needs of the technology sector is needed;

- the region's technology sector is heavily, but not totally, dependent on the federal government. Increased volatility and unpredictability of the federal budget, e.g. defence build down and/or deficit reduction proposals, are forcing considerable business restructuring and re-engineering in the technology sector.   Given its high level of dependence, the region should develop a strategy to manage its relations with the federal government to ensure sustained economic development;

- local and state taxes are a minor but symbolically important factor in the location of technology businesses in the region. Issues of tax cost have been considered, for example, in Northern Virginia and Fairfax County. However, there is a large tax burden differential between the District of Columbia and the lower burdened outer parts of the region. The combined effect of coupling higher taxes with lower quality public schools and higher crime rates has constrained technology business development in the District and has reinforced the heavy concentration of technology firms in the outer parts of the region; and

- technology firms are subject to a wide variety of federal rules and regulations that are barriers to their development. These range from anti-trust (e.g. telecommunications) to the Food & Drug Administration (biotechnology and biomedicine) to product liability issues (e.g., aircraft and aerospace industry) to intellectual property (e.g. software engineering and bio-technology/bio-medicine) to rules set by the

Federal Accounting Standards Board and defence procurement reform (e.g. defence and aerospace). Barriers related to these issues are not specific to the Greater Washington region's technology sector. Regional organisations and leaders are, however, in a position to provide national leadership because of their location where federal policy is made. Providing such leadership would both help elevate the external perception of the region's technology sector and would, by helping to improve competitive conditions in general, contribute to increased competitiveness of technology businesses here.

From this analysis it can be seen that the growth in new technology and its associated jobs reinforces the dispersed peripheral structure of the regional metropolitan economy and that this dispersion is *not* a function of residential distributions alone. Further, from this pattern infrastructure, associations are explicit and clearly linked to new economic growth patterns and vice versa.

Societal Considerations

One part of the region's economy is partly dependent on other parts of the National Capital Region for labour, markets and services. The quality of physical environment is in part dependent upon the levels of residuals (airborne and water) generated in other parts of the National Capital Region and even beyond to include the watersheds of the Potomac and Chesapeake basins as is the environmental quality of these larger areas dependent in part on activities in sub-parts of the region. Similar arguments could be made in terms of quality of life, where factors such as crime, education, entertainment options, and so on are important. In short, it is important to recognise that parts of the region are part of a larger frame of reference, that the frames vary depending upon the purpose or problem being considered and that the future of the region will depend in part on how its relations with these other frames of regional reference are managed.

Patterns of Development in the Region

There has been a significant divergence in the development paths of the District of Columbia and the Northern Virginia and Suburban Maryland parts of the region. Table 6.1 shows the population of the District decreasing from a high of 763,956 in 1960 to 606,900 in 1990. During this period the Maryland and Northern Virginia suburban areas grew from

1,203,979 to 2,586,997 (115 percent). While employment levels were similar in 1970 (645 thousand in the District; 715 thousand in the suburban areas) by 1990 suburban employment was 1,508 thousand (a nil percent increase) with the District increasing slightly (14.7 percent) to 740 thousand (Table 6.2). Similar changes occurred in personal income, commercial construction, and retail sales.

Table 6.1   National capital region population by jurisdiction and by major sub region

Jurisdiction	1960	1970	1980	1990
Northern Virginia	580,369	887,738	1,075,662	1,437,208
Suburban Maryland	698,323	1,184,528	1,244,124	1,486,295
District of Columbia	763,956	756,668	638,432	606,900

Source: US Bureau of Economic Analysis, Summary Economic Data, 1969-91

Table 6.2   National capital region employment by place of work 1970-1990 (full and part time wage and salary)

Jurisdiction	1960	1970	1980
Northern Virginia	372,735	544,879	881,268
Suburban Maryland	385,092	549,990	755,656
District of Columbia	644,933	670,385	740,090

Source: US Bureau of Economic Analysis, Summary Economic Data, 1969-91

Beyond these more obvious quantitative indicators other structural changes occurred. Until the late 1980s unemployment in the District tended to be at about the national average (Figure 6.1). Since then unemployment rates have increasingly exceeded the national average. Over the same period suburban unemployment rates have decreased relative to the District. Crime rates per 100,000 population in the District are nearly twice as high as in Northern Virginia or Suburban Maryland (US Federal Bureau of Investigation, Uniform Crime Reports, 1985 and 1992). High school drop out rates are nearly twice as high as in the District (US Bureau of the Census, Summary of Social and Economic Indicators, 1980 and 1990). The fiscal base of the District is seriously jeopardised with almost daily reports that it will need a 'bail out', make ever more severe cuts in expenditures to balance the budget or become insolvent. Finally, business formation rates, an indicator of innovation levels, have historically been low (about 22 percent of the regional total) in the District compared to much higher levels in the suburban jurisdictions (see Table 6.3). These rates have decreased in the District relative to the outer parts of the region over the past several years (at the same time the rates in Suburban Maryland have decreased relative to Northern Virginia). Given these significant distinctions between the District and other parts of the Metropolitan Region one would expect some economic structural differences to exist.

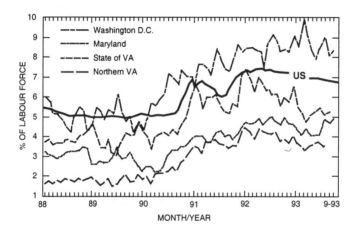

Figure 6.1 Monthly unemployment numbers, Washington metropolitan area

Figure 6.2 illustrates the economic structure of the economies of the District, Northern Virginia, Suburban Maryland and the U.S. in 1991 using personal income as an indicator of the size of different sectors. The data show that the whole National Capital Region may be described as a government, and business and technical services centre and that manufacturing is relatively *unimportant*. When the services are examined in more detail (Figure 6.3) notable differences appear. Business and engineering/management services are much more important in Northern Virginia and Suburban Maryland; membership organisations and legal services are much more important in the District. Further, the federal sector, while important throughout the region, is considerably more important in the District although nearly half of all direct federal employment in Northern Virginia is in the inner suburb of Arlington.

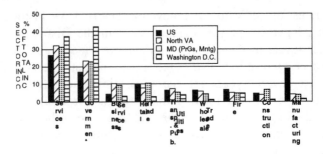

Figure 6.2   The US, Northern Virginia, MD and Washington DC 1991 main sector incomes

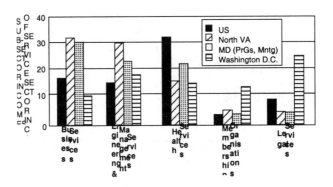

Figure 6.3   The US, Northern Virginia, Maryland and Washington DC 1991 detailed service sector incomes

Table 6.3   New business formation in the national capital region percentage by major sub region

Year	Virginia	Maryland	District
During 1980s	43.0	35.0	22.0
Since 1991	56.4	28.3	15.3

Source: Fuller, 1994

This analysis shows that the District is the home of the federal government and as such the superordinant locus of public policy making in the US. More than 40 percent of income generated in the District is paid directly by the federal government, Further, while the service sector generated nearly 40 percent of the income 25 percent of this is in legal services—a large amount of which is in such government related activities as lobbying and regulation. Beyond this, engineering and management accounts for nearly 20 percent of the services (most of this is in management) . The other major components of the service sector in the District are education (a number of universities are based there) and amusement and recreation services, although in the latter case the proportion is less than for the US, as a whole. In conclusion, the District economy is dominated by the federal government—the business of making and executing public policy and regulation—with some additional semi-independent components such as visitor and educational services.

In contrast, Northern Virginia has only about half as much of its income generated directly by the federal government as the District which, by the way, is still a somewhat greater proportion than for the US. The core of the Northern Virginia economy is business and engineering/ management services of which a significant part is in, advanced technology enterprises. Approximately 124 thousand work in the technology sector which focuses on technology services such as systems integration, systems architecture, systems design, and information technology, including the development of network goods (hardware and software) and services (design, installation and maintenance of networks).

The distribution of technology firms in the region in terms of number of employees per firm is shown in Figure 6.4.

The spatial distribution of these firms is shown in Figure 6.5 along with locations of major transport infrastructure. The clustering of firms along major transport routes as listed earlier is evident, particularly along the Dulles Toll Road, including Reston, the Capital Beltway, and interstate routes.

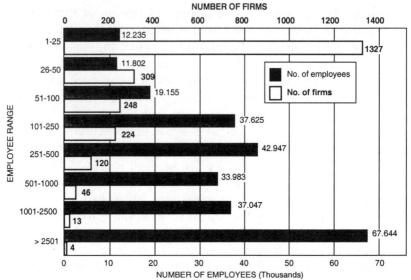

Figure 6.4   Greater Washington Region Technology Survey, number of employees and number by employee range

Source: Center for Regional Analysis, TIPP, George Mason University

The Donut Metaphor

The above analysis shows the relative decline of the economy and quality of life in the District. We may illustrate this with a donut metaphor which treats the District as the 'hole,' and Northern Virginia and Suburban Maryland part as the 'donut'. In adopting the donut model it is an easy next step for some to conclude that the hole is no longer needed, i.e., that it is possible for Northern Virginia and Suburban Maryland to chart development paths essentially independent of the District. In short, with this view, not only is the District considered to be irrelevant but by continuing to treat it as part of the region some believe that it will drain resources from the future development of the donut. The donut model is part of the mind set of more than a few leaders.

The donut model raises two kinds of questions. First, 'what explains the fact that we can even suggest a donut metaphor to describe conditions in the region?'. This question is considered in the next part of the paper. Second, we must ask 'is the donut a viable metaphor for policy formation for the future of Northern Virginia or is not a more collaborative approach more appropriate?'.

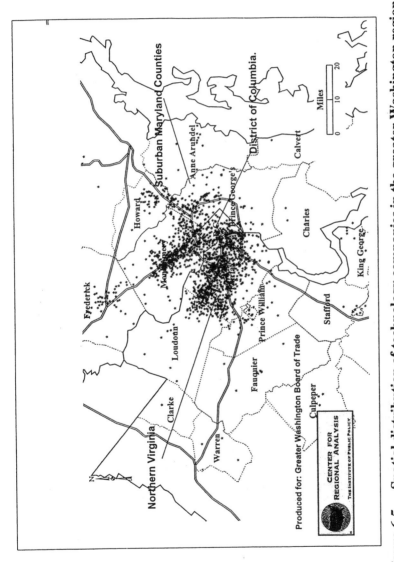

Figure 6.5   **Spatial distribution of technology companies in the greater Washington region**

Source: Center for Regional Analysis—Technology Survey

This donut model may have more relevance to some metropolitan regions in the US than in some other western nations where regions are more integrated in terms of public sector funding decisions, and inner cities are more socially and economically consistent with surrounding suburbs. In these other regions, the inner city can be attractive to producer services, personal services, company headquarters, tourism and residential development, and is attracting further development in this sense.

Why the Donut Model

There are several factors that have led to the differences between conditions in the District and other parts of the National Capital Region. One is a long-term national trend to locate new development on the edge of metropolitan regions.   The renewed vigour of this trend over the past 20 years is described in a recent book by Joel Garreau (1990) *Edge Cities*. The trend has its roots in transportation developments in the early part of the twentieth century, namely with the advent of reliable trucks and automobiles, and highways; and with policies that have kept the cost of operating vehicles relatively low.   There are also cultural and social values and policies that have contributed to concentrations of the less well off in the interior parts of metropolitan regions.   Thus, part of the reason for the difference in conditions between the District and other parts of the region is historical due to intra-urban migration and business location trends toward the periphery.

A second reason for the divergence between conditions in the District and the outer parts of the region has been the inability of the historical core to link development on the periphery to its institutions. There is a tendency on the part of core cities even in the best of circumstances (e.g. the unigov environment of Indianapolis) not to recognise growth on the periphery, especially when state and/or local boundaries intervene, until that growth has become quite sizeable relative to the core. This has certainly been the case in the National Capital Region. The boundaries between the District and the two states veiled the significance and the regional impact of growth in the outer areas from institutions such as the Greater Washington Board of Trade (which did not add the 'Greater' to the organisation name until the late 1980s), the Washington Post, etc.   In fact, it is only recently that these institutions have recognised the need to significantly reshape their agendae to more fully align themselves with the altered economic geography of the region.   The fact that the growth in outlying areas occurred very rapidly (growth in the outer parts of the region grew at or above four percent annually for the past

20 years) made it even more difficult for the traditional institutions to fully appreciate the changing geography of economic activity until quite recently.

In the 1960s and even in the early 1970s development activities in the outer parts of the region were not large and were confined to a few locations. Jurisdictions in these outer areas operated relatively independent from one another as they always had in their rural and agricultural dominated past. About the only thing they had in common was that they served as bedroom communities for those who worked in the District. The fact that economic growth in these areas unfolded very rapidly meant that it was very difficult for the government and non-government institutions (e.g. chambers of commerce) to adjust in time to provide more regionally integrated leadership. Consequently, not only is the District separated from the donut, but the parts of the donut are highly fragmented among themselves whether one views this from state or local government levels. In short, there is a high level of fragmentation throughout the National Capital Region and it exists at many levels. This is an issue in social infrastructure development.

Convergent or Divergent Development Paths?

We must now ask if there are any compatibilities and necessary complimentaries between the District economy and the Northern Virginia economy? If the answer is no then the development paths of the donut and empty core could diverge with minimal or no affect to either part. On the other hand, if the answer is yes then it is important for Northern Virginia and Suburban Maryland leaders to recognise that it is part of an inter-related whole and to develop strategies and tactics for charting a more collaborative future.

David Rusk in a recent book, *Cities Without Suburbs* (1992), examines this pattern throughout the US. He observes that when population loss in the traditional core city area falls by more than 20 percent and when income falls below 70 percent of the median income of the outlying areas conditions throughout the whole metropolitan region, which will have already deteriorated, become extremely resistant to change. By conditions he means a whole gamut of problems ranging from crime and education to tax base and growth to environmental conditions. In short, if the 'hole' is allowed to deteriorate below some threshold the whole region will experience negative spillovers that are very difficult to manage. The National capital Region is below the threshold with respect to population loss (about 26 percent) and moving toward the income threshold although it is still well above it at 88 percent. However, Rusk notes that even at the 88 percent income differential negative spillovers tend to occur and become increasingly difficult to manage. Rusk's analysis based on data from 100 US cities suggests that outer parts of metropolitan areas need to pay attention to what is happening in the interior and help address deteriorating conditions. Failure to do this may result in the export or diffusion of conditions in the interior to outlying areas and thus deterioration of conditions there.

This is probably the strongest reason for taking a more interjurisdictional approach. Some have estimated that about 60 percent of the Northern Virginia economy is dependent either directly (employment and/or contract) or indirectly (via multiplier effects of the directly generated demand and spending and re-spending) of the federal sector. The high level of dependency on federal policy making and budgeting have been important to Northern Virginia in the recent past (last 20-30 years) and will be important for Northern Virginia's present and future. The locus of policy making and budgeting is in the District, For this reason it is also important to improve and enhance the District as a place where federal policy is executed and developed. After all, the largest market for Northern Virginia goods and services (after internal Northern Virginia consumption) is the federal government.   Further, by improving the quality of the environment (physical and social), the District's attractiveness for other activities like, for example, touristic and related visitor services, will be enhanced. Yet the regional leadership and institutional capacity to move in this direction is not well developed.

Should the Donut Model Guide Regional Development Policy?

The donut model suggests that the outlying parts of the region and in particular Northern Virginia should adopt an independent development path.   However, the arguments presented above suggest that blindly following this path of independence would gradually lead to a wide variety of negative spillovers and to deterioration of the highly successful economy and high quality environment the region has enjoyed over the past 20 years. Thus, some degree of interdependence must continue to evolve.

Despite the rapid development path that has hindered the emergence of a more integrated and cohesive region some activities aimed at helping the National Capital Region build cohesive leadership have been undertaken. The Washington Council of Governments recently executed a consciousness raising project that included several hundred people participating in a variety of meetings throughout the region. The effort surfaced a wide variety of issues and identified a number of barriers to developing a more cohesive approach to regional problem solving and governance (not necessarily government). The Washington Board of Trade has formed a senior leadership development process now called the 'Potomac Conference.' The purpose of this group is to develop a more cohesive leadership for addressing region-wide economic, social and environmental problems. To the group's credit it has formed a region-wide programme to market the National Capital Region globally. However, its ability to focus resources on other region-wide issues has been limited. Beyond these two efforts activity to build a more cohesive ability to deal with problems throughout the National Capital Region has been insignificant.

While more efforts of the type undertaken by the Washington Council of Governments and the Greater Washington Board of Trade are needed progress will be slow because each of the three major subregions have very different institutional and statutory foundations and are highly fragmented themselves, particularly in the cases of Northern Virginia and Suburban Maryland. A more likely intermediate term possibility to build the capacity to more reasonably and effectively address region-wide issues would be the development of more cohesion within each of the three major sub-areas. Certainly it will be easier to pull the leadership of Northern Virginia together to address common issues, including relations with the District (and for that matter, Suburban Maryland or even Baltimore) and the State of Virginia, than it would be to achieve cohesion at the National Capital Region level. If this were to occur in each of the major parts of the National Capital Region we would then have three groups somewhat capable of expressing their region's priorities, goals and visions and acting on them. One might envision region-wide development strategy and problem solving being steered by the interaction of the three groups—much like the interaction that occurs among giant tectonic plates. As one moves the others gradually adjust (sometimes violently but usually through a series of smaller tremors) and then the whole system settles down until another plate makes an independent change in course. The tectonic plate metaphor appears to be a much more viable model for steering the future development of the National Capital Region than the donut model which captures a good bit of the current reality. The tectonic plate metaphor allows each major entity to enjoy a good bit of autonomy in its development path but at the same time ensures that the development path of the whole will be conditioned by checks and balances generated by the other two 'plates.'

Alternative Models

Besides the 'Donut' and 'Tectonic Plates' perspectives, some have advanced the concept of a metropolitan area made up of a non-hierarchical network of specialised nodes (Haynes and Stough, 1997). Finally, and not in jest, a new perspective of the leap frogged and abandoned edge cities with external satellite cities has been proposed by Stough in *Edge City News* (Jan./Feb. 1996). This model maximises the expanded transportation structure and is dependent on effective use of new telecommunication technology and efficient application of Intelligent Transportation Infrastructure.

The social implication of these systems in terms of spatial class and income reorganisation for the US society in general and urban social systems in particular is well beyond the discussion that most groups have been willing to confront.

Alternative forms for 21ˢᵗ century cities are also presented in Chapters 11, 13 and 14.

Conclusion

Any assessment of the developing structure of the National Capital Region must come to grips with the physical economic 'hard' infrastructure that both reflects the existing distribution of economic activity, but it must also recognise the social / institutional infrastructure that will guide the investments in new infrastructure which will provide the framework of the pattern of economic activity in the next round of private capital investments.

7 Strategic Planning and the Competitive City: Adelaide, South Australia

STEPHEN HAMNETT and MICHAEL LENNON

Introduction

This chapter considers the planning of Adelaide, a state capital city and its metropolitan region, in the context of urban Australia, diminished regional growth and the global economy. It contrasts in several ways with the development of the National Capital Region of the USA (chapter 6), Stockholm (chapters 8 and 9), Tokyo (chapter 10), Melbourne (chapter 11). It reflects upon recent processes of planning in Adelaide, capital of the State of South Australia. It describes, in particular, two significant planning exercises in which the authors were centrally involved, places these against a broader background of change in the context for urban governance and draws together some themes and preliminary conclusions for further work. It explores, through a case study of one city, the changing role of cities and nation states in a global and informational economy; tensions inherent in the redefinition of public and private roles in urban coalitions and partnerships; and conflicts between the inevitable short-term pressures for development and a longer-term strategic planning which seeks to maximise environmental amenity and urban quality of life.

From the broadest perspective, the experience of Adelaide over the past 30 or so years has been the experience of many cities in the developed world as they have sought to adapt to the changing international division of labour and new spatial patterns of consumption. This period has seen the decline of old manufacturing regions and the emergence of new or regenerated regions, often based on new high-technology industries; the emergence of new, more flexible organisational forms, accompanied by changes in the nature of skilled and unskilled employment; and dramatic developments in global communications which have facilitated, amongst other things, the increased mobility of financial capital and of firms.

In recent years in Australia, there has also been a move by federal and state governments to deregulate key sectors of the economy, reduce government responsibility for the provision of social infrastructure and simplify or remove regulations in the attempt to pursue new investments and jobs. Privatisation and deregulation have gone hand in hand with a new emphasis on competition and public entrepreneurship, well explained by Harvey (1989), Hall (1995), (Brotchie *et al.*, 1995), Borja and Castells (1997) and others and, in the Australian context, by Berry (1990) and Forster (1995). At the same time, the urban policy agenda has been subject to other influences, including the renewed salience of environmentalism, the definition of new (or rediscovered) approaches to strategic planning and pressure to acknowledge a wider diversity of influences and values in the policy process.

Against this background, this chapter focuses on two major planning exercises within Metropolitan Adelaide—the South Australian Planning Review which produced, amongst other things, proposals for a reformed planning system and a metropolitan planning strategy between 1990 and 1992; and the Adelaide 21 project, which commenced in the first half of 1996 and produced a development strategy for the City of Adelaide, the central city area of metropolitan Adelaide.   Both exercises resulted in spatial planning proposals, amongst other outputs, but both were conceived as much more than physical planning projects, seeking to encompass spatial planning and broader economic and social processes.   Both also focused on issues of urban governance, although in this respect, the five or so years which separated them saw some significant changes in the political and economic context, reflected in differences between them in the expectations which they held for the role of government in the urban development process and in the implementation of strategic plans.

The core of the chapter deals with these two planning exercises. It is preceded by a brief historical summary of planning in Australia and South Australia before the 1990s and followed by a discussion of the events of the past few years, their implications for the pursuit of integrated strategic planning in a somewhat remote Australian city and some speculative conclusions about relationships between governments, public planning and the market economy in Australia at the end of the twentieth century. This chapter seeks, in particular, to provide the basis for a discussion about the role of metropolitan planning. Is this simply to adjust constantly to changing forces and conditions, over which planners and governments can exercise little or no influence? Or is it to argue for certain outcomes rather than others, for certain styles of governance and for certain notions of social justice and inclusiveness? Is it, in short, to follow or to lead?

Metropolitan Planning and Urban Policy in Australia: A Brief Summary

Australian cities went through a dramatic period of population growth, economic development and outward expansion between the end of World War Two and the early 1970s. It had taken over a century for the population of Australia's five major cities to reach their 1947 total of four million. By 1971, that total had almost doubled. And 'as well as growing very rapidly, the cities changed radically in structure. The basic character of Australian urban development may have been set during earlier periods, but the sprawling, decentralised, automobile-dependent, ethnically diverse cities most of us live in today are mainly a legacy of the 1950s and 1960s' (Forster, 1995, p.15).

Metropolitan planning before the Second World War in Australia amounted to little more than the *ad hoc* efforts of housing, road building and other infrastructure agencies to provide services (Alexander, 1986; Logan, 1987). The first metropolitan plans were adopted by most states in the 1960s and were typically land use zoning plans writ large—trend-based plans which sought to facilitate suburbanisation, with negative controls to prohibit developments seen as undesirable. Protectionist manufacturing policies and immigration programmes were of more influence in shaping Australian cities.

State governments were primarily responsible for these early plans, since 'those who framed the Australian constitution did not anticipate that the Commonwealth would participate directly in the development of Australia's cities and regions' (Lloyd and Troy, 1981, p.1). However, the Whitlam Government, in office from December 1972 to November 1975, placed urban issues on the Commonwealth's agenda for a while and was significant in shifting thinking about urban planning to a broader plane. A major preoccupation of the Whitlam period was with issues of urban inequality and how to address them. Whitlam's Department of Urban and Regional Development (DURD) pursued an ambitious agenda which relied, to a considerable extent, on the use of federal grants and loans to encourage state governments to pursue new urban policies and programmes. Major initiatives included encouragement to establish land commissions to support public land development on the fringes of capital cities; to pursue decentralisation through the development of regional cities; and to address deprivation in outer suburbs through area improvement programmes and the decentralisation of employment and services.

Most of the urban policy reforms proposed under Whitlam led to only modest achievements, in the face of hostility from some States, poor management of inter-governmental relations and because, by their nature, programmes to bring about major changes in urban areas could only be expected to produce results in the longer-term (Orchard, 1995). However, DURD, in its very short-life, was effective in placing new notions of planning on the agenda where they have mostly stayed—in particular, the broadening of planning away from physical land-use considerations towards a greater concern for the social and economic processes which shape cities. But perceptions of DURD's shortcomings in style, ambition and performance, after the fall of the Whitlam Government, made it difficult for subsequent Labor governments to revive an urban policy focus at Federal level for some considerable time (Badcock, 1995; Alexander, 1994).

The late 1970s and early 1980s saw Federal policies in the hands first of the Fraser Conservative government and then of the Hawke Labor governments. Neither saw a focus on the cities as a high priority. The Fraser government saw planning as the preserve of State governments. When the Hawke government was elected in 1983, some expected a revival of urban policy at the Federal level, but Hawke's priorities were on macro-economic issues—dealing with high unemployment and the need to restructure key industries in particular. Despite the lack of an explicit urban policy, however, other Federal policies during the 1980s were to have profound effects on Australian cities—in particular, policies related to the deregulation of finance and banking, foreign investment in Australian property, tariff reduction and the restructuring of industry.

A dominant housing priority under Hawke was 'affordability' and reform in the planning field was seen initially in terms of simplifying planning procedures and economising on the provision of land and services in pursuit of 'more affordable' housing. Continuing concerns about rising housing costs and house prices led to more substantial measures around 1989 to improve land-supply in the major cities.

Brian Howe, Minister for Social Security and Minister assisting the Prime Minister for Social Justice in the Hawke government was a minority, but increasingly influential, voice arguing for the extension of the government's social justice agenda to cities and for the return to a broader approach in which policies to check the outward growth of cities and reduce the costs of new urban development could be better integrated with policies intended to address emerging environmental and transport concerns.   Out of this came the announcement of a 'Better Cities' programme in the 1991-92 Federal Budget which provided $816m to fund a series of area-based projects in inner and outer suburban areas throughout Australia, intended 'to improve the economic, social and environmental aspects of our cities' (Howe, 1992, p.20). Key urban issues which 'Better Cities' was supposed to address included adapting the housing stock to the presumed needs of an aging and a more diverse set of households, while limiting fringe growth and pursuing the already well-established approach of urban consolidation for a mixture of economic and environmental reasons. Better coordination and integration between all levels of government—a new cooperative federalism—was to underpin Better Cities:

> All spheres of government must work together in a cooperative way to effect the changes which are necessary to improve the outcomes in our cities. While each sphere has its own important and legitimate role to play in the development and management of our cities, each can only be successful in pursuing this if it is coordinated with the others (Howe, 1992, p.30).

In 1995 the Australian Urban and Regional Development Review, another Federal initiative carried out under Howe, by now Deputy Prime Minister to Keating, who had replaced Hawke as Prime Minister at the end of 1991, produced a review of major challenges facing Australian cities at the end of the 20th century. These included:

- the challenge of providing infrastructure, services and a high quality environment in areas of rapid growth while also addressing the future of areas in decline;
- the dramatic changes in metropolitan labour markets which have accompanied economic restructuring;
- the historic decline in levels of investment in our urban infrastructure and the potential consequences for business costs, especially in our internationally traded sector;
- the emergence of significant pockets of long-term unemployment in key suburbs of our major cities and the growth in these areas of communities which can only be described as significantly socially disadvantaged;
- the challenge of addressing our declining urban air and water quality, and our continued treatment of storm water, sewage and garbage as wastes rather than as resources; and

- the challenge of properly addressing in governance the conflict between short-term and longer-term objectives (AURDR, p.2).

    A Better Cities II Program was announced in 1995, allocating a further $236m, this time with a priority on strategic planning, with funds primarily provided initially for detailed planning strategies and feasibility analyses for infrastructure investments required in selected areas of the nation's major cities. Three sorts of 'selected areas' were identified: major 'International Economic Gateways'; areas facing substantial pressure from increasing population; and areas of high social and economic disadvantage

    The funds available under Better Cities I and II were modest. Better Cities I was primarily about 'demonstration projects'. Better Cities II emphasised, as did other government policy initiatives of the period, the increasingly important role of private sector infrastructure provision, with the role of government being to provide coordination and a framework for investment. Hence, the rationale for a focus on planning strategies in Better Cities II:

> Good project appraisal is essential, but alone is not enough. Infrastructure investment must take place within well-defined strategic frameworks. What is needed is a professional approach to infrastructure strategic planning and a commitment to such planning by governments. This planning must not be only physical or engineering planning, but also better pricing and access planning on an integrated basis (EPAC, 1995, p.184).

    The pattern of urban development in Australia in the 1990s is rather different from that of the 1970s and significant changes have included a redistribution of growth, away from the major cities of Sydney and Melbourne, which grew by about 10 percent between 1981 and 1991. Brisbane and Perth, over the same period, grew by 30 percent and 27 percent respectively. The inclusion in Better Cities II of a focus on international gateways, areas of substantial population growth and areas of high social and economic disadvantage reflected the different concerns of different cities, but also masked a tension between a policy emphasis on efficiency or on redistribution (Orchard, 1995). For example, while an efficiency view might see larger shares of infrastructure investment going to Sydney as Australia's principal city and an important centre for the emergence of the new information economy, equity concerns would argue for greater priority being given to the 'rust-belt States'—Victoria, South Australia—hard-hit by industrial restructuring.

The MFP project (see below and also Hamnett, 1995)—initially a joint Australian-Japanese proposal to build a major new city in Australia was located in Adelaide in 1991 after a competition between States which exemplified some of the tensions between competing localities and between various Commonwealth policy priorities. As Stimson commented in 1993

> ...government policies and decisions on where public expenditures occur spatially will continue to have substantial impacts on the locations where some significant new and emerging activities might locate. The decision to locate the Multi-Function Polis in Adelaide, a city that is poorly linked globally and with a struggling regional economy and low levels of population growth, is a case in point, even though initially a site between Brisbane and the Gold Coast had been selected in a region that appears to be more oriented to the future than trapped in the past (Stimson, 1993, p.87).

Adelaide proponents of MFP argued that locational choice for service and informational activities is much more flexible now and that international experience is increasingly that such activity can favour smaller places like Adelaide which lack the congestion and pollution of larger cities.

The Keating Labor government was replaced by a Liberal-National coalition led by John Howard in 1996 and national attention to the cities ceased once again. The Howard Government had no explicit urban or regional development policies on taking office, apart from a lukewarm commitment to urban design, since abandoned, and took the traditional conservative view that urban policies are a state concern and that strategic urban planning has no real place in a programme which emphasises continuing deregulation and small government.

South Australia

Since its establishment in 1836 as 'a community systematically settled by balancing land, capital and labour' following the ideals of Edward Gibbon Wakefield, South Australia has had a distinctive history. According to Hutchings, the early settlers were a curious mixture of radicalism and conservatism—

> On the one hand was their strong advocacy of religious freedom and their willingness to experiment, not only with the techniques of public administration, but also with the very philosophies of governance itself,

even to the point of republicanism; on the other was their strong sense of the central role of property... (Hutchings, 1986, pp.1-2).

The physical form of the city was planned from the outset along the lines of William Light's Plan, well-known internationally, not least because of its inclusion in Ebenezer Howard's celebrated work on Garden Cities, and substantial government intervention in other aspects of the economic and social life of the State has also been a constant feature of South Australia's development.

> In the twentieth century the idea of 'government-led' industrialisation came to be widely accepted. The State government became an active investor in physical infrastructures for the State's economic development, as well as establishing a network of public enterprises, regulating industrial relations and encouraging industry by manipulating taxes and other charges to attract manufacturing activities. Much attention was paid at the same time to securing community consensus for the industrialisation (Sheridan, 1986, p.215).

In the mid-1930s the South Australian government began explicitly to control housing rents on the grounds that 'stable rents could indirectly contribute to a lowering of the production costs of manufacturers in South Australia' (Badcock, 1986), thereby providing an incentive to firms to locate or remain in South Australia, as well as dampening cyclical swings in the local building industry. Thereafter, the South Australian Housing Trust grew to play a major role in the provision of the State's housing stock, and in the 1950s and 1960s, functioned as a post-war development corporation with a major influence on the form of the expanding metropolitan area.

It was in the 1960s that Adelaide acquired its first Metropolitan Development Plan (MDP). The planning system in the 1960s was primarily concerned with land use regulation and property rights, but the Dunstan Labor government pursued a new range of initiatives in the 1970s which went beyond land use planning, especially after the election of the Whitlam Government at Federal level. South Australia enjoyed substantial Federal support at this time as the only mainland state with a Labor government and took full advantage, in particular, of the opportunity to establish a Land Commission. In the three years 1973-74 to 1975-76 South Australia took 43 percent of the Commonwealth funds under this programme (Badcock 1986, p.176).

The City of Adelaide, under the provisions of the MDP, was simply the 'Central Business Zone' in which development decisions were largely the responsibility of the Adelaide City Council. However, the decline in residential population in the City, concerns about the loss of older buildings and proposed road improvements led the City Council in 1972 to prepare an advisory plan which was to become the first modern City of Adelaide Plan. That Plan was adopted in 1976 and enabling legislation was passed to give the Council powers to implement it.

In the latter part of the decade, the State Government established a Department of Housing and Urban Development (later Housing and Urban and Regional Affairs). Clearly influenced by the rationale for the Federal DURD, by then defunct, HURA was conceived as a small policy unit within the Premier's Department that could coordinate housing policy and planning and monitor and review the State's urban development programmes in such a way as to balance efficiency with equity. Probably the major achievement at this time was the establishment of a 'Staging Study' as an integral part of the urban development planning process to provide a framework for staging urban development and the coordination of land development operations. The staging study concentrated on the spatial pattern and timing of development, and on the implications of this for the public sector in terms of infrastructure spending. Later renamed as the Metropolitan Development Program, it became the basis for a highly-regarded and effective approach to monitoring metropolitan growth and coordinating the provision of infrastructure.

At the end of the 1970s, the State Labor government lost office for a short time and was replaced by the Tonkin Liberal government. Tonkin moved to reduce the role of the government in land and housing policy, abolishing the SA Land Commission and replacing it with an emasculated Urban Land Trust, on the basis that land development was largely a task for the private sector to lead. HURA was disbanded, housing policy contracted to public housing concerns and urban development to narrowly-conceived land use planning functions.

The broader context of the late 1970s and early 1980s was one of increasing concern at all levels of government with the impact of structural change and unemployment. Constraints on public resources meant that a new role for bodies like the Housing Trust was inevitable and a greater willingness to embrace public-private joint ventures became manifest. Such joint ventures were not new, but they became the preferred vehicle in the1980s for government involvement in major housing and redevelopment projects, initially on terms which in retrospect seem extraordinarily favourable to the private sector partners. Badcock (1986) commented that '...in tight times there is a readiness to secure the commitment of development finance within the urban economy at almost any cost' and more recent events support this view.

A new Planning Act was introduced in1982 by the recently elected Bannon Labor government. Essentially about development control, it also introduced a system of environmental impact statements for major projects and gave more responsibility for planning and development control to local authorities. The metropolitan development programme continued to evolve as a valuable tool in managing urban expansion, linking population growth and housing demand; land development; physical and social planning; and the capital works programmes of State agencies. But it was not a long-term plan in its own right and the lack of any long-term strategic framework for the metropolitan area's future growth became a matter of growing concern as significant development decisions were taken in an apparently *ad hoc* manner. Forster and McCaskill describe the early 1980s as a time of 'Planning by management', characterised by

> ...incremental growth, urban consolidation, 'realistic' objectives and by the idea that planners should cease to get in the way of adjustment and profitability'..... 'There is a danger that recognition of the power of general economic trends on one hand and of well-organised pressure groups on the other, may become an excuse to opt out, and it is vital that this should not be allowed to happen.....Adelaide has a strong tradition of far-sighted public intervention in the process of urban development. After something of a battering in the late 1970s we need to regain confidence in the role—albeit much changed—of metropolitan planning and we need the will to support its research capacity. Otherwise there is a danger that metropolitan planning may simply become infrastructure provision responding to the imperatives of individual bureaucracies and the windshifts of political expediency, with local councils tending their own patches, legitimately but sometimes with wider inequitable or inefficient consequences (Forster and McCaskill, 1986, p.107).

Some partial attempts to revive long-term planning were made in the mid-1980s, resulting eventually in a long-term strategy for Metro Adelaide which included a policy of urban consolidation to promote more compact development and provision for limited expansion of the metropolitan area to the north and south. But the 'long-term' emphasis was still on land for residential development, with expansion 'managed' through the Metropolitan Development Program. The challenge at the end of the 1980s was to create a long-term vision for the metropolitan area's development which went beyond the identification of new housing areas.

Within the central area a 'development debate' arose in relation to a number of projects and urban development issues (Orchard, 1992) and by 1988 this had broadened into a general debate about the planning system and about the government's commitment to the orderly development of the city. In most Australian cities in the 1980s, special legislation was used to by-pass approved plans, often in order to 'fast-track' projects supported by foreign investment. In Adelaide such legislation was used to facilitate the ASER project, a casino, new hotel and office complex on North Terrace, in which the giant Japanese construction company Kumagai Gumi was a major partner. The City Council at this time was generally perceived to be developer-dominated and tension between pro-development and resident groups continued through the major review of the City of Adelaide Plan in 1986-87.

Several significant development proposals failed to gain approval in the latter years of the decade, in some cases after protracted assessment procedures, fuelling a view, encouraged by the local press, that major development projects were almost impossible to achieve in South Australia in the face of organised opposition from resident and conservation groups and because of delays inherent in what was increasingly characterised as a cumbersome planning assessment system. Orchard (1992, p.153) notes that

> The scene had been set for the Bannon Government to respond to the 'development debate' and..... to develop a strategy for the future development of metropolitan Adelaide. A Planning Review was established in March 1990 with a broad mandate to look at policy objectives for the development of metropolitan Adelaide for the next 25 to 30 years, strategies to implement those objectives, the need for statutory change and the need for improvements in the procedures and structures of the development control system.

The debate about development in the city generally had its public focus on the planning system at this time, with arguments about bureaucratic and planning delays at the forefront. But the broader context was also one in which the State Government was actively promoting property development in the city centre and elsewhere with the State Bank and its subsidiaries as major players.

The deregulation of banking in Australia in the mid-1980s had provided the basis for substantial expansion of the banking sector.

As a group the large State Banks grew more rapidly than the major banks (the Big Four—Westpac, NAB, ANZ and the Commonwealth). However the State Bank of South Australia grew at more than twice the rate of the State Bank of NSW and nearly 80 percent faster than the State Bank of Victoria (Scott, 1992, p.88).

The SBSA was told to act commercially and to foster the economic development of SA. SBSA decided that it was going to play with the big banks—and its experience proved again the truth of the maxim that it is far easier to lend than it is to be repaid. To cap it off, the big banks soon decided that they had to play overseas...For the relatively inexperienced newcomer, the field thus became even more dangerous (Scott, 1992, p. 90).

At the outset of the Planning Review in 1990, however, the potential for disaster to overtake the State's financial institutions was not yet obvious.

The Planning Review

The South Australian Planning Review was carried out between 1990 and 1992. Its major products were a metropolitan planning strategy, a new Development Act, a new Court and Appeals System, and proposals for a 'new style of planning'. Its draft metropolitan strategy drew upon extensive public consultation to distil and express a set of broad values and choices, followed by strategies about 'living', economic activity, the use and conservation of natural resources, access, heritage and design. It recognised the need to transform the city's economic base and to attract certain emerging IT and data processing industries. It proposed measures to slow the outward growth of the metropolitan area and to shift the balance of future urban development to the northern suburbs, away from the vulnerable vineyards of the Willunga Basin to the south (Figure 7.1). It sought to promote a more diverse housing stock and to redevelop old public housing areas with a mix of public and private dwellings; and it argued for the promotion of a multi-centred city, with regional centres taking a greater share of employment and public services and developing as 'real town centres' for their surrounding suburbs. The draft Metropolitan Strategy produced by the Review was cautious about the scope for limiting car use, but espoused a series of travel demand management strategies intended to make better use of the existing road network and firmly ruled out any future expressway development.

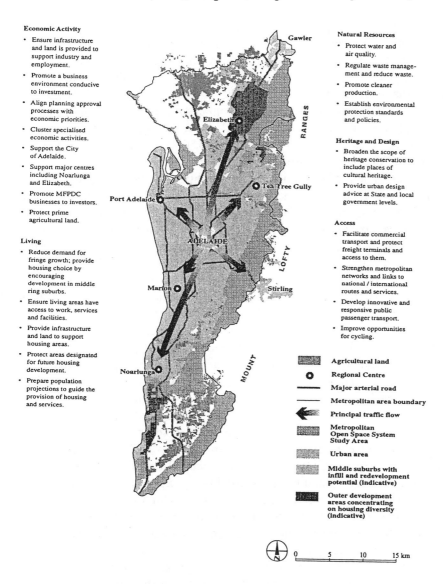

Economic Activity

- Ensure infrastructure and land is provided to support industry and employment.
- Promote a business environment conducive to investment.
- Align planning approval processes with economic priorities.
- Cluster specialised economic activities.
- Support the City of Adelaide.
- Support major centres including Noarlunga and Elizabeth.
- Promote MFPDC businesses to investors.
- Protect prime agricultural land.

Living

- Reduce demand for fringe growth; provide housing choice by encouraging development in middle ring suburbs.
- Ensure living areas have access to work, services and facilities.
- Provide infrastructure and land to support housing areas.
- Protect areas designated for future housing development.
- Prepare population projections to guide the provision of housing and services.

Natural Resources

- Protect water and air quality.
- Regulate waste management and reduce waste.
- Promote cleaner production.
- Establish environmental protection standards and policies.

Heritage and Design

- Broaden the scope of heritage conservation to include places of cultural heritage.
- Provide urban design advice at State and local government levels.

Access

- Facilitate commercial transport and protect freight terminals and access to them.
- Strengthen metropolitan networks and links to national / international routes and services.
- Develop innovative and responsive public passenger transport.
- Improve opportunities for cycling.

Gawler
Elizabeth
RANGES
Tea Tree Gully
Port Adelaide
ADELAIDE
LOFTY
Marion
Stirling
Noarlunga
MOUNT

Agricultural land
Regional Centre
Major arterial road
Metropolitan area boundary
Principal traffic flow
Metropolitan Open Space System Study Area
Urban area
Middle suburbs with infill and redevelopment potential (indicative)
Outer development areas concentrating on housing diversity (indicative)

0   5   10   15 km

Figure 7.1   Metropolitan planning strategy

The Planning Review also made some explicit statements about what it regarded as an appropriate style of planning. It proposed a new system in which strategic planning had a central role. Other cornerstones of this system were new legislative controls and procedures for regulating private and public development, and a new set of arrangements within government to ensure that the actions and budgets of individual government agencies were directed towards the agreed purposes of metropolitan development. This was intended to go beyond the coordination of land release and infrastructure planning of the Metropolitan Development Program and to encompass a 'whole of government' approach which would integrate economic, social and environmental priorities by placing the Planning Strategy at the heart of government decision making.

The system of planning for Metropolitan Adelaide, introduced in the 1960s, was still mainly concerned with providing land for different uses and with setting up a system of development control to guide private and public development and investment. The Planning Review sought to go beyond this and to respond to the demands increasingly voiced in the 1980s for a broad statement of long-term goals for metropolitan development to provide a context for the assessment of development proposals and for the more detailed plans of local councils. The Planning Strategy was intended to provide such a context, and also to establish links between spatial planning and economic and social policy.   Once adopted, it was to be substantially revised and updated at regular intervals, as new information came to hand from demographic forecasts, land supply monitoring, environmental audits, studies of changing transport demand and the like. The responsibility for maintaining the Strategy was to lie with an agency close to the centre of government—the Premier's Department—and this responsibility was to include continuing and extending the arrangements for public involvement developed during the Review. Of greater importance than the strategy itself was to be the recognition of the importance of adopting strategic planning as a continuing participatory process. Also important was to be the progressive extension of the strategic planning approach beyond the metropolitan area to the rest of the state; and the adoption at local government level of local strategic plans to give effect to the metropolitan strategy.

One of the major purposes of the legislative changes which were proposed by the Planning Review was to create a framework in which the many approvals needed for private development of land could be brought together. An important objective of these changes was to remove duplicated or unnecessary controls, and to establish clear and consistent procedures for seeking approval for development with the emphasis on convenience to the users of the system. Significant changes were also proposed to the way in which disputes over planning matters were to be resolved, to the processes through which local development plans were amended and to a range of other matters, all intended to contribute to the achievement of a simpler and clearer system of guiding and regulating development in order to provide more certainty to developers and the community.

The Planning Review also addressed the need to resolve some of the role ambiguities of state government departments, charged with both promoting and regulating development. The Review encouraged some reorganisation of agencies to bring together most of the government's urban development functions and responsibility for the following activities in a single portfolio:

* the development and management of the public housing stock (the Housing Trust);
* the assembly and release of land for new urban development (Urban Land Trust);
* new community planning;
* the management of major public development projects;
* government office and accommodation leasing and purchase; and
* the construction and maintenance of government buildings.

The importance of coordinating these and other government activities in pursuit of the aims of the Planning Strategy was stressed.

> For example, within the next decade it is proposed to release a substantial amount of currently under-used government land to accommodate new development, particularly within the existing metropolitan area. It is most important that such land is released at the right time and at the right price to encourage its appropriate development. That a particular piece of land is owned by one government department or another ought not to make too much difference and conflicts within the bureaucracy cannot be tolerated. At the end of the day, it is public land (Hamnett and Parham 1992, p.84).

Government's own locational decisions were also seen as important. Government in its various forms was an important employer in South Australia. Proposals in the Strategy to increase the amount of employment in regional centres were dependent to a significant extent on the willingness of government to locate more of its activities in metropolitan regional centres. Incremental locational decisions were intended to be taken within a long-term strategic framework and to lead, eventually, to the achievement of a polycentric or 'multi-centred' city.

The Planning Review's report supported the continuation of the public-private joint venturing approach to urban development which, especially since the 1980s, had provided the basis for most large new residential developments, on fringe land acquired and assembled by the Urban Land Trust or on surplus government land within the metropolitan area. The future application of such an approach to the redevelopment of old public housing areas was also advocated. The Review favoured a pragmatic approach to the question of how infrastructure should be funded, allowing scope for negotiation at the time of establishing joint ventures. Overall, however, it aligned itself, for the most part, with arguments in favour of retaining a strong public presence in the funding and provision of urban infrastructure on equity grounds:

> The State Government has long used its role as the provider of infrastructure services, such as roads, water and sewerage mains and energy to influence Adelaide's development. It has funded these services from general revenue or through low interest loans. In other places, there is now a growing tendency to charge the costs of providing new urban infrastructure to land developers who, in turn, pass these charges on to the purchasers of new housing. The problems with this sort of approach are largely to do with equity—why should new home buyers pay for things that residents of existing suburbs have not had to pay for? And how can imposing such costs on new homebuyers who, typically, are not the most affluent members of the community, be reconciled with other aspirations like fairness and housing affordability? (Hamnett and Parham, 1992, p.85).

Reflections on the Planning Review

The Planning Review in retrospect was a somewhat heroic and, perhaps, over-ambitious attempt to bring together major elements of emerging planning orthodoxy at the beginning of the 1990s. It sought to provide a 'community-shared' vision of the future metropolitan area as a context for short and medium-term development programming, and to provide the long-term development framework which had been argued to be lacking in the 1980s. It sought to place equity considerations firmly back on the metropolitan planning agenda and to resolve tensions between economic investment and environmental planning within a single 'integrated strategy', although it was hampered in this regard by the lack of an explicit State economic development policy. The 1980s in Adelaide, in retrospect, had been a decade of economic development led by 'major projects'—the

Adelaide Grand Prix, the Australian submarine contract and, after 1991, the Multi-Function Polis—and the institutional arrangements were lacking for the development of a credible economic strategy which could complement the spatial strategy of the Planning Review.

The Planning Review's central notion of strategic planning provided a clear parallel to (or, some would say, precursor to) the rediscovery of strategic planning at federal level, and elsewhere. Strategic planning was meant to symbolise a shift from reactive, short-range thinking, dominated by sectoral issues, to a proactive, long-range and citizen-oriented style of planning, tackling multiple issues and their inter-relationships and seeking to build consensus around community priorities and aspirations. A long-term perspective was justified, in particular, because of the acknowledged significance of environmental issues and of the long time scale involved in bringing about changes to the physical structure of the city, presumed by the Review to be necessary to achieve a more sustainable urban form.

The Review's proposals to streamline the development assessment processes through new legislation could be seen as the latest in a series of regularly recurring attempts to simplify the regulation of development and provide developers with greater certainty on the (often disputed) premise that planning delay is a major impediment to investment. There was also a specific reform proposed by the Review to abolish the separate planning legislation which had applied to the central city area since the mid-1970s and integrate the central city more closely with the plans and planning arrangements for the rest of the metropolitan area.

Overall, the Planning Review consciously aligned itself with its interpretation of South Australia's tradition of a sound public sector framework for private sector investment, allied to an inclusive and socially just focus appropriate to the 1990s. The roles of the Urban Land Trust and of the Housing Trust were strongly reaffirmed.

But economic disaster overtook South Australia as the Review's preliminary conclusions were being drafted. The State Bank of South Australia had grown dramatically between 1985 and 1990, increasing its total assets by an average annual rate of 43.9 percent (Scott, 1992). In the year to 30 June 1991, however, huge losses were recorded and write-backs of $2.2 billion were undertaken, covered by a cash injection by the government. Federal government assistance was also urgently required. According to Scott (1992, p.92)

> The saga of the State Bank of SA has many lessons for government, business and taxpayers. Its extraordinary growth, the very specialised nature of its lending, and a perception that it was to an important degree saddled

with responsibility for SA's economic development, contributed to the ultimate disaster. The Bank tried to become a large full-service bank at a time when bank lending (and hence bank risk) was more competitive than it had been this century. The speed with which it attempted this transition was unwise and this seems to have been compounded by management structures and systems that delayed an awareness of its grave position.

The State Bank collapse undermined confidence in government and the public sector generally. Radbone (1992, p.110) noted how, in the 1980s

...public sector entrepreneurialism became fashionable. Pursuing profits became more important than serving the community. Now, with the profit-seeking approach seen to have gone disastrously wrong, there is the danger that any role for the public sector will be seen to be illegitimate.

The major preoccupation of South Australian governments since then has been to deal with the consequences of substantial debt. A new Liberal Government took office at the end of 1993 and adopted, with minor rewording, the Planning Review's Metropolitan Planning Strategy, as well as most of its legislative reform proposals, but with little conviction (and with the inclusion of a new southern expressway which went contrary to the general thrust of the metropolitan strategy). The period since then has also seen accelerated attempts to privatise and outsource state government infrastructure and service functions, notably in water supply and public transport, reducing, some would argue, the government's capacity for implementing metropolitan planning proposals in an integrated way.

The Multi-Function Polis

No mention of Adelaide's planning in the 1990s can ignore the remarkable history of the Multi-Function Polis project which dates back to early 1987 and a somewhat imprecise proposal to the Australian Government from Japan's Ministry of International Trade and Industry to collaborate in the construction, somewhere in Australia, of a new city of about 100,000 people. MFP was to be a prototype for cities of the twenty-first century, combining new industries based on computer and information technology, biotechnology and health sciences with activities based on leisure, resorts, conventions and tourism.

After the obligatory round of interstate rivalry and acrimonious competition, a decision was taken to build MFP on a site near the

Queensland Gold Coast, but the Queensland government was unable or unwilling to comply with the Commonwealth's conditions about land assembly and the project was awarded to Adelaide instead, in mid-1990. In the well-crafted South Australian government submission, the whole of Adelaide was nominated as the MFP, but a specific site within the existing urban area, a crescent of degraded and contaminated land centred on Gillman and Dry Creek, 12 kilometres north of the city centre, was designated as the core site for new urban development. Unlike the Queensland site, the chosen Adelaide site had no obvious potential for resort or tourist development. But it was in public ownership and adjacent to a city with good universities and with some significant high technology research and development enterprises already established. It was not unreasonable to suggest, as the submission did, that the opportunity existed to build upon existing strengths in information technology, health and medical science and that MFP could be a vehicle for further encouraging developments in these areas.

Integration with the existing metropolitan area and the advantages which this could offer through connections with existing urban infrastructure were central elements of the submission. In the words of the South Australian submission, the MFP was to be 'a large, new and surprising urban development that will become an integral part of the existing metropolis' (South Australian Government, 1990, p.31).

While seriously contaminated in parts, the Gillman site also included substantial and significant stands of mangroves and important fish breeding grounds. The problems of reclaiming and rehabilitating the degraded parts of the site and preserving its remaining mangroves and the adjacent marine environment were fundamental to the rationale for proposing such a difficult 'brownfield' site. It was seen as an opportunity to demonstrate that such environmental challenges could be overcome, and, in the process, to develop new environmental management techniques and expertise which could find commercial application elsewhere.

Castells and Hall commented on MFP's progress at that point as an example of a large and ambitious project:

> ...some would say so large as to be almost foolhardy. That, we would argue, misses the central point. In order to build any prospect of establishing a genuine innovative milieu, competing with established centres of technological innovation, such projects almost have to be launched on a huge scale. And, at any rate in the early days, they will inevitably have a speculative element. That is why they need to involve the full faith and support not only of regional or state governments, but also of national

governments ....(They) need time to fulfil their potential—and even to demonstrate that the potential is indeed there. So a verdict on them will be due perhaps in the year 2010 at the earliest. They could demonstrate potential results before then, in the form of physical developments on the ground; but the crucial judgement, as to whether they constitute milieux of innovation, may have to wait that long. And since most political and economic actors are not interested in such long-term perspectives, it is highly unlikely that the blueprints underlying these projects will ever be fulfilled. Thus, their lessons could lie more in their failure than in their success. Technodreams can become technocities only if governments and corporations have a vision of the future, want to follow it and marshal enough political support to endure the speculative moves and political manoeuvres that will undoubtedly try to derail the project for the immediate benefit of short-sighted personal interests. As with all major projects of innovation, the construction of technocities is necessarily embedded in the political battles of the city, of the region, and of the world (1994, p.220).

But MFP, to be successful, needed to be an effective exercise in planning under uncertainty, and to match its proposed innovations in urban development with innovations in institutional reform which could strengthen the capacity for government to act strategically. Instead, the focus of successive governments appeared to be on MFP as a *project* —the next 'Grand Prix'—underpinned by the belief that change to decision-making processes could be avoided if another big project could be secured.

Work on proposals for the Gillman site continued until the beginning of 1994, helped considerably by substantial Commonwealth 'Better Cities' funding (in effect a diversion rather than an addition of national funds to the State), much of which went to pay for large and impressive artificial wetland areas. But the Brown government, after its election in 1993, moved quickly to play down the importance of Gillman and, in the light of growing concerns about the viability of the project, shifted the planned first phase development to a drier site, adjacent to South Australia's Technology Park and the University of South Australia's Levels campus. A consortium led by the Delfin Group, partners with the State government in three major housing joint ventures in the 1970s and 1980s, has now been given responsibility for developing this site (renamed 'Mawson Lakes' after a celebrated Antarctic explorer). The Federal Government withdrew from the project in 1996, but the MFP Development Corporation was given a temporary vote of confidence by the State Government at the end of 1996 and expanded to incorporate a number of other State Government functions, including those of the Urban Projects Authority (which had earlier subsumed the Urban Lands Trust). In May 1997, MFPDC assumed responsibility for a series of development projects in the city centre and elsewhere in the metropolitan area, with 'Mawson Lakes' as only one— albeit a significant— project amongst many. Most recently, current Premier John Olsen has announced that the name MFP is to be dropped and the organisation is to be absorbed into the state bureaucracy, with a project-delivery brief focused strongly on the renewal of established areas, including the city centre, in addition to Mawson Lakes. After a long and expensive decade of activity without achievement, the MFP appears to have been laid to rest.

Adelaide 21

As noted earlier, the Adelaide City Centre was brought within the State's Planning arrangements on the recommendation of the Planning Review and the City of Adelaide's separate planning legislation, dating from the 1970s, was abolished, as part of the move towards a simplified system. The Planning Strategy prepared by the Planning Review envisaged a multi-centred city, with the CBD retaining its dominant position in the hierarchy and 'recognised as the main focus of the State's government, commerce, cultural life, learning, retailing, entertainment, recreation and tourism. It should continue to fulfil these roles for the South Australian community and be a strong expression of its community life'. A further, more detailed strategy for the City Centre was foreshadowed in the Metropolitan Planning Strategy and a 'City-State' forum was set up in late 1992 to begin the work of bringing city centre policies together with those for the broader metropolitan area.

By 1994, however, it had become apparent that a number of major and unanticipated forces were undermining the viability of the centre (mirroring trends elsewhere): declining employment as a consequence of the increased use of information technology, corporate restructuring and public sector 'downsizing'; declining retail expenditure and the demise of department stores; a glut of office space from the late 1980s boom and streets of protected but vacant heritage-listed buildings; and static property values

A paralysis seemed to develop in the management of the City Centre in the light of diminishing confidence in the parochial city council and the absence of organisational mechanisms to draw State-local government and private activity in any coherent direction:

> It seems that the planning approach is lurching from a systematic series of statements about the form, character and design of the city which had little to drive them once economic growth and state and municipal prosperity fell away, to a series of urgent statements about leading projects of various kinds (Hayes and Bunker, 1995, p.168).

The city centre's problems were not helped by apparently uncoordinated state government attempts to lure significant new businesses into suburban locations—some to the MFP core site and others to sites which appeared to have no relation to any extant plan or strategy. Locational considerations played little part in economic policy or attempts to attract new investment.

In the period leading up to the 1996 Federal election, two further strategic planning exercises were conceived in the spirit of 'cooperative Federalism'. The first of these was a joint Federal-State Infrastructure Investment Strategy, launched by the Prime Minister in March 1995, with the object of establishing a 'long-term framework for interaction between Federal, State and the community...a marriage for the future'.   This resulted in the identification of a somewhat eclectic list of 'hard' and 'soft' infrastructure investment projects, loosely related to the metropolitan strategy and with an emphasis, in particular, on improvements to freight movement; a series of water management projects to support viticulture and horticulture and, at the same time, to strengthen Adelaide's growing capacity as an international centre for water management; the establishment of a multi-media centre; and a range of projects to support the State's educational institutions in strengthening their overseas markets.

The second was *Adelaide 21*, a project jointly instigated by the Federal, State and City governments. As explained earlier, in the mid-1970s the newly-adopted City of Adelaide Plan brought in a planning system and policies for the City Centre which established a relatively sophisticated planning framework for the time which served the City of Adelaide fairly well. By the mid-1990s, however, the City of Adelaide Plan was widely perceived as being primarily a statutory development plan for the City.

Adelaide 21 was about providing a new context for development decisions, appropriate to the conditions of the mid-1990s.   It sought to position the city centre on the basis of an enhanced understanding of factors affecting the City's activity base—globalisation, new information technologies and new relationships between the public and private sectors. While spatial in scope, it was much less concerned with physical elements than previous plans and strategies for the city. Governance, organisation, marketing and image were prominent in its proposals and culture, creativity and innovation were strong themes.

The Adelaide 21 study proposed a strategy which encouraged a concentration of activity in the city centre 'to promote synergies which help generate self-sustaining growth. Focus, critical mass and agglomeration are fundamental to success' (Hayes, 1997, p.37).

The strategy suggested that Adelaide's distinctive competitive strengths, focused in the City Centre, included a low cost business environment; a strong higher educational base; a focus for tourism and conventions; a concentration of cultural facilities and prominence in the Arts; and an outstanding quality of life reflected within the City Centre with 'previously separate considerations of housing, workspace, learning, leisure and social life converging to create a new kind of urban environment'. There was also a strong emphasis on cultural diversity:

> In planning for the future of the City Centre, diverse needs will be respected to ensure that it provides a welcoming and secure environment as the pre-eminent meeting place for all South Australians. This is in keeping with the social traditions of the State. Rapid technological and economic change, with its propensity to widen the divisions in society, will demand a strong commitment. However, Adelaide will thrive on the social and cultural diversity, respect for individual rights, and longer term social harmony that tolerance, respect and support engenders (Adelaide 21, 1996, p.9).

Area strategies were also included, reinforcing distinctive concentrations of activity in the north-east quarter, central market and the West End and seeking to enhance the qualities of the southern residential and mixed use precincts and the parklands, and a number of 'landmark projects' for early implementation were described.

Adelaide 21 limited its public participation efforts to about 300 'key stakeholders', a leadership group to provide support in key places to carry the strategy into action. A distinctive recommendation of the Adelaide 21 report was for the establishment of an 'Adelaide Partnership' as a separately constituted body with a small project management staff to promote and facilitate initiatives in accordance with the strategy, and to draw in the commitment and the involvement of the private sector.

The Adelaide 21 project, like similar projects in Melbourne and Perth, took the view that a local council could not realistically draw key Federal and State interests, together with other private and public interests, into a new vehicle for managing urban development. The 'Adelaide Partnership' was to be such a vehicle instead, grounded in the corporate business world, rather than in the public sphere. In this it sought to build on the Town Centre Management and Downtown Associations of the UK and

USA. It sought to respond to a climate in which public sector entrepreneurial activity had been widely discredited—fairly or unfairly— and to design an organisation which could meet the requirements of a prevailing ideology which favoured the private sector. It was also a response to the continuing decline of confidence in the City Council. The Adelaide Partnership was intended to 'position' the City better in the eyes of investment managers—nationally based, mostly in Sydney.

However, the Adelaide Partnership proposal became bogged down in just the sort of parochial local political tussles that it was intended to circumvent. Local council members saw it as a clear threat to their power. The State Government responded with a misconceived, premature and poorly-handled attempt to sack the City Council which was rejected by the Parliament. A new State Premier was installed largely as a result of these events and a review of city governance was instigated. At the time of writing, this review is still to be completed, but the alliance of the new Premier with a recently-elected populist Lord Mayor has given some renewed momentum to the Adelaide 21 process and work is proceeding to implement some of its proposals. The future arrangements for the central city's governance are to be resolved before the end of 1997.

Implications and Prospects

As mentioned at the outset, Adelaide's experience, in many ways, is not remarkable. Changes in production and consumption systems have wide social and spatial implications. Adelaide's recent attempts to restructure its policy processes at metropolitan and city level, and, for example, to secure and implement a project like the Multi-Function Polis, are explicable in terms of the interplay of the global processes which have taken us beyond the 'Keynesian city' and which have encouraged cities to seek wider access to global markets and to compete to offer attractive regulatory climates to investors.

Other significant elements of the recent context have been demographic change—lower fertility rates, an ageing population, increased mobility of the young and debate about the size of immigration programmes and the locational preferences of migrants; the emergence of a new urban hierarchy in Australia; and evidence of new patterns of inter- and intra-regional inequity. South Australia is amongst those states which are struggling with debt burdens left over from the financial crisis of the early 1990s, and, with its dependence on manufacturing and the car industry in particular, is especially vulnerable in the short-term to the dismantling of tariffs, as one part of the continuing move to smaller government and a greater role for market forces.

Against the background of these circumstances, and of the description of recent planning history in Adelaide which makes up this chapter, a number of areas for further discussion and study can be suggested. These are sketched below:

The Entrepreneurial Role of Local and Regional Governments

Writing in 1989, David Harvey noted the shift to entrepreneurialism in urban governance as local civic leaders joined with business and other groups in coalitions to mobilise investment in response to deindustrialisation. Harvey noted also the tendency for such investment to go into 'credit-financed shopping malls, sports stadia and other facets of high consumption, high risk projects that can easily fall on bad times' (Harvey, 1989, p.13).

Adelaide's experiments with new State financial institutions, and the State Bank in particular, can be easily understood as a common response by cities in similar circumstances, and illustrate the danger involved in the inappropriate transfer of risk from private to public hands, the use of public assets for private purposes and the threat to good governance inherent in the diversion of resources and attention from long-term investment purposes to immediate and transitory ones. Despite attempts to establish more 'strategic' planning frameworks in South Australia, the State government has become enmeshed in recent years in development projects in retailing, tourism and entertainment, speculative in nature and ultimately publicly-funded or guaranteed. Some of these projects led urban policy rather than the reverse. (The latest version of the metropolitan planning strategy, released for comment in April 1997, has been rewritten to make provision for the creation of a 'landmark icon' in the city's main shopping street.) Not all such development projects are successful by any means, but, even when they are, the critics of civic entrepreneurialism note 'the contrast between the surface vigour of many of the projects for regeneration of flagging urban economies and the underlying trends in the urban condition'...and the need to recognise 'that behind the mask of many successful projects there lie some serious social and economic problems'. 'Success' can also be ephemeral as:

> The huge investments embedded in the built environment to support hallmark events and fashionable lifestyles are quickly devalued as fashions

change and new events, spectacles, and cultural innovations spring up elsewhere. Furthermore, new inequalities and impoverishments create pockets of local opposition and resistance, the basis of anti-development alliances which often have ready access to the lowest levels of government (Berry, 1990, p.136).

But what alternative exists to building new kinds of public-private organisation which go beyond city marketing to 'a progressive urban corporatism, armed with a keen geopolitical sense of how to build alliances and linkage across space?' (Harvey, 1989, p.16; and see also Albrechts, 1991). The proponents of Adelaide 21 and its proposed 'partnership' would argue that it rests on a pluralist view of modern public life, in which conflicting interests can be partially reconciled and the public-private divide bridged by creating networks and alliances, rather than through formal structures; and that it aims to place risk and reward on a sounder footing, rather than requiring the public sector to bear unacceptable levels of responsibility for the actions of footloose investors. A less generous view might be to see it as simply a new vehicle for speculative development projects by local property developers and financiers.

A critical factor is the creation of a coherent policy framework. The responsibility of a city partnership or public-private coalition is to define and promote an agreed competitive position, concentrating on industry sectors with the greatest growth potential and channelling scarce resources into key initiatives. This is especially so when the attraction of private capital has become the dominant priority. And a key component of the policy framework must be a spatial development programme. Unfortunately, neither national nor state levels of government conceive public sector infrastructure programmes in this way at present.

Institutional Reform

In the mid-1980s Adelaide's political leaders were well aware of the forces which threatened the progress of the City and State. The new State Bank was clearly intended to provide a means of stimulating the State economy at a time when the State was losing some of its long-established locally-based investment houses. The State Bank was seen as a new vehicle through which private business behaviour and management could be harnessed through an entity created by, and ultimately accountable (insufficiently so in retrospect) to, the Parliament.

In the field of urban policy, the generally perceived success of major urban project delivery vehicles—joint ventures like West Lakes and Golden

Grove, together with the Urban Land Trust and the Housing Trust—had all become models for other States, emulated not only in Australia but also overseas. That the Multi-Function Polis should follow a new model of public-private joint activity was, in a sense, the continuation of a pattern.

The MFP Corporation, enshrined in its own legislation, was to use an urban development and land reclamation project as a means of leading Adelaide into the new era of traded services in education, environmental management and information technology. The new corporate structure was to provide a means of reconciling federal and state ambitions in a single vehicle, overcoming jurisdictional issues, whilst snaring international business and trade involvement. Parallel legislation was passed by federal and state parliaments to secure this. Through inertia, seemingly endless debate, poor leadership, changed economic conditions and a transfer of political control at national and state levels, the MFP has now become a component of the State bureaucracy. An expensive experiment which is effectively over, with little to show for a decade of effort.

MFP initially represented to some the continuation of an approach to the generation of new activity, driven not by demand but by the power of ideas. Some can see a link in this back to Adelaide's origins as a community of free settlers and as a place which has always 'lived on its wits'. Yet the recent history of attempts to create new institutional forms has shown little of South Australia's 'conscious purpose'. Three separate attempts to reform the State's bureaucracy have faltered as the dual priorities of cutting costs and economic restructuring have clashed. A state and city with historically strong public sector institutions has been left rudderless as the ideology of small government has assumed ascendancy with neither business nor political leadership to replace it. A recent state election (October 1997) saw an unparalleled drift of votes away from major parties and the election of a minority government. In terms of city policy and development, it seems clear that leadership at the civic level is a vital precondition for achieving investment. In this light, the continuing delay in resolving the future governance arrangements of the City of Adelaide may be symptomatic of a deeper malaise.

Self Determination and Globalism

Given the scale of the factors being dealt with, one can clearly question whether a relatively small and isolated economy and society like South Australia's can reasonably make the necessary adjustments to manage its future or whether some wider basis of intervention is required.

As noted earlier, the restructuring of the Australian economy is producing distinct spatial variations. The approach of successive recent national governments of differing political persuasions has primarily been to pursue growth and efficiency in aggregate terms leaving the states and the cities to manage regional variations in performance. This is markedly the case now as the Liberal-National government has dismantled the modest urban programmes of its predecessor, devolved responsibility and withdrawn funding.

At the same time the national government has continued to resist the notion that spatial analysis has much place in macro-economic considerations. However, recent debates over the impact of tariff policy on particular cities and regions, and on the effects of the decision by BHP to close its steel works in Newcastle (NSW) with the loss of 3000 jobs, have caused some rethinking of national industry policy which could broaden into a debate about a more active and interventionist policy and a return, perhaps to an explicit national development strategy. The recent Mortimer Report on industry policy in Australia has fuelled such a debate, but it is not clear where this will lead at this stage.

And beyond national considerations are questions of broader relationships within the Asian region. In Britain the rejuvenation of cities like Glasgow, Manchester and Dublin appears to have entailed some active intervention and alliance between these cities and a supra-national level of government. The relevance of this to Australian cities may not be immediately obvious, but the development of relationships within the Asia-Pacific region between Australian cities and states and overseas counterparts which largely by-pass the Federal level of government is already under way and is likely to gather speed as changes to the structure of states and regions within Australia occur.

The Northern Territory is widely anticipated to move from 'Territory' to 'State' status before long. North Queensland and Northern New South Wales are conceivable units for new States and the separatist movement in Western Australia has gained momentum in recent years. Paralleling the pressures for the break up of federations in the UK, Canada and the Eastern Bloc, future urban governance arrangements in Australia might well involve a realignment of political power upwards into supra-national political institutions and downwards into region-based States, operating more freely beyond current national boundaries.

The Planning Review of the early 1990s made little attempt to question the traditional levels of federal, state and local government responsibilities in Australia, although it took place at a time when the relationship between levels of government was supposedly changing from a hierarchical to a cooperative one. Adelaide 21 seems to rest more explicitly on the presumption of the declining role of the national government—the view that nation states are really too small to influence global flows of power and technology, yet increasingly remote from the diverse social and cultural interests of their cities and regions. According to Borja and Castells (1997) the changing relationship between local and national governments and private sector partners can be summarised thus:

> Producing and managing the habitat and the collective facilities that form the social base for economic productivity in the new informational economy is fundamentally the responsibility of local and regional governments. The link between private companies and local governments, in the framework of global relations regulated by negotiations between nation states, is the fundamental institutional and organizational foundation for wealth-creating processes (Borja and Castells, 1997, p.3).

The Relationship Between Economic Conditions, Political Change and the Nature of Planning

A final question which arises from this review of recent planning in Adelaide is that of the relevance of planning itself—of the usefulness of attempts at conscious management of urban change in the face of the structural changes and ideological forces which typify the mid-1990s. Is planning an anachronism, an instrument left over from another era? Alternatively, is it more helpful not to talk about planning in the abstract, but to recognise that different styles of planning will inevitably be closely related to different types of economic and political context? The following table attempts to provide a rough basis for discussion by attempting to trace the changing relationship in Australia over recent decades between economic conditions, politics and the style of planning which has been pursued.

What goes into the next box in this table? More 'urban boosterism? Or a reinvented strategic, long-range and citizen-oriented style of planning which, following the South Australian Planning Review, looks to tackle multiple issues and their inter-relationships. The question is not one which can be answered simply. Yet there is evidence to suggest that successful cities typically have strategic plans. The style of strategic planning for the future will need to seek consensus around community priorities and

Table 7.1   Planning, politics and the economy

	ECONOMY	POLITICS	PLANNING
1950s to 1960s	• Strong & Growing • Positive Future	• Stable • Secure • Traditional Liberal Conservatism	• Physical • End State
1970s	• Fluid • Inflationary	• Fluid • Uncertain • Radical Social Democracy	• Land Use • Government Led • Urban Management
Lat 1970s to mid-1980s	• Drifting • Weak	• Unstable • Minority Interests Emerge	• Regulatory • Project Driven • Fragmented Effort
Mid-1980s to early 190s	• Uncertain • Unparalleled Change • Protectionism Removed	• Highly Unstable • Pluralist • Reformist Social Democracy	• Integrated • Dynamic • Strategic
Mid-1990s	• Open • More Competitive • Highly Variable Performance	• Market Oriented • Smaller Government • New Conservatism	• Uncertain • Conceptually Divided • Requiring Re-definition
Late 1990s	?	?	?

aspirations, while weaving these into broad strategies for the development of cities and regions, with a particular concern for those otherwise likely to be left behind by globalisation. It will also need to demonstrate clear thinking about implementation and about mobilising effort and resources in pursuit of a preferred future. It will need to address competitiveness by intensifying the synergies in the city between, for example, economic, educational and cultural elements and capitalising on activities and public spaces which contribute to quality of life. And, in one way or another, it will need to be supported by vehicles for bringing together the concerted actions of public and private partners and for resolving tensions between, for example, short-term development pressures and longer-term objectives of sustainability; between promotion and marketing of short-term initiatives and projects and longer-term objectives related to redistribution and social cohesion; and between a deregulation which favours private initiatives and the need to protect the rules and institutions which safeguard collective interests.

Postscript

Some Scenarios for Adelaide

An interesting feature of the Adelaide 21 Project was the use of scenario planning in the process of assembling an urban strategy. These were not forecasts of what would happen and they were not mutually exclusive. Rather, they were written as plausible pictures of what the future could look like if particular actions were taken along the way. As a postscript, a similar attempt is made below to postulate alternative urban planning, policy and governance arrangements for Adelaide over the next 15 years.

Scenario 1: Contract City. In the drive towards greater efficiency, lower costs and competitiveness the withdrawal of government involvement in urban service provision was concluded by the final transfer of all remaining services to private sector providers in the year 2005. A new political orthodoxy had removed tenured and contract public servants. The ideal political structure was seen to be Cabinet and a single Department of Contract Administration which managed the interface between the public and private sectors.

In the field of urban planning, a network of private infrastructure providers now prepares a five-yearly advisory programme of new land development to assist government in its contracting (somewhat in the style of the New York Regional Plan Association).

A de-regulated approvals process, allowing community notification via the web, requires contract planners to prepare recommendations on development applications within sharply defined time periods.

Scenario 2: Federalism Revived. Following the creation of the Republic of Australia, the Federal Government has pursued major initiatives to balance and distribute growth across the country, with a measure of devolution to strong and vibrant centres of governance based upon metropolitan areas and regional economic units. Increasingly these units are pursuing direct cooperative relationships with regions in neighbouring Asia-Pacific countries and the future role of the national government is uncertain. There is some talk of a Federation of Australasia—covering Australia, Papua-New Guinea, some Pacific Islands and New Zealand— and proposals are under discussion for a major initiative to balance and distribute growth across the Region. But meanwhile, at the federal government level, active programmes of differential taxation and infrastructure investment aim explicitly to:

• balance the evolution of the urban hierarchy in economic, environmental and social terms;
• promote industry growth on a targeted spatial basis; and
• ensure the provision of funds for necessary capital investment.

Scenario 3: The Entrepreneurial City—Mark II. From the quagmire of inter-governmental complexity and declining resources, a series of larger and well resourced municipalities began to emerge in the late 1990s— leaner with firm tax bases and more flexible in scope than other governments, thanks to broadly-based constitutional and legal reforms. These were characterised by less formalised party organisations and much stronger connections to key industry and interest groups.

Following earlier experiments with sister-city and other civic relationships, a network of business-based trade networks emerged through which regional centres assumed a higher level of inward investment and growth. Building business from existing strengths was, however, the clear priority. By these means the pattern of decline was slowly, but surely reversed.

New coalitions of private and public interests emerged, providing focused effort for the development and growth of industries with competitive cost and market strengths. These arrangements were assisted by the creation of a new generation of plans and strategies, at once physical, financial and organisational in scope and in turn blending with new networks of private and public activity.

The style of urban planning and management within these new municipal authorities seeks to:

- avoid the bureaucratisation of the past;
- focus as much on implementing as on planning;
- ensure high levels of transparency and accountability;
- secure the benefits and efficiencies of private sector service provision;
- provide new models for public involvement; and
- integrate economics, financing and industry development within a spatial strategy.

8 Net, City and Locality— Technological Impacts on Stockholm

REZA KAZEMIAN

Introduction

Electronic networking, while increasing time, place and work flexibility, is becoming an important factor for the general transformation of cityscapes. This new mode of development, though at an early stage of diffusion, shows signs of being able to alter many vital social, cultural and spatial relationships. It is embedding new conditions for many companies and individuals to become 'footloose' (Sassen, 1991). Out-sourcing routine office information-handling operations to remote areas and teleworking in flextime are becoming accepted concepts in 'Post-Fordist' labour and production management philosophy (Forester, 1989).

The emerging development is causing new tensions between 'space of flows' and 'space of places' (Castells, 1996). It is creating a new segmented spatial structure of technologically 'favoured' and 'less-favoured' urban patterns, engendering crucial problems for disadvantaged inhabitants in the form of a new wave of displacements and rootlessness. It is even providing a new complicated situation for urban and regional planners to choose appropriate locations with respect to social and cultural diversity and to reconcile the two diverging spatial logics: *localities* and *nets*.

> The dominant tendency is toward a horizon of networked, ahistorical space of flows, aiming at imposing its logic over scattered, segmented places, increasingly unrelated to each other, less and less able to share cultural codes. Unless cultural *and physical* bridges are deliberately built between these two forms of space, we may be heading toward life in parallel universes whose times cannot meet because they are warped into different dimensions of a social hyperspace (Castells, 1996).

In the context of Stockholm, the main research problems are to know: how the city and its regional hinterland, the Mälar, are adapting to the flows of new information and communication technologies? What kind of planning efforts at this early stage should be made while there is potential for the information technologies to be optimally diffused, and a sustainable-democratic transformation of this city region to be safeguarded?

Stockholm in Informational Wraps

Over the past two decades, information technologies, though continually on the verge of turmoil, have become important forces of change in urban-regional settings in advanced capitalist systems. It is expected that by the year 2000, the telecommunications industry is to reach seven percent of the Gross Domestic Product of Western Europe compared to two percent in 1984; and more than 60 percent of all employees are to be supported by IT (Mulgan, 1991; Graham, 1996).

Since the early 1990s, Sweden has become one of the leading countries in Europe both in development and application of the new means of communication and information exchange took serious steps forwards. The use of information technology is growing very fast among different social categories. Today, Sweden has one of the highest rates of growth per capita of personal computers in the world.

Stockholm has a long tradition in welding informational infrastructure in urban-regional settings. At the end of the nineteenth century, the city had more telephones per capita than large European cities like London, Paris and Berlin. Today, the inhabitants in Stockholm city-region rank highest in the world in their access to the Internet, fax and mobile telephone. About 60 percent of the people in this city-region are using computers in their daily activities. A major flow of the European Internet goes via Stockholm. In 1996, more than 10 percent of the inhabitants in Stockholm were working, in one way or another, with information technologies. Information-based economic sectors are expanding rapidly and are considered to be the most important source for economic development of this city-region in the near future. There are already signs indicating the impacts of IT on existing work and housing locations; transforming them into a new type of socio-spatial order, following both recentralisation and decentralisation patterns.

After the building boom in the 1980s a period of recession in building activities occurred in Stockholm. Ideas that Stockholm is 'ready-built' have gained momentum and created a doubtful attitude among the construction companies. At the same time, the number of urban renewal schemes increased and became a dominant part of construction activities in Stockholm.

Despite the lower rate of new building production, substantial transformations are taking place in Stockholm. One such trend is the gradual replacement of outmoded ports and industrial activities with residential and new types of work-places and houses in central parts of Stockholm. 'Left-over' plots are being reconsidered for urban development schemes, for upgrading and densification of the urban landscape. The city core is becoming more attractive for a growing number of people as a cultural focus, as a place for shopping or meeting in restaurants, cafeterias and pubs. More and more, higher income citizens are moving into Stockholm's inner areas as more secure and favourable places for living. In contrast with many capital cities in the world, Stockholm's central zones, areas within the *malmar* as it is called, are socially and physically divorcing from its generally low-income suburbs.

At the same time, on a larger scale, a social and demographic transformation is taking place in Stockholm's semi-peripheral suburbs and regional hinterland, specially in modern areas built during the construction boom of the One Million Housing Unit Program (*Miljonprogrammet*) within a decade, between the mid-1960s until the mid-1970s. These areas are especially on the verge of sever transformations. For a few of these neighbourhoods and communities, the new transformation means to adapting rapidly to new technological and economic niches with renewed prospects for development and prosperity; for many other low-income communities, transformation means economic decline, unemployment, social adversity and a struggle to find a basic means of survival. Several peripheral suburbs around Stockholm are losing the functional necessities that brought them into being. The public services and employment opportunities are deteriorating and the areas are becoming unfavourable for living. Concentrations of low income people, unemployed and immigrants in certain suburbs are contributing to socio-spatial tensions and to an increase in ethnic, economic, cultural and spatial segregation.

Some suburban communities, built upon the spatial logic of modernism, are undergoing general functional changes. They are evolving from previously dormitory towns to become sites for secondary headquarters, allocating low price locations to the back-offices of often

non-production services and information-intensive manufacturing enterprises. These suburbs, such as Kista, Husby, and, to some extent, Akalla, in
the northern part of Stockholm, now provide homes and workplaces for
both well-paid professionals and re-skilled low-waged, blue collar service
and informational workers. While these new trends are 'favouring' a
portion of its low-income, youngest, and reskilled inhabitants, it is
intensifying the difficulties for unskilled and unemployed segments of these
suburban people. The latter social group are facing the threat of a new wave
of poverty, segregation and displacement. They are losing their sense of
place, their cultural identity. An apathy toward the 'system' and
'establishment' is growing among these disadvantaged citizens.

Since the early 1990s, the local authorities, together with the national
government and many manufacturing and service companies, have tried to
redirect and promote the infrastructural potential of the Stockholm city
region to combat the negative impacts of transformation and have made a
great effort to speed up the transition towards an information society.
Currently, several pilot teleworking projects are being experienced, testing
the application of telematic devices in daily activities, such as for the
elderly and disabled in private- and municipality-owned dwelling areas, in
modern suburbs, in small towns and villages around Stockholm—in order
to control the social and demographical transformations in a rational way.
Applying a teleworking schedule for the employees of the municipality in
the harbour town of Nynäshamn and the Telematic Scheme in Vällingby
suburb are among these projects being carried out through a cooperation of
several partners including academia, local governments, private and public
IT companies and housing agencies. Particularly important are the
infrastructural IT schemes and investments at the county and regional
levels where the impacts are more profound.

In 1991, the Stockholm County Council's Regional Plan, a regional
strategy scheme mainly for land use and infrastructure in the county, was
incorporated to development of strategic plans of other counties and
municipalities around the Mälar Lake. The Regional Plan of 1991 shows a
15 year development programme and is coordinated by the Mälar Regional
Council. The Council established in 1989 comprises the representatives
from 51 municipalities in the Mälar region.

It is estimated that over $7.6 billion will be invested in developing
transportation and communication systems in Stockholm and the Mälar
Region. The ambition is to limit the travel time required to reach any part
of the region to less than two hours. Great emphasis is placed on the
expansion of telecommunication networks and the rapid development of a

high-speed electronic infrastructure. This scheme is very important and sensitive because it is affecting a large region with nearly 2.5 million population—that is 30 percent of the total population of the country. Already, potential industrial jobs are offered in this region. Over 50 percent of Sweden's research and university training activities are located in the Stockholm-Mälar region. The Scheme is designed to mainly favour the Swedish multinational companies such as ABB, Ericsson, Astra, Pharmacia, Atlas Copco and Electrolux. These enterprises have their origins in the region and it is thought that this gigantic infrastructure investment would eliminate the relocation wave of these companies and that these multinationals might continue to run a proportion of their business operations in the region.

However, the scheme is very weak in some other aspects. One is its sectoral view of planning. No one knows what would happen with this huge social and spatial intervention if one day these multinationals reject investment in the region and if they decide to move their activities away from the regional or even outside national boundaries. The scheme's other weak aspect is its substantial impacts on the locality through eventual relocation of homes and workplaces in the region. The major risk is that the societal and spatial fabrics of many less-favoured rural communities, towns and cities at the national level will be affected by this project. There are already traceable signs of social and spatial transformations that are connected either directly or indirectly to this regional strategic plan. If nothing special happens in the other regions, this expansive and critical scheme would have a great negative effect on localities, on environment, on regional patterns, greater than experienced during the age of the automobile. The deeper problem with the scheme, however, can be found in difficulties its planners and decision-makers have expressed to diverge from the modernist planning doctrines. The scheme still contains a variation of the sectoral planning, abstractisation and compartmentalisation methods inherited from the age of the Modern Movement with its familiar general outlook on territory and living spaces.

As Robert Sack in *Human Territoriality: Its theory and History* (1986) argues: the very way modern economic systems were structured gave the planning system a dualistic role with 'obfuscat tendencies' to compartmentalise spaces to overshadow the structure of power. It means that in such sectoral economic planning systems, regions and urban places are planned with a sense of abstraction that regards places as easy to empty and refill. Planning authorities try to preserve and extend their territorial power and control by thinning out the spaces of places:

The basis of (modern) planning relies on abstracting things from space, that is, on conceptually separating events and spaces. It relies on our coming to think of space (...) That important among the uses of territoriality which can be expected primarily is capitalism and the modern era are the sense of an emptiable space, the increased uses of territorial hierarchies to further impersonal relationships, and the use of territoriality to obscure sources of power.

The cases of treating territory as an emptiable and fillable mold multiply as we approach the present and the same trend is seen when we look at territories in smaller geographical scales within neighborhoods and buildings (Sack, 1986).

New Hopes

The choice of appropriate locations is an important part of urban planning and it is becoming a vital issue in emerging informational societies. Well thought-out and insightful location decisions might bring about new opportunities for synergetic urban planning with symbiotic coexistence of electronic nets and localities but, in contrast, narrow-minded, short-living sectoral location decisions can result in irreversible social, cultural, and spatial damages.

Some visions for the future of localisation strategies in the Stockholm city-region will continue to be guided by utopian, dystopian, futuristic, simplistic, linear, and confusing 'technology-will-fix' attitudes as we witnessed in the Modernist era. Nevertheless, compared to the rigid and constraining urban design methodologies of the 1960s, 1970s and 1980s, the new mode of development promises greater potential for creating places in sync with current concepts and realities, places of integrated cultural, social and spatial diversities. Planners should employ influential impacts of information and communication technologies in placemaking in order to replace, rebalance and redensify urban spaces, for reducing urban traffic congestion and allowing a more culturally and socially effective use of places. But these steps should be taken with a great deal of patience and care. Planners have to deal with uncertainties, to accept that their knowledge about the future is very limited. They have to deal with local resources, with cultural identity, with the space of places, with the socio-spatial multifunctionality that combines employment opportunities, cultural activity, socio-ethnic diversity, recreation, and housing in order to preserve the decaying community life and to answer the problems of compartmentalised cityscapes.

It is widely accepted that the diffusion rate of new information and communication technologies should be in pace with the democratic principle of giving citizens access to, and control over, the flow of information to increase their awareness and making the planning process more participatory and its solutions more contextual. The democratisation of planning in the form of informational empowerment of disadvantaged segments of society is needed, and this should be the primary source of planning inspiration in every urban-regional planning scheme. It is a challenging task for planners to reconcile different spatial logics, to discover how new opportunities can best be diffused, success be achieved, and pitfalls be avoided at this early stage. Any success will surely depend on our ability to establish a well-thought out and far-sighted curriculum to re-educate those with the power of making decision and planning locations in information societies.

9 The Sustainable Network Society—A Scenario Study of Transport and Communications

FOLKE SNICKARS

Introduction

A major contemporary policy issue in Sweden as in other countries is the emerging conflict between the mobility of commodities and people and environmental sustainability. There is an increasing understanding that we are currently undergoing a fundamental change in the global economic system away from the industrial society and into the post-industrial society, the communication society, the knowledge society, or the network society, whatever you might call it. We have witnessed communication and transportation increase dramatically alongside one another. Whereas communication will not damage the environment, transportation will.

What are the mechanisms that cause structural change in the global, national and regional economy in the future? What role does technical change in the information technology and telecommunication industries play in this context? What are the prospects for those nations, regions and cities that have become inextricably tied to transportation modes using fossil fuels? How can we design a policy mix consisting of economic incentives, environmental restrictions, and value changes to save the environment without sacrificing economic efficiency?

A futures study has been performed under the auspices of the Swedish Institute for Futures Studies on the relationship between transport, communications and long-term environmental sustainability. The project has involved a scenario study where a group of experts have been asked about their assessments of driving forces and consequences for society at large, and for themselves.

A major parliamentary government investigation has been performed in Sweden about sustainable transport. It has involved a number of research projects, among others the current one. There are government studies in other countries in Europe as well. However, the question of sustainable transport at the European level remains to be politically addressed. Sweden has a number of reasons to protect its interests in a situation where north-south contacts in Europe are being replaced by east-west ones. The race goes east with the Nordic countries, the baltics and Russia as historical partners.

The study has involved a scenario analysis which aims to investigate the views of four groups of experts on future transport policy, government experts, researchers, practitioners of transport planning, and university students who study transport-related subjects. The scenario study has been developed using ideas from strategic planning in the business sector, especially as regards the treatment of uncertainty (see also Makridakis, 1990 and Snickars, 1990, 1992).

A questionnaire has been designed in nine parts. In the first part, a thought model is presented. Thereafter, seven areas of society which are important for sustainable transport and communications are singled out. In each of them four types of questions are asked concerning general tendencies, Sweden's role in Europe, forecasts of transport-related phenomena, and personal transport and communications futures. In a concluding part there are a number of questions about comparisons among scenarios.

The questionnaire has been filled in by 156 persons, one-third government experts and researchers, one third practitioners, and one-third students. Among the government experts there is a group which has been centrally involved in the preparation of the documents for the new sustainability-oriented Swedish transport policy. The researchers have been selected from address lists of persons connected as experts to the Swedish Transport and Communications Research Board. Practitioners have been selected at random from membership files of the Swedish Association of Traffic Engineers. The students have been selected among persons enrolled in courses at the graduate level within the Royal Institute of Technology with a specialisation towards transport. The respondents mainly come from the Stockholm region. They are between 20 and 70 years old. There are more men than women in the group of respondents. Many participants have a university degree.

Theoretical Framework of the Study

The study has been conceived in the spirit of the scenario analysis of European transport futures performed by Masser *et al.*, 1992 and Nijkamp *et al.*, 1995, 1996. The control-model paradigm employed is presented in

Figure 9.1. The figure distinguishes five interconnected analysis components. There is a public policy actor in charge of instruments within a prespecified range of policy formation possibilities. The state of the society relevant for the assessment of the consequences of public action is determined by the mixing of policy and external factors.

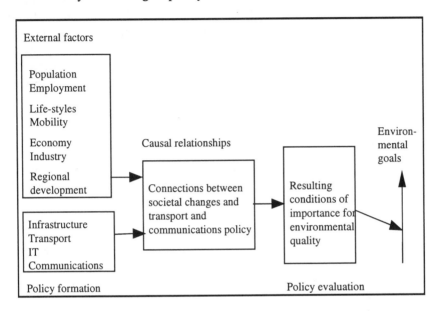

Figure 9.1 Structuring of the cause-and-effect framework of transport and communications policy in a control theory setting

The causal relationships between societal changes and transport and communications policy, defined in accordance with the best available scientific and experience-based knowledge, result in conditions of society relevant for the assessment of environmental quality. The policy evaluation involves the monitoring of the resulting state of society by defining operational environmental goals. The fulfilment of these goals will be determined in a complex way by the interaction among policies and external factors to produce anticipated societal and environmental effects via the causal relationships.

The classical policy-analysis problem is to choose that element in the policy formation set which will yield the highest level of goal fulfilment given forecasts, conditional or unconditional, of the external factors within the set of possible external developments. The relationships between policies, forecasts, resulting states, and goal measurements are usually specified via some kind of model, mental, qualitative, or quantitative. In the forecasting and planning literature, scenarios are used both to specify the future state of external development factors, and to describe a complete combination of external factors and public policies, and their consequences.

The latter use of scenarios often is associated with the use of partly, or completely, qualitative methods of analysis and presentation. In the former mode of thinking, scenarios are often seen as congruent with conditional forecasts, forecasts which are such that the conditioning factors are not assumed to be associated with uncertainty of risk. In the latter mode of thinking, there is seldom reference made to uncertainties at all. Instead, the basic idea is that the scenario should be internally consistent, i.e., the components presented, and statements made, of consequences which will result should not be contradictory.

In the current study the thought model presented above is fundamentally assumed to be a mental model of the respondents to the survey (see also Snickars, 1995). As experts, the persons who are exposed to the questions will have knowledge about earlier forecasts and their uncertainties. They will have studied the field and are therefore aware of the common knowledge among experts about the causal relationships between societal development and transport system performance. Furthermore, they will normally be well aware of current public policies, implemented and considered, and will have a good understanding and knowledge of the environmental goals adopted or being discussed at the political level.

It is an important idea of the questionnaire method that the respondents should reveal not only their actual behaviour, and their preferences for policy alternatives, but also their knowledge about policy alternatives, about causal relationships, and about earlier studies of external factors driving the transport system in certain long-term directions. We are interested in getting knowledge about the cognitive mappings of the transport-environment nexus into the minds of the respondents. The idea is not, as in classical Delphi studies, to present the experts with their statements in a comparative context so as for them to be able to change their views. It is to perform a new form of survey, which might be called a 'stated-knowledge' study, borrowing one of the terms in contemporary transport research.

In this process, we wish to give the experts the opportunity to state their own level of confidence in the answers they have given. It is logical that some persons feel that they have studied one aspect more thoroughly and therefore feel more confident in their causal knowledge or even forecast. For others, the question posed might be new, or the effort they may have spent in making a forecast less comprehensive. It is therefore logical that they should be allowed to weigh that effort. The idea is thus not the one of classical decision theory to state the probability that a forecast will come true but to make a subjective assessment of the degree of certainty in the forecast, or the confidence the experts are willing to place in it. The fact that a number of respondents will respond to the same questions about external factors and causal relationships will imply that a spread will occur which can be associated with the differences in knowledge, and in some cases opinion, between different experts.

Figure 9.1 shows that four areas have been selected for the description of the external milieu for transport-environment policies. Population and employment conditions are, of course, important since age, income, and family conditions influence the transport needs. These are also influenced by life-styles and customs as regards mobility given the socio-economic context. An important factor here, for instance, is the development of the volume and composition of car ownership in the population. The economic and industrial developments will have direct influences on the goods transport systems via technical and market changes in production, distribution and trade. In the modern service society the economic development will become more and more associated with business travel.

Since transport and communications are both there to bridge distances there will be a strong need to understand both how regional development will give rise to different needs for interaction and how regional development will be affected by those policies. One aspect of particular interest here is the future direction of the urban system of Europe. The question is whether urbanisation will proceed or whether rural areas will be gaining more in importance in view of their environmental traits.

The policy areas selected for the study are transport and communications in a broad sense. The public actor at the centre of interest is a national Swedish agency in charge of preparing for decisions to be made about infrastructure investment, and operation and maintenance, for the different transport modes, and for telecommunications. The policy set includes administrative regulation as well as economic policy instruments. The recent government investigations in Sweden have employed a broader view of transport policy than earlier. In particular, new instruments have been considered which will be conducive to a higher degree of environmental sustainability. The logic behind this is that the policy evaluation will have to embody the environment.

There are two perspectives possible here. One sees the environment as an aspect of goals for the transport and communications sector. In this mode of thinking the main goals are economic efficiency, industrial development, traffic safety, regional development, and environmental impacts. The other approach would be to see the environmental situation as the object of the policy. Then the transport policies will be included among a number of actions to reduce the burden on the environment. The policy discussion in the later years states that the transport sector is not taking its full environmental responsibility. Obviously, the two perspectives overlap one another and need to be kept in the discussion concurrently.

Figure 9.2 illustrates another view of the survey study, viz. the connection of Swedish transport and communications policy to international development. Both international socio-economic development and international policy development in transport and communications are external factors in the model framework of the study. However, they are distinguished from each other. Goal fulfilment in Sweden, at the right end of the figure, is determined by the economic and social development at the European level including, of course, Sweden. In the fast economic growth alternative, Europe will gain growth momentum from the inclusion of the new members in the north and east, Finland, Sweden and Austria. Further growth prospects appear in the future through the change of eastern Europe's political system in the beginning of the 1990s. Slow growth will materialise if the unemployment problem in Europe cannot be solved, the EU cannot work efficiently to create equal conditions in the capital markets, and Europe's competitiveness with America and Asia will not remain.

Transport policy at the European level can basically be of two types, market-oriented or environment-oriented. The same two alternatives exist for Sweden. The market-oriented policy alternative is strong in Europe for the moment. There is a long-term goal to increase Europe's competitive edge by building a new generation of infrastructure systems to support trade and mobility. Examples are found in the so-called Trans-European Network (TEN) programmes. At the same time the strategy is to remove bottlenecks and regulate transport so that free competition can be attained in the transport sector at large. A rapid development in this respect is taking place in the freight forwarding market. Similar developments are foreseen in the air transportation sector implying a privatisation movement for both airlines and airports.

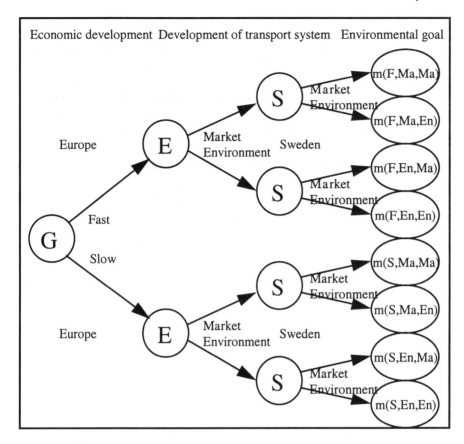

Economic development   Development of transport system   Environmental goal

**Figure 9.2   Sweden's alternatives for transport and communications
policy in an international context**

The Figure illustrates the fact that the level of environmental goal
fulfilment for Sweden, when pursuing its national transport and
communications policies, will be influenced by policies around the country.
The policies will also function in different ways depending on the pace and
direction of economic development. If Europe and Sweden jointly select
the market strategy in transport and communications under the scenario that
a fast economic development will demand this, the resulting economic
development might still be slow. There will be an environmental cost or a
benefit associated with the deficient forecast which is measured by the
difference between the goal values for the two branches in question. In
reality, long-term policy action will have to be taken ahead of demand, i.e.,
there is always a risk of having to pay for the regret of a false forecast.

In the following sections we will give examples of results of the scenario study in particular as regards the development in association with urban and regional development. A number of tables and graphs will be presented which illustrate the view of the selection of Swedish experts about the inter-relation between transport, communications and long-term environmental sustainability. Evidently, the results are not representative of any other group of individuals. To the extent that the knowledge base of the Swedish experts is international, however, the results of the study might reflect also the perceptions of experts in other countries or other fields of research.

The sample of experts includes people with different educational and professional backgrounds. It is therefore instructive to investigate to what extent the views differ depending on age, gender, education, profession, or social networks of the expert. The null hypothesis in this context, however, will be that these differences are small. It would be somewhat disturbing if the views of the experts were highly dependent on their personal rather than their professional characteristics.

Population and Employment

In the survey, a set of questions has related to population and employment conditions. An obvious reason for this is the central role that population-related projections normally play in futures studies and forecasting. Figure 9.3 shows the forecasts made by the experts of the male and female labour force participation rates. The thin lines in the figure are the standard deviations for the two forecasts respectively.

The respondents were presented with the figure exclusively as a basis for their forecasting. Their task was to mark two points on the vertical line representing 2010 as their forecasts. They were also asked to give an assessment of how confident they were in their forecast by stating a number between zero and one hundred for the each of the two forecasts. No restriction was placed on the method of forecasting. Most respondents worked directly on the graph but some made calculations at the side.

The figure shows that the respondents have been cautious with their forecast on average. It is revealing to note that very few believe that the seminal increase in the female labour force participation will continue. Instead, there is a certain tendency for them to reduce the pace of reduction in the male participation rates. One would expect that a forecast made in the beginning of the 1990s, before the dramatic slump in the rates for both genders in Sweden, would have been considerably higher, especially for women. From a more detailed analysis of the results, it appears that respondents have not generally forecasted a substitution within the labour force. A high forecast for men is almost always associated with a high forecast for women.

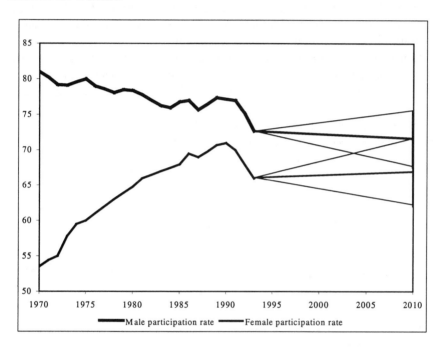

Figure 9.3   Share of men and women aged 16-74 years in Sweden 1970-93 who are members of the labour force and forecasts to 2010 (percent)

The respondents were asked a number of questions about the position of Sweden's labour market in the European context. It was a general characteristic of the answers to these questions that respondents believed Sweden would not retain its position as a country with high participation rates and low unemployment.

Table 9.1 provides a summary of the views expressed by the experts on future traits of mobility in the labour market. Labour mobility, of course, will have a direct impact on transport and communications, and on urban development. The table shows how all experts and two subgroups, students and women, each making up about a fourth of the group, differ in their views on future geographical and occupational mobility. More than 90 percent believe that people will have to change occupation and almost everyone thinks that recurrent education will be common.

The table shows that there are marked differences in the responses between the average respondent and the statements made by students and women, at least in some dimensions. As mentioned earlier, it is not to be expected that there would be major differences in opinion since the experts' answers are unlikely to be flavoured by their personal characteristics. Instead, differences might occur as a consequence of different educational backgrounds or different working experiences. The intention is, of course, that the statements made should not be value judgements but represent forecasts. For this reason these questions have also included statements concerning the level of confidence that the respondent places with the response. The table shows rather small differences in the response patterns. The female respondents seem to have assessed the mobility levels to be generally somewhat smaller than the average expert.

Table 9.1   Views expressed by respondents about likely future traits of labour market mobility

Share of yes to statement to consider to 2010	All	Students	Women
Many more will have mobile work-place in own region	73	69	77
Many more will have mobile work-place in country	81	82	77
Many more Swedes will work in western Europe	84	80	79
Many more from western Europe will work in Sweden	64	63	65
Many more will have changed their occupation	91	90	85
Many more will have had recurrent education	97	97	94

It is obvious that the respondents believe that more people will have mobile work-places where they move across the country rather than within their home region. As many as four out of five express the view that the Swedish labour force will find jobs in the rest of Europe and two out of three foresee an inflow of people from western Europe into the Swedish labour market. The impression is that the respondents envisage a future labour market where people spend part of their time in other regions of the country or in other countries. Smaller changes seem to be foreseen for the short-term dynamics of the local and regional labour markets. The consequence is likely to be an increased demand for long-distance travel at the national and European scale.

Life-Styles and Mobility

The modern life-style seems to be one of combining a relatively stable residence with mobility to reach supplies of both jobs, service outlets, and recreational and cultural amenities. For some groups of high-income households in Sweden the situation in the 1990s is already that they spend as much on transport and communications as on housing. The tendency is for more people to move into those socio-economic brackets where such behaviour is typical. Historically, the life-style and mobility patterns have been characteristic of cohorts of the population. Persons who have adopted a behaviour in their youth seem to retain that over time. In this way a mobile generation will keep being mobile when people get older. Seen in this perspective, it may be equally important for environmental policy to address the question of altering the life-style of older people as it is of teaching the young generation to adopt a less mobile one. Both tasks seem to be very difficult indeed.

Figure 9.4 contains information of the long-term trend in mobility in Sweden during the latest 25-year period. The stable increase in distance travelled is associated almost exclusively with increased speeds of movement. The average time spent on transportation each day is still around one hour as it has been since the 1950s. The figure shows that the serious economic recession in Sweden in the 1990s has entailed a stagnation, and even a reduction in, the average mobility trend. The average distance travelled, as measured by the so-called travel habit surveys which are performed on a regular basis in Sweden, has been around 35 kilometres per person and day since the later part of the 1980s.

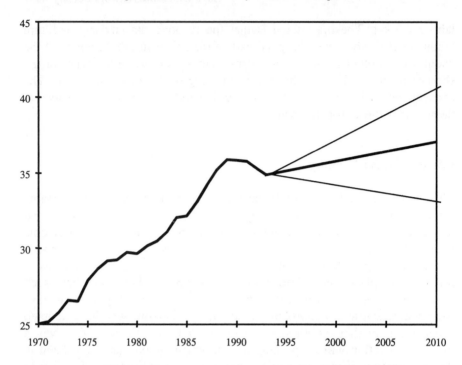

Figure 9.4   Average distance travelled in Sweden 1970-93 in kilometres per person and day. All movements including walk and cycling are included except short walks at the home and forecasts to 2010

Figure 9.4 shows that the average respondent has produced a forecast with a continued increase in mobility but at a slower pace. The span between respondents is relatively large. Since the forecasts take their starting points in the situation in the middle of the 1990s, at the end of a recession which ended around 1995, the experts have not seen the slump in the curve as an episode. The knowledge available in the later part of 1996 when the survey was performed would have been such that respondents could have adopted the episode view and increased the forecasted rate of change.

Figure 9.5 provides an example of the information gained from the question concerning the confidence the experts place in their forecast. For each observation, i.e., forecast of the mobility level in 2010, there is a number between zero and one hundred stating the degree of certainty of the respondent. The figure shows that on average those experts are more confident in their forecast who have stated a continuation of the increasing trend. Those who have forecasted a decline in mobility, or a level below the average of the forecasts, have stated that they are not as certain about their assessment. The figures represented in Figure 9.5 can be seen as further information on top of the actual forecast. In principle, the individual forecasts could be weighed with these numbers to produce an adjusted one where each observation has been corrected with the credibility of it as assessed by the experts. In the current case, the average forecast of mobility will be slightly higher if this information is added.

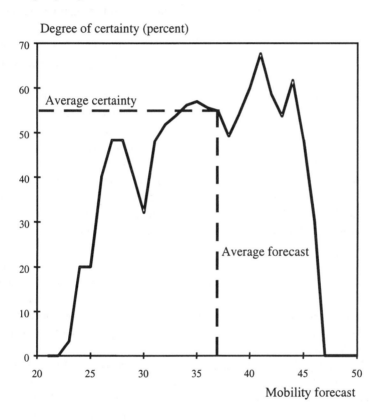

Figure 9.5   Degree of confidence in forecast made of individual mobility in 2010. Average share of respondents who have stated the degree of certainty as a function of forecast value of mobility (percent)

It should be noted that empirical observations in the corporate sector, reported by Makridakis (1990), show that the level of confidence of a forecaster in a projection is not a perfect measure of the goodness of the forecast. In fact, the use of a more sophisticated forecasting technique, or the bringing in of a more experienced forecaster, tends more to raise the confidence of the forecaster in the statement made about the uncertain future than enhancing the accuracy of the forecast itself.

This empirical observation is verified to a larger degree for long-term forecasts than for short-term ones. In the short-term the result is rather that the use of sophisticated modelling techniques will reduce the uncertainty because it removes the chance of the expert judgement being biased by personal views about the importance of external driving forces and recently occurring events.

There is a dominant role of private cars in supporting the individual mobility in Sweden as in almost all high-mobility countries. There are a few exceptions at the urban level where some metropolitan regions have managed to create a public transport system which is so competitive that it carries a substantial part of the urban travel task.   Some cities in Switzerland, some Nordic cities and, possibly, some Japanese cities could be placed in this range, see also Wegener (1995). However, in a geographically extended country like Sweden, cars and trucks, are essential to connect the geographically dispersed settlement and production system.

This fact is exacerbated by the recent economic and political changes in Europe at large. Continental Europe is Sweden's top market both for manufacturing, and for tourist travel. The market for cars is an increasingly global one. Sweden will be even more integrated with the rest of Europe in the market for private cars during the next decade. For the moment there are considerable differences in the car ownership intensity in different countries (see also Figure 9.6).

The results of the questionnaire study for car ownership is presented in Figure 9.7. The figure can be interpreted to mean that Swedes need to use some 3.8 cars to produce a million of their GNP (in 1985 prices). The trend has been steadily increasing even during the beginning of the 1990s. There was a boom in the beginning of the 1970s which was curbed by the global oil crisis. It had a substantial effect on the costs for car-driving both directly through petrol prices and indirectly through government taxation and ensuing changes in behaviour.

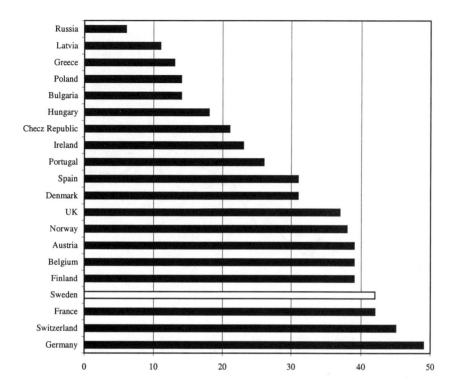

Figure 9.6 Car ownership expressed as number of cars per one hundred inhabitants 1990. Germany does not include the eastern part and Russia is the former nation excluding the Baltic countries and the Ukraine

Again, the Figure illustrates the tendency for the average expert to be moderate in the forecasting activity. A slight increase in the long-term trend is forecast with a large standard deviation. A possible explanation for the conservative nature of the forecast could be that the ratio employed is not the most well-established one for car ownership forecasting. Some of the experts would be used to seeing and interpreting a time series for car ownership among the population. Sometimes, the measure is cars per person and sometimes it is persons per car (see also Figure 9.6.)

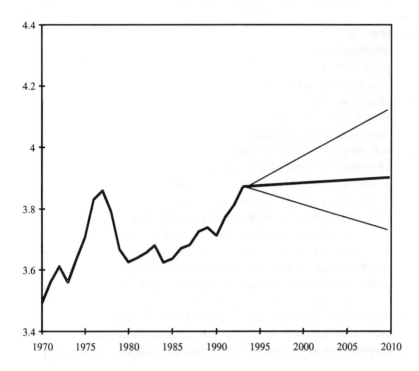

**Figure 9.7   Car fleet in operation in Sweden 1970-93 in relation to
GNP and average forecast to 2010 including standard
deviation in forecast**

The question in the survey was intentionally constructed to relate the car ownership to GNP. One way to interpret the result would be that the respondents are not certain about the development of GNP, which might fluctuate between years more than population. It is obvious that the development in the 1990s is a reflection of the slump in GNP which occurred during that period, see also Figure 9.8 below. In the above analysis car ownership is a stock variable with relatively slow changes and GNP is a flow variable with relatively fast changes.

It should also be noted that the estimates by the respondents reported in Figure 9.7 are not to be seen as forecasts of an external driving force in the model framework employed here. It should rather be seen as an example of a parameter forecast in a policy evaluation model, or as a part of a set of observations to be used to construct an econometric model to forecast car ownership.

Table 9.2 illustrates another technique used in the survey to assess the experts' knowledge, or perception, of the relationship between driving forces for mobility and consequences for the transport sector. The results summarised in the table show the share of respondents who have stated that the respective travel modes will gain in ridership if the stated events will materialise. Thus, more than 90 percent of the respondents have the view that the car and air modes will gain in particular from the combination of real-income and leisure-time increases. On the other hand, if both real incomes and leisure time will stagnate or decrease, the car and air modes will not be favoured at all. This is the situation when buses, trams, undergrounds, and trains will prosper according to the experts. It may be noted that the changes foreseen by the respondents as a result of the changes stated in the rows and columns of the table are rather large. These are the implicit prior views held by the experts as a component of their experience-based knowledge.

Table 9.2   Assessment by respondents of the relative competition between travel modes as a function of real income and leisure time (share of respondents giving the answer)

	Leisure time increases	Consequence	Leisure time decreases	Consequence
Real incomes increase	Car	93	Car	79
	Train	26	Train	26
	Air	95	Air	75
	Bus & track	44	Bus & track	26
	Walk and cycle	71	Walk and cycle	39
Real incomes decrease	Car	26	Car	20
	Train	88	Train	75
	Air	5	Air	4
	Bus & track	92	Bus & track	80
	Walk and cycle	57	Walk and cycle	28

The experts have been asked about their own mobility futures for several reasons in the questionnaire. Questions such as the ones listed in

Table 9.3 are standard ways of finding patterns of current and future behaviour in a population as it is normally done when surveys are made of stated and revealed preferences.

Table 9.3   Statement of personal situation as regards life-style and mobility 2010 (percent of respondents)

Share of yes to statement about behaviour to consider to 2010	All	Students	Women
I will change residence	64	71	65
I will buy a new car	86	82	80
I will have a summer house	53	37	48
I will watch TV more than today	14	3	0
I will more often buy food in bulk	33	50	50
I will buy more from local shops	53	44	62

The earlier questions do not contain requests that the respondents should relate the answers to their personal values and behaviour. The questions concern their knowledge about current tendencies in their field and the answers should relate to their role as experts. Their views on future developments are thus collected not because they might have a particularly interesting mobility future themselves but because they represent expertise in the field.

The experts are close to unanimous in their determination to buy a new car. Since students and women both are found to be below the average of the other groups, people in the work-force and male respondents are more determined than the average. Very few see their future time-use connected to the television medium. An observation here is that the media industry will most certainly be aggressively attempting to challenge this forecast. There are marked differences between the responses of the students and the average, especially as regards purchasing habits. The observation may be made that the pattern of behaviour sketched in the responses is well in line with current trends in behaviour in Sweden.

Economy and Industry

Economic development in Sweden is intimately connected to the international division of labour. The Swedish economy has passed through

The Sustainable Network Society 239

a period of rapid structural change during the period 1970-95. There have been recurrent business cycle swings but some of these have been strengthened by national economic policies, especially during the later part of the period.

Sweden's economic development will, among other things, as a result of the membership in the EU, be valued in relation to the rest of Europe. Economic policy may be expected to be directed towards attaining economic growth equal to the one in other countries. A particular reason for this is credibility in the financial policies. There is a discussion in the country about how to strategically manage the emergence of the European Monetary Union. The stability in the economic development will influence people's expectations and thus their attitudes towards consumption and saving. Through this mechanism there will be a penetrating effect on transport and communications.

Figure 9.8 summarises one part of the questions raised with the experts on economic development. The request has been to provide a point estimate of the yearly rate of change in real GNP in the year 2010. The background has been the text provided above plus the information contained in the figure below. The respondents, furthermore, have had the information about the recovery of the Swedish economy during the second half of the 1990s to consider as an experience-based input.

The result of the exercise is that the persons who were involved in the survey on average assume that the yearly GNP change will be the same in 2010 as it was in 1995, in spite of the fluctuations in the curve and the slightly downward-sloping trend in the long-term. The theory for decisions under uncertainty tells us that in normative terms the rational decision-maker will make the forecast zero change in a situation of high uncertainty. It is, therefore, in a way, quite rational by the respondents to state a zero rate change. Of course, not all of the respondents have acted in this way. A more detailed analysis of the response patterns reveals that the government experts, the researchers and the practitioners have been more conservative than the students.

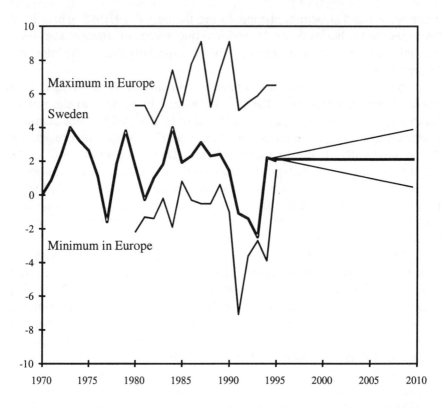

**Figure 9.8   Yearly percentage change in Sweden's real-price GNP
1970-95 in relation to the maximum and minimum growth
rates in western Europe during the corresponding years
(percent) as well as average forecast for 2010**

At the same time it should be noted that earlier research on Swedish
economic development produced as a part of the long-term economic
forecasting and planning has indicated that 2 percent per year is a likely
level of economic growth for Sweden in view of its natural and human
resources and its global specialisation.

The income development has a central role in determining the
demand for transport and communications among households and thus the
environmental impact. When demand weakens in the economy the firms
will reduce their production plans which will entail a smaller demand for
transport and communications. In forecasts of car ownership the disposable
income of households plays an important role. Long-term assessments of
those incomes have to be made in a macroeconomic context where the

room for private consumption in the economy is assessed. This means that forecasts of the development of car ownership, disposable income, and private consumption will be intimately connected to the GNP forecasts reported above.

The study has contained independent forecasts of the development of private consumption. The ambition has been to compare the forecasts of external driving factors for car ownership and person transport work made by the experts. The idea behind this is to provide alternative views on the uncertainty analysis. The results show that there is a general consistency among the answers provided by the persons involved in the survey. Those who have made high GNP forecasts have also normally provided high forecasts of private consumption. The level of consistency, however, differs markedly between different categories of respondents. On average, respondents have made somewhat lower forecasts for private consumption than for GNP development. The obvious reason for this is that forecasts were made in level index values for private consumption and for yearly percentage changes in the case of GNP. The GNP forecasts were then transformed to index values. Although respondents were generally able to connect the two forecasts, the GNP ones, made in terms of the rate of change, turned out to be more optimistic.

The freight transport work depends directly on industrial activity in the economy. As the value content of Swedish, and international, production increases a rising demand for goods and services in Sweden will not give rise to a corresponding growth in the freight transport work. Figure 9.9 shows the development of the freight transport work in relation to real GNP in Sweden during the period 1970-93. There is a general falling tendency. The development during the 1990s shows a slower reduction of the ratio which is partly a reflection of the recession in the Swedish economy. Since the figure plots two flow variables against one another, the tendency is not similar to the car ownership case with its sharp increase during the early 1990s.

Again, the forecasts provided by the experts as regards freight are conditional ones and might be interpreted as inputs into the specification of an econometric model for the relationship between transport and the economy. In the context of freight there are three components which determine the development in the graph above, volume, distance, and value. The curve represents the alteration of the value content in terms of the ratio tons/GNP multiplied by the average shipment distance which should increase as the level of international trade rises. Given the current best-practice information about the value content of production, therefore, the result may be interpreted to imply that the average respondent has forecasted a slight increase in the shipment distance.

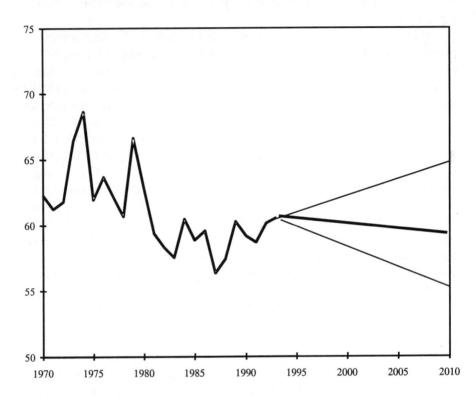

Figure 9.9   Development of freight transport work in relation to GNP in the Swedish economy 1970-93 (ton/km per SEK and year in 1985 prices)

Regional Development

There is often mention of the future of Europe as being in the regions, the regional mosaic emerging as one of Europe's most important cultural and economic assets. At the same time concepts such as territorial competition are being used to describe how regions and cities compete with one another about firms, jobs, culture, and public investments in a variety of fields. A number of futures scenarios have been put forward by different groups of actors in the European arena. Catchwords such as the blue banana, the new

Hansa, the Atlantic arc, the Mediterranean sunbelt, and the Bothnian arc, have been launched nationally and internationally (see also Löwendahl *et al.*, 1994). At the political level there have emerged spokesmen for a new regionalism in opposition with the national states, based on historical traditions.

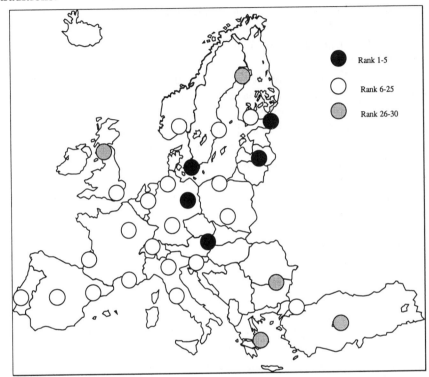

Figure 9.10 **The assessment of the regional development prospects of thirty European regions up to 2010 according to a selection of Swedish experts. Rank order based on selection of three high-priority projects and three low-priority ones**

The survey has included a number of questions about regional development. The responses to the question most directly related to the above discussion about the Europe of regions are summarised in Figure 9.10. The question posed to the experts was simply to indicate those three regions which, according to their view, would, on average, have the largest yearly increase in the gross regional product during the period up to 2010.

Correspondingly, the respondents were asked to select those three regions with the bleakest economic development prospects in the same terms.

Figure 9.10 contains an indication of those regions which came out among the five with the highest average priority and the ones which came out among the five with the lowest average priority. The result is revealing in several respects. It shows that the Swedish experts have made a ranking which differs substantially from the current common knowledge. It illustrates the influence of basic knowledge of a region and the role of cognitive maps.

The result which emerges is that regions in the north and eastern parts of Europe are foreseen to have the most rapid economic development. The Baltic countries are ranked considerably higher than any other region of Europe. The Vienna-Prague-Budapest region comes second before Berlin and the Copenhagen-Malmö area. The Benelux countries end up only as the seventh highest ranked growth region. At the bottom end of the scale we find the peripheral regions of northern and southern Europe, including the Swedish north. The national experts have used their more thorough knowledge to rank down the Swedish north while the reason for giving the other peripheral regions a low ranking may also relate to ignorance about their resources.

There is no common view in Europe about how the European city will look and function in the future (see also Table 9.4). During the last 50 years the urban fabric has changed dramatically to support life-styles and economic functions typical of a car-driven society. In certain European cities there has been a policy to keep high densities and complement those with the development of competitive urban rapid transit.

A main reason for the anticipated growth of cities in Europe is the demand for business and household services in the market-place. Also, the general belief is that the European cities of the future will be incubators for creative processes and arenas for knowledge production. They will thus, according to this reasoning, be more important to the economic competitiveness of the nations than ever before.

In the main, urban growth has been characterised by a sprawl of new settlements to fulfil the demand for dwelling space. A result has been a sparse and nature-oriented residential pattern. Concerns have been raised during the later years that this urban pattern will not be conducive to long-term sustainability. A number of arguments have been put forward both to validate and to reject this hypothesis. Table 9.4 contains the results of questions asked of the experts about the role of telecommunications for the total growth and the inner differentiation of the European cities up to 2010.

The first observation is that the Swedish experts do not generally see the city as becoming more competitive in the future. They qualify their statement by almost unanimously pointing out areas with nice living environments as attractors of new businesses. Evidently, this may not be said about some of the European urban environments for the moment.

Table 9.4   Statements about urban regional development tendencies to 2010 as a consequence of the introduction of information technology made by selection of Swedish experts (percent)

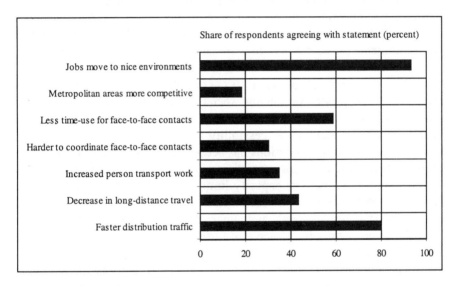

The table also contains information about the views expressed by the respondents on future trends in travel and freight systems. Only one-third suggest that there will be a marked increase in person transport work and this is supported by the view held by two out of five that long-distance travel will decrease in importance. At the same time the experts see telecommunications leading to less time to be spent in face-to-face contacts rather than those communications creating difficulties in coordinating personal contacts. There is a considerable consensus in the view that distribution traffic will become more effectively organised.

Even though the survey has not involved questions about the composite impact of telecommunications on urban growth, the responses as regards person contacts and distribution seem to indicate future conditions which are quite likely to prevail in many urban areas. The response that urban areas will not become competitive thus seems to stem from the cognitive map of the respondents of metropolitan areas as areas fraught with traffic, environment, and social problems.

Infrastructure and Transport

The capacity utilisation is close to the limit for several infrastructure systems in Europe. In the transport system, critical links exist in several places, such as the Channel, the Danish sounds, the Alps, the Pyrenes, and the east European mountain areas. The possibility of creating extra capacity is limited within national investment programmes. There has been a central ambition in the EU to build so-called Trans-European Networks to promote the attainment of economic and social goals (see also Grübler and Nakicenovic, 1993 and Spiekermann and Wegener, 1994).

The development of air traffic constitutes a mirror of Europe's transition to a service-producing society. Medium- and long-distance contacts can be materialised much quicker via air than by using any other means of transportation. Accessibility to airports with good flight connections to central destinations has become a location factor for contact-intensive firms, and for firms specialising in high-value manufacturing. The air transport system is at its capacity limit at several of the major airports. There has emerged a hierarchy of airports which compete with each other about positions in national and international transport systems. The deregulation underway in Europe will further increase the competitive edge between airlines, and between airports.

The air transport sector is intimately connected with the development in the telecommunications sector. Since extended contacts via telecommunications at longer distances will lead to contact needs, there is no competitive transport alternative. Currently, there are a number of formerly national airlines which are attempting to merge and form strategic alliances so as to gain a strong position as network operators. At the same time deregulation in the freight sector has spurred an internationalisation of the land transport sector as well. Formerly national forwarding companies are competing with one another about the long-distance haulage market. It seems that companies in the peripheral countries of Europe have a competitive disadvantage in this game.

The survey has contained a number of questions concerning the future of the European transport system. One aspect of this system is which infrastructure projects should be promoted and financed at the all-European level with the involvement of the EU. Table 9.5 contains a list of 20 such projects which have been discussed in documents from the EU during the middle of the 1990s. They are not identical to the ones more recently selected for EU short lists. Some of them have already been decided but have not come into full long-term operation.

Table 9.5 Twenty infrastructure projects in Europe which have been given high priority in EU considerations during the middle of the 1990s

Project	Description of project
1	Railway tunnel through the Brenner pass
2	High-speed railway Amsterdam-Brussels-Calais
3	High-sped railway Madrid-Barcelona-Perpignan
4	Tunnel under Fehmarn belt
5	High-speed railway Paris-Strasbourg
6	High-speed railway Karlsruhe-Frankfurt-Berlin
7	Betuwe railway line Rotterdam-Ruhr area
8	High-speed railway and motorway Lyon-Turin
9	Motorway Nuremberg-Prague-Berlin
10	Motorway Warsaw-Lvov
11	Motorway Thessaloniki-Sofia
12	Motorway Barcelona-Perpignan
13	Motorway Bari-Brindisi-Trento
14	International airport Athens
15	Canal Rhine-Rhône
16	The Seine canal
17	Canal system Elbe-Oder
18	Motorway St Petersburg-Vilnius
19	Öresund bridge Copenhagen-Malmö
20	High-speed railway along Gulf of Bothnia

Of course, since the Nordic countries have only relatively recently been involved in these priority discussions few projects from the north are found in the official documents. Therefore, some Nordic projects have been added to the list given to the experts to rank order. The rank order has been done, as above, by assigning three pluses and three minuses for the highest- and lowest-priority projects respectively. Figure 9.11 shows the result of the exercise in the form of indications of the high-priority projects, and the ones getting least attention. The index for ranking has been based on positive mention of a project, negative mention, and no mention at all.

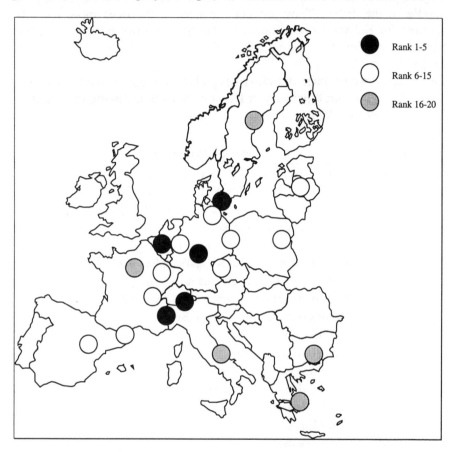

Figure 9.11   Rank order of twenty infrastructure projects in Europe according to a selection of Swedish experts. Rank order based on selection of three high-priority projects and three low-priority ones for being in full operation in 2010

The Brenner pass connection is regarded to be the most important one by the experts. An overwhelming majority of respondents expressed that they thought this project had the highest chance of being in full operation well before 2010. The other projects mentioned as important ones were the rapid railway connections between Karlsruhe and Berlin, and between Amsterdam and Calais. The Öresund connection was mentioned as well as the combined rapid railway and motorway connection between Lyon and Turin. Again, projects in the European periphery were not given bright prospects and not projects involving European waterways. It may be noted that the Swedish government decided to go ahead with the rapid railway project along the coast of the Gulf of Bothnia a short time after the completion of the survey.

The impression is that the respondents were well-informed about the potential infrastructure projects. Many of them will have had personal experience of the European transport system through business and tourist travel. This may have influenced their conception of the most important bottlenecks, additional to the professional knowledge that they might have or the information they would have from courses and conferences.

Information Technology and Communications

The use of information technology and telecommunications as a substitute for travel is an alternative which has been there throughout history. The industrial revolution saw the emergence of the telephone and the telegraph. We have witnessed a dramatic change in the capacity to send and receive information electronically to our work-places and homes during the last twenty years. In the future, the spatial consequences of the information revolution are potentially enormous, with a global spread of information services, international telecommunications systems, tele-shopping, a society based on geographically distributed small-scale production and consumption, the virtual city, and the global village.

The different transport means are influenced in different ways by the introduction of information technology. The number of transports in a given time period can be affected via changes in the volume transported and through the differentiation of each transport into specialised units. The distribution of transports over the day and the week can be affected both for travel and freight transport. Information technology can exert an influence on the distances commodities and persons are transported and on the selection of means of transportation to be employed. There will be a potential influence on traffic safety and on the ability to adhere to predetermined time-schedules (see also Lind, 1997 and Höjer, 1997). It is by no means clear what will be the direction and magnitude of impacts on information technology on these fundamental components of the transport system (see also Capello, 1994).

Impacts embedded in forecasting models will often beg the question in impact analyses in that the model estimation often employs a predetermined view on the causal relationships. In a situation of rapid technological change it will neither be possible not advisable from a decision-making point of view to use historical data to address these questions. The current situation in policy analysis seems to be that a large amount of emphasis is placed on analysing the existing transport systems, where we have relatively little uncertainty about the technological options. At the same time the lack of stable information about the emerging information technologies is often put forward as a reason for not studying their societal impacts. During the industrial revolution there was also a period when the new developments were seen in the context of the old farming society. Over time this perspective became more and more irrelevant. The situation is largely similar now with regard to the division of attention between transport and communications in research and policy. It is therefore reasonable to assume that the experts will have less long-term personal experience to use when making their forecast judgements.

Table 9.6 contains the reactions of the experts to questions about the effect of an introduction of information technology on some central indicators of transport system performance. The table contains the share of respondents who have stated that they are in agreement with a selection of statements concerning the anticipated effects of the introduction of information technology in society at large. The table contains information both for freight and person travel.

An analysis for each of the transport modes indicates that there are differences among types. In freight the majority of positive agreement statements are made for just-in-time and traffic safety. Respondents thus believe that information technology will, in particular, make freight more reliable and safe. The same response pattern holds for distribution traffic although there is also a fair mention of speed and increase in shipment numbers. The impression is that the respondents have thought of increased flexibility.

Information technology will, ceteris paribus, make commuting distances longer, more reliable as regards actual time spent in transport, and safer. It will also reduce their number. Also, the faster means of transport will gain. Information technology will, in particular, boost the number of recreational trips and enhance their safety. They are also forecasted to spread over time by a large group of experts. Finally, traffic safety is regarded by a large share of the respondents to be a positive consequence for shopping trips. They also feel that these trips will reduce in number and be more concentrated in time.

Table 9.6   Share of respondents in agreement with six statements about the effect of information technology on transport patterns up to 2010 (percent)

	Freight	Distribution	Business Trips	Commuting Trips	Recreation Trips	Shopping Trips
Transports increase in number	35	46	34	11	50	16
Transports concentrate in time	34	41	29	24	12	23
Transport distances increase	48	32	53	50	41	27
Transports just in time	77	76	54	51	38	35
Fast means of transport gain	46	49	60	45	33	35
Traffic safety increases	70	65	52	54	53	47

As seen from the analysis of Table 9.6 above, telecommunications will, according to the respondents, continue to influence our daily life in a more and more profound way during the next decades. It is important for a futures study on transport, communications and long-term environmental sustainability to reflect on the personal relationship to the technologies which are being introduced, accommodating the demand from pioneering groups among the youth, and among urban dwellers with modern life-styles. Table 9.7 provides a summary of the results of some personal questions about the future use of telecommunications and information technology.

The respondents to the questionnaire can all be characterised as high-education people with urban life-styles with a generally positive attitude towards cultural innovation. The responses of the students differ in some respects from the average in this question. Students seem to be most prone to use teleconferences, engage in telecommuting, and use electronic banking. They do not intend to order food electronically to the same extent as the other groups but are, on average, when it comes to expressing the usefulness of face-to-face contacts. More students than other respondents state that they will work with information-technology development.

Table 9.7   Share of respondents in agreement with six statements about the impact of information technology on personal behaviour up to 2010 (percent)

Share of yes to statements about IT to consider to 2010	All	Students	Women
I will use teleconferences	87	93	91
I will engage in telecommuting	74	80	82
I will use electronic banking	94	100	97
I will order foodstuff electronically	37	30	44
I will substitute face-to-face contacts	41	38	41
I will work with IT-development	29	43	32

The observation might be made that even though the respondents have adopted a positive attitude towards the new technologies, the likely outcome would seem to be that they are underestimating the penetration. The chances are that there will be stronger pressure from the supply side to introduce electronic systems for cost-saving reasons. The development is likely to continue to be technology-driven for some time yet.

Environmental Conditions

Carbon dioxide is emitted from mobile road traffic vehicles, and other transport vehicles, and is spread over long distances which makes it difficult to identify sources. Nitric oxides are emitted in the same way from transport vehicles in use. The nitrogen is spread over long distances which makes it difficult to identify the sources in a distinct way. Introducing catalytic converters has proved to be an efficient way of achieving considerable reductions in the emissions containing nitrogen. There are a range of other substances, such as ground-level ozone, particles, soot, rubber, and chemical compounds emitted to air during the operation of the transport system. Furthermore, transport generates noise pollution and represents a visual externality. The transport system restricts alternative land-uses for long periods of time and cuts off natural environments through its network character.

The survey has contained a number of questions aimed at identifying the experts' knowledge about the relationships between transport and the environment. They have also been asked to make forecasts of the future development of the environmental burden from transport. Unlike in the earlier sections the forecasts are here to be seen as judgements concerning the likelihood that the environmental goals formulated at the national level will be attained in the long run. In particular, two goals have been put under scrutiny in the investigation, the carbon dioxide goal and the nitric oxides goal.

The national goal for carbon dioxide from mobile sources is that it is first to stabilise at the current level and then to recede. A reduction of 10 percent in comparison with the level of emissions in 1993 has been put forward. For the nitric oxides the goal is considerably stricter. The emissions should be at least halved within the medium-term. The goal for 2010 is that the level should be 75 percent less than in 1993. We will illustrate the forecasting and goal fulfilment dilemma by presenting the analysis for the carbon dioxide goal. The arguments will be similar for the nitric oxides case.

Figure 9.12 provides a picture of the results of the survey when respondents were asked to make a direct forecast of the level of carbon dioxide emissions from mobile sources in Sweden in 2010. The figure shows that the respondents have on average forecast a slight increase in the emissions compared to the situation in1993. The 10 percent reduction goal is within the lower standard deviation limit but the mean judgement of the experts is that the goal will not be fulfilled. In fact, relatively few persons in the survey made the forecast that the government would be successful in its activity to reduce the emission so that the goal would be fulfilled. The implementation of such a policy will demand the participation of national government agencies, municipalities, and other public actors. It will also require that households change their behaviour with regard to transport, and that Swedish industry will see it in their long-term interest to work with the government in fulfilling the political obligation.

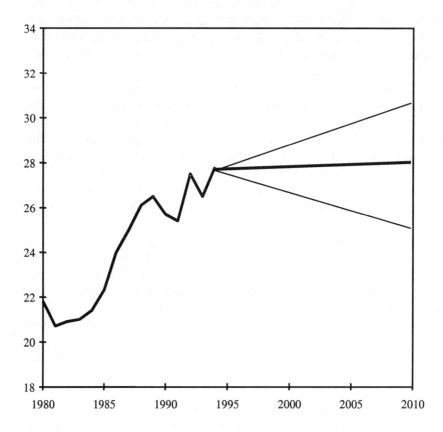

Figure 9.12   Generation of carbon dioxide from mobile sources in Sweden 1980-93 (million tons per year) and forecast including standard deviation to 2010

In general, however, the participants in the survey associated little value with the explicitly given information about the government commitment. The same pattern occurred, but even more clearly, for the forecast of emissions of nitric oxides. Very few respondents were prepared to let their forecasts come down to 25 percent of the current level. Emissions have stayed at that high level during the last decade. Even though the experts had the information, the result again shows the considerable degree of conservatism, or cautiousness, that the experts have employed when they participated in the study. Of course, it may be that the ex ante goal fulfilment forecasts that the respondents made will ex post turn out to be good estimates of the ultimate policy achievement. Evidently, such a development is not seen by the respondents as being exclusively influenced by national environmental goals.

The transport means have different technical properties which leads to different profiles as regards their environmental impact. Not only do the technical properties differ but also the volume carried by the different means involved and the time profiles of their use. For petrol-driven vehicles, for instance, cold starts are environmentally detrimental. The heavy trucks cause proportionally more environmental damage than small vehicles.

Five environmental threats associated with transport are listed in Table 9.8, carbon dioxide, ozone, nitric oxides, particles, and noise pollution. The idea of the question is to have the experts assess the relative importance of a set of environmental policies in the transport sector to amend these problems. The answers are given in terms of the number of respondents who regard the policy in question as important for the handling of the environmental problem.

Table 9.8   **Assessment of relative importance of different environmental policies with regard to transport and communications up to 2010. Share of respondents who regard the policy as important for the handling of the corresponding environmental problem (percent)**

Relative importance of environmental policies	CO_2	O_3	NO_x	Particles	Noise
New fuels	82	69	70	83	13
New motors and vehicle design	77	64	75	81	78
Fewer new roads	31	25	27	23	30
Maintenance of roads & streets	26	19	22	23	54
Increase real costs of car-drive	75	63	65	60	55
Change youth attitude to mobility	40	34	33	31	31
Change youth attitude to car-drive	52	42	44	40	41
Extend telecommunications nets	33	28	28	27	26

The table can be interpreted in both a horizontal and a vertical mode. The first mode of analysis addresses the question whether the policy is anticipated to have a strong impact on the environmental problem in question. The second mode compares the ability of different policies to solve the environmental problem at hand. We will use the second entry point into the analysis here.

The majority of respondents regard new technology, including fuels, as the ultimate solution to the carbon dioxide problem. They also promote the use of economic instruments to reduce the amount of car use. The same pattern holds for the problems associated with ozone, nitric oxides, and particles so that the experts, in the main, see relatively little conflict between the first four areas. The rank order between new fuels and new motor technologies is different for nitric oxides than for the other two. The respondents to a lesser degree believe that the particles problem can be reduced by increases in the real cost of car-driving. For the noise pollution problem the experts recommend new motors and vehicle designs as well as increased car-driving costs and enhanced road and street maintenance.

On average, the respondents have not seen the promotion of alternatives to car-driving as a high-priority alternative. It is as if the cognitive pattern among the respondents is that letting policies operate via communications rather than transport will not get to the transport and environment goal. However, such a view will tend to underestimate the potential damage to the environmental cause that may result if that highly expansive technology area is left out of the discussion of protecting the environment.

Actions to environmentally adjust the transport system can lead to consequences for the household choice of dwelling and work-place and their selection of means of transportation (see also Gordon and Richardson, 1994 and Hall *et al.*, 1994). Some of these consequences can strengthen the effect of the policies but others can counteract them. In some cases the intention behind a policy is that it should affect environmental goal fulfilment via a behavioural change, for instance, as regards the choice of means of transportation to go to work. There is often a difficult problem in identifying unwanted side-effects of a policy. Some of these effects will be created by actors who wish to protect themselves from the impact of the policy. Other consequences will be unwanted because they hit actors who have little possibility of taking compensatory measures. There is a balance to be struck between general and selective policies.

Table 9.9 shows the anticipated effects of the policies presented in Table 9.8 with regard to typical household choices. Are the respondents in agreement with the observation that the policy will primarily act through choices in the long-, medium- and short-term, respectively?

Table 9.9: Assessment of relative importance of different environmental policies with regard to transport and communications up to 2010. Share of respondents who foresee the main effect of the policy occurring in the respective decision field (percent)

Relative importance of environmental policies	Dwelling choice	Commute choice	Modal choice
New fuels	11	22	43
New motors and vehicle design	7	24	43
Fewer new roads	51	59	55
Maintenance of roads & streets	29	42	43
Increase real costs of car-drive	84	85	92
Change youth attitude to mobility	39	37	36
Change youth attitude to car-drive	39	40	59
Extend telecommunications nets	57	57	85

The common knowledge among the experts is that new fuels and new vehicle technologies will affect mainly modal choice. A reduction in road construction is likely to have an even and quite substantial impact across the long-, medium- and short-term decisions, respectively, whereas a maintenance strategy for roads and streets will be less inclined to lead to relocation impacts. The highest level of consensus is achieved for the effects of increases in real costs of car-drive affecting modal choice. A high reading for modal choice effects is also attained for the telecommunications policy. The generally high values for the importance of the latter policy across the time spans is an indication that the respondents feel that effects will become diluted if that policy would materialise. This is in agreement with the observations made in conjunction with the earlier table.

The attitude policies in the table are intended to represent a whole range of activities to influence the value schemes of youth as regards mobility and car-use. The respondents have not given these the potential impact gauge that they would seem to deserve in the long run. In fact, they have associated the highest impact reading with the shortest-term individual choice process.

Economic instruments have been put forward as necessary and efficient to reach goals concerning the carbon dioxide emissions (see also

Button, 1994). There is a specially constructed carbon dioxide tax in Sweden. There have been suggestions to raise the petrol tax by considerable amounts. The economic instruments are supposed to work through giving households and firms the incentive to substitute for transport modes which are especially damaging to the environment. At the same time, households and firms which are especially dependent on transport can be unduly affected by the instruments if their substitution possibilities are smaller than anticipated when the policy was designed and they can only change their behaviour in the long-term. The result might be a more uneven distribution of income and welfare. It might also affect Sweden's competitive edge if the transport-intensive industries are at the same time the main export earners.

In this perspective, the economic instruments will tend to encourage relocation of firms and raise claims for compensation payments, thus, decreasing the benefit-to-cost ratio of that particular public-spending opportunity. They might be regarded as a punishment for Swedes and Swedish industry in a situation where other countries would not follow along. In principle, then, this would be an example of how Sweden would select the environmental alternative in transport and communications policy at the same time that Europe as a whole would go for the market alternative.

The question posed in the survey was which household groups, and which industries, the respondents considered to be most vulnerable to substantial petrol price increases. Table 9.10 summarises the results.

The perception among the group of respondents is that rural households, and car-owners in general, would receive the largest negative impacts from petrol price increases. Metropolitan households receive a much lower score than the others. This is, in a way, surprising as a result, since car-use is at least as typical of an efficiently functioning urban area as it is necessary to uphold a rural life-style. The urban residents might have alternatives but petrol price increases will certainly have important distributional consequences within the metropolitan areas as well.

The respondents associate the largest impact from petrol price increases with the transport-intensive manufacturing industries, and with the transport services sector itself. The impact assessments for the service sectors is remarkably low. It is as if the respondents have not connected, for instance, consulting with high mobility.

At the same time, the largest increases in transport task has come, and will come, from person movement in the future. The cognitive pattern seems to be that goods movements are more crucial to the economy than movement of persons. The conclusion among the experts at the same time is quite clear in its pointing out the goods-producing sectors as the main impact receivers.

Table 9.10 Relative needs of adjustment to 2010 to large petrol price increases among household groups and industrial sectors. Share of respondents who have stated the corresponding impacts to be important (percent)

Relative needs of adjustment to large petrol price increase	Share of Responses (percent)
Rural households	94
Metropolitan households	13
Car-owning households	83
Two wage-earner households	60
Low-income households	70
Forest industry	79
Iron and steel industry	60
Vehicle industry	85
Wholesale trade	63
Retail trade	57
Transport services	87
Telecommunications	13
Consulting	14
Education and research	8

Some Conclusions for Urban Development

The chapter has addressed the question of the role of transport and communications in the sustainable network society. Since the post-industrial society has been developing during the last 20 years it should be safe to say that we have by now already emerged into a new global regime. This regime bears the typical characteristics of a multi-layer network society where node and network operators develop their schemes of maintaining supremacy over economic and social functions across networks and within nodes. The political function is historically connected to the node function and the territory. It will presumably remain with this connection. The operation range of the network operators may vary from the local to the global. It is actually not the globalisation which is the most important aspect of the emerging society. It is the increasing speed, and the enhanced reliability, of fast connections over long distances.

There was a fundamental break in the economic development in the 1970s when the multinational companies decided to outsource their manufacturing from the high-demand regions in western Europe, North America and Japan. This has implied a new and more complex network of international interdependencies. The new strategy was made possible by the emergence of control and monitoring systems which enabled the corporate sector to become global at the strategic level. As a consequence, commodity production became more or less footloose at the global level. This, in turn, spurred the development of telecommunications and information technology.

The consequences of this development are many and far-reaching. Some of the most important ones relate to the emergence of a global urban system. Urban areas traditionally used to be seen as top-hierarchy members of a national settlement system. Now the most logical way of seeing them is as members of a network-based global system of central places.

Some infrastructure systems are more important in determining the long-term characteristics of this emerging urban system than others. In transport the obvious candidate is the combined airline and airport system. Continued large changes are going to take place in this system during the coming years. They are connected with the development in the most important network infrastructure systems of all, the regional, national and international telecommunications systems. It is important to understand that changes are occurring at all three geographical levels of these systems concurrently. The interconnectedness of them makes it necessary not to separate the perspectives but to keep them together to understand how they work. This is basically the essence of the network aspect of the so-called global village concept.

The most important nodal infrastructures for the future will be the education, research, and innovation ones. They can develop in a private mode as with many of the classical infrastructure systems of the industrial revolution as the telephone, the car, or even the train. There is also room for collective action at the regional, national and international level to construct knowledge-creation institutions which adhere to the network rather than the node paradigm. There is also a role for an active political strategy in this area which will need a new structure at the democratic base.

The current scenario study of the sustainable network society should be seen in the light of the theoretical views expressed above. The ambition of the study is to address the question of the emerging conflict between mobility and environment from a somewhat different way than in other studies. By mustering up a conflict between the industrial way of production and consumption, and an environmentally sustainable one, and between an industrial and environmental way of thinking, there is a risk that the solutions will be sought in obsolete policy areas. The challenge is not to carefully calculate the emission volumes of current transport vehicles, but to attempt to understand the driving forces of future mobility. To spend all effort in the traditional dimension is fundamentally wasteful in a context of limited public resources for research and development.

The paradigms of viewing and analysing societal changes are as slowly changing as people's values themselves change. The current field of transport, communications and the environment is no exception. The ultimate objective of the scenario study has been to point to the difficulties in forecasting in a context where perspectives may need to be more fundamentally changed.

The experts are surprisingly conservative in their answers. There are not so large differences between the different groups of respondents which implies that they have been exposed to the same body of knowledge in their field. The experts are influenced by their mental maps of Sweden, Europe, and the world when they make their considerations. Ignorance about the development prospects of a region or about the discussion around an investment project leads to a low priority of this factor. The practitioners are more reluctant than the other groups to express radical views or make forecasts which deviate from the mean. The opposite is true for the students where there are persons who have made more drastic forecasts.

The level of certainty expressed by the experts varies considerably. These uncertainty expressions can be used to adjust forecasts according to the stated knowledge value of the information given by the expert. Trend breaks generally are given lower certainty values than trend continuations. The respondents with a long professional experience seem to be more reluctant than others to adopt novel perspectives. They provide the body of conservative stability also when it comes to perceptions of directions of future change.

The views of the experts do not seem to be strongly dependent on their personal characteristics. This is illustrated by the fact that there is a rather high degree of correspondence between answers to different questions from one person. There seems to be support for the view that there is an experience-based knowledge in the form of mental models. Even though the students are new to the field they are often not much more radical in their answers to the questions posed than the other respondents. One reason for this may, of course, be that the survey was designed in such a way that creativity in these respects was not promoted. The other explanation is that the education system's propensity to give priority to the established body of knowledge does not promote lateral thinking to the extent warranted.

The experts in the study are somewhat sceptical of the role of the urban areas as cores of the sustainable network society. Instead, they have a tendency to promote response alternatives which are typical for decentralised systems and smaller regions. It may be argued that this is simply a reflection of the cultural attitude of a selection of members of the Swedish population rather than a result which would be portable to other expert communities. This can be tested by performing the study also in other regions.

PART III

URBAN

AND

ENVIRONMENTAL

AMENITY

10 Environmental and Urban Amenity in a Growing Mega-City—Tokyo as a Blend of East and West

MAMORU TANIGUCHI

Introduction

Mega-cities in developing Asian countries face very rapid urban growth that most Western cities have not experienced in the recent past. Most of these Eastern cities suffer from inadequate urban infrastructures, such as roads, sewerage and parks. For these cities to achieve better urban amenities for the coming 21st century and to fully benefit from the information economy, the strategy for infrastructure improvement is very important.

This study focuses on the urbanisation of Tokyo. It is assumed that Tokyo might be perceived as the city that acts as a bridge between Western and Eastern cities. This can easily be understood from Figure 10.1, which shows the growth patterns of several typical cities in East and West. Tokyo is located at the mid-point between Eastern and Western cities from an urbanisation point of view. As the total population of the metropolitan area (four prefectures) is now more than 30 million, Tokyo is also one of the most populated metropolitan areas in the world. It has, like other Eastern cities, also experienced rapid urban growth, but it is now almost saturated like Western cities. We should, of course, consider the individual character of each city, but Tokyo could be one of the most suitable cities from which to extrapolate an evaluation of rapid urban growth. The discussion in this paper is built on three different analyses.

Firstly, this study focuses on the urbanisation and infrastructure improvement process in Tokyo. The term *gap,* the incompatibility between urban growth and infrastructure improvement, is defined and calculated in each region of the metropolitan area. By comparing the gap in each region, effects of rapid urban growth and the results of planned infrastructure improvement are discussed. Secondly, the cost of rapid growth, namely urban sprawl, is estimated. Usually, sprawl areas have large *gaps*. Infrastructure improvement to minimise these gaps in sprawl areas seems to cost too much compared to the same improvements undertaken before such rapid growth. The effectiveness of action in the early stages of the urbanisation process is discussed in this section. Thirdly, the meaning of *infrastructure improvement* in the age of the information society is discussed. Tsukuba Science City, in the north-east region of the Tokyo metropolitan area, is the focus of this section (Figure 10.2). New investment is discussed, especially for the ways in which it might have changed people's perceptions of the metropolitan structure.

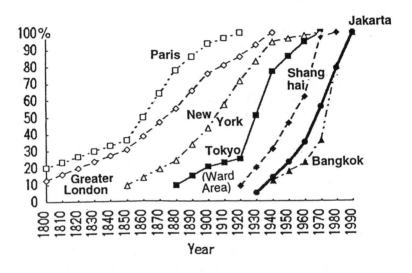

(100 percent: maximum population to date)

Figure 10.1   Population increase in eastern and western cities
Source :   Mitchell, 1995, Chandler, 1987

Growth Pattern of Tokyo and its Character

The population density of the Tokyo metropolitan area is relatively high compared to that of metropolitan areas in Western countries. The population density of the Tokyo Metropolitan Government (2,168 km²) is 5,430 persons/km². That of Greater Tokyo, a very large metropolitan area

(4 prefectures: 13,947 km^2), is 2,323 persons/km^2. Figure 10.3 shows the growth pattern of the Tokyo metropolitan area over the last 30 years. Tokyo expanded in accordance with its economic growth. Though Tokyo has expanded very quickly and densely, the well developed railway network has supported its expansion very well. From this point of view, as Newman and Kenworthy (1989) pointed out, annual gasoline consumption per capita in Tokyo is estimated to be very low in comparison to cities in Western countries.

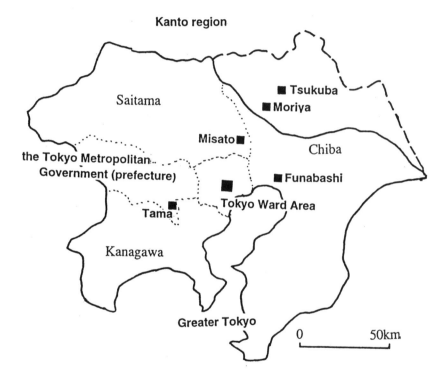

Figure 10.2   Definition of the Tokyo metropolitan area

On the other hand, the railway congestion rate in Tokyo is still infamously high. The number of railway passengers has increased about 3.2 times during the 30 years from 1955 to 1985. The improvement of railway capacity has, however, been executed at a much faster speed (3.9 times) than passenger increase.[1]   Consequently, the congestion rate has improved

---

[1]   In peak hour, most crowded section of each commuter rail.

gradually during those 30 years. Meanwhile, infrastructure improvement of amenities, such as roads, parks and sewerage, could not always keep up with the speed of urban growth.

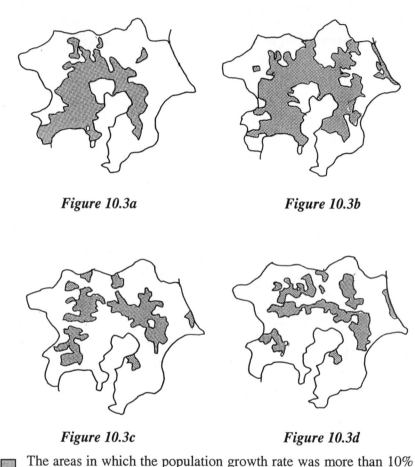

Figure 10.3a   *Figure 10.3b*

Figure 10.3c   *Figure 10.3d*

▨ The areas in which the population growth rate was more than 10% per 5 year period

Figure 10.3   Growth pattern of the Tokyo metropolitan area
**   *Figure   10.3a—1960-1965   10.3b—1970-1975***
**   *10.3c—1980-1985   10.3d—1990-1995***
Source: The City Planning Institute of Japan, 1992, National Census

Gap Between Urban Growth and Infrastructure Improvement

In this chapter, roads, parks and sewerage are recognised as three indispensable elements of the urban amenities infrastructure. In order to identify their service level in each region, the term *gap*, as the incompatibility between urban growth and infrastructure improvement, needs to be defined. To compare these elements with urban population growth, it is desirable to define *gap* on the basis of population scale (see Figure 10.4). The *gap* in each region is defined as the difference between population and *satisfied or serviced population* for each infrastructure element. The *satisfied population* is calculated from the *infrastructure level* in each region divided by the *long-range goal* as announced by the Ministry of Construction (Ministry of Construction, 1986). Data was collected for 115 municipalities around Tokyo from 1955 to 1990.

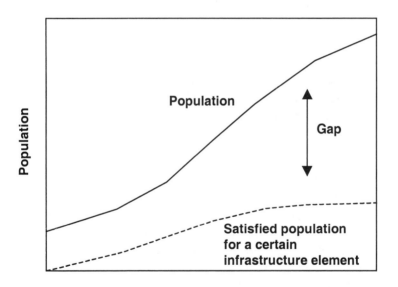

Figure 10.4 Definition of gap

The results from each municipality can be classified into several groups, and several typical patterns are shown in Figure 10.5 Misato (10.5) is a typical example of a rapid growth city. This city began to be urbanised from 1970 with an already insufficient infrastructure. After 1980, the speed of population growth became a little slower, but infrastructure improvement has not yet progressed. In the case of Funabashi (Figure 10.5), where the population has now risen to more than half a million, difficulties are faced in improving the infrastructure. In almost 30 years, its population has grown about three times, but the *satisfied population* remains at the same level as previously. These two cases, which show rapid growth without enough infrastructure improvement, are not faced with a one-time problem, but one that will continue into the future.

There are also some examples with much better conditions in the Tokyo metropolitan area. Tama (Figure 10.5) has been mainly planned and developed by the public corporation as a new town, and its gaps are relatively small compared to other cities, in spite of its fast growth. Tsukuba (Figure 10.5) which has been developed as a new science city, also shows evidence of good performance in infrastructure improvement. These planning-based new towns could evade the problem of urban sprawl caused by rapid urban growth.

Cost of Rapid Growth: Problem of Urban Sprawl

As sprawl areas are formed by rapid urbanisation, they usually have large gaps. Infrastructure improvement in sprawl areas to minimise these gaps becomes very difficult and is usually inefficient once the sprawl area has formed. In this part, the effect on cost reduction by executing pre-urbanisation infrastructure improvement before the outbreak of urban sprawl (namely, *sprawl cost*) is calculated.

In order to calculate sprawl costs, three types of urban conditions are assumed (as shown in Figure 10.6): (1) the *first condition* (before rapid urban growth); (2) the *present condition* (urban sprawl after rapid urban growth); and (3) the *improved condition* (planned urban development with matched infrastructure). The pre-urbanisation improvement cost for infrastructure, before the outbreak of urban sprawl, is calculated as the necessary expense to improve directly from the *first condition* to the *improved condition*. On the other hand, the post-urbanisation improvement cost of sprawl is calculated as the total cost between the cost from the *first condition* to the *present condition* and the necessary cost from the *present condition* to the *improved condition*.

The case study in this section is Moriya, located near to Tsukuba Science City, in the north-east part of the Tokyo metropolitan area. This is a typical sprawl area in an outer suburb, and infrastructure improvements

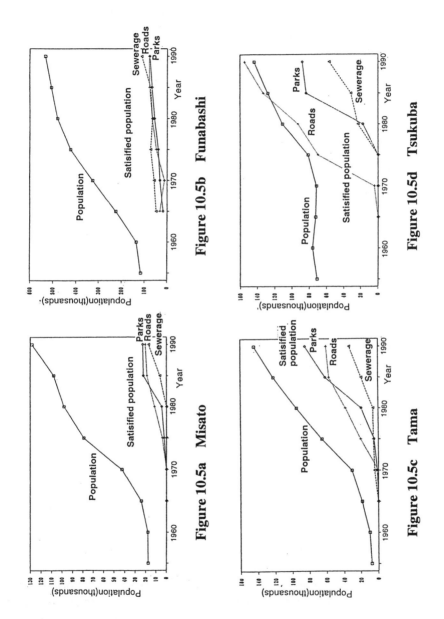

Figure 10.5   Results of gap calculations in several cities

Source: Taniguchi and Hori, 1996

under the *Land Readjustment Project* (387,000m²) are being executed now. It is assumed in this analysis that pre-improvement should have taken place in 1970 before rapid growth and that post-urbanisation improvement should have taken place in 1993. It is also assumed that the *first condition* is the urban situation at 1970, as estimated from an aerial photograph and other data. The *improved condition* is the plan shown in the *Land Readjustment Project*.

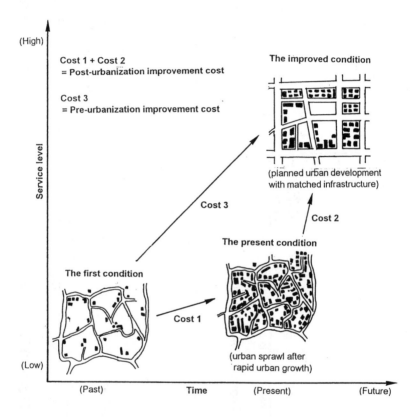

Figure 10.6   Assumption of urban conditions (scenario)

Cost is estimated in three parts (land purchase cost, compensation cost and construction cost) on each infrastructure element (roads, parks and sewerage). As shown in Table 10.1, the total post-urbanisation improvement cost is about five times more expensive than the total pre-urbanisation improvement cost. Among infrastructure costs, sprawl cost for roads is the most expensive. As the area has already become built up, compensation becomes the largest part of the cost. This shows how early actions are necessary in the process of urbanisation. Although not taken into consideration in this study, if the attendant increase in property tax was to be increased in the calculations, the income of local government could also increase with the pre-urbanisation improvement.

Table 10.1   Costs of sprawl (rate and difference)

	Land Purchase		Compensation Cost		Construction Cost		Total Cost	
Roads	3.6	(46.2)	8.8	(104.7)	3.5	(22.5)	5.3	(173.4)
Parks	2.5	(4.3)	4.9	(3.4)	4.0	(0.7)	3.1	(8.4)
Sewerage	3.0	(0.2)	1.0	(0.0)	5.7	(6.7)	5.5	(6.9)
Total	3.4	(50.7)	8.6	(108.1)	3.8	(29.9)	5.1	(188.7)

Rate : (post-urbanisation improvement cost)/(pre-urbanisation improvement cost) (Difference) : (post-urbanisation improvement cost)—(pre-urbanisation improvement cost) (million $: 1993 price)

Infrastructure for Amenities in the Age of the Information Society

As discussed in the previous section, some parts of the Tokyo metropolitan area could be provided with certain infrastructure amenities in spite of rapid urban growth. According to classical location theory, infrastructure improvements, such as highways and ports, could attract more heavy industries to the region. These have been big factors for change in regional structures. Now we have to ask questions, *How can infrastructure improvement of amenities, such as local roads, parks and sewerage affect a present regional structure?* In this age of the information society, *could an infrastructure for amenities become an important factor for regional competition in rapid growth metropolitan areas?* If so, how can we prove it? In order to answer this question, Tsukuba Science City, about 60 km north-east of Tokyo (on the fringe of the metropolitan area) is the focus of this chapter. The method used here to examine regional competition is not based on industrial location, but on people's perception of the region.

In September 1963, the Japanese Government, with two main objectives, decided to establish a new academic city in Tsukuba. One was to create a national centre for advanced research and higher education. The other was to relieve over-population in central Tokyo and to help balance development of the metropolitan area. The land, 2,700 ha, was developed for research and educational institutes, commercial facilities and housing. Development of the city has been carried out with the close cooperation of national, prefectural and local governments. The National Land Agency has played the role of overall project coordinator and the Housing and Urban Development Corporation has been responsible for the basic development, such as the master plan, land purchase and preparation. On the locational base, 47 government research institutions have already located, and it is becoming one of the most important cores of the information industry.

In order to investigate the people's perception of the region, the *land names* utilised by offices at all business sites are adopted as the indicator in this analysis. Telephone directories in each zone are the data source of these office names, and probabilities of selection for each land name are calculated. The most dominant name in each zone is considered as the most commonly perceived regional name in that zone. By using this method, the change of regional structure, on the perceptional level, could be traced.

The time frame of this analysis is from 1963 to 1994, and the area for analysis is the north-eastern part of the Tokyo metropolitan area around Tsukuba Science City. From the analysis, perception of regional structure in this area has completely changed during these 30 years because of infrastructure improvements in Tsukuba. Before the investment (1963), only a few zones (about 30,000 ha) were recognised as being the Tsukuba region (as a small local community). All other perceptional regions in this area were also small (from 15,000 to 40,000 ha) and not so different from each other in size. Following investment (1994), Tsukuba has become a very dominant region (about 150,000 ha). Many of the small perceptional regions in 1963 have since been subsumed into the Tsukuba region. Though we could not ignore non-infrastructure effects, such as the announcement effect by the media of Science City, it could be concluded that the relatively affluent infrastructures in Tsukuba could change people's perception of the metropolitan structure. On this point, the small, ancient community of Tsukuba, from a perceptional point of view, changed into one of the strong sub-regions of the Tokyo metropolitan area, from a perceptional point of view. Such a perceptional change is having a positive impact on the Tsukuba region. Private research institutes have accumulated one after another as Tsukuba comes to be accepted as the principal competitive region in their sphere of activities.

Conclusion

This analysis of the Tokyo metropolitan area shows how infrastructure improvement of amenities is important for rapidly growing cities, especially in the early stage of urbanisation. It is estimated that the post-urbanisation improvement cost of infrastructure for amenities is more than five times as expensive as that of pre-urbanisation improvement. Moreover, this estimation is based on the assumption that post-urbanisation improvement can be done immediately. In reality, the results show that it is very difficult to execute post-urbanisation improvement to decrease gaps if rapid urban growth has already occurred and urban sprawl has already formed. On the other hand, the results with respect to Tsukuba also clarify that infrastructure amenities have a very important role, not only in creating a better urban environment, but also in regional competition. It has been found that investment in Tsukuba Science City has changed people's perception of Tokyo's metropolitan structure, and that this is predicted to affect the locational behaviour of further companies/institutions in the information industry in the metropolitan area.

11 Cities and Air Pollution

PETER NEWTON and PETER MANINS

Some mornings in the back of the jeepney on her way to work near Cubao in Metro Manila, Maria Francisco can see a long way down the broad EDSA ringroad. But today is a common experience: she has a handkerchief clutched to her face to keep out the choking black fumes belching from the vehicle and hundreds like it as they jostle with careering buses and dilapidated rushing lorries. A dark grey cloud of diesel and petrol particles hangs over EDSA like a blanket for as far as she can see.

The same morning Mr Lee Gwan-ju sets out to work on foot from the Keukdong Apartment Complex in Kwangjung-dong, a suburb of another mega-city: Seoul. He lives in Apt. 17, on the 9th floor of Block 11 of the Complex. He hurries along the street choked with cars and buses to the subway entrance where a twenty minute journey will drop him close to his employer. The sky is, as usual, pale and lifeless due to a persistent haze of smog from the traffic and industry.

Cities may well be the engines of modern economies, central to the delivery of services that permit ongoing increases in gross domestic product (GDP). But with these increases generally there is found also to be a strong correlation with that other meaning of GDP—garbage, dust and pollution (gdp).

Air pollution knows no boundaries. Local activities not only lead to local problems, but also to national and international consequences lasting for hours to decades:

- industry, transport and other modern urban systems require energy. Consequent emissions of carbon monoxide, carbon dioxide and nitrogen oxides from fossil fuel combustion blanket the earth, trapping excess heat and leading to global warming, climate change, rising sea-levels, changes in vegetation and severe weather events;
- use of oil and coal fuels for this energy generation additionally leads to the emission of sulfur dioxide. Combined with copious emissions of fine particles, the resulting deadly miasmas in London in the 1950s shocked England into action to control air pollution. The same lessons had to be re-learnt in Japan in the 1970s and again in Korea in the 1980s. They have yet to be heeded in South Asia and China;
- but these oxides of sulfur and nitrogen emitted to the atmosphere have had a far wider and more insidious effect: acid rain. Acting over

277

decades, it has killed lakes and forests in north America and northern Europe hundreds and thousands of kilometres from the major emission centres in eastern USA and in Central Europe. Energy development plans in southern China in particular, have yet to come to grips with the expected deleterious consequences of acid deposition;

- before they return to the surface as acid rain, the sulfur emissions are transformed into fine particles that scatter and reflect light very effectively. It is believed that these sulfate particles are a major cause of *reducing* global warming in the northern hemisphere;
- although their consumption is now essentially banned worldwide (in developing countries by 2005), chlorofluorocarbons have been the mainstay of foam blowing, refrigeration and fire fighting systems. The past release of these chemicals continues to cause destruction of the ozone layer each Spring far above the surface. Parts of the earth are consequently unprotected from strong ultra-violet radiation for several months each year until mixing restores the ozone distribution; and
- in 1997 the weather event El Niño brought drought, famine, and heavy pollution from fires in Indonesia throughout the countries of South East Asia. Levels of fine particles in the air in cities such as Kuala Lumpur and Singapore on occasion reached frightening levels: 10 or more times as high as dangerous levels defined by the World Health Organization.

Sources of Air Pollutants

As an example of the case for all major developed cities of the world, Table 11.1 shows that in Sydney a high percentage of emissions for most pollutants is due to motor vehicles. Most of the emissions of nitrogen oxides (NOx) and of volatile organic compounds (VOCs) arise from motor vehicle sources. These two pollutants generate secondary pollutants such as ozone and other smog products.

Although about one-third of all particle emissions in Sydney are reported to be due to vehicles, the influence of road traffic is far more marked for the fine particles. In 1990 in Greater London, for example, it is estimated that 86 percent of emissions of particles less than $10\,\mu m$ in diameter (important for human health effects) arose from this source (QUARG, 1993).

Table 11.1 Percentage of air pollutant emissions due to different sources in Sydney

Pollutant	Vehicles	Industry	Domestic, Commercial
NOx	82	13	5
VOCs	49	10	41
Particles	31	36	33
CO	91	2	7
SO$_2$	14	64	22

Source: SOE, 1996

In some countries the issue of transboundary influx of polluted air is frequently a major confounding issue: in Germany, for instance, it is estimated that approximately 50 percent of the air pollution burden is due to cross-border influx (BMU, 1996a). And acid rain and bushfire smoke reaches out to countries far away.

There can be large differences in relative importance of emissions sources between cities of developed and developing countries, depending on the level of motorisation and the level, density and type of industry present:

- vehicles continue to be the most significant contributor to air pollution in most newly industrialising countries, and that contribution is growing rapidly, with fleet sizes doubling every seven years. In South Korea vehicle numbers have grown from 3.4 million to over 10 million since 1987, and half of all vehicles are in the Seoul area (Manins, 1992b). There, most vehicles are relatively young and hence 'clean' compared to a country such as Australia where the average vehicle age is over 12 years;
- cities in Latin America tend to have higher vehicle densities than those in other developing regions. However, in cities in Africa and in cities located in cooler regions dependent on coal or biomass fuels for space heating and other domestic purposes, emissions from vehicles are relatively less important;
- highly polluting diesel vehicles and two-stroke motorcycles are common in many of the less developed countries (45 percent of vehicles are diesel in South Korea compared with 7.4 percent in Australia; two-stroke motorcycles are rampant in Taiwan, as are auto-rickshaws in India—they are both rare in Australia);

- sulfur dioxide pollution due to use of poor quality coals and cheap oils is a feature of pollution emissions due to energy production in cities such as Manila. Only in the more affluent newly industrialising countries has there been a shift to use of cleaner natural gas; and
- cities such as Jakarta and Calcutta have very large emissions of smoke from indiscriminate burning and poorly controlled vehicles, but the authorities are in denial, not even acknowledging that there is pollution and that it is due to urban and industrial activity.

Air Pollution

Emissions of air pollutants lead to the production of smogs that destroy sensitive tissues (in people, animals and plants), the formation of inhalable carcinogenic particles, reduced lung function, and are responsible for many untimely deaths each year. Pollution degrades building materials such as rubbers and stonework, and reduces the visual amenity of scenic vistas. Air quality comparisons for selected global cities are shown in Figure 11.1. Although annual average total suspended particulate matter (TSP) is only a crude indicator of air quality, it is notable that over the past decade there has been some improvement in Sydney. Overall, the risk of detriment from air pollution in Australia's largest cities is probably similar to that in New York or Tokyo (Manins, 1992a).

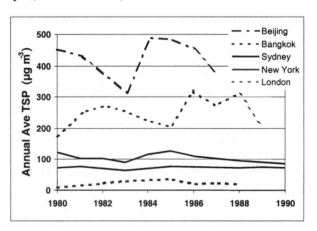

Figure 11.1   Annual average TSP concentrations in selected international cities

Source: SOE, 1996

A finer measure of air quality for cities is the number of days on which ozone levels exceed recommended levels. In 1991, residents of Mexico City were exposed to 1400 hours of high ozone, compared with the World Health Organization guideline of one hour. In Sydney there were four such occasions that year. Some American cities experienced: five days, Atlanta; 16 days, Chicago; 135 days, Los Angeles; 29 days, New York; two days San Francisco (Ahmet and van Dijk, 1995).

Figure 11.2 shows the dramatic success since the 1960s achieved in London in reducing fine particles and sulfur dioxide in the air. Similar successes have been achieved in other cities such as Los Angeles, Tokyo and, to a lesser extent, Moscow (UNEP/WHO, 1992).

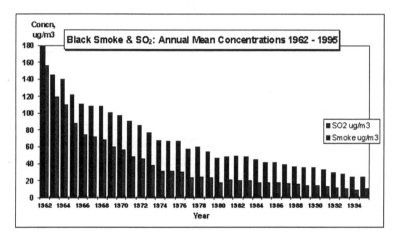

Figure 11.2   Measured mean black smoke and sulfur dioxide levels in London air

Source: AEA, 1996

The contrast with the worsening situation in many Asian cities except in Japan and South Korea (where there have since been major improvements) is all too stark. A measure of the problem is the number of times each year that World Health Organization air pollution guidelines are exceeded. Table 11.2, from ADB (1991), summarises past annual air quality in some Asian cities from data from the UNEP/WHO Global Environmental Management Systems project.

Table 11.2   Exceedances per year to 1990 of WHO guideline values for sulfur dioxide and airborne particle concentration in selected Asian cities

	SO₂ –Days above recommended level		TSP –Days above recommended level	
	Ave.	Max.	Ave.	Max.
Shanghai	16	32	133	277
Shenyang	146	236	219	347
Hong Kong	15	74	...	...
Calcutta	25	85	268	330
Manila	24	60	14	225
Bangkok	0	0	97	209
Seoul	87	121	...	...

Business as Usual

A striking difference in urban environmental quality between developed and less developed countries is the trend in premature urban deaths due to atmospheric concentrations of fine (PM10) particles. An interpretation of what continues to be a controversial relationship is shown in Figure 11.3 from a presentation by World Bank (1996).

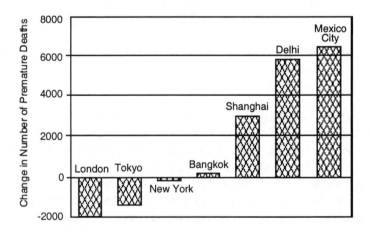

Figure 11.3   Change in number of premature deaths caused by change in concentration of PM10 (1980-1990)

Recently the Asian Development Bank released an assessment of the state of the environment in Asia (ADB, 1997). It points to dismal progress over the last ten years and increasing threats to human health in Asia's cities.

> Asia's environment has become so polluted and degraded that it poses a threat not just to the quality of life of its people, but also to its economic prospects. Of the world's 15 most polluted cities, 13 are in Asia, as are the most populous countries.
>
> Despite rapid and steady growth in income, at least one in three Asians still has no access to safe drinking water, and at least one in two has no access to sanitation. The costs of this neglect of the environment are massive. Children that ingest lead lose precious IQ points. They and their parents also suffer from chronic respiratory conditions and other ailments. Unsanitary living conditions and polluted water cause a variety of other gruesome conditions.

The report says that Asia's environmental crisis is in large part the result of failed policies and neglect. Those countries where incomes have lagged have environmental records that are just as bad as those where incomes have grown quickly. As in eastern Europe, rising incomes seem eventually to herald an improvement as growing popular demand for a better environment forces a favourable policy shift. South Korea is a notable example of this. It is entirely possible that Asia may become even dirtier, less forested, and less ecologically diverse in the future. The prospect of continued urbanisation poses yet further problems. The share of Asia's population living in urban areas will rise from 35 percent in 1995 (see Figure 11.4) to around 55 percent in 2025. While urban life will offer people greater opportunities and will probably mean less pervasive poverty than in rural areas, Asia's particular style of urbanisation—toward mega-cities rather than mid-sized cities (13 of the world's 20 biggest cities are in Asia) is likely to further exacerbate environmental and social stresses.

The ADB characterised much current environmental policy as 'misguided and badly implemented' and 'overly ambitious and inflexible'. Even before the economic collapse in several Asian countries in late 1997, it predicted dire consequences with global implications (e.g. air emissions from Asia will grow by up to 10 times by 2030) if better environmental management is not employed.

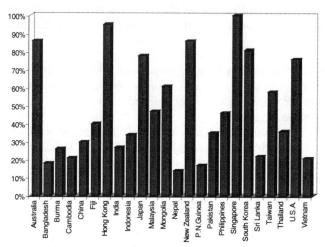

Figure 11.4   Percentage of populations in urban areas of selected countries
Source: AsiaWeek, 1997

A Better Future

Does this have to be the common experience? No.

Some governments have shown enlightened development policies, recognising the interconnectedness with interlinking environmental problems. For example, western Germany has broken the nexus between growth in GDP and the other gdp, as shown in Figure 11.5. But given the huge effort that Germany has made (much of which has had to be repeated in eastern Germany), Figure 11.5 also illustrates the difficulty that modern States face. It is hard to *reduce* energy consumption (as measured by CO_2 and NO_x emissions) as is essential for mitigation of the enhanced greenhouse induced climate change.

Other developed mature cities also have had some successes. In recent years some urban pollution levels (particularly of airborne lead, sulfur dioxide, and particles—see e.g., Figure 11.2) have decreased in many cities, probably due to better emissions management. However, increases in vehicle ownership, distance travelled each year, and the change in mix towards diesel from other fuel-type vehicles, leads to the expectation that gross urban pollution emissions and air quality levels may soon rise in developed countries unless further interventions occur. Major innovation and restructuring of transport, service delivery, and commercial activities will be required.

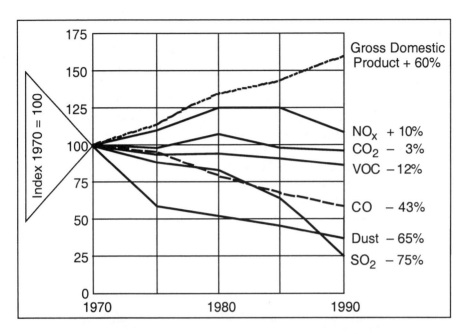

Figure 11.5   Decoupling increasing GDP and air pollution in Germany
Source: BMU, 1996b

Alternatives

Do we just accept that the growth in pollution and energy consumption is inevitable and inexorable in the long term? Or do we recognise that there are alternatives? Alternatives such as radically cleaner vehicles ('zero emission vehicles' and 'hypercars', see, for example, Manins, 1997) or change in the 'shape' or structure of our cities (Newton, 1997a, b). With changes in urban form and infrastructure it is possible to reduce congestion by reducing the need for transport in the first place.

Debate concerning what constitutes desirable urban form continues to stimulate widespread academic interest (viz, in the United States—Gordon and Richardson, 1997; Canada—Bourne, 1996, the UK—Breheney, 1996; and Australia—Troy, 1996; Newman *et al.*, 1992). This is as it should be, given the environmental, equity and efficiency implications associated with different archetypal city forms—the most prominent of which are illustrated in Figure 11.6. These may be described as follows (after: Pressman, 1985; Minnery, 1992; Newton, 1997a)

- *Business As Usual*—extrapolation of current patterns into the future;
- *Compact City*—increased population and density of an inner group of suburbs;
- *Edge City*—encourage increased population, housing densities and employment at selected nodes within the city; increased investment in orbital freeways linking the edge cities;
- *Corridor City*—a focusing of growth along linear corridors emanating from the CBD and supported by upgraded public transit infrastructure;
- *Fringe City*—where additional growth is accommodated predominantly on the fringe of the city; and
- *Ultra City*—where additional growth is accommodated primarily in provincial cities within 100 km of the principal (capital) city and linked by high speed rail transport.

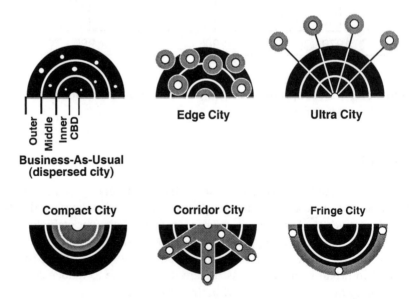

Figure 11.6   Archetypal urban systems

Which of these urban forms is most desirable, from an environmental perspective? All cities, irrespective of their geographic location, can be re-shaped to generate greater liveability.

Research undertaken specifically for the recently completed Inquiry into Urban Air Quality in Australian Cities (Newton, 1997a) attempted to explore, for the first time, the nexus between urban form and three key dimensions of the environment, namely: ambient air quality (for six criteria pollutants—SO_2, NO_x, particles, ozone, lead and CO), greenhouse gas emissions, and transport energy use.

The research employed integrated landuse-transport-emissions (LUTE) modelling to appraise the 'performance' of Melbourne in the year 2011 (from an environmental perspective) in the context of contrasting urban development scenarios.

The Environmental Performance Appraisal Model

Since urban development and urban form can be characterised by changes in land use, this inquiry used the TOPAZ 2000 integrated land use–transport model as the tool for evaluating the impact on air quality of different urban growth scenarios (see Figure 11.7).

Under the land use component, a region is divided into zones, with the list of land uses or activities specified. A scenario is then defined by specifying the population engaged in each activity within each zone, for a given time period. For each land use scenario, the area-based emissions are obtained by multiplying the activity population with the corresponding per capita emission factor. Point-based emissions are then added from sources that fall within the zone. Unfortunately, biogenic emissions could not be considered due to unavailability of data. Emissions of volatile organic compounds (VOCs), nitrous oxides (NO_x), carbon monoxide (CO), sulfur dioxide (SO_2) and fine particles with effective diameters of 10 microns or less (PM_{10}) were modelled.

Link emissions are obtained by applying a transportation gravity model to the land use component. The gravity model generates and distributes trips between each pair of zones, depending on the trip generation and travel impedance properties of each pair of activities. The trips are then loaded into a road network to produce traffic flow. The level of congestion on each link determines the amount of emission produced for that link. The aggregation of zone and link emissions onto grids then follows.

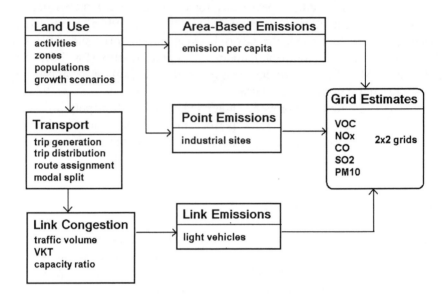

Figure 11.7   Integrated landuse-transport-emissions model

Point emissions are obtained from data on stack sources that fall within a grid. A zone's area-based emissions are divided equally among grids that fall within the zone. Link emissions are calculated based on the proportion of each link that falls within the grid. The grid emissions are then passed on to a prognostic three-dimensional photochemical airshed model for dispersion analysis (see Figure 11.8).

The example region used for this study was the Melbourne metropolitan area. The region was divided into 26 zones, as used in a 1991 national study of *Journey to Work* (Gipps *et al.*, 1997). These zones, shown in Figure 11.9, are consistent with the recently amalgamated municipalities in the inner, middle and outer rings of Melbourne. The zones in the outer ring or suburban fringe are large. However, the location of existing development within them is considered for calculation of trip lengths and zone centroids

Alternative future scenarios can then be distinguished largely on the basis of the type of future development that is assigned to each of the rings and their associated zones.

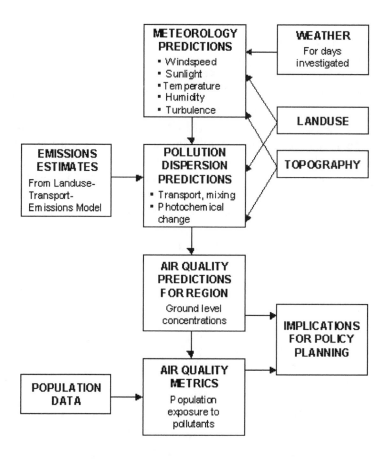

Figure 11.8   Prognostic meteorological and airshed model

Urban Development Scenarios

Modelling Future Scenarios related to Alternative Urban Systems

A range of scenarios that relate to alternative urban forms, defined in terms of land use changes and service improvement, were applied in modelling Melbourne's development to the year 2011. The key challenge relates to the accommodation of an additional 500,000 people in Melbourne by 2011 to a base population of 3,168,300 in 1991. The input data and assumptions for each scenario are summarised in Table 11.3.

Business as Usual

In the business as usual scenario, the new half million population is distributed across the 26 JTW zones in the Melbourne metropolitan area (Figure 11.9) in proportion to the 1991 base, as shown in Table 11.4.

This essentially continues a dispersed pattern of 'constrained' development (i.e., growth is accommodated within the confines of the Melbourne Statistical Division (MSD) as presently defined) with population increased proportionately in each ring. The increase in outer Melbourne could be as green-field development at the fringe, given the significant amount of land which remains available for residential or commercial development. Consolidation trends associated with dual occupancy and infill development would have some limited influence. As such, this scenario models many of the current trends operating in Melbourne, including a slight increase in density.

Figure 11.9   The 26 journey to work (JTW) zones of Melbourne classified into inner, middle and outer rings

Table 11.3 Scenarios and assumptions

Scenario	Transport		Population Distribution			Employment Distribution (%)		
	Infrastructure	% Public Transport	Ring	Percent	Density (persons/ha)	Manufacture	Producer Services	Social Services
Base case 1991	Existing network	20	Inner	7		22	53	32
			Middle	58		55	36	47
			Outer	35		23	11	20
Future to 2001	Upgrade			Growth			Growth	
Business as usual[a]		19	Inner	7	40	22	33	32
			Middle	58	40	55	36	47
			Outer	35	40	23	11	20
Compact city[b]	City freeway links	30	Inner	100	300	0	100	100
			Middle	0		33	0	0
			Outer	0		67	0	0
Edge city[c]	Freeway-level ring road radial rail	16	Inner	0	80	0	0	0
			Middle	86	80	33	83	83
			Outer	14	80	67	17	17

a Increases density proportionally throughout the city—increasing congestion on existing road networks, and travel times and fuel consumption as a consequence.

b Concentrates growth in inner city well served by public transport but in the highest concentrations of pollutants.

c Places new activities in edge city centres—further from concentrations of pollutants.

Table 11.3 (Contd.)

Scenario	Transport Infrastructure	% Public Transport	Population Distribution			Employment Distribution (%)		
			Ring	Percent	Density (persons/ha)	Manufacture	Producer Services	Social Services
Corridor city[d]	Radial road/rail link upgrades	32	Inner	0	60	0	0	0
			Middle	0	60	0	0	0
			Outer	100	60	100	100	100
Ultra city[e] (including Regional centres)	150 mkh rail, Freeways		Inner	2	60	7	16	10
			Middle	17	60	17	11	14
			Outer	11	60	7	3	6
			Regional	70	60	70	70	70
Fringe[f] (balance of homes and jobs)	Radial road/rail link upgrades	28	Inner	0	40	0	0	0
			Middle	10	40	10	10	10
			Outer	60	40	60	60	60
			Fringe	30	40	30	30	30

d   Similar to edge city but with growth channelled into growth corridors—increasing trip length, emissions and fuel use but further from pollutant concentrations.

e   70 percent of growth in regional cities (in separate airsheds)—linked by fast electrified rail carrying 80 percent of cross-commuters (20 percent of new commuters). Electricity also generated in separate airshed.

f   Places 30 percent of new homes and service jobs in fringe corridor green-field locations connected to radial highway/freeway and rail links. Balances new homes and jobs in each zone.

Compact City

In this scenario, the new population is distributed to the eight statistical local areas that comprise inner Melbourne.

The density of new residential development or redevelopment in these zones is 300 persons/ha, significantly above business as usual levels for the inner city. Higher densities are premised on the capacity of the transport and personal services in the 'transit city' section of Melbourne to accommodate such an influx of people.

Multi-Nodal or Edge City

In this scenario, new population is allocated to six major district centres within the MSD connected via a major ring road. The district centres are located in zones situated within or close to the middle ring of Melbourne.

Table 11.4   1991 distribution of land and residential population

Zone	Land area (km^2)	Residential population (000s)	Density (persons/ha)
Inner Melbourne	81.7	227.4	27.8
Middle Melbourne	1041.1	1831.8	17.4
Outer Melbourne	6708.5	1109.1	1.7

The ring road is the same as in the base case except that, in this scenario, improvements have been made in order to bring it to freeway status. The six nodes are also on radial rail networks centred on the CBD. These edge city zones are assigned medium-density housing up to 80 persons/ha.

Corridor City

In this scenario, the new population is added to three corridor zones in the outer ring of the city. The three corridors received transport infrastructure upgrades (of a radial nature) to both road and rail.

Fringe City

In this scenario, 30 percent of new population is added to the three development corridors in new green-field sites on the urban fringe. Of the remaining 70 percent, 10 percent is added to the middle ring of zones, 60 percent is added to the outer ring.

New manufacturing and service industries are also distributed to these same zones and in the same proportions, providing a balance between new homes and new jobs. The times of development of new homes and jobs will also be similar, increasing the opportunities for selection of a home and job in the same local area, thereby increasing self-containment of commuting, as well as of shopping, and other trips.

The new corridor development and distribution to existing middle and outer zones is another variation of present and recent trends, except that there is no addition to the inner city zones.

The new corridor fringe development is connected to the rest of the city with radial freeway/arterial links and with upgraded heavy rail links, thereby reducing travel times to these zones below what they would be without these upgrades.

Ultra City

In this scenario, 70 percent of the new population is added to four provincial centres within a 100 km radius of Melbourne's CBD (Ballarat, Bendigo, Seymour, Warragul); the remaining 30 percent is dispersed throughout the 26 zones in proportion to the base-year distributions. As such, it is business as usual, but with a twist. The twist is that the concept of ultra-city developed here represents a 21st century solution to a late-20th century problem. The problem relates to the future viability of many of Australia's provincial cities which were established in an earlier era to service the needs of a predominantly agrarian–extractive economy which is diminishing in significance (Newman *et al.*, 1996). These centres are struggling to find a new economic base, yet they represent environments of high residential amenity and liveability much sought after by sections of the capital city's population. The proposed solution (scenario) involves linking (selected) provincial centres with their capital city via high-speed rail, thereby making them part of the functional urban region of that city (functional urban being defined by patterns of daily commuting to work). The availability of 350+ km/h high-speed transport could effectively transform each provincial city into the equivalent of a middle ring suburb of their respective capital city where travel time to work is of the order of 30 minutes (Newton., 1997a). Prospects then exist for country lifestyle with access to urban employment and services or urban lifestyle with access to employment located in the provincial centres ('suburbs'). They effectively become part of the engine of the 21st century economy—the capital city. The demand for housing and commercial–industrial space is diminished in cities with 'spill-over' into the provincial cities. In the scenario modelled, the four provincial centres are linked by fast train (150 km/h) and freeway to the CBD.

Telecommuting (Info-City)

In addition to the six urban form scenarios outlined above, it is also possible to 'superimpose' additional urban scenarios that relate to the form of work that sections of the population can be expected to be engaged in by 2011. We anticipate that a higher proportion of the population will be engaged in telework than at present—overall perhaps as high as 20–30 percent, with perhaps equivalent levels of reduction in vehicle kilometres travelled (some being substituted by soft travel modes—walking and cycling—within local village contexts) and resultant emissions.

We expect that substitution of telecommunications for travel will be greatest for producer services, where much activity involves the manipulation of 'symbols' rather than physical goods. Social services is relatively lower, given that it also includes personal services, requiring a high level of face-to-face contact. Social trips (residence-to-residence) can be expected to fall with the penetration of videotelephoning, but perhaps not greatly. The objective here, in any case, is to be speculative with a view to examining possible impacts. As new 21st century scenarios are examined, challenges also emerge for modelling and the incorporation of new urban systems concepts, trends and relationships (viz, an increased role for commercial vehicles in a teleshopping age; the relative shares and linkages of urban travel between work, social and other activities).

Urban Form Matters!

Within the stated limitations and assumptions associated with the land use–transport–air quality modelling, we can advance the following conclusions related to air quality and urban form:

Urban Form and Photochemical Smog

Any one of several strategies designed to deliberately channel and
concentrate additional population and industry into specific 'zones' within
a large city such as Melbourne (viz. corridor, edge, compact inner city, etc.)
when supported by the simultaneous installation or upgrading of
appropriate transport infrastructure will deliver environmental and
efficiency benefits that consistently outperform those associated with a
'business as usual' approach. In the case of photochemical smog, for
example, a corridor model for Melbourne's metropolitan development in
2011 on a summer day of adverse meteorological conditions delivers a 55
percent improvement over the base situation on the same day for that city in
1991. Where new development is primarily concentrated at nodes on the
fringe, within the inner suburbs or at key nodes within the city, the air
quality enhancements are also significant (respectively, 39, 24 and 21
percent reduction in population exposure to smog compared to the base
case for the same adverse summer meteorological conditions). For business
as usual development, the result is an increase by 71 percent in the
population exposed to smog at levels above those considered appropriate by
present air quality standards (see Figure 11.10).

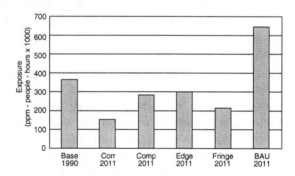

**Figure 11.10   Exposure to photochemical smog on a day of adverse
conditions in Melbourne in 1991 and for different urban
development scenarios in 2011**

Urban Form and Particle Concentrations

PM_{10} *emissions* for the compact city scenario are little changed from the
1991 base model. However, since *all* the additional half million population
gain proposed for Melbourne in this scenario is to be accommodated in

these inner suburbs, more people will be exposed to the 'umbrella' of particle emissions. Hence the considerably higher levels of population exposure represented in Figure 11.11 on a winter day of adverse meteorological conditions for the compact city.

Indeed, on a modelled day of adverse meteorological conditions in 2011 the compact city delivers a 160 percent increase in population exposure to particle emissions compared to the Melbourne base case (1991). For business as usual development, the level of increased population exposure is 61 percent. Edge, corridor and fringe developments all deliver improvements as far as population exposure to PM_{10} particles is concerned.

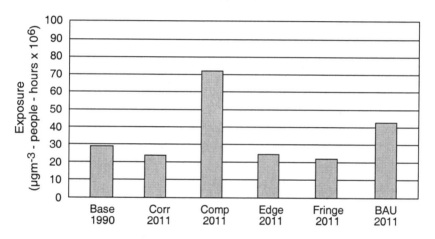

Figure 11.11   **Exposure to fine particles on a day of adverse conditions in Melbourne in 1991 and for different urban development scenarios in 2011**

Urban Form and Carbon Dioxide Emissions

Two of the key contributors to greenhouse gas emission by cities are demands on transport and electricity. For most Australian cities, electricity generation occurs in locations outside metropolitan airsheds, a trend which has occurred over the past 25 years as advances in transmission technology have permitted electricity production at greater distances from the market. However, the late 1990s are witnessing the emergence of a new set of forces in the electricity utilities industry in Australia (privatisation and deregulation of the gas and electricity industries) that may see an increase in the number of gas turbine generators embedded in the larger cities. This is likely to have a positive effect overall on greenhouse gas emissions, but would have a negative effect in relation to NO_x emissions.

In this context, then, it is the link emissions which become the primary focus for reducing CO_2 from urban areas. Figure 11.12 illustrates that a compact city form delivers the lowest output of CO_2 emissions, due to greater use of public transport and fewer vehicle hours (and kilometres) travelled (see Figures 11.13 and 11.14), compared to other forms of urban development. A shift by 2011 from business as usual urban development to a compact city form may give savings in CO_2 emissions of the order of 11.5 million kilograms each day (11,500 tonnes).

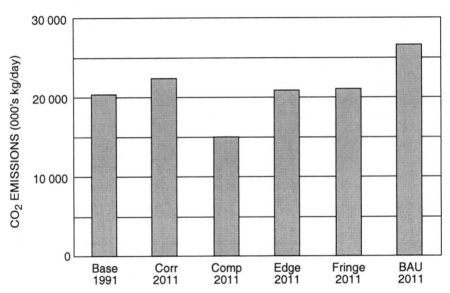

Figure 11.12   Daily CO_2 emissions from link sources in Melbourne

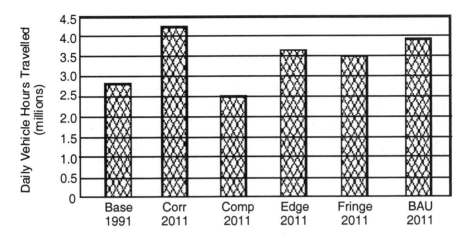

Figure 11.13 **Daily vehicle hours travelled for base 1991 and five future scenarios for Melbourne**

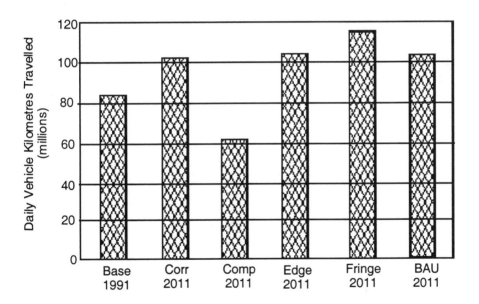

Figure 11.14 **Daily vehicle kilometres travelled for base 1991 and five future scenarios for Melbourne**

Urban Form and Energy Consumption

As one might expect from discussions in the section above, the compact city emerges as the most fuel efficient of all urban forms (see Figure 11.15) with 43 percent less fuel consumption than a business as usual form of development. The fact that in the corridor city scenario infrastructure investment was primarily radial in nature is the reason why higher levels of daily travel were generated than in other scenarios (i.e., limited prospects for cross-town trips). The addition of a higher order ring or orbital transport network to the current corridor city infrastructure, however, could be expected to generate positive benefits in travel time and energy consumption outcomes.

Indeed, it is this type of strategic planning and evaluation which is notably absent at state government level as attempts are made to chart the future infrastructure investments required for their major metropolitan areas into the 21st century. By way of contrast, in the United States, for example, the federal Clean Air Act is requiring a closer linking of funding in areas such as urban transport with a set of goals. These goals include air quality. Integrated land use–transport–environment models represent the only means by which impacts of proposed urban development can be evaluated across the spectrum of dimensions relevant to the key goals of economic efficiency, social equity and environmental sustainability.

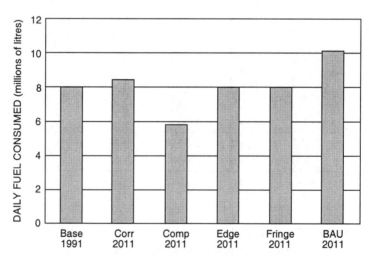

Figure 11.15   Daily fuel consumption for base 1991 and five future scenarios for Melbourne

Urban Form in an Information Era

The form of 'the city' towards the middle of the 21st century is likely to be different in many significant ways from those with which we are presently familiar. With each new technology transition there has been a significant change in the form and structure of cities, as Figure 11.16 illustrates— although key elements from previous eras often remain as functioning artefacts (viz. the higher density 'walking city'—typically the historic cores of modern cities; the 'transit city' with its radial train and tram networks and associated residential development; the 'automobile city' and its extensive low density suburbs).

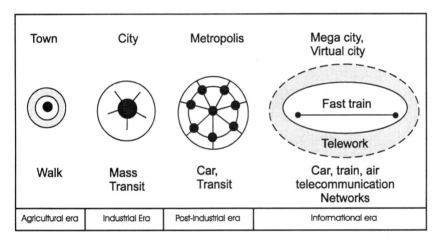

Figure 11.16   Technology transitions and the changing space economy

Change in urban form is due to the fact that the key drivers that underpin human settlements have also undergone radical change from one technological/societal era to another, as Table 11.5 shows.

However, an interesting feature is that the time people are prepared to spend in travelling to and from work has remained essentially invariant throughout. According to Marchetti (1992) it is an instinctive or anthropological human characteristic. With essentially constant travel time budgets (on average, 30 minutes commuting either way between residence and workplace), the size of the city has been influenced by the distance which can be travelled within that time budget. Thus, with each transition, an increase in travel speed has been provided by new technology and this has facilitated an increase in urban scale, with transitions, from walking city to transit city to automobile city to telematic city.

Table 11.5   Transition to an information society

	Societal Transitions		
	Agricultural →	Industrial →	Informational
Industry location	Dispersed	Centralised	Centralised with decentralisation
Industrial process specialisation	Handcraft	Mass production	Flexible
Economic engine	Human muscle	Machines	Human knowledge
Product	Customised	Uniform	Personalised
Work conditions	Informal	Formal	Team
Dominant mode of interaction	Face-to-face	Hierarchical line management	Information networks
Type of information transfer at work	Verbal	Paper	Electronic
Market orientation	Local	National	Global

For workers and residents in the (future) telematic city the *prospects* for collapsing space and time are now evident—given that broadband networked computing provides the technology platform to support telepresence and real-time wide area collaborative working. This will be more likely for some classes of work than for others. We *speculate* that workers in producer services industries have the greatest prospect of substituting telecommuting for travel given that their jobs are concerned primarily with the collection, processing and distribution of information, in contrast to the in-person services that demand face-to-face attention (Reich, 1993). As evidence begins to emerge from research and surveys as to which economic activities can be more readily substituted by electronic rather than face-to-face interaction (in whole or in part), it will be possible to modify the telecommuting assumptions in our land use–transport–environment modelling.

Given the assumptions that were used (viz. due to substitution by telecommunications, travel by producer services workers would decline by as much a 50 percent by 2011; social services would decline by as much as 30 percent; manufacturing up to 10 percent; and residential (social) trips by five percent), the results of the modelling suggest that telecommuting would make a positive impact on the metabolism of cities—reducing energy consumption (Figure 11.17), greenhouse gas emissions (Figure 11.18) and population exposed to criteria air pollutants such as photochemical smog and fine particles.

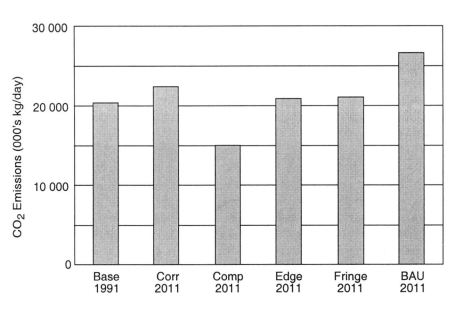

Figure 11.17   Daily fuel consumption for base 1991 and five future scenarios with telecommuting for Melbourne

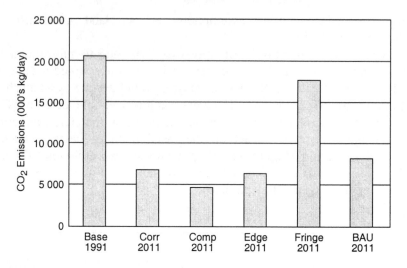

Figure 11.18   Daily CO$_2$ emissions from link sources with telecommuting for Melbourne

Conclusion

Finally the verdict is in. It *is* possible to break away from the nexus of rising GDP and garbage, dust and pollution. Urban form *does* matter. And not just for urban air quality. In relation to indicators such as energy consumption, self-containment of sub-urban regions and vehicle kilometres travelled, there appears to be universal concurrence from the land use-transport-environment modelling that to maintain a business as usual model of urban development (viz. relatively laissez faire, low density, dispersed) is to condemn the population and industry of that city to a sub-optimal living and working environment into the future.

On many measures a trend to a compact city will lead to the greatest improvement in the indicators considered. However there is a sign that the situation is more complex: higher population density leads to higher concentrations of health-impairing fine particles, a factor of concern in winter in particular (Figure 11.11). Perhaps in the scenarios studied here this is just a consequence of the urban density not being high enough! But it is here that the social acceptability of different living arrangements enters into the debate. And it is one which is not readily resolved.

12 Privatising Climate: First World Cities in South East Asia

HOWARD DICK and PETER RIMMER

Introduction

The long cherished notion that South East Asian cities were Third World cities and different in kind from those of the First World can now be seen as ill-conceived and fallacious. Apparent variations between American or European and South East Asian cities has reflected differing market conditions, rather than a fundamental difference in culture. The technology of the high-rise city has turned out to be just as transferable to the Third World as the motor vehicle.

Historically, Westerners could transfer people, capital and technology to South East Asia but they could not simply transfer their familiar living environment. They had to adapt to local conditions. This is no longer the case. Westerners can now fly to South East Asia in air-conditioned comfort, transfer to a hotel by air-conditioned taxi and live in an air-conditioned hotel or private house while working in air-conditioned offices. Except for brief periods outdoors, they need be no hotter or colder than in their home environment.

By the same token, wealthy and middle-class South East Asians are no longer constrained by local conditions to live like 'natives'. They, too, can now afford air-conditioning in their homes and cars, work in air-conditioned offices, and visit shopping malls and restaurants. In fact, there is no longer any technological reason why middle-class South East Asians and Westerners should lead lifestyles that are substantially different. The enhanced flow of information is also breaking down cultural differences.

This ability to produce temperature controlled environments is redefining the fundamental relationship between people and place in urban South East Asia. Daily life in cities means, for the most part, being inside. Paradoxically, most urban analysts look only at relations in the external environment. There has been no attempt to link technological transfer in building and construction to urban form. Not that the emerging high-rise

305

cities of South East Asia are unfamiliar in the West. That very familiarity has probably diverted attention from the importance of timing and content of this technology transfer.

Previously, most discussion of technological transfer has been confined to industrialisation and not extended to urbanisation. This neglect leads here to examination of the impacts of technological transfer on urban land use and its social implications. The emerging dualistic character of urban society is highlighted as the hallmark of the new 'colonial' city. Before discussing technological transfer it is important to conceptualise the exterior and interior geography of cities.

Conceptualising Inner and Outer Space

There is extensive demographic literature about the rapid growth in South East Asia's urban population (Fuchs, Jones and Pernia, 1987; Ogawa, Jones and Williamson, 1993; ESCAP, 1993). Before the Second World War the largest city in South East Asia was Manila with one million people in 1939 (UN, 1995a). By the mid-1990s, Jakarta had 11.5 million people, Manila 9.3 million and Bangkok 6.6 million (UN, 1995b). Within less than two generations there has been an increase by an order of magnitude.

The degree of urbanisation within these countries has also increased sharply. Between 1970 and 1995 the percentage of population residing in urban areas in the Philippines increased from 33 percent to 54 percent, in Indonesia from 17 percent to 35 percent, and in Thailand from 13 percent to 20 percent (UN, 1995b). By 2025 it is expected the Philippines will have an urban population of 74 percent, Indonesia 61 percent and Thailand 39 percent.

Other literature refers to transport, housing and the urban environment (e.g. Rimmer, 1986; Douglass, 1996). Recently, there has been a growing interest in the emergence of a middle class and rising income levels (Robison and Goodman, 1996). All of this can be set within the context of a general literature which discusses the broad trends of globalisation, economic restructuring and industrialisation.

Globalisation, whose impact on South East Asia has almost become a cliché, has unquestionably transformed the urban environment. This phenomenon is apparent in the explosion and size of cities, and the level of urbanisation. Yet analysis of the impact of globalisation has so far been focused on the external environment of cities, in particular the highly visible built environment and traffic problems. Most literature on economic restructuring and industrialisation scarcely acknowledges the city as a coherent and functional unit. Further, demographers are content simply to quantify; they make little attempt to understand the city as a system.

Discussions of traffic, housing and other social services are problem focused and take the city itself as given. Even geographers, whose discipline best equips them to analyse the relationships of people and space, have unwittingly restricted themselves to a bird's eye view that looks only at the 'external environment'.

Most geography is actually 'external geography', that is to say, the geography of external space or the relations between buildings. Although human geographers profess to study 'real people', they have focused for the most part at a community or micro level and have tended to lose sight altogether of the city as a functional system. Conceptually, one may also conceive of an interior geography. Hitherto the latter has been the realm of the architect rather than the geographer.

Architects show an intimate awareness of how people live and work within the interior built environment. Here, design combines both theoretical and applied knowledge of materials, technology and human behaviour in a social and environmental context. The leading exponents, therefore, do understand in microcosm the nature of the changing society. This is the cutting edge of globalisation, economic restructuring and industrialisation.

Yet architects, for the most part, speak only to each other. Outside their profession the impact of architects is not in what they say and write but in the structures they create, which become the built environment. Although some architects are town planners, there is still a cleavage between inner and outer space. The architect's writ extends into the external environment not much further than the car park.

Conversely, town planners have little say in building design. When urban growth is slow, this is merely an inconvenience. However, when urban growth is explosive, as in modern South East Asia, this awkward disjunction gives rise to all kinds of externalities, such as environmental pollution, which are regarded as the bane of modern cities.

This specialisation renders any integrated analysis impossible. Even brief reflection suggests that there is a key link between the transfer of technology, which gives rise to new building styles, and the changing patterns of urban land use and transport systems. The way forward in conceptualising urban space may be to blend the knowledge and perspectives of the geographer with those of the architect. Any building of more than one-storey involves a replication of space. Indeed, in a market economy it is precisely this ability to replicate space which escalates land prices at urban cores or places of prime accessibility.

Geography can, therefore, be extended to encompass an interior geography of the built environment, which hitherto has been the realm of the architect. Although the architect's vision of land use planning takes account of the externalities generated by buildings and groups of buildings it has hitherto been a bureaucratic concern, often ineffectual, local government. The architect's vision would become more persuasive if supported by the analysis of geography and economics. Thus, the interior geography of multi-storey buildings, which are so characteristic of the urban capitalist economy, has been neglected.

One of the crucial links between architecture and geography, is technology. Space can be replicated only by means of technology. Very tall buildings were technically infeasible until the invention of reinforced concrete. They were also economically dependent on the elevator and escalator. In tropical South East Asia, the technology of air conditioning has also been crucial. Technology is therefore a necessary but not sufficient condition for the emergence of high-rise central business districts. Nevertheless, the opportunity to readily transfer a specific package of technology applicable to high-rise buildings, has allowed the emergence of familiar Western urban forms in booming South East Asia.

Technology Transfer

There is a growing literature that links the rapid industrialisation of South East Asia to world trade, direct foreign investment and technology transfer. However, this literature is aspatial below the level of the nation state and takes no account of cities. Since rapid urbanisation is almost a defining characteristic of these South East Asian countries, this literature has obvious limitations. Nevertheless, it does suggest the scope for a parallel inquiry into the connection between urbanisation, rising living standards, direct foreign investment and technology transfer in building and construction and changing urban forms.

The tenfold growth in just over one generation of cities such as Jakarta, Manila and Bangkok could not have been accommodated without significant investment in embodied technology. The widely deplored symptoms of urban breakdown (congestion, pollution and loss of amenity) may also suggest how much worse the situation would be if investment and technology had remained as they were in the 1940s.

In other words, the symptoms are not good indicators of the extent to which private building stock and public infrastructure has been upgraded. As various writers have argued, it is the very success of these cities in maintaining rates of investment and employment growth faster than the rural areas that has increased the rate of urbanisation. This is a dynamic process of cumulative causation, not a sad tale of failure. Indeed, those who so vigorously criticised the 'breakdown' of South East Asia's big cities are, for the most part, Westerners who come from cities which are economically stagnant by comparison. Most Indonesians, Filipinos, Malaysians and Thais, who have a very different yardstick of comparison, see their capital cities as symbols of achievement.

The technology which has accommodated South East Asia's rapid urbanisation has, for the most part, been acquired by technology transfer from the West. The literature has emphasised the importance of new modes of transport, especially the motor car. Equally dramatic has been the application of imported technologies to the built environment, especially in construction, internal transport (elevators, escalators) internal communication (telephone networks, computer systems) and temperature control (heating, ventilation and air-conditioning). This package of technology can be seen in office buildings, hotels, shopping malls and airports.

To understand the role of technological transfer in the evolution of South East Asian cities, attention needs to be focused on the timing of development. Three phases are critical: classical architecture; tropical architecture between 1910s and 1950s; and foreign high-rise since the 1960s.

Classical and Vernacular Design

Classical South East Asian design emphasises the adaptation of buildings to the harsh external environment (Table 12.2). This was achieved in various ways. Court cities were set in modified micro climates. Often these cities were located next to natural water sources such as rivers, whose cooling effect was enhanced by canals (klongs) and lakes. Shade also reduced ambient air temperature. Courtyards were of swept earth, not harsh heat absorbent or reflective surfaces such as concrete and asphalt.

Buildings were either set on stilts or raised platforms. Porous walls admitted air flow, high ceilings with apertures, deep shaded verandahs, wide openings and external rattan blinds ('chicks') facilitated ventilation, and marble or tiled floors were cool underfoot (Edwards, 1990; Yeang, 1987; Powell, 1993; Tan, 1994). Despite high ambient air temperatures, air flow was maintained and hot air transferred away from the interior, ensuring personal comfort by non-mechanical means.

Public and private buildings employed all of these techniques where they could be afforded (Table 12.1). Materials used included wood, matting and thatch. These materials were not heat absorbent and were porous to air flow. Sparse furnishing, light clothing and the rhythm of daily activities were adapted to local conditions. In the mid-nineteenth century, cities such as Bangkok were built entirely to this principle (Tettoni, Warren and Liu, 1989).

Europeans brought less sympathetic materials (such as stone and bricks) but adapted their buildings to the rigours of a tropical climate. Long experience in India had taught the British, Dutch and Portuguese the benefits of local design. The colonialists brought with them new forms of vernacular architecture such as the verandah and bungalow (King, 1990a,b). Towards the end of the colonial period, many of the principles were formulated as the study of tropical architecture, which became a recognised specialisation within the profession (Beng, 1994; Tan, 1994).

Tropical Architecture

By the interwar years, the Dutch had vigorous schools in tropical agriculture, medicine, law and administration in Leiden and Amsterdam. In a curious reverse technology transfer, local students who studied in Britain learned these ideas formally as part of their training. These studies matched those in tropical geography and tropical medicine. The proconsuls of Empire were being trained by 'experts' who themselves had first-hand experience of the colonies and recognised that technology transfer was a two-way process.

The florescence of tropical architecture occurred in Indonesia (then Netherlands Indies) from the 1910s to the 1930s and in Malaya and Singapore during the 1950s (Dawson and Gillow, 1994; Edwards, 1990; Yeang, 1992). From the 1910s Maclaine Pont and Karstens, two colleagues working in Indonesia, incorporated better techniques of ventilation into modern design. In Java the Dutch applied the ultra-modern principles of the Bauhaus movement to create an exciting new variant. These were typically whitewashed buildings, with minimalist facades, whose lofty interior spaces and inner courtyards were designed for natural cooling and ventilation assisted only by ceiling fans. Many of these buildings still survive as an unique architectural heritage.

Table 12.1 Past adjustments/adaptations and present alterations to hot/wet climate

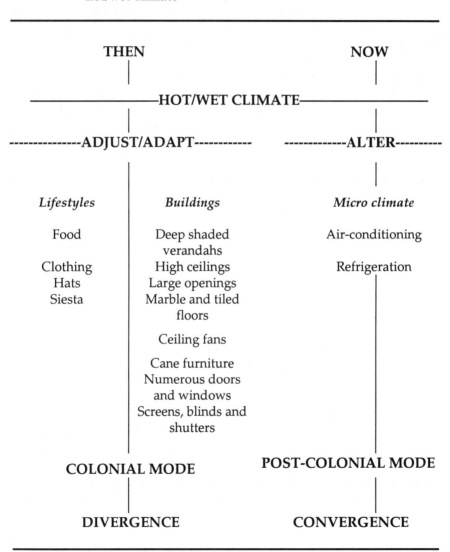

THEN   NOW

——————————HOT/WET CLIMATE————————

--------------ADJUST/ADAPT------------   --------------ALTER----------

Lifestyles	*Buildings*	*Micro climate*
Food	Deep shaded verandahs	Air-conditioning
Clothing	High ceilings	Refrigeration
Hats	Large openings	
Siesta	Marble and tiled floors	
	Ceiling fans	
	Cane furniture Numerous doors and windows Screens, blinds and shutters	

COLONIAL MODE   **POST-COLONIAL MODE**

DIVERGENCE   **CONVERGENCE**

The British designed their public buildings, private offices and luxury dwellings with modern materials such as reinforced concrete, but designs were adapted with ingenuity to local conditions. Several leading local practices played an influential role such as Palmer and Turner, which had offices not only in Singapore but in Hong Kong and Shanghai until the outbreak of the Second World War (Powell, 1988). Local architects who had received overseas training were also involved in grafting Chinese and Malay features onto European designs in the post-war period (Beamish and Ferguson, 1985; Lee, 1984; Powell, 1988; Yeang, 1992).

Unexpectedly, these hybrid designs turned out to be an evolutionary dead-end. The 1950s were a time of rapid decolonisation. In Indonesia the process of technology transfer was interrupted when the Dutch lost all influence after Independence. In the mid-1950s students of architecture at the prestigious Bandung Institute of Technology (ITB) were sent to London for a six-months postgraduate course in Tropical Architecture at the Architectural Association (H. O'Neill, pers. comm.). The economic crisis meant that little funding was available for large buildings of innovative design. A rare exception is the Bank Indonesia building in central Jakarta. In Malaysia and Singapore the influence of British architects persisted much longer but tropical architecture was being overtaken by imported 'modernism'. The battleground between tropical architecture and imported modernism was high-rise.

High-rise

Pre-war buildings in South East Asia were no match for those in New York. There were few buildings in South East Asia much taller than six storeys (Table 12.2). In 1928 Singapore's new Hill Street Police Station was eight storeys. In 1939 the record passed to the Cathay Building with 12 storeys. No buildings exceeded this height in Indonesia, Malaya, Indo-China and the Philippines. In 1953-54 the Bank of China Building in Singapore reached 18 storeys and was regarded as the first skyscraper in Asia (Powell, 1988). These buildings still took account of the principles of tropical architecture, featuring high ceilings and natural ventilation. However, high ceilings in a tall building necessarily multiplied the cost. Once air-conditioning systems became available, much more accommo-dation could be built for a given height and a given cost.

**Table 12.2 Development of high-rise buildings in New York,
Singapore and Kuala Lumpur**

	New York	Singapore	Kuala Lumpur
First 10-storey	1840 (Duane Street Broadway)	1939 (Cathay)	1957 (Federal Hotel)
First 20-storey	1889-90 (Pulitzer)	1963 (Selegie House)	1969 (Federal Hotel Extension)
First 30 storey	c1909 (City Investing)	—	1972 (KL Hilton)
First 40 storey	c1909 (Singer Tower; Municipal)	1975 (Hong Leong)	1987 (Maybank)
First 50 storey	1913 (Woolworth)	1975 (PBS)	—
First 60 storey	1931 (American International)	—	1987 (Komtar)

Sources: Beamish and Ferguson, 1985; Beedle, 1986; Edwards, 1990; Landau and Condit, 1996; SIAJ, 1984; Yeang, 1992

As early as the late 1950s the future design path had already been determined. The development of high-rise South East Asian cities awaited only the mobilisation of the necessary investment. In 1968 the 24-storey Chokchai tower was erected in Bangkok (Askew, 1994). By 1970 Singapore's first high-rise boom was underway. Kuala Lumpur followed soon after with the 28 storey UMBC Building in 1971 and the 36 storey Hilton Hotel in 1972. In the Philippines high-rise began with the development of Makati in the 1960s but was held back by the economic and political crisis of the later Marcos years. Jakarta's first high-rise, the

Nusantara Building, was commissioned by President Sukarno with Japanese assistance but it remained a rusting skeleton until the 1970s. The boom in Indonesia did not begin until the 1980s.

In the mid-1990s a high-rise construction boom characterised every large city in South East Asia and city skylines changed dramatically by the year. The two tallest buildings in the world are the Petronas Twin Towers in Kuala Lumpur completed in 1996 (Dupré, 1996). In fact, there was so much tall construction underway that Asia accounted for 70 percent of the world's elevator market (UT, 1997). By 2000 six of the world's 10 tallest buildings will be in Asia. This compares dramatically with none in 1980 (when they were all in North America) and one in 1990—the Bank of China Building in Hong Kong (Table 12.3).

There is a familiar rationale for high-rise buildings, whether in Kuala Lumpur or Manhattan. Buildings are a capital good which are used as inputs in the production and consumption of goods and services (except in the case of monuments and ceremonial buildings). They are constructed to meet what economists refer to as derived demand. It, can, therefore be predicted that in any market system where there is rapid growth in real income and rapid social change, the built environment will also be rapidly transformed. This is particularly so in the city centre where land is most valuable. Albeit with some time lag, the market will reallocate urban land to its most highly valued use. As land increases in real value it becomes economic to construct a larger area of floor space upon a given plot of land.

As witnessed in Asia and North America, the process is not entirely 'rational'. Competition for commercial prestige, especially among high profile corporations such as banks, has been an important spur in the race for the sky. Height matters. There is also an important speculative component. The developers relentless quest to gain maximum profit from site consolidation feeds off the demand for prestige space in the sky.

Privatised, high-rise urban space is the core of the market economy. This space commands the highest land price and has to attract custom. It therefore has to be a comfort zone. In South East Asia the easiest way to achieve this is to air-condition the space. The aim is to create a micro-climate for which people would be prepared to pay a premium to enjoy. A classic case of climate control is the shopping mall. The market economy works best in a controlled temperature environment. Air-conditioning allows people the opportunity to stay and browse. It is a comfort zone creating a physical well being that people wish to seek out.

Table 12.3   World's 'top 10' tallest buildings, 1980, 1990 and 2000

	1980			1990			2000		
	Building	Place	m	Building	Place	m	Building	Place	m
1.	Sears Tower (1974)	Chicago	443	Sears Tower	Chicago	443	*Petronas Tower 1*	*Kuala Lumpur*	456
2.	World Trade Center North (1972)	New York	417	One World Trade Center	New York	417	*Petronas Tower 2*	*Kuala Lumpur*	456
3.	World Trade Center South (1973)	New York	415	Two World Trade Centre (renamed)	New York	415	Sears Tower	Chicago	443
4.	Empire State New York (1931)	New York	381	Empire State	New York	381	*Jin Mao*	*Shanghai*	420
5.	Standard Oil Indiana	Chicago	346	*Bank of China Tower*	*Hong Kong*	*369*	One World Trade Center	New York	417
6.	John Hancock Center (1968)	Chicago	344	Amoco (renamed)	Chicago	346	Two World Trade Centre	New York	415
7.	Chrysler (1930)	New York	319	John Hancock Centre	Chicago	344	*Plaza Rakyat*	*Kuala Lumpur*	*382*

Table 12.3 (Contd.)

	1980			1990			2000	
Building	Place	m	Building	Place	m	Building	Place	m
8. American International (1931)	New York	290	Chrysler	New York	319	Empire State	New York	*381*
9. First Bank Tower (1975)	Toronto	285	Texas Commerce Plaza	Houston	305	*Bank of China Tower*	*Hong Kong*	*382*
10. 40 Wall Tower (1976)	New York	283	Allied Bank Plaza	Houston	295	*T&C Tower*	*Kaohsiung*	*349*

Note: Buildings italicised are in the Asia-Pacific Region.
Source: Beedle, 1986; Dupré, 1996

Air-Conditioning

In South East Asia air-conditioning and refrigeration have been the critical elements in the timing of technology transfer among the package of technological innovations introduced in high-rise buildings (Table 12.4). Natural ventilation, assisted by ceiling fans, served the purpose so long as investors were prepared to pay a premium on capital cost to construct the additional space required for the high ceilings and perhaps courtyards and verandahs. This was the frontier of tropical architecture. Air-conditioning was impracticable in such buildings because their volume was too large for efficient cooling. At most, individual offices of top managers and officials were partitioned off and fitted with individual wall units. A similar approach was taken to fitting individual units to the walls of bedrooms in expatriate bungalows. High-rise buildings require a sophisticated ventilation and air-conditioning system if they are to be productive work and comfortable living environments.

Air-conditioning came into use as a common term in the mid-1900s but it was the mid-to-late 1920s before summer cooling was applied to state and commercial buildings in the United States (Arsenault, 1984). However, the use of air-conditioning for high-rise buildings did not become economic until the development, in 1939, of forced draught cooling systems. Hitherto, high-rise office buildings were fitted with central heating for winter but in summer relied upon rather inefficient natural ventilation (opening the windows for cooling). Despite the 1939 invention, and because of wartime disruption, it was not until the 1950s that air-conditioning systems became standard. In 1951 cheap wall units became available. In 1952 all rooms in the first Holiday Inn in continental United States were air-conditioned. This immediately became the yardstick for the hotel industry. Air-conditioning also became a standard fitting in motor cars by the early 1950s.

> By the mid-1970s ... air conditioning had infiltrated more than 90 percent of the [United States] South's high-rise office buildings, banks, apartments and railroad passenger coaches; more than 80 percent of its automobiles, government buildings and hotels; approximately two-thirds of its homes, stores, trucks, hospital rooms; and roughly half of its classrooms (Arsenault, 1984: 156).

The only city in South East Asia which by then approached such rates of market penetration was Singapore. Air-conditioning was still a luxury in other cities.

Table 12.4   Technology transfer table

Innovation	New York	Singapore	Kuala Lumpur
Electric Light	1878	1906 (replaced oil lamps)	
Ceiling fan		1906 (replaced punkah wallahs)	
Elevator	c.1855 (steam-driven) 1870 (hydraulic) 1889 (electric) 1903 Geared Traction Electric Elevator		
Air-conditioning	1902 Carrier air conditioner 1920s Unit air conditioning 1939 Conduit Weathermaster skyscrapers 1951 Window units	early 1930s (replaced mechanically ventilated ducts)	1940s/1950s air conditioned offices
Refrigerators	1918 Automatic refrigerator 1928 GEC Hermetic Automatic Refrigerator	late 1920s (kerosene refrigerator)	

Sources: Althouse *et al.*, 1956; Jones, 1973; Jordan and Priester, 1949; Landau and Condit, 1996; Sheridan *et al.*, 1963; Stoecker and Jones, 1986

The first air-conditioned high-rise building in Singapore was the Bank of China Building (1953-54), whose ceilings had later to be lowered to achieve energy efficiency (Beamish and Ferguson, 1985: 150). It is likely that the first systematic use of full air-conditioning systems was applied not to office buildings but to luxury hotels built in Singapore in the 1960s—Cockpit (1960), Marco Polo (1963) and Ming Court (1970) (SIAJ, 1984; Powell, 1988; Edwards, 1990). By the 1960s there was an expectation that first-class hotels would have fully air-conditioned systems which involved a good deal of retro-fitting. Indonesia's first air-conditioned hotel was Jakarta's Hotel Indonesia opened in 1963 which was built by the Japanese. In Thailand the influx of air-conditioning in hotels in Bangkok (and in upcountry towns) coincided with the arrival of US forces engaged in the Vietnam War during the late 1960s.

A parallel occurrence to air-conditioning in South East Asia was the development of commercial and domestic refrigeration. Commercial refrigeration was introduced in Singapore in 1906 with the opening of the Singapore Cold Storage Co. This was essentially a wholesale and distribution outlet. Even expatriate households continued to use ice chests until the 1950s (Edwards, 1990: 194). The first domestic refrigeration units were kerosene powered. In 1928 the first hermetic refrigeration unit was produced by General Electric. This was followed in 1938 by the first low-cost domestic unit, the Kelvinator. These became common among expatriate households in South East Asia during the 1950s.

The high penetration rates of refrigeration and home air-conditioning among expatriates in South East Asia point to the fundamental difference with the United States, namely the absence, until recently, of any large high income group. Only with the rapid industrialisation and high rates of economic growth since the 1970s has there been a critical mass of purchasing power to generate investment in a modern built environment. It is now the emerging middle class of South East Asia, rather than the quite small expatriate community, which is driving the market. This high income group has both a rapid rate of growth of real income and a high income elasticity of demand for physical comfort, whether at work, home or recreation.

The Emerging Middle Class and New Urban Forms

The rapid growth of the middle class has been accompanied by an important shift in cultural attitudes. In the colonial and early post-colonial period, when most urban dwellers were, at best, of modest means and lived in cramped and poorly ventilated accommodation, each family's private space was very restricted and public space was shared. In the evenings when it was cooler outside than inside, people moved out onto the pathways and streets to carry on their lives in a social atmosphere. Those who stayed inside, preoccupied with private activity (unless ill or immobile) were viewed with suspicion or distrust. This way of life used to be observed from the crowded rows of shophouses in Singapore and

Penang to the *kampongs* of Jakarta, the *barangays* of Manila and the *sois* of Bangkok. How much has changed!

Such scenes can still be seen today though it has become more acceptable for people to stay inside and watch television. Now the new middle class, almost as a matter of self definition, have moved out of these community environments and into their own private, controlled space. The middle class live typically as nuclear families and enjoy their own private recreation with their own consumer durables behind fences, locked gates and barred windows. This phenomenon can be described as the privatisation of the means of consumption (Dick, 1990). In spatial terms it can be equated with the privatisation of space; both withdrawal from and encroachment upon public space.

This increased size and exclusivity of the middle class has given rise to new urban forms (see Dick and Rimmer, forthcoming). These include gated suburban communities, shopping malls, cinema complexes and high-rise offices. These are all private spaces, provided through the market, and their characteristic, except perhaps in the case of crowded shopping malls, is the ability to restrict access to like people. Middle class people minimise their presence in public space by travelling in private motor cars. The market facilitates social exclusivity by locating these gated communities, offices and recreation centres in places which are readily accessibly only by motor cars. This is strongly reminiscent, not only of the behaviour patterns of colonial and expatriate communities, but also of white collar middle class communities in the United States and other Western countries. There is a direct technology transfer from middle class White America to middle class South East Asia. The common link is fear of the urban poor.

An important aspect of the high-rise building, though not one that is commonly remarked upon, is that it is a modern fortress. Except for off-street service offices of airlines and banks, offices are accessible only by elevator—fire escapes do not permit entry from below. Security in South East Asia is controlled at ground level and often on each floor by personnel. These may be receptionists but are usually security guards who are often armed. They are reinforced by a phone link to armed police, military and even riot squads. Unauthorised entry is almost impossible. Many of these office towers no longer advertise a street address. Their advertising is their corporate logo on top of the building. Car access is restricted to regular staff. Those of visitors are allocated to a parking bay and their drivers paged on the intercom when they are ready to depart the building.

Air-conditioning is one of the most important technologies which makes this social exclusivity possible. The urban space occupied by the middle class is not only private space and thus secure space, but also temperature controlled space. The middle class can now buy climate. This is more than just an opportunity to incidental enjoyment of a cool night's sleep or lunch in an air-conditioned restaurant during the heat of the day. Income and technology now make it possible to live in a tropical South East Asian city in one's own micro climate. Except for a few moments stepping between home and car, or car and office, there is no need to be outside the comfort zone. Indeed, for much of the day executives or officials may live and work in a climate which is much closer to colleagues in Europe or North America than to ordinary people in the same city.

Air-conditioning and the built environment that goes with it has actually widened the temperature difference between the 'man-in-the street' and denizens of the urban comfort zone. The use of heat absorbent and heat reflective building materials, combined with the paving of vast areas of the city as roadways and carparks (and the associated loss of shade), has transformed the once benign external microclimate of the city into a blazing inferno for many hours of the day. The internal built environment of small concrete boxes, most efficiently heated by a large area of windows and fitted out with heat absorbent materials (such as carpets and soft furnishings) can only be made bearable by the continuing use of air-conditioning. The exhalation of hot air becomes yet a further burden upon the external environment. The consequences of this effect are known as 'heat islands'; cities become several degrees warmer both day and night. To this is added the massive pollution that results from motorised traffic and industry. The wealthy and middle class can insulate themselves. The less wealthy have to make do in living conditions which are hotter, less comfortable and more densely packed than ever before.

Conclusion: The New Colonial City

Colonial geographers of Asia took climate as their starting point. In the case of South East Asia, they emphasised its tropical climate and seasonal monsoons. The importance of climate was that it seemed to establish beyond reasonable doubt that South East Asia was very different, to the point of being exotic. Period photographs confirm this perspective. South East Asian cities were characterised by shophouses, bungalows, shady kampongs, tree-lined streets, man-powered and horse-drawn vehicles, and a colonial elite. In the late 1990s this colonial perspective seems remarkably quaint. South East Asia's leading cities, such as Bangkok, Jakarta, Kuala Lumpur, Manila and Singapore are today typified by high-rise buildings, streets heavily trafficked by motorised vehicles and, until very recently, a thriving middle class.

To all intents and purposes the urban middle class in South East Asia is no longer part of the Tropics. When air-conditioning was first applied in the United States, it was a matter of summer cooling and was the counterpart to the much older technology of winter central heating. The combined effect in the United States was to enable people to live and work in a comfortable average temperature all-year-round. In South East Asia, by contrast, air-conditioning is beneficial only if it can be maintained all-day and all-year-round. Failure of air-conditioning systems, as during the brown-outs in Manila during the late 1980s or in April 1997 in Jakarta, are catastrophic. Many buildings have no natural form of ventilation and become intolerable living and working environments if standby generators are unavailable.

In South East Asia this technological fix has brought about a dramatic and permanent reduction in temperature for those who can afford to buy their way into that upper level of society. The new fault line in South East Asian cities is between those who can live within the temperature controlled middle class and Westernised society, and the less wealthy whose enjoyment of that comfort is, at best, occasional. Poorer people may, in humble capacities, work in an air-conditioned environment, and they may, with their families, spend time in an air conditioned shopping mall or cinema, but they go home to a hot and stuffy home in a crowded urban community.

This widening gap between the privileged and underprivileged, is epitomised by the redistribution of urban land. In Jakarta, in Manila, and in Bangkok developers have managed, with government backing, to remove low-income people from well located urban land and to consolidate it for high-rise construction. The former occupants are paid, if they are lucky, the market value of the unconsolidated land, from which they must try to rehouse themselves in other crowded communities or on the urban fringe. The betterment value, of course, is captured by the developers. The excluded and underprivileged are therefore also the dispossessed. While South East Asia's modern cities boast of their new skyscrapers that rival or surpass the scale of New York's once mighty Empire State Building, the mass of the struggling urban poor look on with increasing bitterness. In simple terms, this phenomenon may be described as a new form of urban dualism. In social and historical context it may, without too much exaggeration, be described as the new colonialism.

There are two challenges to the modern South East Asian idyll. The immediate and unanticipated threat is the currency crisis of 1997-98. The construction industry can be expected to remain depressed for the next few years while excess capacity is absorbed. This is likely to interrupt rather than alter the trajectory of urbanisation in South East Asia.

The long-term challenge is still that of environmental sustainability. Air-conditioned high-rise is a crude technological fix which demands high or very high inputs of energy to maintain it. The environmental cost of meeting the rate of growth in demand for energy has already become a burden in many South East Asian countries. Even without power crises or global warming, the burden of externalities continues to increase exponentially (Samuels and Prasad, 1994). This results not only from the growth of emission of specific pollutants but also from synergistic effects between different forms of pollution. Although traffic congestion has been the externality most to preoccupy urban planners over the past generation (and as yet is without solution) even more costly will be the investment in infrastructure to deal with problems of air and water pollution, salinity, subsidence and flooding.

Ultimately, even the privileged middle class will be affected by environmental breakdown, though the burden will continue to be borne most heavily by the less well off. This is not a prediction of imminent urban collapse. It is a matter of correctly identifying a trend. As South East Asia's largest cities absorb and account for an increasing share of national production, income and wealth, and as the middle class continues to increase, the environmental and ultimately economic cost of artificial climate change will impose an increasing liability on future generations.

The only professionals in South East Asia who have so far shown the way to a possible solution are a small group of visionary local architects. These architects, though seeking to draw on the best of local science and technology, passionately believe buildings should be integrated with their external environment. This means not only reducing the environmental load in terms of energy consumption and emission of pollutants but also using the building to mobilise energy, such as sunlight, to generate its own energy and improve the external environment. This is the concept of an organic building adapted to a tropical climate. Such design harks back to the classical and vernacular forms, and recovers the idealism of that transitional school of tropical architecture. Some of the best examples are the campus of the University of Indonesia at Depok in South Jakarta and the new Jakarta international airport (though the designers are French!).

Whether such idealism has any hope of success beyond the construction of a few prestige or demonstration buildings depends upon whether South East Asian leaders, both political and business, can be persuaded to share that commitment to a uniquely tropical built environment and life style. This would be truly revolutionary. The trend towards international homogeneity, like the trend towards an average indoor ambient air temperature, seems for now to be irresistible.

PART IV

EAST WEST

COMPARISONS

13 The Global City and Sustainability—Perspectives from Australian Cities and a Survey of 37 Global Cities

PETER NEWMAN, JEFF KENWORTHY and FELIX LAUBE

Introduction

Cities are shaped by technological, economic and cultural forces. The emerging global city—a city formed primarily by the globalised economy and information technology—will also be subject to these forces. Part of the pressure on global cities is for them to be part of the global sustainability agenda. Sustainability is the simultaneous improvement of the economy and the environment (global and local). This chapter will attempt to see whether emerging global city forms are consistent with this agenda, in particular the sustainability agenda to reduce car dependence (UN, 1996).

The chapter will examine how transport and information technology are the primary forces shaping cities and that economic and cultural factors can work through the priority on the provision of infrastructure for these technologies or directly impact through affecting where people choose to live or work. These are obviously linked.

Several postulates are suggested showing how global cities may now be responding to the new combinations of these factors. These will then be examined through the perspective of two recent studies—one which looked at the form of Australian cities for the national State of the Environment Report (Newman *et al.*, 1996), and the other which looked at 37 global cities for the World Bank (Kenworthy *et al*, 1997).

City Form: Technology, Economics and Culture

Technological Forces Shaping Cities

Cities cluster people together so they can do more as a community than as individuals. The technologies for people to move around cities and to share information are critical to how they are formed. One of the critical theories explaining how this happens is that concerning the constancy of time budgets in city travel (Neff, 1996; Zahavi and Ryan, 1980). People in settlements throughout time have shown that they do not like to spend more than around half-an-hour on average travelling to destinations (Manning, 1978; Pederson, 1980). In the UK a government study found that travel time for work trips had been stable for six centuries (SACTRA, 1994). Thus, it is possible to see how this has caused three types of cities to develop as transportation technologies have evolved towards greater speed and freedom of movement:

- *the Walking City* (up to about 1860) could only spread five km and so it tended to be dense (100-200 people per hectare) with narrow streets; many Third World cities retain this walking-based urban form and most cities have some parts with this character, in particular their centres;
- *the Transit City* (1860-1940) could spread 10 to 20 kilometres and tended to be linear and focused on railway stations or along tram lines, with medium-density houses and work locations (50-100 people per hectare) and with a strong emphasis on the CBD; many European cities retain this transit-based urban form and most North American and Australian cities have transit-based areas of their cities; and
- *the Automobile City* (from 1940 on) could spread 20 to 40 kilometres (and sometimes more) wherever roads were built; the density in such cities is subsequently much lower (10 to 20 people per hectare), though a lot of space is taken up by the automobile for roads and parking. The CBD became mainly an office centre with most other types of work dispersing to the suburbs. North American and Australian cities demonstrate this automobile-based urban form and some new parts of all cities indicate this form.

Recent decades may have seen the emergence of a fourth city type:

- *the Nodal/Information City.* This form may be emerging in large global cities where the distance of travel, even by automobile or fast train, is now well beyond the half-hour limit. The Nodal/Information City, it is suggested, may be establishing a range of smaller sub-centres with the global information processing and networking capabilities of the CBD (Newton, Brotchie and Gipps, 1996). Although linked to the rest of the city, these nodal/information sub-centres could be generating a large degree of self-sufficiency in their urban region. This chapter will explore in more detail the new expressions of urban form relating to this technological change.

Economic Forces Shaping Cities

The transportation priorities of a city will obviously be a major factor in shaping a city. However, it is also necessary to have the economic incentive and ability to build such cities. History shows that in some cities, the Auto City kind of urban form was resisted and a more compact, less car-oriented city was facilitated, at least for a large part of this century. Mostly this was due to an economic priority over-riding the priority for road-based infrastructure.

Frost (1991), in an historical and economic analysis of cities, shows there were two distinct types of city in the nineteenth century and into the twentieth century:

- the traditional high density cities of Europe, east coast North America, and east coast Australia (mainly Sydney); and
- the low density 'new frontier' towns of west and southern North America and Australia (Perth, Adelaide and Melbourne).

The reason for this difference is not just the time of development as new cities in these regions followed both patterns. Frost suggests that the major difference was in the way the two cities used their capital. The 'traditional' city directed a high proportion of its capital accumulation into industrial plant and had little left for urban infrastructure, hence housing was dense. The 'new frontier' city directed a far higher proportion of its wealth into urban infrastructure, thus enabling low density to be the major form of development.

The differences in capital availability came from the different wealth base:

- the 'traditional' city developed wealth from an industrial base for import substitution and innovation; and
- the 'new frontier' city developed wealth by servicing a large rural hinterland and just investing in land for suburb building. Jacobs (1984) developed a similar analysis of how capital priorities shape cities.

Political priorities can thus shape cities by favouring how capital is used: for developing innovation or for developing land. The new global economic forces associated with information technology may be a new factor shaping cities today but sources of capital can still be directed toward assisting them for productive innovation or continue to be directed into land for suburb building.

Cultural Forces Shaping Cities

In addition to economic priorities there are cultural priorities which shape cities. Australia is a good example as it is a large country with a small population by any comparison. When the first settlers came to Australia from the densely populated areas of Europe, the one resource which seemed virtually endless was space. The desire for space was also fed by a strong anti-city, pro-rural tradition that came from England in the nineteenth century. This pastoral tradition was partly a reaction to the 'dark satanic mills' and polluted air of the uncontrolled industrial cities of England, and partly a response to poets and writers like Banjo Patterson and Henry Lawson and the painters of the Heidelberg school who projected the vision of a pastoral Australia in which the closer that people are to nature, then the healthier and more socially adapted would be its citizens (Williams, 1985).

Urban development in each of the transport phases, therefore, was under cultural pressure to provide as much space as possible (Carter, 1987). So, density has tended to be relatively low in each period of Australian urban history. In the nineteenth century, the density of Sydney was over 100 people per hectare which is ten times the density being built in new suburbs today; in European cities, however, densities at the same time were around 150 to 200 per hectare (Newman and Hogan, 1981).

The imposition of generous spatial standards in cities had a ready acceptance in the New World cities of America and Australia through modern town planning—a reformist movement designed to create more 'healthy' and 'morally upright' urban residents by imposing standards of density and segregating land uses (King, 1978; Boyer, 1983).

Australia has a long tradition of spacious urban planning. However, it has also had a long urban tradition of residents being equally desirous of easy access to urban services, work and community; and so there is also a history of inner urban living. Many people have left these inner areas for new suburban locations but at the same time many have moved to these areas from outer suburbs. Desirable locations for living in Australia continue to be a combination of these two cultural traditions (ABS, 1981). Data on this are provided in trends outlined below.

Thus, technology, economic priorities and cultural attitudes all impinge on city form through choices made about where people live and work; they are all expressed through the transport and infrastructure priorities of the city as well as the preferred form and location of buildings. These factors are now including a new set of technological and economic forces related to information technology and globalisation. Is this new global city changing its urban form? There is also a new cultural agenda for sustainability which features the need to contain the growth in use of the automobile. Is this agenda complementary or conflicting with that of the global city?

The Global City—An Emerging Form

The major new economic/technological factors in the last years of the twentieth century which are likely to shape our cities are: (a) the increased use of information technology; and (b) the increased globalisation of major cities. These are linked and may begin to work through our cities in a number of ways.

Increased Use of Information Technology

Simplistic notions about information technology first suggested that its impact on cities would be to create 'community without propinquity', to disperse people into 'non-place urban realms' or exurbs, where people only needed to telecommute (Webber, 1963, 1964, 1968). More sophisticated approaches recognised that information technology had the ability to reform cities based on the reduced need for face-to-face interchange in some activities, but the continuing need for some quality human interactions critical to economic and cultural processes (Castells, 1989;

Castells and Hall, 1994). Hall (1997) after several years of being very equivocal on this, now states:

> The new world will largely depend, as the old world did, on human creativity; and creativity flourishes where people come together face-to-face (p.89).

Others have emphasised that 'local milieus' will emerge (Willoughby, 1994) or that local culture will be strengthened as globalised information makes national borders less relevant (Ohmae, 1990; Naisbett, 1994; Sassen, 1991, 1994) or that the importance of face-to-face contact will ensure centres emerge as critical nodes of information-oriented production (Winger, 1997). We would like to build on these emerging ideas.

The mechanism for how information technology could be associated with the concentrating of urban activities into nodal centres, rather than dispersal of cities, is possibly due to a combination of:

- the shifting of intrusive industrial production out of urban centres which means that clustering of information-oriented jobs can occur more easily;
- the need for integration of specialised disciplines to solve most global economy issues which means that face-to-face interaction between professionals is necessary for the critical phases of any project; and
- the purchasing of easy access to quality urban environments by those with the extra wealth, created by being part of the global economy; whether such places will be in central/inner city centres or edge city centres (Garreau, 1991) is pursued below.

It is postulated, therefore, that the emerging future city based around information technology is likely to be more of a multi-nodal city with distinct sub-centres that express a particular cultural and economic identity. The idea of a city with just one major centre (CBD) will become less and less obvious, though there is no necessity for this sub-centering process to be any less urban in character as once was considered inevitable. Other agendas like sustainability, and particularly the need to better manage the car in urban areas, need to be assessed in the light of the global city's changing form.

Some hypotheses are therefore suggested.

HYPOTHESIS 1: The cities of the modernist era, which were scattered by the car and the zoning of industry, may begin to concentrate around central and sub-centred nodes of quite intense urban activity in the global-information technology era.   Figure 13.1 pictures how a car-dependent city may change to being more multi-centred.

HYPOTHESIS 2: These global cities may also begin to slow down in their use of the car and grow in transit as this is favoured by sub-centering. However, this will only occur if infrastructure and urban design are less oriented towards car dependence, not more. Thus, the techno-economic processes may have different expressions due to different cultural forces, especially those shaping what is a quality urban environment and how seriously a city tackles the sustainability agenda.

Increased Globalisation of Major Cities

Cities have always existed as commercial and cultural centres for a region and with links to the broader global arena of other cities (Jacobs, 1984). What is new in our era is the extent of the globalisation and how much of a city's economy can be oriented to that bigger arena rather than just its own region.

Global cities are those which are primarily oriented to global markets and hence the global region, or at least a major part of that, such as the Pacific Rim. With a primary link to a broader region, rather than just the local region, it is possible that global cities will begin to have different outcomes for urban form than cities which are just regional. Thus, a further hypothesis is generated.

HYPOTHESIS 3: Increased globalisation of cities may enlarge the disparity between those in global cities able to participate and those who do not, and heighten the difference between global cities and regional cities in terms of how local economic and cultural differences are expressed, e.g. land prices (and hence population growth) and the ability to meet the new global sustainability agenda.

These hypotheses will now be examined in terms of evidence from two recent studies.

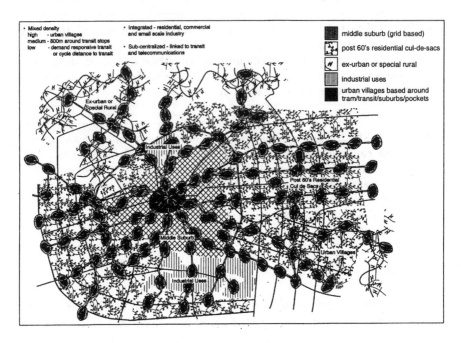

Figure 13.1   Future city—nodal/information city

Evidence in Australian Cities: the State of the Environment Report

The 'State of the Environment Australia 1996' report was a landmark study in Australia conducted for the Federal government by a series of expert panels. The report was also a first in that it contained a whole chapter on Human Settlements. The data collected for this chapter provide some perspective on the above postulates about the form of global cities. The two main economic trends are summarised in the following way.

The Emergence of Sydney as the Main Australian Global City

Evidence from a range of sources shows Sydney has become Australia's number one global city. The 1995 Business Review Weekly top 200 companies in Australia were located as follows: Sydney 83, Melbourne 63, Perth 25, Brisbane 13 and Adelaide 8. Some 46 percent of Australia's outgoing overseas business telephone calls are made from Sydney, 26 percent from Melbourne, 8 percent from Perth, 7 percent from Brisbane and

4 percent from Adelaide (Newton, 1995). Other data on international firms and capital investment show the same pattern (Stimson, 1995a).

The Restructuring of Australian Cities to a More Information-Oriented Economy

In the 10 year period from 1981 to 1991 Australian employment in manufacturing declined by 10 percent, producer services (information-oriented jobs related to globalisation) grew by 51 percent, and people services (personal services and social services also with an information-oriented base but not so related to globalisation) grew by 35 percent (Newton *et al.*, 1996). These are the major urban job shifts (see Table 13.1).

Table 13.1   Trends in employment in Australia, 1981-1991

Employment Category	1981	1991	Absolute Growth	% Growth
Extractive industries	50,925	49,377	-1,548	-3.0
Manufacturing (transformative industries)	1,017,906	914,015	-103,891	-10.2
Distributive industries	927,646	1,115,941	188,295	20.3
Producer services	369,942	560,046	190,104	51.4
People services (social services and personal services)	920,056	1,245,533	325,477	35.4

Source: Newton *et al.*, 1996

Impact on Urban Form and Sustainability

The Increasing Concentration of the Global City. Recent trends in the geography of Australian employment show:

• manufacturing jobs have gone out of the city centres and sub-centres and some have gone out of the city altogether (Beer *et al.*, 1994);

- producer services are clustered in the core and inner area, i.e., they are in sub-centres of activity rather than in the dispersed outer areas; and
- people services are found across the whole city, particularly in sub-centres.

The growth of employment centres in Australian cities based on information-oriented jobs confirms the postulate that information technology can be the means for re-urbanising a city around sub-centres. That it is more urban than suburban is also confirmed by the data below.

The employment data show that global city jobs in producer services are concentrating more in the central core and inner areas than the outer and fringe suburbs. Table 13.2 and Figure 13.2 show that the wealthy residential sectors of Australian cities are also now more concentrated in the core and inner suburbs than in the outer and fringe suburbs.

Table 13.2   Percentage of households earning $70 000 or more per annum by urban sector in Australia's major cities, 1991

	Sydney	Melbourne	Brisbane	Adelaide	Perth
Core	17.1	11.4	9.4	14.7	7.5
Inner	15.1	10.9	7.5	10.3	7.3
Middle	10.7	10.1	8.2	7.3	9.1
Outer	12.6	8.2	5.8	5.3	6.1

Source: ABS 1991 Census

Thus, it appears that people involved in the professional and managerial occupations related to the global city are clustering in central locations near to where their jobs are found.

This has not always been the case as the Australian inner city did go through a significant downturn and population decline in the 1970s which led some to speculate that a 'donut effect', similar to US cities, would set in. This has not eventuated but instead the inner city (and core area) have re-urbanised and now it is continuing with renewed momentum due to global city jobs and associated new residences.

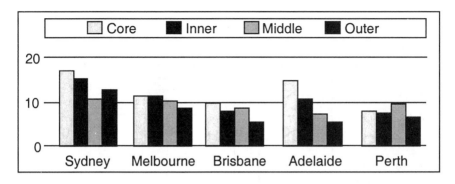

Figure 13.2   Proportion of Australian city households earning $70,000 or more per annum, by urban sector (1991)

Figure 13.1 above also confirms that the most globalised city, Sydney, shows this concentration of wealth in central areas the most. Thus,the inner area in Australian cities is becoming the pre-eminent global city area. This is reflected in housing prices: the inner areas are much higher in price and Sydney again has the highest difference between inner and outer areas with the highest overall average as well (Real Estate Institute of Australia, 1997).

Though suburbanisation continues, reurbanisation in the older areas of Australian cities is now evident, particularly in the form of higher density dwelling construction (see Figure 13.3).

The global city residential concentration effect seems to be most evident within Sydney. By 1994, 48 percent of all residential development in Sydney consisted of medium- and high-density dwellings. This shift to denser dwellings is, however, reflected in Australia-wide trends.

In the 1970s Melbourne and Sydney's inner areas declined both in the number of dwellings and population, but since then the trend has reversed.

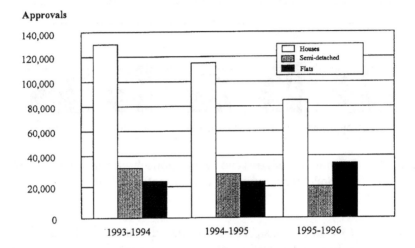

Figure 13.3 Approvals for different dwelling types, Australia, 1993-1994 to 1995-1996

Source: ABS, Building Approvals Australia, November 1996 Cat #8731.0, cited in AHURI (QHM, February 1997)

Table 13.3 Population and housing trends in inner area of Melbourne and Sydney 1971-1991

	Sydney		Melbourne	
	Population	Housing	Population	Housing
1971-76	-11%	-3%	-16%	-2%
1976-81	-4%	-1%	-6%	-1%
1981-86	+1%	+2%	-5%	-1%
1986-91	+1%	+2%	-1%	+1%

In terms of dwelling commencements in Melbourne, since 1985 each year the proportion of housing that has been built through reurbanisation has been around 21 percent of the total housing. In 1994 this was 26 percent. In Sydney the figure is around 25 percent for each year since 1985 with 32 percent in 1993 and 1994, and it is of a higher density than in Melbourne. The situation in Brisbane shows an even more dramatic increase in the process of reurbanisation. In 'Brisbane 2011', the City of Brisbane outlines how its current housing stock is 80 percent detached houses and 20 percent higher density but recent trends are rapidly changing this:

• from 1971 to 1991 the ratio of detached houses to other dwellings in new construction was typically 65:35; and
• since 1988 the balance has been close to 50:50, with some quarters showing higher proportions of non-detached housing.

The Brisbane study concluded:

• housing development is becoming increasingly diverse and is market driven in response to demand;
• the detached house on a large allotment is no longer the dominant form of new housing; and
• a range of housing forms is feasible in old and newly developing areas (Brisbane City Council, 1994).

A study in Perth shows that 38 percent of all housing development (and 21 percent of population) in the past 15 years has occurred in the present built-up area rather than on the fringe (Newman, 1995). This is higher than any of the planners had anticipated or planned for. The same can be seen in all the Australian cities where no facilitative or coercive planning has been involved in this process apart from a few demonstration projects by the Federal Government under the Better Cities programme. Many Australian academics have been vehemently opposed to such reurbanisation (e.g. Troy, 1996 and O'Connor, Darby and Rapson, 1995) and believe it is a government-led process that has no market appeal. The evidence appears to be contrary. Recent data from Melbourne shows that 8000 extra people moved into the central core area in 1996 compared to a loss in all other years for as far back as records go (Australian Financial Review, 1997).

Thus, the increased importance of the global city has been associated with a rapid process of reurbanisation in recent years in Australian cities. The 20 percent to 40 percent of all residential activity outlined above which has reurbanised is associated with more than 50 percent of all commercial activity which has occurred within the existing urban area rather than on the urban fringe. And the data would suggest that it is the top end of the market which is focusing on the core and inner areas. Many commentators suggest that this process is quite small compared to the suburbanisation of housing and work, but this would appear to miss the significant slow down in all-out suburbanisation which characterised the 1970s and early 1980s. To any casual observer the Australian inner city is booming and certainly the real estate market reflects this.

The question remains as to whether this change which has occurred at the same time as the growth of global city information-oriented jobs, is just a coincidence or is an expression of how global city jobs have become more important for face-to-face meetings in central locations. Detailed studies of the firms involved in these processes and the lifestyles they are inducing, would help to confirm or deny the hypothesis. Certainly the global city jobs and housing appear to be associated with quality urban environments offering a range of cultural services. Quantification of this would also be helpful to confirm the greater urbanity of the global city process in its Australian expression.

The concentration of the global city in each Australian city, especially in Sydney, is consistent with the hypothesis that information technology can be a force for reurbanising cities and this can be concentrated in central and inner areas. In the second section of this paper evidence is given of reduced growth in car use associated with this reurbanisation process.

Sydney's economic growth and the size of the city may not be as closely linked any more. For many years, each Australian capital city has been attracting a larger share of its region's population growth. There are signs now that the proportion of this growth is slowing down and in Sydney's case the share of State population is declining. Despite its economic growth, the metropolis no longer dominates the population growth of its State: in 1991, 62 percent of the population of NSW was located in Sydney, but Sydney accommodated only 55 percent of the State's growth between 1986 and 1991 and 42 percent between 1991 and 1993. Sydney has been the major source of interstate migration to the South East Queensland conurbation and to major growth nodes along the mid- and north-NSW coastline.

Among the contributing factors to this change could be the effect of international market forces causing Sydney housing and land values (particularly in reurbanising areas) to rise to international market levels thus pushing many people out to cheaper locations. Therefore, the process of becoming a global city with an orientation to its global region may, to some extent, disconnect a city from its regional economic forces. Land and housing prices in a global city become more strongly related to the global region demand, not just the local region demand. Many people who are not direct participants in the global city economy can then cash in their extra land and house value and shift to other city-regions with a substantial gain. This appears to have been happening with around 60,000 moving from Sydney to South East Queensland between 1986 and 1991.

This global city phenomenon of stabilising or slowing population growth relative to other parts of its region, may be increasingly a feature of other global cities, though evidence for it is not yet clear.

The larger global cities are more able to address the sustainability agenda. Sustainability for a city can be defined as a process which leads to reduced inputs of natural resources (land, energy, water, materials), reduced outputs of wastes (solid, liquid and air emissions) whilst simultaneously improving livability (health, income, employment, housing, education, accessibility, public spaces and community) (Newman and Kenworthy, 1998). The evidence in the SoE Report is that larger cities like Sydney tend to do better at this aspect of the sustainability agenda. They have lower per capita use of resources and production of wastes as well as having higher livability on all criteria (Newman *et al.*, 1996). This is consistent with other studies such as a study of Nordic cities by Naess (1993). The mechanism for this appears to be the economies of scale and density found in larger cities. This means that global cities can have better access to markets and technology for recycling, waste treatment, energy efficiency and public transport as well as the livability criteria which have been traditionally associated with larger cities. Larger cities do reach capacity limits sooner for airsheds and water supply/waste issues, but they also have more ability to tackle such issues in their growth. It could be anticipated that global cities would continue to lead other settlements in these sustainability issues as well as with information-related productivity gains. The 'green Olympics' in Sydney is certainly fulfilling this role in Australia.

The economic (and cultural) disparities within Australian cities are growing. Global city processes are likely to create economic and cultural disparities within a city (as well as between a city and its region as above). The data in Australian cities show that over the past 15 years the difference between the richer and poorer neighbourhoods increased (Gregory and Hunter, 1995). The poorer areas had a significantly higher number of poor and, in particular, unemployed people. These 'pockets of poverty' are not as bad as some ghettos in other countries due to Australian social wage factors, but are of considerable concern. It would not be hard to show that these areas are the least oriented to the global city information economy. Thus, the new global city jobs are just by-passing them. They also have the least cultural services as well as economic wealth. The importance of education in reversing these disparities will become more critical as the global city grows.

The evidence from the State of the Environment Report suggests that the Australian global city with its information-oriented economy is becoming more multi-centred and more urban, with implications for its overall population growth, but there are growing disparities between those who are part of the global city and those who are not. It is not inconsistent with the sustainability agenda.

Evidence in Global Cities: the World Bank Report on 37 cities. This study was commissioned by the World Bank to update to 1990 our study of 32 global cities (Newman and Kenworthy, 1989), to extend it to other Asian cities and to include some new economic and environmental parameters (Kenworthy *et al.*, 1997). The full study will be published in Newman and Kenworthy (1998).

The study allows some conclusions to be drawn of relevance to this discussion about how the global city is being formed in other parts of the world. Some brief conclusions are drawn below and illustrated using data gathered for the study.

Most global cities in the sample are reurbanising and concentrating, thus reversing decades of decline in densities (jobs and population). The trends in activity intensity (the sum of jobs and population), for the period 1960-90 in the 37 global cities are outlined in Newman and Kenworthy (1998). For most cities the previous two decades have seen declines in activity intensity. However, for this last decade (1980-90), the trend towards dispersal has slowed or stopped. There are only two cities which are clearly still declining overall in their activity intensity (London and Brussels). Sixteen cities have levelled off from their declines and are now steady. Thirteen have increased in the density of their activity. The trend could not be followed for the newly industrialising cities for which 1990 data alone have been obtained.

The US cities have all increased in their activity density, apart from Detroit and Chicago which held steady. This increased concentration, however, has not been uniform: the concentration has been in the outer suburbs whilst their inner areas continued to decline, though not enough to lead to overall activity intensity declines as has occurred in previous decades. This is consistent with concentration around edge cities. The continued decline of US inner cities seems to be related to the on-going social problems there.

The Australian cities data show a steadying out of the decline from the previous decades and as the main reurbanisation process seems to have occurred in the 1990s, it is likely that the next decade will show an increase in activity density.

The European city which shows the most reurbanisation is Stockholm which increased in activity in its CBD, inner and outer areas. It is particularly worth noting that this trend is also associated with an absolute and per capita decline in car use across the whole city.

These trends are largely consistent with the postulated changes expected in the global city and they again show that sustainability is not necessarily made more difficult by the emerging global city. As these trends in urban form are only in their early phase it is hard to distinguish on such a large scale and so more detailed internal studies would help to confirm that the process of concentrating, particularly around quality urban environments, is underway.

For example, Cervero (1995) has shown how Stockholm has made its transition to an information-oriented city by stressing its transit corridors and sub-centres. Gehl and Gemsoe (1996) have shown that Copenhagen has had a deliberate strategy for 30 years to build a competitive global city by continuously reducing car-parking and creating more attractive public spaces in their central area. Monheim (1988) has shown that global businesses are attracted to pedestrian-oriented European urban environments which are very intensely active but are largely car-free. Roberts (1989) found similar results for traffic calmed areas in a study of six European cities. Linneman and Gyourko (1997) showed that in US global cities big corporation headquarters are attracted to large central parks.

Most global cities are beginning to slow down in car use growth. The Stockholm example above suggests that it may be possible to see a slow down in car use growth in the emerging global city. There has been a lot of speculation that the US city and the Australian city will begin to stabilise in their car use growth, not due to the postulated ideas above (i.e., reurbanisation), but due to dispersal of work to the suburbs leading to reduced jouney-to-work distances. This is seen to obviate any necessity to restructure the approach to car-based, low density development such as through reurbanisation or changed infrastructure priorities (Gordon and Richardson, 1989; Gordon, Kumar and Richardson, 1989; Gordon, Richardson and Jun, 1991; Brotchie, 1992). In the US these authors pointed to some data which suggested a stabilising in journey-to-work lengths (though it is hard to compare the two surveys they used as they came from different kinds of studies and mostly concerned journey-to-work times that remained roughly half an hour—see Newman, Kenworthy and Vintila, 1995). However, the conclusion that low density sprawl may lead to reduced car use was used to justify the continued sprawl and lack of transit options in these cities.

The global cities data can now be used to provide some perspective as comparative information on the trends in car use and journey-to-work can be examined for the period 1980 to 1990 (when stabilisation in both parameters was predicted in these cities). Table 13.4 summarises the data.

Table 13.4   Growth in car use per capita and journey-to-work trip lengths in global cities, 1980-1990

Cities	Annual car use per capita (km, 1980)	Annual car use per capita (km, 1990)	Journey-to-Work length (km, 1980)	Journey-to-work length (km, 1990)
United States	8806	10870	13.0	15.0
Australian	5794	6536	12.0	12.6
Toronto	4238	5019	10.5	11.2
European	3526	4519	8.1	9.6
Asian (wealthy)	923	1487	?	?

The trend in US cities is to continue to grow substantially in car use and journey-to-work distances. The growth is faster than it was in the previous decade (2.3 percent p.a. in the 1980s compared to 2.2 percent p.a. in the 1970s). The 2113 kms of extra car travel by the average US city dweller in the decade that it was anticipated to stabilise, is similar to the total level of car use per capita found in Tokyo and Singapore in 1990 or Paris and London in 1980.

In US cities the absolute amount of extra growth is far more than in any of the other cities (see Figure 13.4 below). There is as yet no sign of stabilisation in car use or travel distances in US cities.

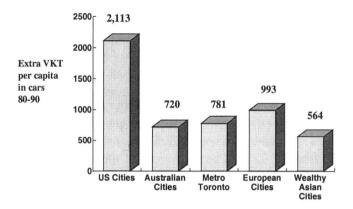

Figure 13.4 Trend in per capita use of cars (VKT) by region, 1980 to 1990

On the other hand, there has been an interesting slow down in car use per capita growth in Australian cities (4.5 percent/yr in the 1960s, 2.3 percent/yr in the 1970s and 1.2 percent/yr in the 1980s). It is possible that the difference is primarily due to the reurbanisation process. Reurbanisation, if it occurs in transit-oriented or walking-oriented areas, means that people are generally going to have far less need to travel and the process also favours other modes. The difference between the reurbanisation which has begun to occur in Australian cities compared to US cities is that the Australian process is largely concentrated in core and inner areas. Thus, when wealthy people move to these areas and/or create businesses there, this is likely to involve reduced car use. On the other hand, creating more concentrated activity in the outer areas is only going to build on an already established car dependence and make it more so. Other related factors could also be involved in the slow down of per capita car travel in Australian cities relative to US cities, such as the quality of urban spaces resulting in safer urban environments for transit users, pedestrians and cyclists (Kenworthy and Newman, 1993).

Similar patterns in slower car growth than US cities are observable in Canadian cities and in the European cities in the global city sample where reurbanisation is also apparent. For example, Stockholm is the only city in the sample to have a per capita decline in car use (229 kms) between 1980 and 1990. It grew in per capita transit by 15 percent in this period and at the same time it increased its density in the city centre, the inner area and the outer suburbs through a range of innovative new compact developments.

However, reurbanisation and more sustainable transport practices only occur together if the cultural conditions for facilitating them are in place. The situation in US cities is not the same as in Australian, Canadian or European cities. Despite strong environmental policies and economic rationale contained in legislation such as ISTEA and the Clean Air Act, there are social barriers to reurbanisation in the inner areas due to the wide disparities in wealth and lack of opportunities associated with racial issues (Massey and Denton, 1993). The abandonment of the inner city by those with the means to move has fed the sprawl and car dependence outlined above. This sprawl appears to be largely continuing unabated and new commercial development is going mostly to edge cities, in some cases 'second generation' edge cities even farther from traditional centres. Thus, although sub-centering and concentration are occurring, it is not associated with transit and walking-oriented landuse. It is just concentrating around areas that were built for the car and few new transit systems are part of the process.

If social policies on US inner cities are not able to overcome their problems, then it is likely that future urban growth will continue to direct US city development into car-dependent edge cites. In such an event the US global city is not likely to be associated with much stabilisation in car use or travel distances, whilst others like Australian, Canadian and European cities probably will. Asian cities are discussed below. The US global city may thus, on current trends, be not as sustainable as those elsewhere.

However, the situation could change and there is some evidence that reurbanisation is beginning to occur in a few US cities (Portland, Boston and Washington). Boston, in particular had 14,000 extra people in its inner area in 1990 compared to 1980, and this was following a decade where they lost 75,000 people. At the same time Boston had the lowest car use growth of all the US cities (1428 kms) and it grew in transit use per capita by 43 percent. Perhaps of greatest significance, Boston's inner city crime rate has dropped dramatically: in 1995 there was not one teenage murder in the City of Boston. These matters seem to be related.

The universal decrease in inner area crime rates in US cities which has occurred in recent years may mean that processes of dispersion there will also begin to reverse. The fledgling inner city reurbanisation process may grow as it has in inner cities elsewhere and hence make their global cities more sustainable. The conditions for US inner cities to reurbanise are not too difficult to imagine. Thus, it is possible to see an acceleration in this process in the 1990s as has occurred elsewhere in developed cities in the 1980s. It would be given extra momentum if the sustainability agenda was adopted more seriously and was associated with new priorities for non-car based infrastructure.

Transit is growing nearly everywhere. Charles Lave (1992) in an analysis on transport trends suggested that: 'The desire for personal mobility seems to be unstoppable—it is perhaps the irresistible force....public transportation has lost the battle against the auto in the US....and it is losing it in Europe too....it is very, very hard to lure people out of automobiles and into transit' (p.9). He continues that there is 'no evidence in the literature' to support the view that this is possible.

Is it the case that the global city will inherently be an anti-transit city or will it begin to favour transit because it will lead to sub-centres that inherently are more transit-friendly? The actual data from most cities seem to indicate the latter—see Figure 13.5.

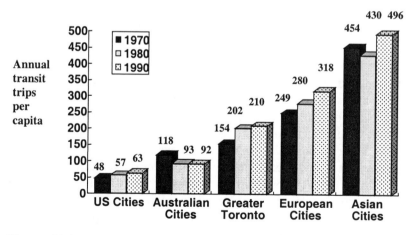

Figure 13.5   Trends in transit use in the world's cities, 1970-1990

Transit in US cities is still very low but the systems in most major global cities are growing again. Toronto, the European cities and Asian cities all grew rapidly in transit. However, Australian cities have hardly changed in the 1980s. Looking at it more positively, the trend down did stop and indeed may have started growing again in the 1990s (Kenworthy and Newman, 1993). But compared to most other cities in the global cities' sample the Australian city and the US city have not done much with their transit systems in recent times. The difference is obviously related to the much greater area of car-dependent urban form in Australian and US cities but it also relates to the level of transit service provided. Two measures of transit service are provided in Table 13.5.

Table 13.5   Public transport service per urban ha in global cities, 1990

Public transport service	US cities	Australian cities	Toronto	European cities	Wealthy Asian cities	Developing Asian cities
Service kms per urban hectare	428	760	4,082	4,474	19,474	19,773
Speed-weighted service kms per urban ha	289	552	3,049	4,803	21,179	15,068

Table 13.5 shows the amount of public transport service that is provided per urbanised ha in the cities in our study. It shows this in two ways. The first is simply the amount of service provided divided by the relevant urbanised area. The second way of describing service provision distinguishes what might be described as a service quality factor which reflects the kind of public transport infrastructure that predominates in cities (e.g. buses on congested streets or rail services on dedicated rights-of-way). This factor takes the first variable and multiplies it by the ratio of the overall public to private transport speed in each city. This weights the service kilometres per ha by how competitive public transport is in speed terms with respect to its main competitor, private transport. Thus, in cities dominated by buses (such as in Australia, the US and developing Asian cities), which are considerably slower than cars, the service is reduced.

Whereas in cities which have good rail systems which boost public transport speed relative to cars, the service provision is increased.

The service data show a considerable difference in commitment to transit. Furthermore, the limited data we have on trends indicate that the Australian and US cities were virtually static in the 1980 to 1990 period, Toronto grew a little (but is reversing in the 1990s), and European cities on the other hand grew by seven percent from their already high position. The wealthy Asian cities grew by 20 percent and of the newly industrialising cities only two, Kuala Lumpur and Manila, had the data and in both cases they declined.

The growth in some European global cities' transit systems has been quite spectacular. Zurich for example, which is the wealthiest city in the global cities sample, grew by 171 trips per capita in the 1980s to reach a level of 515 trips per person per year. The average total trips per capita in Australian cities is 91. In fact the average transit trips per capita *growth* in European cities is more than the *total* per capita transit use in US cities and is similar to the total trips per capita in Perth, Adelaide and Brisbane. In Asian cities the growth was similar. Far from Lave's dismal predictions, growth in transit in European cities is accelerating (2.1 percent in the 1980s cf to 1.5 percent in the 1970s).

The transit pattern in global cities is thus very mixed in different parts of the world. The idea that transit is not associated with the new world of the global city is nonsense. However, the US and Australian cities (and newly industrialising Asian cities) have done little to upgrade their transit systems but have instead continued to put most of their infrastructure funding into roads (see the data below). On the other hand, in European and wealthy Asian cities, the priority has shifted to upgrading their transit. Such trends are a positive sign towards sustainability and, as discussed below, they are associated with improved overall economic performance in these cities.

Asian global cities are expressing two different cultural approaches to their transport task, one car-based the other transit-based. As shown below in Table 13.6 the Asian cities are all uniformly more dense than other global cities in the sample.

In terms of activity intensity, the Asian cities are more than ten times denser than US and Australian cities. However, they are showing different cultural expressions of how they cope with transport within these compact areas. The differences are seen by comparing Hong Kong, Singapore and Tokyo (the three wealthy Asian cities) with Jakarta, Surabaya, Kuala

Lumpur, Manila, Bangkok and Beijing (the newly industrialising Asian cities).

Table 13.6   Density in global cities, 1990

	Australian cities	US cities	Canadian cities	European cities	Wealthy Asian cities	Developing Asian cities
Population Density Per ha	2.3	14.2	28.5	49.9	152.7	166.4
Job Density Per ha	5.3	8.1	14.4	31.5	87.5	65.1
Activity Intensity Per ha	17.5	22.3	42.9	81.5	251.4	231.5

The different transport characteristics are set out in Table 13.7 along with the Gross Regional Product which is a measure of actual city wealth (ie it is not national data).

Table 13.7   Transport patterns and city wealth in global cities, 1990

	Australian cities	US cities	Canadian cities	European cities	Wealthy Asian cities	Developing Asian cities
Car use per person (VKT)	6,571	11,155	6,551	4,519	1,486	1,821
% transit of total passenger transport task	7.7%	3.1%	10.2%	22.3%	62.8%	38.7%
Gross Regional Product per capita	$19,761	$26,822	$22,572	$31,720	$21,331	$2,861

The most obvious characteristic separating the two groups of Asian cities is the level of commitment to public transport. The differences are almost as acute as those between the US/Australian city and European cities. Despite being seven times less wealthy, the newly industrialising Asian cities actually have a little higher level of car use than the wealthy Asian cities; but they do not have nearly the same level of transit which in the wealthy Asian cities takes over 60 percent of all the motorised transport needs. The very successful Asian global cities have thus managed their cities by retaining their compactness and channelling their transport needs into transit. They also have relatively high levels of walking and cycling, e.g. Tokyo has 42 percent of total daily trips by non-motorised means.

The newly industrialising Asian cities are becoming dominated by their traffic problems and are mostly tending to invest in large roads for solutions to their transport problems, rather than the transit systems characteristic of the wealthy Asian cities. Rather than looking to car-dependent cities for their model, these cities would do better to pursue the successful Asian model. Their urban form lends itself to transit, as not only are these cities compact, they are invariably very densely developed along strong corridors which are ideal for rapid transit. Thus, investment in rail systems would produce dramatic improvement to their traffic situations. Their urban forms are also characterised by mixed land use which is ideal for high levels of non-motorised transport. However, the traffic and environmental problems in these cities, as well as lack of investment in non-motorised infrastructure, are forcing pedestrians and cyclists off the streets.

The problem with transport policy in the region is that nations and financing institutions like the World Bank and Asian Development Bank have had an anti-mass transit stance for the last few decades (with little support for non-motorised transport). The reason for this seems to be an inadequate understanding of the economics of transport in cities. This new global cities study now can provide a fresh perspective on this critical issue as it suggests that not only would the agenda of reducing car use growth be met, but the cities would be doing better economically in this emerging global economy. In other words the sustainability agenda would be met in all its dimensions.

Those global cities with better balanced transport systems are doing better economically. Table 13.8 sets out some of the economic data on the various cities in the sample. The indicators are only a few of those obtained but they show the broad patterns.

Table 13.8   Economic data on global cities, 1990

	Australian cities	US cities	Toronto	European cities	Wealthy Asian cities	Developing Asian cities
Amount spent on roads per $1000 of GRP	$7.19	$9.84	$6.65	$4.26	$4.13	$14.76
% transit cost recovery	40%	35%	61%	54%	119%	99%
Transport deaths per 100,000 persons	12.0	14.6	6.5	8.8	6.6	15.0
% of Gross Regional Product spent on all modes transport	13.2%	12.4%	7.4%	8.0%	4.7%	15.0%

The patterns reveal that those cities with the most automobile dependence have the least overall economic efficiency in their transport systems. They spend the most on roads, have to subsidise their transit the most, have the most indirect costs to factors like road accidents (and pollution) and overall they are committing a higher proportion of their city wealth (GRP) for the non-productive purpose of passenger transport.

The World Bank study (Kenworthy *et al.*, 1997) relates these differences to the impact that car dependence has on the efficiency of the city through the costs of infrastructure, direct and indirect costs of the automobile and perhaps to the loss of investment associated with traffic-dominated urban environments compared to quality pedestrian-friendly urban environments.

The difference between the two kinds of Asian cities highlight the point. The wealthy Asian cities are the most efficient overall, while the newly industrialising Asian cities are the least efficient overall. This seems to be related to the high proportion of their money going into roads and relatively high levels of car use (0.637 km/$ of GRP compared to 0.070 km/$ of GRP).

The Australian and US cities with their inadequate transit systems also come out quite poorly in comparison to the European cities and Toronto with their more extensive transit systems. The data support studies by economists such as Aschauer and Campbell (1991) who found that the economic flow-ons from transit were far better than those from highway spending.

The World Bank study suggests that one of the areas of competitive advantage in global cities is the extent of their transit systems. Conversely, one of the factors that will tend to drain the economic life blood of a city is excessive car use. Perhaps it is possible to begin to understand such trends by reference to the emerging global cities form that favours quality urban environments in sub-centres and central areas which are not helped when cities place too much emphasis on facilitating car traffic.

Many commentators on global city urban form have expressed the virtual necessity of growing car dependence if a city is to be competitive, e.g. Stimson (1995b) says that the trends in such cities mean 'an overwhelming dependence on the private car' and thus 'the scenario we face in our cities is that public transport will only be able to service a shrinking proportion of total trip demands' (p.2). The evidence here shows there is no techno-economic imperative for a global city to be more car dependent, if anything it is the reverse—such commentators are only expressing a cultural preference.

Conclusions

We will conclude by discussing the three hypotheses raised at the start of this paper.

Hypothesis 1

Global cities may be concentrating, though in European and wealthy Asian cities this is reinforcing their transit-oriented forms, in US cities it is in car-dependent edge cities, in newly industrialising Asian cities it is in car-oriented dense corridors and centres, and in Australian cities it is more transit-oriented but without the transit support.

Hypothesis 2

Global cities may indeed be able to assist the sustainability agenda, but only if infrastructure priorities enable them to reinforce the concentrating processes in less car-oriented ways.

Hypothesis 3

Global cities may heighten the disparity between those participating and those who do not, they may also mean increased disconnection between a city's population growth and the region's economy, and they could use their growth in wealth as an opportunity for greater sustainability in use of resources and production of wastes.

The two studies which have been used to provide evidence on the emerging characteristics of the global city show some broad patterns which are consistent with the arguments set out under the three hypotheses. In particular they suggest that it is entirely possible for a new alignment to exist between globalisation, information technology and the reduction of car dependence.

There is, of course, a great deal more to do to confirm these patterns. The reurbanising of cities may be well underway across all global cities though it would be better to have more recent data to confirm this trend. Data from inside cities showing how global city firms and residents are working and living would help us to understand how face-to-face contacts are critical to global city economic processes. They could also relate this to the value of urban environmental quality.

14 Sustainability of Eastern and Western Cities

JOHN BROTCHIE, PETER GIPPS, DAVID JAMES,
DON MacRAE and JEREMY MORRIS

Introduction

The development paths of eastern and western cities are converging—in terms of architecture (Chapter 12), urban form and industry mix, and diverging in regard to population size (Chapter 1). Economic and environmental sustainability are increasingly vital to these cities in the global information economy.

The larger cities in Developing Asia are undergoing rapid long-term urban growth from both natural increase and in-migration from villages and smaller towns, attracted by increasing income and employment prospects, and social and cultural opportunities. The current economic crisis is expected to be a short- to medium-term interruption to this urban development and an opportunity to evaluate and revise its directions. Many cities are also undergoing almost simultaneous societal transitions from a largely primary industry base of agriculture and resource development to an industrial and to an information and service base. Urban densities are higher, generally, than in Western cities partly as a result of crowding in low income housing and informal housing in kampongs. There is a shortage of capital for infrastructure, especially water, sewerage and drainage, but also for telecommunications and transport, particularly rail transit—with some notable exceptions such as Singapore and Hong Kong. Formal, low-income housing is also generally in short supply and beyond the means of many low income families. There is an increasing middle income class and a shortage of skilled personnel, increasing car ownership, road traffic congestion, and pollution of urban air, land and natural drainage systems—and, higher urban densities, including office and apartment towers in inner cities. Superblocks with minimal internal movement routes reduce available road space and contribute to congestion. With high rates of income increases in the medium-term some of these problems will be reduced, but the corresponding increase in the use of resources, particularly energy, will continue to create congestion, emissions and sustainability challenges.

Western cities are undergoing urbanisation, re-urbanisation and de-urbanisation forces with different mixes and different outcomes (Harding *et al.*, 1994 and the previous chapter). Their transitions from an agricultural—to an industrial—to an information-based society have commenced much earlier and been slower and sequential. Economic growth is now slow or stable. These societal transitions have seen reversals of fortune, form and movement patterns. Some cities, which prospered in the industrial age, were less well equipped to attract knowledge workers and service industries in the information age. Urban form changed from dispersed agricultural activity to concentrated industrial centres, to again dispersed suburban forms, with transport patterns initially outwards, then inwards, and now a mixture of these, and circumferential trips. Infrastructure is mature and often in need of expansion, replacement or repair. The problems of traffic congestion, air quality and water and land pollution continue to exist but in a more manageable range of growth and change.

Rail transport systems, including urban transit, are generally more developed, reducing road traffic demands in central cities. Telecommunications networks continue to expand in capabilities and band widths. They are converging with computers to form the new urban and global information infrastructure.

Rates of resource use and emissions are stabilising in the West, providing management options for sustainability of urban development.

Rates of resource use and emissions in Eastern cities can be expected to increase towards those in the West. It is doubtful that they will stabilise until they move closer per capita to those of the West (Hooke, Chapter 15), but the rapid rates of growth allow major savings to be introduced—in urban form, infrastructure, activity patterns and transport options, so that sustainability can be an effective part of the development process—leading to a far more sustainable development product. These opportunities are now examined.

Strategies for Sustainable Urban Development

A number of strategies are proposed, in three broad areas, self-containment, integration, and transition to an information economy (CSIRO/Synectics, 1997).

Increasing Self-containment of Urban Activity Patterns or Flows at a Local Level.

1. *House.* Increasing the capacity for home-based activities, e.g. home-based work activities, recreation activities—also telework, tele-shopping, tele-entertainment, teletraining—as telecommunications networks expand in coverage and capabilities and converge with information technologies.

2. *Balancing jobs and homes at the local level.* This can include urban villages, and multi centres. It enables some reduction in commuting travel presently, and more under conditions of travel price increase, or travel restraint—towards the level of complete self-containment.

3. *Providing more centres.* This enables shorter trips for other purposes also—shopping, school, recreation, and access to other services.

4. *Extending water infrastructures.* This means less need for motorised carriage of water, and wastes. Telecommunications can assist with monitoring, meter reading.

5. *Localising energy flows through utilisation of sustainable and renewable energies*—solar, wind, co-generation. Reducing transport energy consumption through the strategies above.

6. *Waste.* Recycling materials, reclaiming air and water pollutants, and solid wastes, reducing energy needed for winning, processing and hauling new resources.

7. *Transport.* Cutting trip lengths as above makes walking, cycling and low energy consuming vehicles more viable and attractive. Use of low energy consuming hybrid or electric vehicles.

Integration or Mixing of Complementary and Synergistic Activities and Land Uses.

8. *Integrating natural and built environment.* This enables cooling and shading of homes and of walking and cycling paths, recreation in or near the home, reduction of urban runoff, retention of rainfall in the

soil, retardation and filtering through vegetation, retention of drainage systems in their natural states, and a more pleasant environment for work and play.

9.   *Mixing and concentrating activities* provides scale and agglomeration economies and increased efficiencies, levels of specialisation, face-to-face contact and innovation, and hence increased income as a result.   Transport costs between these activities are also reduced, and opportunities for face-to-face meetings are increased.

10.   *Linking production / distribution / communications / consumption,* enables inventory management, production on demand, re-engineering of the production process, and substitution of information flows for some movements of people and goods.

Utilising the Transition to an Information Economy

11.   *Improving land use patterns and infrastructure networks using computer-based systems techniques* allows synergistic activities to be co-located, shorter trips between complementary activities, improved networks and network flows, including public transit (rail) networks, channelling of public transport flows to provide higher frequencies along trunks.   Reduction of headways to a few minutes is shown to increase public transit demands.

12.   *Development of increased telecommunications capacities and capabilities, including convergence with information technologies*, enables wider spatial organisation of activities. This includes virtual cities, virtual markets, and virtual organisations, thereby decreasing migration movement to the larger cities, relieving traffic congestion in these cities, enabling substitution of information flows for some trips and for some transport flows.

13.   *Development of global and regional networks* enables this wider organisation of activities, increasing incomes and equity between cities, reducing the need for migration, to the larger cities, enabling a more sustainable development pattern and substitution of information flows for some movements of people and goods.   These latter strategies will take longer to develop in Eastern cities (again with

notable exceptions—such as Singapore), but their impacts can be one order larger.

Demand Management Strategies

14. *Demand management is a further approach to sustainability.* The planning strategies above provide a positive form of demand management through better location and linking of activities. Other methods constrain flows through pricing, regulation, reduction of supply capacity, exclusion or restriction zones for transport and other flows (e.g. water, energy). Pricing policies can be used to constrain demand overall or differentially to reduce congestion and assist productive commercial and industrial flows. These can include pricing of road use, differential pricing of road and rail, differential pricing of inner city roads, pricing or restriction of parking in central cities.

National Socio-Economic Objectives for Sustainable Urban Development

Physical Infrastructure-Related

1. *Housing.* To increase dwelling provision to meet shelter, security, social, psychological and comfort needs at less cost; to improve access to 'social' infrastructure; to increase competitiveness/ attractiveness to new knowledge-based industries and their knowledge workers to increase sustainability and capacity for home based work and other home based activities.

2. *Travel/transport.* To improve public and private transport modes and systems to maximise access to socio-economic opportunities while reducing resource, environmental and other costs; increase access to markets and services; increase efficiency/effectiveness of movement.

3. *Energy.* To improve production and consumption—to yield greater efficiency in residential and commercial sectors, transport, etc., to increase sustainability of energy sources.

4.   *Water.* To increase water quality and access to delivery, urban runoff management, roof water catchment, etc., reclamation, water mining.

5.   *Waste.* To improve sewage sludge treatment and solid waste management, recovery from gaseous stack emissions, recycling, reducing the need for developing new resources.

6.   *Telecoms infrastructure.* To maximise access to socio-economic opportunities and reduce resource / environmental / other costs; increase national competitiveness / access to markets and services; organise activities to increase efficiency / effectiveness / productivity / sustainability/equity.

7.   *Other physical infrastructure*:   to improve other infrastructure, including schools, hospitals, governance, community and social services, etc.

Social Infrastructure-Related

8.   *Health.* To add 'years to life...', increase working days, reduce illness, medical expenditures.

9.   *Education.* To increase access and attainment, training, productivity and assist the transition to an information-based economy.

10.   *Culture.* To preserve or create a spirit of place, cultural experience, wealth generating creativity, innovation.

11.   *Recreation.* To increase mental / physical health, thus reducing health costs and increasing productivity / welfare—'...years to life; improve quality / diversity / synergy of recreational opportunities accessed/ realised, and reduce costs.

12.   *Environment.* To decrease pollutant concentrations, noise; increase amenity, natural vegetation; improve urban setting, etc., improve liveability, quality of life.

Economic Infrastructure

Use the above strategies and objectives to increase social equity, sustainability, attraction, competitiveness, and productivity of cities, and consequently increase GDP.

A Reduced Set

In order to develop and illustrate the techniques in greater depth, only some of these objectives will be considered in particular here.

1.   Improved travel / transport systems improving access and movement efficiency.

2.   Increased information and communication capacities and capabilities, enabling wider organisation of activities, increased access, increased urban, regional and global opportunities.

3.   More efficient and sustainable energy use.

4.   Improve environment and quality of life.

An overall measure of national economic performance is also used: GDP and sector outputs are also evaluated.

The remainder are developed elsewhere (CSIRO/Synectics (1997): Inception Report, Compendium of Issues Papers, Results Report).

Urban Impacts of Strategies

An Urban Impact Model

A two-dimensional model (Brotchie *et al.*, 1995) of urban land-use/ transport interaction is further developed and used to evaluate the urban impacts of the strategies above. The model plots an urban land use parameter against an urban transport parameter.

•   the land use parameter (x) is the ratio of mean trip destination dispersal to mean trip origin dispersal each measured from the city centre, (i.e., mean distance from city centre to each); and

- the transport parameter (y) is the ratio of mean trip distance between these origin and destination pairs over the mean trip distance if all destinations were located at the city centre.

The trip can be the journey-to-work, or to shop or to school, etc. It can be for a particular industry type, e.g. producer services, consumer services or manufacturing, etc.

It can also be for a particular trip mode: car, train, bus, etc., or a communication mode, e.g. telecommunications.

It can also be for a particular city. A particular trip type, journey-to-work, and particular city are shown by the Point D in Figure 14.1.

The parameter x is the ratio of mean distance to all jobs (from city centre) divided by mean distance to all homes (from city centre).

The parameter y is the ratio of mean commuting distance to mean commute if all jobs were at the city centre.

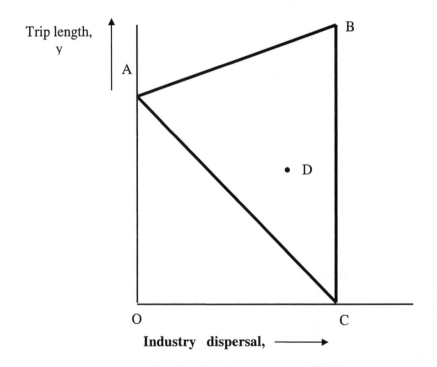

Figure 14.1   Urban triangle ABC: plotting industry dispersal versus mean trip length

D	=	Particular city e.g. Jakarta—particular trip type, commuting
ABC	=	limits to location of city (D)
AB	=	trip length for zero unit travel cost
AC	=	trip length for infinite unit trip cost
A	=	single centred city
BC	=	house/job balance (equal dispersal of each)
C	=	cottage industry
B	=	virtual city—all teletravel—actual travel = point C
AD	=	present travel cost/behaviour
x	=	mean radius of jobs—from city centre (or ratio of mean radius of jobs to mean radius of homes—0C)
y	=	mean trip length (or ratio of mean trip length to mean radius of homes 0C) or mean tele-trip length

The Triangle ABC represents the limits to the location, D, of a city in this x, y space.

Point A represents a single-centred city.

Line BC represents balanced development or equal dispersal of homes and jobs.

Line AB represents zero transport costs.

Line AC represents infinite transport costs.

Ray AD represents present transport costs.

Point C represents cottage industry or a job (or more) in every home.

In the case of telecommunications, Point B represents telecommuting with an equal dispersal of homes and jobs.

Point D represents the major Australian (or Indonesian) metropolitan cities and their commuting trips.

For other types of trip, e.g. shopping, school, or recreation, the Point D would change. For particular types of industry it also changes. Point D also varies between cities. Examples are later shown.

The point D has also moved over time for Western cities. With the shifts from an agricultural or cottage industry economy (Point C) to an industrial economy with industry concentrated near the centre (Point A) to an information economy in which jobs are largely dispersed into the suburbs and edge cities. This trajectory is illustrated (by the line W) in Figure 14.2. In Europe, the two transitions occurred about 200 years apart.

For (Developing) Eastern cities these transitions are occurring almost simultaneously, suggesting the trajectory E in Figure 14.2.

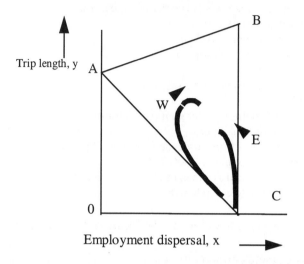

Figure 14.2   Urban development trajectory over time
W :   Western cities—agriculture to industry to information economy
E :   Eastern cities—agriculture to industry/information economy

The present trip length (e.g. Melbourne) shows savings over a single-centred city of about 37 percent (Figure 14.3). These savings increase by another 12 percent (to almost 50 percent) for balanced home/job location on the line BC. Scope for further savings is also shown.

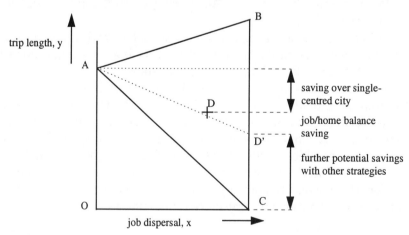

Figure 14.3   Urban triangle—evaluation of strategies

SURD Strategies Impact—on Travel:

Self- containment	1. *housing density increase*:	– reduces mean dispersal of homes; absolute trip length, y
	2. *resident/job balance*:	– moves D to line BC at D', reducing trip length
	3. *more centres*:	– moves D and D' towards AC—for commuting. D and D' still lower for other trip types—reducing trip lengths
	7. *sustainable transport*:	– shift to lower energy modes including cycling, walking for shorter trips—through trip shortening above
Integration	8. *natural and built environment.*:	– moves D towards C for recreational trips—reducing trip lengths
Information economy	11. *optimum land use*:	– moves D towards AC, BC, reduces trip length y
	12. *virtual city:*	– separates travel and information flows: D for telecommuting towards point B, D for travel towards C

Complete self-containment, although unattainable, indicates the potential for further savings. For a single-centred city and complete self-containment, the trip length ratio is 1.0 (Figure 14.4). For four equal centres, with job/home balance, the mean trip length reduces to 0.5, for nine centres it reduces to 0.33, for 16 centres it reduces to 0.25, and for 64 centres and full self-containment to 0.125.

Removing the present economic impediments to changing homes would allow further trip length savings, further increasing self-containment. Increased self-containment and increased centres provides further savings. Better planning of job and home locations will produce further savings still.

In the limit, locating a job in every home, so that commuting is eliminated, returns D to the Point C. Telecommuting can have this effect. For 30 percent telecommuting, mean trip length reduces below the point D by 30 percent. Teleshopping can have a similar effect for shopping trips, etc. In Eastern cities, the high proportion of home-based work has this same effect.

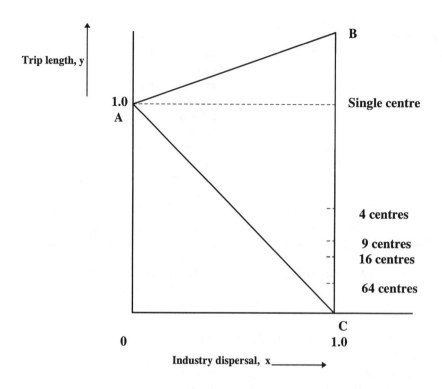

**Figure 14.4   Full self-containment: trip length vs number of equal
centres—balanced dispersal of homes and jobs (x = 1.0)**

The relative dispersal or concentration of various industry types, producer services, consumer services, manufacturing, can also be plotted (Figure 14.5). The relative locations of destinations for work, shopping, school and recreation trips are illustrated in Figure 14.6.

Urban Impacts

The potential for trip reduction, energy saving, air quality improvement, reduction in greenhouse emissions and savings in resources and costs with the various strategies above is substantial.

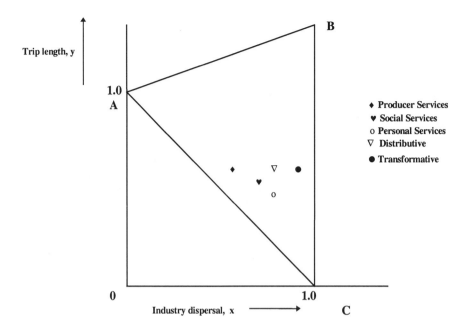

Figure 14.5   **Trip length vs industry dispersal—for different industry types in major Australian cities (Sydney, Melbourne, Brisbane, Adelaide, Perth)**

Self-Containment

- increasing home-based activities for income generation and recreation, can eliminate relevant commuting and recreational trips;
- balancing jobs and homes at a local level reduces mean trip length potentially by almost 20 percent for major Australian cities. Potentially similar savings can be expected in major Asian cities;
- increasing the number of centres offers a similar potential saving for shopping and other trip types; and
- full local self-containment is not realisable—particularly under present market conditions, but its potential savings are large—reducing trip length ratio substantially as given in Figure 14.4.

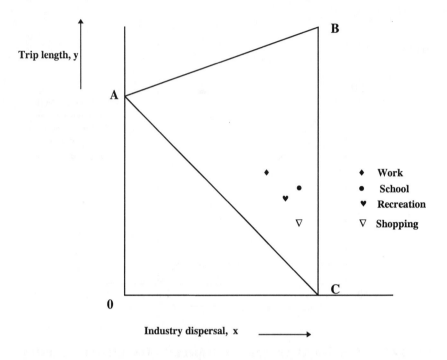

Figure 14.6   Trip length (time) vs destination dispersal for different trip purposes—(Melbourne/Sydney data)

These limits will be more closely approached in futures of energy use constraint or increased travel price.

Reducing the barriers to changing homes or even to changing jobs can increase degree of self-containment. Incentives can also be provided for living and working in the same area. Staging of provision of homes and employment simultaneously can also assist substantially.

Trip shortening can also allow use of lower energy consuming modes such as walking, cycling, or low energy consuming vehicles such as small, hybrid and electric cars.

Recycling of materials can also result in energy savings—in winning, hauling and processing new raw materials.

Integration.   Integration of natural and built environments enables increased recreational opportunities locally, reducing need for external recreational trips. Natural vegetation can also shade and cool the home, and walking and cycling paths, encouraging use of these and further energy savings. This integration also allows drainage systems to be retained in their natural states. Vegetation filters water entering drainage channels, or recharging aquifers. It also retards and retains rainfall runoff, reducing flooding and flash flooding.

Integrating like complementary and synergistic activities provides scale and agglomeration economies and increased incomes, and also reduces time and cost of work trips between these activities, and allows easier face-to-face contacts.

Integrating production/distribution/communication and consumption produces further savings—in inventory management, reduced re-handling, production and distribution on demand, re-engineering of production processes to further reduce resource waste, and tradeoffs between scale and distribution economies. Increased efficiency and competitiveness are outcomes here.

Using the Transition to an Information Economy. Better location of land use activities and transport routes between them can make significant further improvements—to trip distance, and modes used. Placing home and work locations in close proximity, including in mixed use zones, can make savings of 5-20 percent in trip length—from previous land use optimisation studies. Some of these benefits would already be realised from the strategies above. Better location of networks between land uses can provide similar savings. Further savings in energy come from the fact that some of these trip lengths will be reduced enough for a shift to walking or cycling, or use of other low energy consuming modes.

The wider organisation of activities by means of telecommunications and computers can provide further savings. The increasing capacities and capabilities of these networks means that some substitution of these for trips may be made—for interactions between work activities, and for telecommuting, teleshopping, etc.

Perhaps even greater is the benefit resulting from inclusion of other smaller towns in this virtual city or virtual organisation—allowing people to work in—and access services from—these smaller towns, reducing urbanisation pressures on the larger cities, and hence congestion, pollution and the demands for new urban development and infrastructure.

This organisation can extend even wider regionally and globally, yielding increased opportunities at each of these levels, for employment, and access to services, and interactions leading to increased innovation and competitiveness. Substitution of information for movement of people and goods at each of these levels increases sustainability, reduces resource use, and allows increased social equity also—particularly between cities. However, it can also stimulate increased travel and transport and provide more evidence of differences in access and equity.

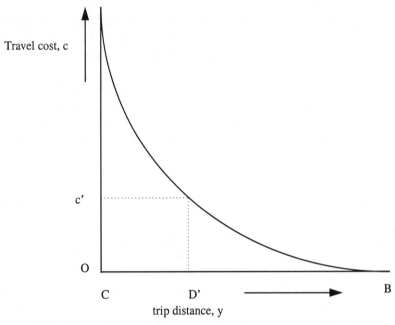

Figure 14.7   Mean trip length, y, vs unit trip cost, c—at line BC of Figure 14.1 or 14.3.
Trip length is y' = CD' for present unit trip cost, c'
Trip length is 0. for infinite cost
Trip length is y = CB for zero cost

Demand Management—Pricing Policies

The impacts of an increase in the price of travel can also be evaluated from the two dimensional model of Figure 14.1. Consider for simplicity of explanation the line BC of balanced jobs and homes. The Point C represents infinite unit transport cost. The Point B represents zero unit transport cost, and the Point D' represents present transport costs. The resulting (exponential) distribution of unit trip cost vs mean trip distance is shown in Figure 14.7. An increase in unit transport costs will result in a corresponding decrease in mean trip length (or number of trips in the short-term) leading to longer-term changes in location or mode to reduce these impacts.

National Impacts

In Australia, a study of impacts on national GDP of efficiency changes in the various service sectors was made for the Australian Government by Stoeckel and Quirke (1992).

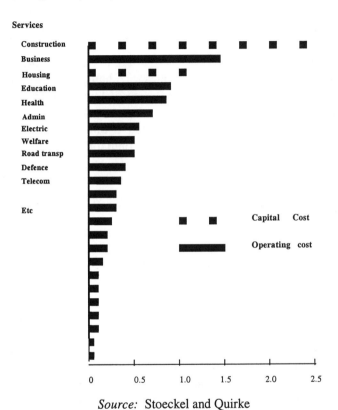

Source: Stoeckel and Quirke

Figure 14.8   Long-term impact on GDP (%) for 10% cut in service costs

This study utilised a national economic model of the Australian economy and examined the impacts on GDP of 10 percent cost savings in each of the various service industry sectors in Australia, including construction, housing construction, business services, the various transport sectors, utilities, and social services. A 10 percent reduction in each of these, independently, provides the increments of GDP shown in Figure

14.8. This provides a total increment in GDP of just over 10 percent if each is assumed to act independently.

These service sectors can also be considered as contributing to capital goods (e.g. via construction and house construction sectors)—providing a 3.7 percent increment in GDP and those providing services which may have some input to capital costs but represent largely operating benefits and costs—providing a further 6.3 percent increment, or more, to GDP.

In major Western cities, service sectors represent the dominant component of GDP. However, the rates of change in urban form and transport networks are slow as a consequence of low (or zero or negative) rates of population growth.

In major and mega (Developing) Eastern cities, the service sectors are smaller, but expanding, and the rates of population and income growth, and construction growth, are much higher. Hence, the benefits derived from sustainable urban development assisted by the strategies above, could be higher, substantially reducing capital and operating costs with a consequent increase in GDP.

In Indonesia, no equivalent national economic model was available and an alternative assessment of national economic performance had to be developed. One basis for evaluation of national economic impacts of the savings above, is to assume an idealised economy in which resources saved in the strategies above are redeployed to produce additional GDP. A 19 sector input output model was developed based on the Indonesian Government's 1990 Input Output Tables—expanded to 22 sectors by break up of the utility, energy and transport sectors—using more detailed data from 66 sector and 161 sector input output tables (CSIRO/Synectics, 1997). The model projected the economy to 2018 based on Government projections for growth in each sector. It further related these projections (in further matrices) to the 12 national objectives and the 13 SURD strategies. The outcomes projected are a 10-fold increase in GDP to the year 2018 from a 1990 base, an 18-fold increase in the construction sector and an 8-fold increase in services. A conservative application of SURD strategies to urban areas is projected to provide a 10 percent increase in urban housing construction costs, a 30 percent reduction in urban travel and a 20 percent decrease in urban energy use. Using these and other national objective impacts as inputs to the national economic model—results in a 4.4 percent increase in national GDP. If housing cost is reduced 10 percent through minimising pavements and through retention of natural environment, GDP increase rises to 5 percent. These results appear to be essentially consistent with those of the Australian study above (Figure 14.8) and the arguments below. The model is Excel-based allowing parameter changes to be evaluated instantaneously and providing a convenient planning aid.

In Indonesia, the service sector is 40 percent of national GDP, with manufacturing 20 percent, but in the major cities these two sectors would contribute a larger share to GDP. Urbanisation is a major force, nationally, and is claimed to represent about 30 percent of national GDP. Savings in its costs of establishment and operation can therefore contribute significantly to GDP. Forty percent of the population is now urban and it will rise to nearly 50 percent by the year 2018. Much of this new urbanisation is in the larger cities. Substantial savings are feasible in some sectors of the economy on the basis of the potential urban cost savings outlined from the SURD strategies above

In Western countries, the proportion of population in cities is much higher and the gross capital investment in cities is also much higher on a per capita basis, but the rate of increase is less. These offsetting effects mean that the reductions in capital and operating costs are similarly significant in their impacts on GDP.

The higher rates of urban development in Eastern cities also means that sustainable development can provide larger proportional savings.

The trip length ratio y, also appears to reduce with city size (e.g. Figure 14.9 for Australian data—but USA and UK data show similar trends), so that larger Asian mega-cities can be expected to have lower values of trip length ratio, y.

These higher growth rates mean that expenditures of capital, energy, greenhouse emissions and air pollutants, etc., will also increase—but the potential savings due to sustainable development strategies will substantially reduce these outputs and rates of emission growth. Even so, creation of a stable state will take much longer in view of the gap that still exists between Eastern and Western per capita incomes, GDP and expenditure of resources. These differences are indicated in Figure 14.10 where Western cities are in a much better position to meet emission reduction targets, but are expending more resources per capita than their Eastern counterparts. Some recognition of this difference is required and is given in global policy for sustainable development and greenhouse emissions.

Trip length

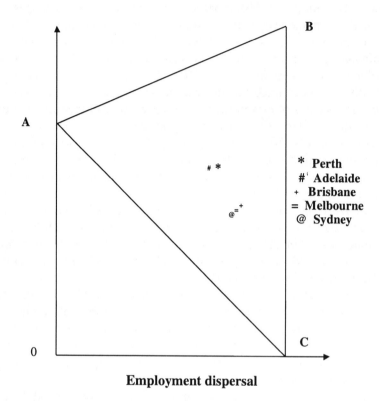

Employment dispersal

Figure 14.9   Comparison of Australian cities

The national economic model developed for this project has some useful additional features:

- it covers all sectors of the economy with finer subdivision in urban related sectors;
- it can be applied more widely to evaluation of national development projects;
- it allows the project parameters to be varied to maximise impact on national economic performance;
- each SURD strategy similarly can be separately evaluated;
- the impacts of this strategy on value added in each national economic sector is evaluated;
- its impact on GDP is also evaluated; and

- the XL base for the model allows these evaluations to be essentially instantaneous—adding to its value as an interactive decision aid.

The national economic model provides a snapshot of the economy in 2018. Cumulative effects over the period to 2018, such as those of capital expenditure on infrastructure which will contribute to productivity and GDP, are evaluated separately (CSIRO/Synectics, 1997).

This model allows integrated planning at the urban, regional and national levels.

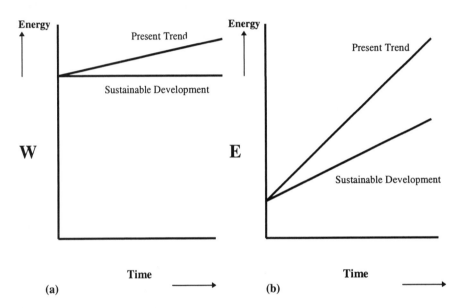

Figure 14.10   Sustainable development impacts—Western and Eastern cities

(a)   Western—high base value, low growth, stable with moderate savings
(b)   Eastern—low base, high growth, still rising even with large savings

Conclusion

Urban Level

This study (for APEC) proposes and examines firstly strategies and objectives for sustainable development at the urban level, especially in the larger urban centres where urbanisation forces are greatest. The study potentially applies to various mega-cities and other major cities and smaller urban centres in Asia. Indonesian cities are considered in particular.

The strategies proposed are capable of making substantial contributions to sustainability of urban development in terms of reduced costs of—development, transport, energy consumption and water supply and drainage needs. These cost savings can be evaluated from land use transport interaction modelling and optimisation, including congestion and air pollution impacts (Newton and Manins, Chapter 11).

The potential savings in transport costs, transport task or energy consumed can be further illustrated and evaluated with the simple, two dimensional urban triangle model which plots land use dispersal against transport trip length. Under current transport costs, substantial transport energy savings can be made with the strategies proposed. Under futures of higher transport costs, or restraint to motorised travel, even larger savings will be made—as a consequence of higher levels of self-containment of travel and transport flows (and also of energy and water flows).

National Performance Impacts

The impacts of these strategies on Indonesia's national economic performance are evaluated in collaboration with University of Indonesia and BAPPENAS using a long-term national modelling approach.

Stoeckel and Quirke analysed the impacts of improved efficiency in Australia's service sectors on national GDP using a national input output based economic model—for Australia—providing the bar chart of Figure 14.8. The national model outputs for Australia show a slightly over 10 percent increment in GDP for a 10 percent reduction in all service sector costs, including urban development (capital costs) and other urban services or urban operating costs (the resources saved are assumed to be employed to produce additional GDP).

A similar result is obtained for the Indonesian national economic modelling study, allowing the national impacts on GDP of the various urban sustainable development strategies proposed herein to be evaluated. For the proposed SURD strategies, applied to urban centres and their evaluated cost changes (positive and negative), the net increase in GDP is about 4.4 percent to five percent. The national economic model gives only a snapshot of the economy in 2018. Inclusion of cumulative effects of capital expenditure on infrastructure will contribute further to productivity and GDP. Additionally, the increased traffic congestion costs for the business as usual scenario were not evaluated. Inclusion of these would increase further the projected relative benefits of the sustainable development scenario.

In Indonesia, the service sectors represent a smaller proportion of GDP, e.g. 40 percent (cf Australia's 70 percent) —but urbanisation is a much larger factor and resource user in Indonesia, representing 30 percent of GDP. The rapid rate of urbanisation from a lower base means that the opportunities for savings in urban development and operating costs are larger, and the potential improvement to national economic performance and GDP are again substantial. In this way, strategies for sustainable urban (and regional) development provide resource savings, which may be redeployed to increase national economic performance, including GDP. In an expanding, resource restricted economy such as Indonesia, the opportunities for this redeployment are large—in the longer term—and can allow backlogs in urban housing and infrastructure to be reduced and export activities to be increased.

The study shows that sustainable development strategies can substantially improve the environment while significantly reducing overall development cost. National economic performance is improved with these strategies. The contributions of each of the 13 strategies can be separately evaluated in terms of the 12 national objectives, 22 national sectors and the national economy as a whole.

The model developed for this evaluation is Excel-based, providing an interactive decision aid for integrating planning over these three levels and for selecting the most cost effective strategy combination.

These broader findings are applicable to both Indonesia and Australia and have wider application in the region.

They provide an urban development path which can lead to increased economic and environmental sustainability for both Western and Eastern cities—to the benefit of these cities and to the global economy and environment as a whole.

15 Income Shifts Between East and West

GUS HOOKE

Introduction

Until a few centuries ago, a major characteristic of the world economy was the widespread distribution of poverty. Certainly by today's standards, and to a large extent also by the standards of that time, all but a few were poor.

However, especially from about the middle of the 18th Century, countries in Europe and then North America moved onto paths of sustained economic growth. Unfortunately, most of the countries in Africa, Asia and Latin America did not immediately accompany them along this path. Thus, by the end of the third quarter of the 20th Century, there was a stark contrast in living standards between the countries in what the United Nations describes as the 'More Developed Regions' (North America, Western Europe and the Western Pacific [Australia, Japan and New Zealand]) and those in the 'Less Developed Regions'.

The last quarter of the 20th Century has seen a reversal of the per capita income growth poles. The secular growth of per capita income has not declined in the More Developed Regions; it has remained at about 1.5 percent a year.

However, the rate has increased sharply in the developing countries, especially those in Asia, to more than double that in the high income countries. This has been due mainly to technological and managerial transfer associated with the movement of multinationals from the high income nations to the developing countries, but also reflects the activities of multilateral and bilateral aid agencies and the internationalisation of education.

It is likely that the globalisation of the best technologies and managerial practices will see a continuation of this equalisation of per capita incomes among countries in the next Century. Thus, economic power will again reflect the distribution of population. Asia will easily dominate the world economy, with China and India individually producing more goods and services than possibly all the countries in Western Europe and North America combined. The relative scale of the economy of Japan

379

will be about the same as that of Australia today, while the economy of Germany will be considerably smaller. Among those in the present group of high income countries only the United States will be a major economic player.

These changes will have important implications for urban form in the 21st Century. From a world in 2000 in which perhaps 80 percent of the population can be described as poor, we will move into a world by the year 2100, in which the overwhelming majority of a population twice as large will be comparatively rich.

The larger population will add to the demand for residential and commercial land. However, the higher income of this population will place much more pressure on the demand for, land especially in urban areas, and will have a considerably greater effect on the living and working structures people want to build on this land.

We should be concerned, but probably should not panic, at the emerging large numbers for population and income. First, population growth is slowing down. The total may never rise much above 12 billion, and it will probably take the whole of the 21st Century to reach that level. And even if, as a result of rising incomes, population density in urban areas (where the overwhelming majority of the population will live) falls to, say, 25 per square kilometre, the world will require only 475 million square kilometres, or about 3.6 percent of its total land area, for residential and commercial purposes.

Further, even if the increase in urban land was all to come from the existing agricultural and pastoral areas (which would be a requirement for reasonable protection of biodiversity), all urban land would absorb only 10 percent of that total. Most agricultural and pastoral land would still be available for the production of food and it is likely that, over the course of the next Century, farmers would need only a modest increase in the real price of foodstuffs to generate the roughly fourfold increase in food production needed to satisfy the demand of the larger and considerably more affluent population.   Further details of this development scenario follow.

The Demographic Outlook

The main difficulty in forecasting future population levels lies in the considerable uncertainty attaching to the outlook for average life expectancy.

One scenario is that average life expectancy will move to about the current level for a child born today into a high income country—i.e., approximately 100 years. In this case, the world's population might increase to about 10 billion in 2050 and stabilise at about 12 billion from 2100.

However, the view seems to be widening that most medical causes of death could be overcome during the next Century, and that during that period or shortly afterwards, physical and mental deterioration of the human body might be arrested and possibly reversed. On this approach, average life expectancy will rise to, and then increasingly exceed, 100 years. If the scenario is correct, world population might rise above 12 billion in the 22nd Century.

On the first scenario, the average life expectancy of the population will increase to approximately 100 years, with roughly 10 percent of the population in each decile. On the second scenario, the average age will rise continuously.

On both scenarios, family size could be expected to fall, as children under 15 years of age decline to 15 percent of the population (first scenario) and then increasingly below (second scenario).

An Overview of Economic Development

Rapid and geographically unbalanced economic growth may be largely a 300 year phenomenon, coming to an end in the middle of the next Century. Over this period, the world economy will move from a situation of low growth through a period of high growth and back to a situation of low growth (Figure 15.1). It will also move from a position of reasonable income equality at a low average level of income through a period of first increasing and then decreasing income inequality to a new position of reasonable income equality at a much higher level of income.

There appear to be two main external sources of economic growth during the 300 year period: work force increase and technical progress. From about 1975, the transfer of technical knowledge and managerial expertise from the More Developed to the Less Developed Regions, is also adding to the realised growth of world output and income.

The decline in birth rates in virtually all parts of the world, and to replacement rate only in the More Developed Regions, is producing a sharp slowdown in population growth in the lower age brackets. By 2050, this is expected to reduce growth of the working age population, as presently defined in most high income countries (ages 15-64), to approximately zero.

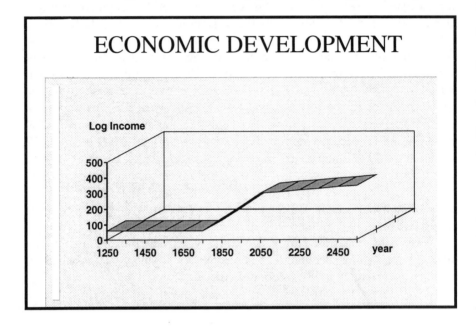

Figure 15.1   World income growth over time
Source: Estimates and Projections by The Australasian Institute

The transfer of technical knowledge and managerial expertise, the main cause of the new phenomenon of economic catch-up, allows developing countries who permit and encourage it to grow at rates much higher than countries in the More Developed Regions were able to achieve at comparable levels of per capita income. However, they seem to be able to do this only until their per capita income reaches about 70 percent of the level in the high income countries. Then their growth rate slows down to about the level in the latter countries.

During the first half of the next Century, more and more countries will reach the 70 percent threshold. By the middle of that Century most countries in Asia will probably be in this category. Only Africa will have a significant number of countries with per capita incomes below the 70 percent level, and many countries on that continent will be approaching that level. By the end of the third quarter of the Century virtually all countries will have passed the threshold.

Thus, the contributions of two of the three main current drivers of world economic growth can be expected to be quite small by the middle of the 21st Century and close to zero shortly afterwards. Outward movements of the world's technical frontier will be the remaining significant driver, and with world production moving away from goods, where the scope for technical progress is high to services, where it appears to much lower, it is possible that world economic growth could fall to about one percent a year from about 2050.

Changes in Output and Income

Compared to developments since then, the world economy was relatively static prior to the middle of the 18th Century. In most countries, both the level and composition of output, as well as the level and distribution of income, were almost unchanged from generation to generation.

The More Developed Regions' Period

Using the United Nations terminology, the period from 1750 to 1975 can be described as the More Developed Regions' period. During these 225 years, the world's work force increased from about 300 million to 1.7 billion, labour productivity rose from about US$200 to approximately US$8,000 and per capita income grew from US$100 to US$3500 (all in 1995 prices).

However, the pace of labour productivity growth, and therefore of per capita income growth, was much higher in the More Developed than in the Less Developed Regions. The catch-cry of the left, that the gap between the rich and poor was getting wider, was powerful mainly because it was true.

The Less Developed Regions' Period

The period from 1975 to 2050 is primarily the Less Developed Regions' period. The transfer to the developing countries over a short period of time of the technical knowledge and managerial expertise that has been built up in the More Developed Regions over a much longer period of time has already resulted in the movement of the world's growth centre to the developing countries of Asia. The centre, which historically has moved from Western Europe to North America to the Western Pacific to Eastern

Continental Asia, appears to be continuing its westward movement, and can be expected to include Africa by the second quarter of the next Century.

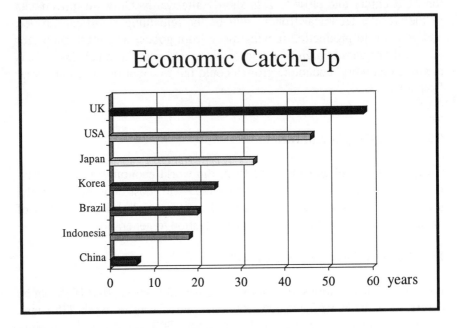

Figure 15.2   Periods for doubling of per capita income in various countries

Source: World Bank's World Development Report, selected issues

The above chart (Figure 15.2) shows how long it took selected countries to achieve the first doubling of their per capita income. It illustrates the strong tendency of the globalisation of economic behaviour to equalise per capita incomes among countries.

The United Kingdom, starting about 1750, took 58 years. The United States, beginning much later, reduced the time by 12 years. Japan, commencing much later still, took only 33 years.

Since then, the performances of the developing countries in this area have easily exceeded those of countries from the More Developed Regions. China took only eight years to achieve its first doubling of per capita income.

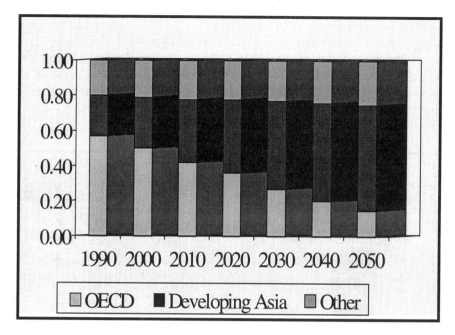

Figure 15.3 **World income shares**
Source: Projections by The Australasian Institute

The Australasian Institute projects that world income will increase from just over US$30 trillion in 1995 to approximately US$300 trillion in 2050 (1995 prices). Per capita income will rise from US$5700 in 1995 to US$30,000 in 2050.

Income in the More Developed Regions will double, to US$36 trillion. However, the share of this group (which includes the United States, Japan, Germany, Italy, France, the United Kingdom and Canada) will fall to only 12 percent.

The share of Developing Asia (Asia excluding Japan, Figure 15.3) will increase from 25 percent to 60 percent, or five times the share of the More Developed Regions. Nevertheless, average per capita income in Developing Asia will still be only two-thirds of that in the More Developed Regions.

These changes are independent of short term developments such as the Asian Meltdown in 1997. Cyclical and other adjustments will cause actual output to fluctuate around the long-term path. However, these adjustments have been occurring for a long time, and their recurrence has already been factored into the Institute's projections.

Among the rest of the world (Africa, Eastern Europe, Central and South America and Oceania) the big gainer will be Africa because of its high work force growth (which is approximated only by that of West Asia) and larger unexploited scope for technical and managerial transfer.

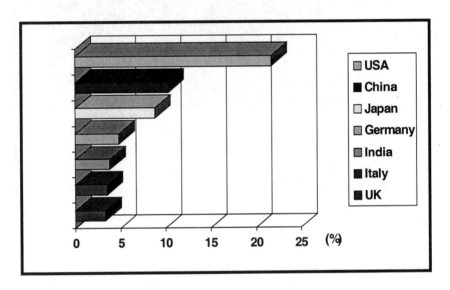

Figure 15.4   Country income shares, 1995
Source: World Bank's World Development Report, 1996

Using the purchasing power method of measurement, the United States had by far the world's largest economy in 1995 (Figure 15.4), with gross domestic product (GDP) amounting to $7 trillion, or 22 percent of gross world product (GWP). The United States also had the highest per capita income among the major countries, of $27,300.

China had the second largest economy, with GDP of $3.3 trillion (10 percent of GWP). Per capita income in China was $2800.

Japan was in third place, with GDP amounting to $2.9 trillion, or just under nine percent of GWP. Japan's per capita income, of $22,700, was eight times larger than that of China but was only four-fifths that of the United States.

Germany's GDP, of $1.6 trillion, was the largest in Europe and fourth largest in the world. It accounted for five percent of GWP. Germany's per capita income was $20,300.

India, with GDP of $1.2 trillion, had the third largest economy in Asia and the fifth largest economy in the world. Its share of GWP was four percent. India's per capita GDP was $1,400.

Italy, the United Kingdom and Brazil each accounted for about three percent of GWP. Then followed Russia, Spain, Canada and South Korea with two percent each.

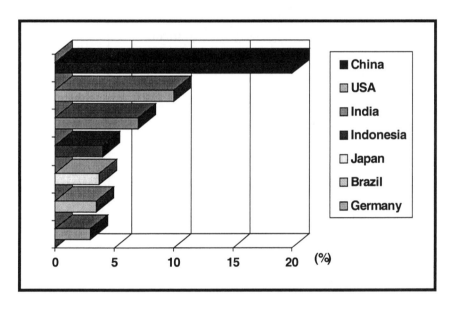

Figure 15.5   Country income shares, 2025
Source: Projections by The Australasian Institute

The Institute expects the GDP of China (including Taiwan and Hong Kong) to pass that of the United States in 2005. Being the world's largest economy will not be a new experience for China. Available evidence suggests that it was also the largest from about the birth of Christ until approximately 1750, and may have had the highest per capita income from the birth of Christ until 1500. Thus, China may simply be returning to a position it has held for most of recorded history.

By 2025 China, with its large work force and demonstrated capacity to absorb new technologies, will probably account for about 20 percent of world income (Figure 15.5). It is expected that the United States will be in second place with 10 percent followed by India with seven percent. Then will come Indonesia, Japan and Brazil with four percent each and Germany with three percent.

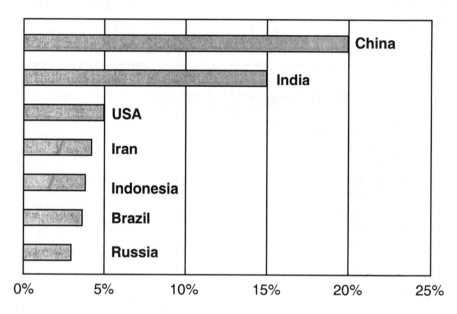

Figure 15.6   Country income shares, 2050
Source: Projections by The Australasian Institute

In 2050, China will still generate about 20 percent of world income (Figure 15.6). India will be in second place with 15 percent. Together, the economies of China and India (assuming the political boundaries of these countries do not change) will be about seven times larger than that of the United States. However, it is likely that per capita income will still be significantly higher in the United States than in China or India.

Iran is expected to have the world's fourth largest economy, with GDP about three quarters that of the United States. Its high position reflects both strong work force growth (currently, about 60 percent of the population is under 16 years of age) and a capacity, which was demonstrated clearly in the 1960s and 1970s, to both absorb and develop new technologies.

Four of the world's five largest economies will be in Asia: China (North East Asia), India (South Asia), Iran (West Asia) and Indonesia (South East Asia). These do not include Japan, whose relative importance in 2050 will not be much greater than that of Australia today.

Some Implications for Urban Design

The main influences of these income shifts on urban design are the impact of population and income growth on the availability of land, especially in Asia, and the effect of widespread high incomes on the kind of structures that will be put on this land.

Asia has a low ratio of land to population. With 60 percent of the world's population, a share that is not likely to change significantly, Asia has only 20 percent of the world's land area. It also has 20 percent of the world's agricultural land which, partly for historical reasons, is the most preferred for urban development. In addition, it has 30 percent of the world's pastoral land, the next most preferred part.

Between now and 2050, population growth will probably increase the demand for urban land in Asia by about 50 percent. However, rising per capita incomes can be expected to raise the demand for land by several hundred percent.

For the world as a whole, there will be considerable pressure on urban land in the early part of the next century. If, because of income increases, average urban density was to fall to 25 persons per hectare, then total demand for urban land would be 400 million hectares in 2050 or three percent of the world's land area. It would increase to about 475 million hectares by 2100, using up 3.6 percent of total land area.

In 2050, urban land would be the equivalent of 33 percent of agricultural land. With technical progress in the area of water provision and with growth of the world's transportation infrastructure, there could be some movement of expanding urban populations onto pastoral land, which is more than twice as abundant as agricultural land (3.3 billion hectares for pastoral land compared with 1.4 billion hectares for agricultural land).

Currently, the value of annual per capita consumption of farm products (measured at the farm gate) is about US$500 for the world as a whole and US$1000 in the highest income countries. If per capita consumption for the world as a whole increases to the latter figure, and the population doubles to 12 billion over the course of the 21st Century, the demand for farm products can be expected to rise fourfold and then stabilise.

This implies an average annual rate of growth of 1.4 percent. Given the considerable scope that still remains for increasing land productivity and the responsiveness of realised productivity to the real (or relative) price of farm products, the world should have little difficulty realising this growth rate, even with a decline in farm land. The greater problem is still likely to be that of keeping farmers happy with the price they receive for their products, not of having enough land or other resources to feed the world's larger, high income population. Thus, there should be few real constraints on the availability of quality land for urban developments.

But technical progress is not limited to structures that must be built on Earth. Nanotechnology offers a range of exciting opportunities. Already the scope for building cities of 100,000 people and more in space is being explored, and with all the resources that are available outside Earth, it can be expected that such cities will be a further and possibly very attractive option by the second half of the 21st Century.

Epilogue

JOHN BROTCHIE, PETER NEWTON, PETER HALL
and JOHN DICKEY

Global Change

The world is undergoing several major societal transitions. One is the globalisation of its markets and economies, facilitated by the development and expansion of global networks for information and communication and for fast transport, and their convergence. Another is the consequent transition to an information- and knowledge-based economy changing the very nature of work activities. This has also enabled a shift in technology, production, and the income it generates, from the Western World to Developing Asia. These transitions are occurring rapidly and almost simultaneously with differing urban impacts between developed western and developing eastern regions. These changes are accompanied in these developing regions by large scale urbanisation, creating major cities, mega-cities and urban-industrial agglomerations (Chapters 1, 2 and 3).

Changes in Living and Working

The transition to an information and knowledge-based economy is creating fundamental changes in working and living activities. The rapid development and introduction of information and communication technologies and their use in combination are transforming the workplace. This is increasing flexibility of production processes, changing skill requirements and transforming management structures to less formal, less hierarchical, increasingly virtual, networked teams. It is linking production with distribution, communication and computing, manufacturing with services, and supply with demand. It is increasing flexibility of workplace location, including telecommuting. It has out-sourced service activities from manufacturing, creating producer services, and increasing their levels of specialisation and locational choice within and between cities.

It is changing shopping patterns and marketing processes, and education and recreation with technologies such as home computers, CD ROM and Internet. It is influencing almost all forms of human activity, and

391

is the most profound of all technological transitions to date. It is also diffusing more quickly, via its global networks for information and fast travel and their integration with information processing, allowing global organisation of activities. It is increasing the importance of cities in this global information economy. Cities are the new engines of this economy.

The information economy is raising incomes and increasing equity between regions, and between cities, and enabling increased efficiency, sustainability and affordability of urban development. Within cities, however, it is widening income gaps between information or knowledge workers and those involved in more routine service and manual tasks, or whose skills are no longer in demand.

The Drivers of Change

Each technological transition and its dissemination has influenced urban form and structure at a global, regional and city level. The development of agricultural implements allowed a shift from hunting and gathering to agriculture, and residential concentration in permanent settlements—for security. The development of mechanised production plants powered by fossil fuels allowed concentration of production at the city centre and growth of larger cities with the introduction of rail transport. The motor car and road networks has allowed even larger cities with multi centres and peripheral manufacturing plants. Telecommunications and information technology and their integration, and fast air, rail and road transport, have created the global markets and networks, and allowed the integration of production of both goods and services, with communications, information technology and fast transport.

This is allowing a wider spatial organisation of activities, including global markets and production systems, production and distribution on demand, and even virtual cities and virtual firms; and a reduction of income differentials within these wider organisations and between cities.

It is also changing working and living patterns. It is introducing flexibility in space and time, allowing locational shifts within these global firms, including movements of production to Developing Asia, with lower factor costs, and the transfer of production technologies from the West to the East. Rapid movement of capital is also facilitated on global communication networks. At the individual level, it is also allowing more flexible employment conditions, including part-time work, flexi-time, and potentially telework, teleshopping, and information based recreational activities.

Consequences

The societal shifts from agriculture to manufacturing to information, which took two centuries in Europe, are occurring later and faster and are converging in Developing Asia. And the income differentials, which developed with these transitions, are now beginning to close (Hooke, Chapter 15) The result may be a return to more equitable yet higher levels of income as these transitions mature. These income differentials are also reducing between cities, producing greater social equity in this regard. Access to new technologies is similarly becoming more widespread: mobile telephones and future low earth orbiting satellites (LEOS) may extend this access even to remote regions.

The increasing problem, however, is that incomes within cities are diverging between the highly skilled knowledge-based workers in 'high tech' industries and less skilled workers performing routine tasks in manufacturing and personal services—the 'high touch' activities, and those whose skills are no longer required, including the retrenched and the retired. There is an urgent need to focus on this problem of social and economic inequalities within cities if the benefits of new technologies are to be shared and enjoyed, and social dysfunction is to reduce (Chapter 2).

Human Behavioural Influences

Both this volume (Chapter 13) and the previous one (Brotchie *et al.*, 1995) have noted the influence of invariant human behavioural characteristics over time: through an agricultural, an industrial and an information age, and probably through the much earlier hunting and gathering age. Particularly relevant to the scale and form of cities are human travel time budgets (Chapter 13). The mean time allocated by individuals for journey to work has been shown to be essentially invariant at about half an hour per one-way trip—since the development of recorded data.

In the agricultural age where the journey to work was on foot, villages and towns were limited in scale by the distance which could be walked in this time. In the industrial age, the introduction of steam trains, on tracks radiating from the industrial hub, allowed urban expansion and formation of residential suburbs. The motor car and fast road networks allowed further extension and infill, and the formation of suburban centres, edge cities and peripheral production as earlier noted. The development of fast rail has allowed further extensions along intercity corridors and formation of urban agglomerations—based on longer distance trips within this same travel time.

The development of information technologies and telecommunications has combined with the technologies above to facilitate a still wider organisation of activities and production systems for both goods and services, including virtual organisations and virtual cities, and larger urban/industrial systems.

The times allocated to other daily activities such as sleep and work have also tended to be relatively constant. But artificial lighting and air conditioning (Chapter 12) and information and communication technologies have allowed shifts in these times during the day, and in location, and hence shift work and flexible hours, allowing higher productivity of facilities and more flexible work and recreation times for many with telework, teleshopping and teletraining. The net result is more flexible, less formal organisation of work activities, with flatter organisational structures, greater individual autonomy, increased productivity and a wider spread of working, shopping, and recreational activities throughout the day and week, and a reduction in distinction between these activities. The changes above are also blurring distinction between male and female roles, and between full and part-time work, and in the US at least, enabling longer working lives.

Regional Impacts—A Return to City States?

Globalisation has also seen a reduction of national barriers and a shift of production to the cities. Cities are the engines of the information economy, competing with other cities nationally and internationally for provision of goods and services and attraction of new industries and skills (Brotchie *et al.*, 1995). Cities are generators of wealth and ideas. They are innovation centres. The formation of a European Union de-emphasising national roles provides the conditions for at least a partial revival of city states—a post-industrial counterpart of the pre-industrial, fourteenth century Hanseatic League. In North America, Australasia and Asia (Lindfield and Stimson, Chapter 4), the economic roles of cities will also increase. They compete for primacy as transport and communication hubs, market places, finance centres, regional centres, entertainment and major event centres and centres for major projects, company headquarters, producer services, and high tech firms.

Company headquarters and producer services are attracted to the larger global and regional cities on major nodes of global information and transaction networks and fast travel routes. They attract the more highly skilled knowledge workers and pay the highest incomes. They are also attracted to centres of high urban and environmental amenity. These may be centres which prospered in the agricultural economy as market or service centres, or centres of education or government, or indeed, earlier city states, rather than those which developed as industrial towns with lower urban and environmental amenity.

These new larger information- and communication-based cities are generally financial, corporate, business and knowledge centres and centres of innovation, with higher income levels. They are also more self-contained and offer higher participation rates for their residents.

Urban Form

Corporate headquarters and producer services generate ideas, earn the highest incomes and can select the best cities and best locations within cities. In many cities, this is the CBD at the centre of earlier developed radial rail and road transport hubs, or new metro centres nearby, with good access to global communication and fast transport nodes.

Consumer services and retailing tend to follow residential customers to the suburbs creating multi-centred cities, with these new centres often at transport nodes, increasing opportunities for self-containment of travel movements, or use of lower energy modes.

Technological change is creating winners and losers—between cities and also within cities. Some industries move away, often overseas, to lower cost labour markets, while 'high tech', or knowledge-based activities expand in other locations, changing the balance of income and employment opportunities within and between cities (e.g. Stockholm; Kazemian, Chapter 8). Cities are both the incubators of new information industries and the graveyards of old and obsolete ones.

Global Economic Activity Shifts

Major shifts are also occurring in economic activity from the developed Western world to the developing eastern nations. This can be viewed as part of a larger global sequence of societal transitions (see Table below). The shift from an agricultural to an industrial society began in the 18th Century and saw major change in production processes and growth in income and output capacity in the Western world, and trade in resources for this production. It began in Europe, then North America and later in the Western Pacific—Japan and Australasia. This created widening income differentials between the developed West and less developed Eastern nations until a further, more recent shift to Developing Asia.

Technological transitions and societal impacts

Period	Age / Transition	Drivers	Societal Impacts		
			Global	Regional	Urban
-1750	**Agriculture**	Population, technology	Permanent settlement, generally low incomes globally	City states—formation of nation states	Small, dispersed villages, Towns
1750-1950	**Industrial**	Technology, trade links, fossil energy	Shift in production capacity to west: Europe, Nth America, then Australasia, Japan,	Western income growth in Europe, then Nth America, then Aust., Japan	Growth of cities, rail transport, urban income/capita.
1950-2050	**Information transition**	IT,T, Global networks, markets, population	Further shift in production capacity to west: Pacific, Asia	Western Pacific, Asia Industrial-ised, income growth. Cities competing	Growth of Asian mega-cities, industrial/urban agglomerants.
2050-	**Global Information economy**	IT,T, Global networks, markets, population, Resource and environment capacity constraints	Further shift west: to Africa: incomes rising then levelling, sustainability	Transition to a more even distribution of per capita income between regions, but not within regions, cities. Formation of virtual city states?	Reduced urbanisation pressures, increased sustainability of development, but more social unrest unless income equity increased

The transition to a global information economy has seen a further growth in economic activity followed by a further diffusion of this activity from the West towards the developing nations, particularly Asia, resulting in higher rates of income growth and, potentially, a more even global income distribution at a higher level in the next century (Chapter 15).

These two transitions started almost two centuries apart in Europe, less in Northern America, and are occurring almost simultaneously in Developing Asia.

Income Shifts

Incomes in Developing Asia, though rising relatively quickly over the long-term, have a very low base in comparison with the developed world. Over the next half century these income differentials (between West and East) are projected to reduce (Chapter 15), resulting in a more even distribution of per capita income between the developed world and developing nations, particularly Asia, and between cities in these regions, if not within these cities, with even greater demands for housing, urban land and infrastructure, and with increasing capacity to pay for each of these.

At the individual city level, income levels are diverging as the premium paid for knowledge workers increases, while the salaries of manual and routine service workers remains low—creating decreased social equity and the potential for urban unrest. The recent economic problems in Asian nations and the resulting downturn (meltdown) in their economies has added greatly to this inequity.

Contrasting Urban Impacts in the West and East

The convergence of the industrial and information transitions in Developing Asia has consequences for urban development.

In Europe and North America, each transition had time to produce its own imprint on urban form. The agricultural age saw the development of small agricultural centres and villages where production was in the surrounding fields and urban travel movement was primarily by foot, which restricted urban scale. The industrial revolution enabled the formation of larger manufacturing centres where production was concentrated near the urban centre and the construction of radial urban rail links allowed the development of larger cities.

The later introduction of the motor car allowed infill between rail lines, the movement of large manufacturing plants to the city edge, and the development of suburban retail and service centres.

The growth of the information economy, including increasing telecommunications capabilities, information technologies and their convergence, has reinforced these suburban centres. It has allowed the move of back offices of major companies to lower rent suburban centres with less traffic congestion, and the shift of document processing to smaller centres, and its concentration regionally or nationally in these centres.

The outsourcing of various service activities from manufacturing has created specialised producer services serving various companies in the same or different cities allowing these services to be flexible in location and to choose larger cities with global access via global network nodes.

In Developing Asia (e.g. Jakarta, Chapter 5) these transitions are occurring almost simultaneously. Urban form is developing along current western city lines with producer services and company headquarters generally in the central business district, with good access to telecommunications and to fast travel nodes (e.g. airports). Multiple (e.g. suburban) centres are forming for retail and consumer services, with large manufacturing plants at the periphery of the city or in nearby smaller cities with transport nodes.

Urbanisation is occurring at a higher rate in these larger Asian cities, with higher incomes, increased services and employment opportunities and larger national populations and their growth rates. This is creating large urban concentrations including mega-cities such as greater Jakarta (Jabotabek—nearly 20 million people) and industrial/urban agglomerations such as the Pearl River Delta (over 30 millions—Hall, Chapter 1). By the year 2000, more than half of the world's mega-cities (of over 10 million population) will be in Developing Asia, including China and India; and this proportion is increasing.

Urban Development and Infrastructure Backlogs

These enormous urbanisation pressures are creating backlogs in urban development and infrastructure, particularly in low-income housing and urban infrastructure—water supply, sewerage, drainage, urban street pavements, and public transport. Urban densities are also relatively high with over-crowding in low-income homes and informal housing kampongs. The future movement to more formal housing and urban development with increasing household incomes will also see a spatial expansion of these cities as they continue to generate a larger share of national income. The provision of infrastructure at the time of urban development is shown in Chapter 10 to reduce these costs by a factor of about five, and will be feasible as incomes rise.

Design of Cities

Asian cities with increasing urbanisation and income levels, and impacts of technological change, have seen both a development boom in offices and apartments and a change in architectural styles of city buildings which is rapidly changing the cityscape (Chapter 12). There has been a shift from low rise buildings designed to harmonise with the climate and natural vegetation, creating minimal external impact—to western high rise office and apartment buildings supported by high energy technologies of full air-conditioning, fast elevators, artificial lighting and multi-storey structures.

These new buildings are creating artificially cooled microclimates within, but adding to urban heat island effects externally. They are creating two societies; those who can afford to select this cool micro climate within their offices, cars and homes, and those who cannot, and whose micro climates are made worse by these added external heat loads, and by traffic congestion, overcrowding, and air and water pollution.

Need for Sustainable Development

There will be increasing need for economic and environmental sustainability of urban and regional development and urban livability (McGee, Chapter 2) as resource limitations become more binding and the receptors of urban waste—the atmosphere, waters and land, become increasingly polluted. In the chapter by Newton and Manins (11) a range of alternative urban forms common to cities in East and West are examined in relation to key dimensions of environmental sustainability, namely: energy consumption, greenhouse gas emission and air quality. The current recession in Asian development activity, may provide an opportunity to evaluate and implement more innovative, environmentally and economically sustainable urban development options and strategies, such as those which follow. Will it be realised or will short-term self-serving remedies dominate?

Strategies for Sustainability of Development

Increased economic and environmental sustainability of urban (and regional) development is needed—and might utilise a number of strategies which may be grouped as follows (Chapter 14).

Increased opportunities for self containment through:
- facilitation of home based activities;
- better local balance of homes and jobs;
- increased local centres for services of various kinds;
- retention and retardation of rainfall run-off, reducing need for piped supply and drainage networks;
- local generation of renewable energies; and
- reclaiming and recycling of solid/liquid/gaseous wastes.

Integration of synergistic elements including:
- *natural and built environments;* to reduce urban heat islands; increase shading and cooling of homes, paths, roads; filtering of air and water, oxygenation of each, retardation of water flows, retention of these flows, reducing flooding and piped water imports/exports, facilitating local recreation and use of walking and cycling paths;
- *grouping of complementary activities;* homes and jobs, like activities for increased specialisation and income, complementary activities to assist innovation, productivity, face-to-face activities, strategic alliances;
- *coordination of housing, commercial, and infrastructure development*—to maximise efficiency, reduce development costs, eliminate development backlogs, enable mass production techniques, capacity building, choice of home and job in one location, public transport use.

Utilising the shift to an information economy—including information technology, telecommunication and systems techniques to:
- simulate, optimise urban land use patterns and development staging;
- create virtual organisations, virtual cities, which link smaller centres into the major city and its firms, allowing teleworking, teleshopping, teletraining and reducing urbanisation pressures and congestion—potentially the most effective strategy of all; and
- developing telecommunication and information technology networks to facilitate these virtual cities and firms, and extend them to more remote

areas using mobile telephony and low earth orbiting satellites (LEOS)—increasing social equity.

Demand management:
- each strategy above influences demand through shorter, lower energy trips, reduced heat island effects, etc.;
- pricing is a further mechanism for constraining demand through increased costs of travel, carparking, energy use, etc.; and
- regulation is another, restricting road or parking facilities, times, or speeds.

Potential Outcomes

The aim of these strategies is to increase urban amenity, efficiency and sustainability and environmental quality, provide increased livability, urban competitiveness, reduced development costs, and minimal housing and infrastructure backlogs. The strategies are also expected to reduce urbanisation pressures through creation of larger virtual cities and virtual organisations, thereby providing increased locational choices, including smaller cities and towns. The local balancing of homes and jobs and increased teleworking, teleshopping and teletraining, increases the robustness of cities in terms of their capacity to function at lower energy levels under possible futures of transport energy constraint.

In this post-industrial economy, information and knowledge are key resources, reducing reliance on land, energy and material resources, and the potential for conflict over these. The information economy is also increasing socio-economic equity between regions and cities, although not within them.

These strategies have been shown to improve national economic performance (e.g. GDP—Chapter 14) through reduced urban development and operating costs. These benefits are generally assisted by the tide of global technological and economic change.

Unfortunately, this tidal flow is not increasing social and economic equity within cities or between cities and rural areas, where the income gap is widening between 'high tech' knowledge workers and 'high touch' personal service and routine manual workers, together with those whose skills are no longer in demand. It is a challenge which must be met if cities are to be economically, environmentally and socially sustainable, and the benefits of the new information society are to be more widely shared.

Bibliography

Abaya, A.C. (1996), 'Decongestion: the key to improving urban environment', *Cities and the New Global Economy*, International Conference presented by the OECD and the Australian Government, AGPS, Canberra, vol. 1, pp. 1-4.

ABS (1981), *Housing Survey 1978, Sydney, Newcastle, and Wollongong—Part 3, Anticipated Residential Movement and Satisfaction with Current Housing Conditions*, No 8713.1, ABS NSW, Sydney.

ADB (1991), *Asian Development Outlook*, Asian Development Bank, Manila.

ADB (1997), *Emerging Asia: Changes and Challenges*, Asian Development Bank, Manila. See also: http://www.asiandevbank.org/pubguide/emergingasia/emerasia.htm

Adelaide 21 (1996), 'City centre strategy for the new era', Adelaide 21 Steering Committee / Project Team, Adelaide.

Advisory Commission on Intergovernmental Relations (1992), *Significant Features of Fiscal Federalism*, vol. 11, Washington, DC.

AEA (1996), *Long Term Trends in Pollutant Concentrations*, National Environmental Technology Centre, AEA Technology plc, UK. See: http://www.aeat.co.uk/netcen/airqual/networks/trends.html

Ahmet, S. and M. van Dijk (1995), *Ambient Air Quality in the Port Phillip Control Region, 1979–1993: Compliance with Objectives and Observed Trends*, Environment Protection Authority of Victoria, Publication 468, October 1995.

Albrecht, J. (1995), *The Mega-City: Metropolis or Monster?* Deutschland, Special Issue, 36-9.

Albrechts, L. (1991), 'Changing roles and positions of planners', *Urban Studies*, vol. 28, No.1, pp.123-37.

Alexander, I. (1986), 'Land use and transport planning in Australian cities: capital takes all?', in J.B. McLoughlin and M. Huxley (1986) (eds), *Urban Planning in Australia: Critical Readings*, Longman Cheshire.

Alexander, I. (1994), 'DURD revisited? Federal policy initiatives for urban and regional planning 1991-94', *Urban Policy and Research*, 12(1), pp. 6-26.

Althouse, A.D., Turnquist, C.H. and Bracciano, A., 1956, *Modern Refrigeration and Airconditioning*, Chicago, Goodheart-Willcox.

Amin, A. and Thrift, N. (eds) (1995), *Living in the Global, Globalization, Institutions and Regional Development in Europe*, Oxford University Press, New York.

Ando, Y. (1983), Kanagawa-ken Keizai no Tokucho nitsuite (Characteristics of Kanagawa Prefecture's Economy), in Kanagawa-ken Kenmin2bu Kenshi Henshu-shitsu (ed.) *Kanagawa Kenshi Kakuron-hen 2 Sangyo Keizai*, 3224. Yokohama: Kanagawa-ken Kosai-kai.

Anon (1993), 'Megacities'. *Time*, January 11, 28-38.

Anon (1996), 'Global city regions: searching for common ground', *Landlines (Newsletter of the Lincoln Institute of Land Policy), 8/1*, 1-7.

Armington, C. 'The changing geography of high-technology business', in J. Rees (ed.) *Technology Regions and Policy*, Totowa, New Jersey: Rowman & Littlefield, 1986, 88-9.

Arsenault., R. (1984), 'Cooling the south', *The Wilson Quarterly*, Summer: 150-9.

Aschauer, D.A. (1990), 'Why is infrastructure important?', in *Is There a Shortfall in Public Capital Investment?*, A.H. Munnel (ed.), Federal Reserve Bank of Boston, Boston.

Aschauer D A and Campbell E J (1991), *Transportation Spending and Economic Growth– The Effects of Transit and Highway Expenditures,* American Public Transit Association, Washington, DC.

AsiaWeek (1994), *'Vital Signs'*, 13 April 1994. See also: http://pathfinder.com/Asiaweek/98/0206/vital.html

AsiaWeek (1998), *Vital Signs*, 6 February 1998. See also: http://pathfinder.com/AsiaWeek/98/0206/vital.html

Askew, M. (1994), 'Bangkok: transformation of the Thai city', in M. Askew and W.S. Logan, *Cultural Identity and Urban Change in Southeast Asia: Interpretative Essays*, Deakin University Press, Geelong, 85-115.

Australian Financial Review (1997), *Inner City Resurgence*, Special Feature, August 29th.

Australian Housing and Urban Research Institute (AHURI) (1995), *Strategy for Trade and Investment, Far North Queensland Region Economic Development Strategy*, AHURI publication, August.

Australian Urban and Regional Development Review (AURD) (1995), *Urban Australia: Trends and Prospects*, Research Report No. 2, Commonwealth of Australia.

Badcock, B. (1986), 'Land and housing provision', in Sheridan, Kyoko(1986) (ed.) *The State as Developer: Public Enterprise in South Australia*, Wakefield Press, Royal Australian Institute of Public Administration.

Badcock, B. (1995), 'Towards more equitable cities: a receding prospect?', in P. Troy (1995) (ed.) *Australian Cities*, UP, Cambridge.

Batten, D.F. and R.Thord (eds) (1989), *Transportation for the Future*, Springer-Verlag, New York.

Beamish, J. and Ferguson, J. (1985), *A History of Singapore Architecture: The Making of a City*, Graham Brash, Singapore.

Beedle, L.S. (ed.) (1986), *High-Rise Buildings: Recent Progress: Council on Tall Buildings and Urban Habitat*, Lehigh University, Bethlehem.

Beer, Andrew (1995), 'Never mind the content, let's understand the process: an alternative perspective on recent federal urban initiatives', *Urban Policy and Research*, 13, 2, pp.107-12.

Beer A, Bolam A. and Mande. A, (1994), *Beyond the Capitals: Urban Growth in Regional Australia*, AGPS, Canberra.

Beng, T.H. (1994), *Tropical Architecture and Interiors: Tradition-based Design of Indonesia, Malaysia, Singapore and Thailand*, Page One Publishing, Singapore.

Berry, M. (1990), 'The politics of Australian cities', *Arena 91*, pp.126-37.

Biro Pusat Statisitk (BPS) (1994), *Tren Fertilitas, Mortalitas dan Migrasi*, BPS, Jakarta.

Biro Pusat Statistik and United Nations Development Programme (BPS and UNDP) (1997), *Laporan Pembanguanan Manusia (Report on Human Development), 1996*, United Nations, Jakarta.

Blakely, E.J. (1994), *Planning Local Economic Development: Theory and Practice*, 2nd edition, Sage Publications, Thousand Oaks, London.

Blakely, E.J. and Stimson, R.J. (1992), 'Interdependencies and the new urban form in the Pacific Rim cities', chapter 1 in E.J. Blakely and R.J. Stimson (eds), *New Cities in the Pacific Rim*, Monograph No. 43, Institute of Urban and Regional Development, University of California, Berkeley.

BMU (1996), 'Environmental policy in Germany', Chapter C. The German Federal Environment Ministry. See: http://webindex.hsl.com/bmu/gesamt/umpolit02/c7%/5Fe.htm

Borja, J. and Castells, M. (1997), *Local and Global: Management of Cities in the Information Age*, Earthscan, London.

Bourne, L.S. (1996), 'Reurbanisation, uneven urban development and the debate on new urban forms', *Urban Geography*, 17, 690-713.

Boyer, M.C. (1983), *Dreaming the Rational City: The Myth of American City Planning*, Cambridge, Mass.

Breheny, M. (1996), 'Centrists, decentrists, and compromises: views on the future of urban form', in M. Jenks, E. Burton and K. Williams (eds), *The Compact City: A Sustainable Urban Form?*, E&FN Spon, London.

Brisbane City Council (1994), *Brisbane 2011*, BCC, Brisbane.

Brosseau, M. (1994), 'Entrepreneurs probing uncertainty', in: Y.M. Yeung, D.K.Y. Chu, (eds) (1994), *Guangdong: Survey of a Province Undergoing Rapid Change*, 175-205, The Chinese University Press, Hong Kong.

Brotchie, J.F. (1992), 'The changing nature of cities', *Urban Futures*, Special Issue 5, 13-26

Brotchie, J.F. Anderson, M., and McNamara, C., (1995), 'Changing metropolitan commuting patterns', J.F. Brotchie, M. Batty, E. Blakely, P. Hall and P.W. Newton (eds) (1995), *Cities in Competition—Productive and Sustainable Cities of the 21st Century*, Longman, Melbourne.

Brotchie, J.F., Batty, M., Hall, P. and Newton, P.W. (eds) (1991), *Cities of the 21st Century, New Technologies and Spatial Systems*, Longman-Cheshire, Melbourne.

Brotchie, J.F., Batty, M., Blakely, E., Hall, P. and Newton, P.W. (eds) (1995b), *Cities in Competition : Productive and Sustainable Cities for the 21st Century*, Longman, Melbourne.

Brotchie, J.F., Hall, P. and Newton, P.W. (eds) (1987), *The Spatial Impact of Technological Change,* Croom Helm, London.

Brotchie, J.F., Newton, P.W., Hall, P. and Nijkamp, P. (eds) (1985), *The Future of Urban Form—The Impact of New Technology,* Croom Helm, London.

Bryson, J.M. and Einsweiler, R.C. (1988), *Strategic Planning: Threats and Implications for Planners,* American Planning Association, Planning Press, Chicago.

Bureau of Industry Economics (BIE) (1994), *Regional Development: Patterns and Policy Implications,* Research Report No. 56, AGPS, Canberra.

Buhr, W. and M. Koppel (1986), 'Regional investment functions of material infrastructure: theoretical issues and selected empirical case studies', *Environment and Planning* 18:491-509.

Bums, L.S. and Grebler, L. (1982), 'Construction cycles in the United States since World War II', *Journal of Real Estate and Urban Economics,* 10: 123-15 1.

Bureau of Transportation Statistics (1995), 'The economic performance of transportation', *Transportation Statistics Annual Report 1995,* US Department of Transportation, Washington DC.

Button, K, (1994), 'Transport, communications and the environment: is current infrastructure pricing optimal?', Working Paper, Department of Transport Technology, Loughborough University.

Capello, R. (1994), *Spatial Economic Analysis of Telecommunications Network Externalities,* Avebury, Aldershot.

Carlton, D. (1983), 'The location and employment choices of new firms: an econometric model with discrete and continuous endogenous variables', *The Review of Economics and Statistics,* 65, 440-49.

Carlton, D. (1979), 'Why new firms locate where they do: an econometric model', in W. Wheaton (ed.), *Interregional Movements and Regional Growth* (Coupe Paper 2, 15-6), Urban Institute, Washington, DC.

Carter, P. (1987), *The Road to Botany Bay: An Essay in Spatial History,* Faber and Faber, London.

Castells, M. (1989), *The information City, Economic Restructuring and Urban and Regional Process,* Information Technology, Basil Blackwell, Oxford.

Castells, M. (1992), 'Four Asian tigers with a dragon head: a comparative analysis of the state, economy, and society in the Asian Pacific Rim', in R.P. Appelbaum, J. Henderson (eds), *States and Development in the Asian Pacific Rim,* 33-70, Sage, Newbury Park.

Castells, M. (1996), *The Rise of the Network Society,* Blackwell Publishers, Cambridge and Oxford.

Castells, M. and Hall, P. (1994), *Technopoles of the World: The Making of 21st Century Industrial Complexes,* Routledge, London.

Cervero, R. (1995), 'Sustainable new towns: Stockholm's rail served satellites', *Cities,* 12(1), 41-51.

Champion, A. G. (ed.)(1989), *Counterurbanization: The Changing Pace and Nature of Populahon Deconcentratio,* Edward Arnold, London.

Chan, M.K. (1995), 'All in the family: the Hong Kong-Guangdong link in historical perspective', in R.Y.-W. Kwok, A.Y. So (eds), *The Hong Kong-Guangdong Link: Partnership in Flux*, 21-63, M.E. Sharpe, London.

Chan, R.C.K. (1995), 'Development strategy in an era of global competition: the case of Hong Kong and South China', in G.Y. Lee, and Y.W. Kim (eds), *Globalization and Regional Development: In South east Asia and Pacific Rim*, 202-27, Korea Research Institute for Human Settlements, Seoul.

Chandler T. (1987), *Four Thousand Years of Urban Growth, An Historical Census*, Second Edition, The Edwin Mellen Press, New York.

Chatterjee, L. (1983), 'Technology choice in the construction sector of developing countries', in M. Chatterjee *et. al.*, (eds), *Urban and Regional Change in Developing Countries*, Gower Publishers, Hants.

Chatterjee, L. and Hasnath, S.A. (1991), 'Public construction expenditures in the United States: are there structural breaks in the 1921-1987 period?', *Economic Geography* 67:42-53.

Cheung, P.T.Y. (1994), 'Relations between the Central Government and Guangdong', in Y.M. Yeung, D.K.Y. Chu, (eds), *Guangdong: Survey of a Province Undergoing Rapid Change*, 19-51, The Chinese University Press, Hong Kong.

Chiu-Ming, L. (1994), 'Transport and communication', in Y.M. Yeung, D.K.Y. Chu (eds), *Guangdong: Survey of a Province Undergoing Rapid Change*, 301-25, The Chinese University Press, Hong Kong.

Chu, D.K.Y. (1994), 'Synthesis of economic reforms and open policy', in Y.M. Yeung, D.K.Y. Chu, (eds), *Guangdong: Survey of a Province Undergoing Rapid Change*, 449-68, The Chinese University Press, Hong Kong.

Clawson, M., Hall, P. (1973), *Planning and Urban Growth: An Anglo-American Comparison*, John Hopkins UP, Baltimore.

Coburn, C. (ed.) (1995), *Partnerships: A Compendium of State and Federal Cooperative Technology Programs*, Battelle, Columbus.

Cohen, M.A. (1995), 'Cities and the prospects of nations', *Cities and the New Global Economy*, an international conference presented by the OECD and the Australian Government, AGPS, Canberra, vol. 1, pp.165-72.

Corporation for Enterprise Development (1994), *The 1994 Development Report Card for the States*, Corporation for Enterprise Development, Washington, DC.

Cox, K. and Golledge, R. (1973), 'Designative perceptions of macro-space', in R.M. Downs and D. Stea (eds), *Image and Environment*, Aldine Publishing Co.

CSIRO/Synectics, (1997), *Sustainable Urban Development and National Economic Performance –Inception Report, Compendium of Issues, Results Report*, CSIRO Building, Construction and Engineering, Melbourne.

Daniels, P.M. (1985), *Service Industries: A Geographical Appraisal*, Methuen, London.

Davis, L. (1981), 'New definitions "high tech" reveals that U.S. competitiveness in this area has been declining', *Business American*, October.

Dawson, B. and Gillow, J. (1994), *The Traditional Architecture of Indonesia*, Thames and Hudson, London.

DBIRD (1994), *Sectoral Analysis—Queensland Manufacturing*, Department of Business, Industry and Regional Development, Brisbane, June.

Dick, H.W. (1990), 'Further reflections on the middle class', in R. Tanter and K. Young (eds), *The Politics of Middle Class Indonesia*, Centre of Southeast Asian Studies, Monash University, Melbourne, 63-70.

Dick, H.W. and Rimmer, P.J. (1998), 'Beyond the third world city: the new urban geography of Southeast Asia', *Urban Studies* (forthcoming).

Dicken, P. (1992), *Global Shift: The Internationalisation of Economic Activity*, 2ⁿᵈ edition, The Paul Chapman, London.

Dosi, G. and L. Orsenigo (1988), 'Coordination and transformation: an overview of structures, behaviors and change in evolutionary environments', in Giovanni Dosi *et. al.* (eds), *Technical Change and Economic Theory*, pp. 13-37, Frances Pinter, London.

Douglass, M. (1966), 'World city formation, poverty and the environment on the Asia-Pacific Rim: reflections on the work of John Friedmann', unpublished paper presented at a Conference on Planning and the Rise of Civil Society, University of California at Los Angeles, April.

Due, J.F. and Mikesell, J.L. (1998), *Sales Taxation, State and Local Structure and Administration*, Urban Institute Press, Washington DC, Forthcoming.

Dupré, J. (1996), *Skyscrapers*, Black Dog & Leventhal, New York.

EPAC (Economic Planning Advisory Commission) (1995), *Private Infrastructure Task Force, Interim Report*, Australian Government Publishing Service.

ESCAP (1993), *State of Urbanization in Asia and the Pacific, 1993*, United Nations, Economic and Social Commission for Asia and the Pacific, New York.

Edwards, N. (1990), *The Singapore House and Residential Life, 1819-1939*, Oxford University Press, Singapore.

Federal Aviation Administration, Metropolitan Washington Airports (1985), *Master Plan Update: Washington Dulles International Airport*, September, (prepared by Peat, Marwick, Mitchell & Co., San Francisco, CA).

Forester, D. (1989), 'The myth of the Electronic Cottage', Forester (ed.) *Computers in the Human Context,* Blackwell Publishers, Oxford.

Forster, C. (1995), 'Australian cities: continuity and change', Oxford University Press.

Forster and McCaskill (1986), 'The modern period: managing metropolitan Adelaide', in A. Hutchings and R. Bunker (eds), *With Conscious Purpose: A History of Town Planning in South Australia*, Royal Australian Planning Institute, Wakefield Press.

Friedmann, J. (1986), 'The World City Hypothesis, Development Change', in P.L. Knox and P.J. Taylor (1995), *World Cities in a World System, Appendix*, Cambridge, UK.

Friedmann, J. (1993), 'Towards a non-Euclidean mode of planning', *American Planning Association Journal, 59:* 482-86.

Friedmann, J. (1997), 'A look ahead: urban planning in Asia', Keynote address to Asia Planner Association, Bandung, Indonesia.

Frost, L. (1991), *The New Urban Frontier: Urbanisation and City Building in Australasia and the American West*, University of NSW Press, Sydney.

Fuchs, V. (1968), *The Services Economy*, National Bureau of Economic Research and Columbia University Press, New York.

Fuchs, R. J. *et.al.* (eds) (1994), *Mega-City Growth and the Future.* Tokyo, United Nations University Press.

Fuchs, R.J., Jones, G.W. and Pernia, E.M. (1987), *Urbanization and Urban Policies in Pacific Asia*, Westview Press, Boulder.

Fujita, K. (1991), 'A world city and flexible specialization: restructuring of the Tokyo metropolis', *International Journal of Urban and Regional Research, 15*, 269-84.

Fuller, S. (1994), 'Federal spending trends in Northern Virginia, 1984-1993 and the growing importance of small business as sources of employment growth', in R. Stough (ed.) *Proceedings of the First Annual Conference on the Future of the Northern Virginia Economy*, Center for Regional Analysis, George Mason University, 1994, pp. 68-86.

Gappert, G. (1989), 'A management perspective on cities in a changing global environment', in R.V. Knight, G. Gappert (eds), *Cities in a Global Society*, 312-25, Sage, Newbury Park.

Gardiner, P. (1997), 'Migration and urbanisation: a discussion', pp. 118-34, in G.W. Jones and T.H. Hull (eds), *Indonesia Assessment: Population and Human Resources*, Australian National University, Canberra.

Gardiner, P. and Oey-Gardiner, M. (1991), 'Pertumbatian dan Perluasan Kota di Indonesia (Growth Lateral Expansion of Cities in Indonesia)', *Kompas*, 7 May.

Garelli, S. (1995), 'From competitive enterprises to competitive societies', *The World Competitiveness Report 1995*, Geneva.

Garelli, S. (1996), 'What is world competitiveness?', *World Competitiveness Year Book 1996*, Geneva.

Garreau, J. (1991), *Edge City and Life on the New Frontier*, Doubleday, New York.

Gehl, J. and Gemsoe, L. (1996), *Public Space—Public Life, City of Copenhagen*, Copenhagen.

Gershuny, J.I. (1978), *After Industrial Society: The Emerging Self Service Economy*, MacMillan, London.

Giddens, A. (1990), *The Consequences of Modernity*, Polity, Cambridge.

Gilbert, A. (ed.) (1996), *The Mega-City in Latin America*, United Nations University Press, Tokyo.

Gilpin, R. (1987), *The Political Economy of International Relations*, Princeton University Press, Princeton, New Jersey.

Ginsburg, N., Koppel, B. and McGee, T.G. (eds) (1991), *The Extended Metropolis: Extended Settlement Transition in Asia*, University of Hawaii Press, Honolulu.

Gipps, P.G., Brotchie, J.F., Hensher, D., Newton, P.W. and O'Connor, K. (1997), *Journey to Work, Employment and the Changing Structure of Australian Cities*, AHURI, Melbourne.

Glasmeier, A., Hall, P. and Markusen, A.R. (1983), 'Defining high technology industries', Working Paper No. 407, Institute of Urban and Regional Development, University of California at Berkeley.

Goldstein, H.A. and Lugar, M.I. (1993), 'Theory and practice in high-tech economic development', in R.D. Bingham and R. Mier (eds), *Theories of Local Economic Development*, Newberry Park, California.

Gordon, P., Kumar, A. and Richardson H. W. (1989), 'The influence of metropolitan spatial structure on commuting times', *Journal of Urban Economics*, 26, 138-49.

Gordon, P. and Richardson, H. W. (1989), 'Gasoline consumption and cities: a reply', *JAPA*, 55, 342-6.

Gordon, P., Richardson, H.W. and Jun, M. (1991), 'The commuting paradox-evidence from the top twenty', *JAPA*, 57, 416-20.

Gordon, P. and Richardson, H. (1994), *Household Commuting. Department of Urban and Regional Planning*, University of Southern California, Los Angeles.

Gordon, P. and Richardson, H.W. (1997), 'Are compact cities a desirable planning goal?', *Journal of the American Planning Association*, 63, 95-106.

Gottmann, J. (1961), *Megalopolis: The Urbanized Northeastern Seaboard of the United States*, Twentieth Century Fund, New York.

Graham, S. (1997), 'Cities in a real-time age: the paradigm challenge of telecommunications to the conception and planning of urban space', *Environment and Planning*, vol. 29, pp. 105-27.

Graham, S. and Simon, M. (1996), *Telecommunication and the City: Electronic Spaces, Urban Places*, Routledge, London and New York.

Greene, R., Harrington, P. and Vinson, R. (1983), 'High technology industry: identifying and tracking emerging sources of employment strength', *New England Journal of Employment and Training*.

Gregory, R. and Hunter, B. (1995). 'The macro economy and the growth of ghettos and urban poverty in Australia', Paper presented to National Press Club, April.

Grübler, A and Nakicenovic, N (1993), 'Economic Map of Europe: transport, communication and infrastructure networks in a wider Europe', Working Paper, IIASA, Laxenburg.

Guldin, G.E. (1995), 'Toward a greater Guangdong: Hong Kong's sociocultural impact on the Pearl River Delta and beyond', in R.Y.-W. Kwok, A.Y. So (eds), *The Hong Kong-Guangdong Link: Partnership in Flux*, 89-118, M.E. Sharpe, London.

Hall, P. (1984), *The World Cities,* Wiedenfeld and Nicolson, London.

Hall, P. (1994), 'Can we reshape the cities of tomorrow?', *The Human Face of Urban Development*, 2nd Annual World Bank Conference on Environmentally Sustainable Development, September, Washington, DC.

Hall, P. (1995), 'Towards a general urban theory', in J.F. Brotchie, M. Batty, E. Blakely, P. Hall and P.W. Newton, *Cities in Competition: Productive and Sustainable Cities for the 21st Century*, Longman, Melbourne.

Hall P. (1997), 'Reflections past and future on planning cities', *Australian Planner*, 34(2): 83-9.

Hall, P. (1998 forthcoming), *Cities in Civilization*, Harper Collins, London.

Hall, P., Prud'homme, R. and Snickars, F. (1994), *The impacts of the Dennis agreement: Regional development*, Department of Infrastructure and Planning, Royal Institute of Technology, Stockholm.

Hamel, E. and Prahalad, C. (1994), *Competing for the Future: Breakthrough Strategies for Seizing Control of Your Industry and Creating the Markets of Tomorrow*, Harvard Business School, Boston.

Hamer, A.M. (1994), 'Economic impacts of third world mega-cities: is size the issue?', in R.J. Fuchs *et al.* (eds), *Mega-City Growth and the Future,* United Nations University Press, Tokyo, pp. 172-91.

Hamnett, S. (1995), 'The Adelaide multifunction polis in 1993: from technopolis to enterprise zone', in J.F. Brotchie, M. Batty, E. Blakely, P. Hall and P.W. Newton, *Cities in Competition: Productive and Sustainable Cities for the 21st Century*, Longman, Melbourne.

Hamnett, S. and Parham, S. (1992), '2020 vision: the Adelaide planning review', *Urban Futures*, September, pp.78-85.

Hanson, R. (ed.) (1984), *Perspectives on Urban Infrastructure*, National Academy Press Washington, DC.

Harding, A., Dawson ,J., Evans, R., and Parkinson, M. (eds) (1994), *European Cities Towards 2000*, Manchester University Press, Manchester.

Harvey, D. (1989a), *The Condition of Postmodernity, An Enquiry into the Origins of Cultural Change*, Blackwell, Oxford.

Harvey, D. (1989b), 'From managerialism to entrepreneurialism: the transformation in urban governance in late capitalism', *Geografiska Annaler*, 71 B, pp.3-17.

Hasnath, S.A. and Chatterjee, L. (1990), 'Public construction in the United States: an analysis of expenditure patterns', *Annals of Regional Science* 24:133-45.

Hayes, D. and Bunker, R. (1995), 'The changing role of the city centre in Adelaide and Melbourne', *Urban Policy and Research*, vol. 13, No. 3, pp. 159-71.

Hayes, D. (1997), 'Adelaide 21', *Australian Planner*, vol. 34, No. 1, pp. 37-41.

Haynes, K.E. and Stough, R.R. (1988), 'Infrastructure investment for basic research—US patterns in university science and technology', in I.J. Roborgh, R.R. Stough and T.A.G. Toonen (eds), *Public Infrastructure Redefined*, Leiden University Press, Leiden.

Haynes, K.E. and Krmenec, A. (1989), 'A sensitivity assessment of uncertainty in infrastructure expansion', *Annals of Regional Science* 31:301-15.

Haynes, K.E., Krmenec, A., Georgianna, T.D., Whittington, D. and Echelberger Jr. W.F. (1984), 'Planning for water capacity expansion', *Journal of American Planning, Association* 50:359-64.

Haynes, K.E., Krmenec, A., Georgianna, T.D., Whittington, D. and Echelberger Jr. W.F. (1985), 'Community infrastructure expansion', in K.E. Haynes, A. Kuklinski, O. Kultalahti (eds), *Pathologies of Urban Processes*, Finn Publishers, Tampere (Finland) pp. 341-62.

Held, D. (1991), 'Democracy, the nation-state and the global system', *Economy and Society*, vol. 20, pp. 138-72.

Held, J.R. (1996), 'Clusters as an economic development tool: beyond the pitfalls', *Economic Development Quarterly*, vol. 10, No. 3, Aug., pp. 249-61.

Henton, D. (1994), 'Reinventing Silicon Valley: creating a total quality community', *Cities and the New Global Economy*, an international conference presented by the OECD and the Australian Government, vol. 1, pp. 306-26, AGPS, Canberra.

Höjer, M, (1997), *Telematics in Urban Transport—A Delphi Study Using Scenarios. Licaentiate Thesis*, Department of Infrastructure and Planning, Royal Institute of Technology, Stockholm.

Honjo, M. (1991), *The Hub of Japan. Work in Progress*, United Nations University, 13/3, 6.

Housing and Urban Development Corporation (1994), *Land Readjustment*, in Japan, Housing and Urban Development Corporation, Tokyo.

Howard, R. (1996), *Queensland Competitiveness 1995: The Competitive Strengths and Weaknesses of Queensland as a Location for Investment*, Industry Development Branch, Industry and Technology Division, Queensland Department of Tourism, Small Business and Industry.

Howe, B. (1992), 'Building better cities: an information kit', in C. Fletcher and C. Walsh, (eds), *The Impact of Federalism on Metropolitan Strategies in Australia*, Federalism Research Centre, Australian National University.

Hsing, Y.-T. (1996), 'Blood, thicker than water: interpersonal relations and Taiwanese investment in southern China', *Environment and Planning A, 28*, 2241-61.

Hugo, G.J. (1975), 'Population mobility in West Java, Indonesia', Unpublished Ph.D. Thesis, Department of Demography, Australian National University, Canberra.

Hugo, G.J. (1991), 'Recent developments in Indonesian migration', Paper presented to International Conference on Migration in Asia, University of Singapore, January.

Hugo, G.J. (1992), 'Women on the move: changing patterns of population movement of women in Indonesia', pp. 174-96 in S. Chant (ed.), *Gender and Migration in Developing Countries*, Belhaven Press, London.

Hugo, G.J. (1996), 'Asia on the move: research challenges for population geography', *International Journal of Population Geography*, vol. 2, pp. 95-118.

Hutchings, A. (1986), 'Conscious purposes', in A. Hutchings and R. Bunker (eds), *With Conscious Purpose: A History of Town Planning in South Australia*, Wakefield Press/Royal Australian Planning Institute.

Imbroscio, D. (1995), 'An alternative approach to urban economic development: exploring the dimensions and prospects', *Journal of Urban Affairs Review*, vol. 30, pp. 840.

Indonesia Demographic and Health Survey (IDHS) (1987), *Demographic and Health Survey 1986*, Central Bureau of Statistics, National Family Planning Coordinating Board and Ministry of Health, Jakarta.

Indonesia Demographic and Health Survey (IDHS) (1991), *Demographic and Health Survey 1990*, Central Bureau of Statistics, National Family Planning Coordinating Board of Ministry of Health, Jakarta.

Indonesia Demographic and Health Survey (IDHS) (1994), *Demographic and Health Survey 1993*, Central Bureau of Statistics, National Family Planning Coordinating Board of Ministry of Health, Jakarta.

Itakura, K., Takeuchi, A. (1980), 'Keihin region', in K. Murata, I. Ota (eds), *An Industrial Geography of Japan*, 47-65, St. Martin's Press, New York.

Jacobs, J. (1984), *Cities and the Wealth of Nations: Principles of Economic Life*, Penguin, Harmondsworth, England.

Jones, W.P. (1973), *Air Conditioning Engineering,* 2nd edition, Edward Arnold, London.

Jordan, R.C. and Priester, G.B. (1949), *Refrigeration and Air Conditioning*, Constable, London.

Kanagawa Prefectural Government (1985), *The History of Kanagawa*, Yokohama: Kanagawa Prefectural Government.

Kasper, W., Bennett, J., Jackson, S. and Markowski, S. (1992), *The International Attractiveness of Regions: A Case Study of the Gladstone-Fitzroy Region in Central Queensland*, Centre for Management Logistics, University College, Canberra.

Kenworthy, J. and Newman, P. (1993), *Automobile dependence: 'The irresistible force?',* Commissioned report for the University of Technology, Sydney, Faculty of Design, Architecture and Building, Institute for Science and Technology Policy, Murdoch University (49pp).

Kenworthy, J. and Newman, P. (1994), 'Toronto—paradigm regained', *Australian Planner*, 31 (3), 137-47.

Kenworthy, J.R., Newman, P.W.G., Barter, P. and Poboon, C. (1995), 'Is increasing automobile dependence inevitable in booming economies?: Asian cities in an international context', *IATSS Research*, 19 (2): 58-67.

Kenworthy, J. R., Laube, F., Newman, P. and Barter, P., (1997), 'Indicators of transport efficiency in 37 world cities', a report for the World Bank, ISTP.

King, A.D. (1978), 'Exporting planning: the colonial and neo colonial experience', *Urbanism, Past and Present*, 5:12-22.

King, A.D. (1990a), *Urbanism, Colonialism and the World Economy: Cultural and Spatial Foundations of the World Urban System*, Routledge, London.

King A.D. (1990b), *Global Cities: Post-Imperialism and the Internationalization of London*, Routledge, London and New York.

Kirby, A. (1996), 'Editorial: high stakes in the city', *Cities, 13*, iii.

Knight, R.V. (1989a), 'The emergent global society', in R.V. Knight, G. Gappert, (eds), *Cities in a Global Society*, 24-43, Sage, Newbury Park.

Knight, R.V. (1989b), 'City building in a global society', in R.V. Knight and G. Gappert (eds), *Cities in a Global Society*, Urban Affairs Annual Reviews, vol.25, pp.326-34, Sage Publications, Newbury Park.

Knight, R.V., Gappert, G. (eds) (1989), *Cities in a Global Society*, Sage, Newbury Park.

Knowledge in Action (1996), *Globalisation*, http://info.minez.nl/nota/kennisen/hfd2.htm.

Kurokawa, T., Taniguchi, M., Hashimoto, H. and Ishida, H. (1995), *Cost of Infrastructure Improvement on Sprawl Area,* Papers on City Planning, No.30, pp.121-6.

Lakshmanan, T.R. (1989), 'Infrastructure and economic transformation', in A. Andersson, D.F. Battan, B.B. Johansson and P. Nijkamp (eds), *Advances in Spatial Theory and Dynamics*, Elsevier, North Holland.

Landau, S.B. and Condit, C.W. (1996), *Rise of the New York Sky Scraper, 1865-1913*, Yale University Press, New Haven.

Lave, C. (1992), 'Cars and demographics', *Access*, 1:4-11, Transportation Center, UC Berkeley.

Leaf, M. (1996), 'Building the road for the BMW: culture, vision and the Extended metropolitan region in Jakarta', *Environment and Planning A*, vol. 28: 1617-35.

Leaf, M. (1996), *Learning from Shenzhen. Cities, 13*, 195-7.

Lee, K.L. (1984), *Emerald Hill: The Story of a Street in Words and Pictures*, National Museum Singapore, Singapore.

Lee, Yok Shiu F.(1997), 'Facing the urban environmental challenge', in R.F. Watters and T.G. McGee (eds), *Asia Pacific. New Geographies of the Pacific Rim,* Hurst and Company, London, pp. 140-60.

Lim, L.Y. and Malone-Lee, T.C. (1994), 'Singapore as a global city—strategies and key issues', *Cities and the New Global Economy*, papers from the OECD-Australian government conference, Melbourne, November.

Lin, G.C.S. and Ma, L.J.C. (1994), 'The role of towns in Chinese regional development—the case of Guangdong province', *International Regional Science Review, 1*, 75-97.

Lind, G. (1997), 'Assessment of the effects of integrated ITS-scenario', PhD dissertation, Department of Infrastructure and Planning, Royal Institute of Technology, Stockholm.

Linneman, A. and Gyourko, B. (1997), 'Report to the Fairmount Park Commission: The influence of city parks in local firm neighbourhood development', in *Working Papers of the Wharton School of UPenn.*, No 22.

Lipton, M. (1977), *Why Poor People Stay Poor: Urban Bias in World Development*, ANU Press, Canberra.

Lloyd, C.J. and Troy, P. (1981), *Innovation and Reaction: The Life and Death of the Federal Department of Urban and Regional Development*, Allen and Unwin, Sydney.

Lo, F.-C. and Yeung, Y. (eds.) (1996), *Emerging World Cities in Pacific Asia,* UN University Press, Tokyo.

Lo, F.-C. (1991), 'The emerging world city system', *Work in Progress, United Nations University, 13/3*, 11.

Logan, T. (1987), 'Urban and regional planning in a federal system: New South Wales and Victoria', in S. Hamnett, and R. Bunker (eds), *Urban Australia: Planning Issues and Policies*, Mansell, London.

Lugar, M.I., Schubert, U. and Todtling, F. (1991), *External and Internal Factors Affecting the Productivity of European Research Institutes*, Wirtschaftsuniversitat Wien, IIR, Vienna, Austria.

Makridakis, S. (1990), *Planning, Forecasting and Strategy for the 21st Century*, Free Press, MacMillan.

Manins, P.C. (1992a), 'Clean air: an oxymoron?', *Search*, 23, 305-7.

Manins, P.C. (1992b), 'At the Korea Ministry of Environment', *Clean Air (Aust.),* 26, 152-61.

Manins, P.C. (1997), 'Transport—the future is clearer', in *Minerals and Energy*, vol.3, Proc. National Agricultural and Resources Outlook Conference, Canberra, 4-6 February: ABARE Conference 1997, 85-93.

Manning, I. (1978), *The Journey to Work*, George Allen and Unwin, Sydney.

Massey, D.S. and Denton, N.A. (1993), *American Apartheid: Segregation and the Making of the Underclass*, Harvard University Press, Cambridge.

Marchetti, C. (1992), *Anthropological Invariants in Travel Behaviour*, International Institute of Applied Systems Analysis, Laxenburg, Austria.

Marchetti, D. (1987), 'Infrastructures for movement', *Technological Forecasting and Social Change*, 32: 373-94.

Markusen, A.(1967), *Profit Cycles, Oligopoly, and Regional Development*, MIT Press, Cambridge,

Maruya, T. (1994), 'The economy', in: Y.M. Yeung and D.K.Y. Chu (eds) *Guangdong: Survey of a Province Undergoing Rapid Change*, 53-74, The Chinese University Press, Hong Kong.

Masser, I., Svidén, O. and Wegener, M. (1992), *The Geography of Europe's Futures*, Belhaven Press, London.

McGee, T.G. (1985), 'Circuits and networks of capital: the internalization of the world economy and the national urbanization', *Conference on Urban Growth and Economic Development in the Pacific Region*, Academica Sinica, Institute of Economics, Taipei.

McGee, T.G. (1991a), 'Asia's growing urban rings', *Work in Progress, United Nations University*, 13/3, 9.

McGee, T.G. (1991b), 'The emergence of desakota regions in Asia: expanding a hypothesis', in N.S. Ginsburg *et al.* (eds), *The Extended Metropolis: Settlement Transition in Asia*, University of Hawaii Press, Honolulu, pp. 3-25.

McGee, T.G. (1995), 'Systems of cities and network landscapes: new cultural formations and the urban built environment of the Asia-Pacific region', *7th Annual Pacific Rim Council on Urban Development (PRCUD) Conference*, San Francisco, October, pp.1-28.

McGee, T.G. and Griffiths, C. (1995), 'Global urbanization: towards the twenty-first century', New York, Population Division, Department of Economic and Social Information and Policy Analysis. United Nations, pp. 55-74.

McGee, T.G. and Robinson, I.M. (1995), *The Mega-Urban Regions of Southeast Asia*, University of British Columbia Press, Vancouver.

Mera, K. (1973), 'Regional production functions and social overhead capital: an analysis of the Japanese case', *Regional Science and Urban Economics*, vol. 3, No. 2:157-86.

Metropolitan Washington Airports Authority (1990), *Washington National Technical Report on Airport Plans*, May, (prepared by Howard, Needles, Tammen & Bergendoff).

Ministry of Construction in Japan (1986), National long-range plan for construction, Ministry of Construction, Japan.

Minnery, J.R. (1992), *Urban Form and Development Strategies: Equity, Environmental and Economic Implications*, The National Housing Strategy Background Paper 7, AGPS, Canberra.

Minnesota IMPLAN Group, Inc. (1991), *Micro-IMPLAN Users Guides*, Stillwater, MN.

Mitchell, B. (1995), *International Historical Statistics, 1750-1988*, Stockton Press, Stockton Press, New York.

Miyakawa, Y. (1980), 'The location of modern industry in Japan', in Association of Japanese Geographers (ed.), *Geography of Japan*, 265-98, Teikoku-Shoin, Tokyo.

Mizutani, F. (1994), *Japanese Urban Railways*, Aldershot: Avebury, p.21.

Monheim R (1988), 'Pedestrian zones in West Germany—the dynamic development of an effective instrument to enliven the city centre', in C. Hass-Klau (ed.), *New Life for City Centres*, Anglo-German Foundation, London.

Montagnon, P. (1997), 'Total of Asia's "megacities" set to double', *Financial Times*, 21 April.

Moochtar, R. (1995), 'The evolving city', *Cities and the New Global Economy*, an international conference presented by the OECD and the Australian Government, vol. 2, pp. 624-28, AGPS, Canberra.

Mowery, D. and Rosenberg, N. (1989), *Technology and the Pursuit of Economic Growth*, Cambridge University Press, New York.

Mulgan, G. J. (1991), *Communication and Control: Networks and the New Economies of Communication*, Oxford: Polity Press.

Munnel, A.H. (ed.) (1990), *Is there a Shortfall in Public Capital Investment*, Federal Reserve Bank of Boston.

Murata, K., Takeuchi, A. (1987), 'The regional division of labour: machinery manufacturing, microelectronics and R&D in Japan', in F.E.I. Hamilton (ed.), *Industrial Change in Advanced Economies*, 213-39, Croom Helm, London.

Mussey, D.S. and Denton, N.A. (1993), *American Apartheid: Segregation and the Making of the Underclass*, Harvard University Press, Cambridge.

Nadiri, M.I. (1970), 'International studies of factor inputs and total factor productivity: a brief survey', *Review of Income and Wealth* 18:129-48.

Naess, P. (1993), 'Energy use for transport in 22 Nordic towns', *NIBR Report No 2*, Norwegian Institute for Urban and Regional Research, Oslo.

Naisbett, J. (1994), *Global Paradox—the Bigger the World Economy, the More Powerful its Smaller Players*, Allen and Unwin, Sydney.

Naldcenovic, N. (1991), 'Diffusion of pervasive systems: a case of transport infrastructures', *Technological Forecasting and Social Change*, 39:181-200.

Neff, J.W. (1996), *Substitution Rates Between Transit and Automobile Travel*, Paper presented at the Association of American Geographers' Annual Meeting, Charlotte, NC, April (13pp.).

Neilson, L. (1995), 'Partnerships in Australian urban management', Address to the conference on 'Planning Victoria', Bendigo, 12 October.

Newman, P.W.G. (1995), 'Consolidation : mistake?', *People and Place*, vol. 3, no. 3: 45-7

Newman, P.W.G. and Hogan, T.L.F. (1981), 'A review of urban density models: Towards a resolution of the conflict between populace and planner', *Human Ecology*, 9(3), 269-303.

Newman, P.W.G. and Kenworthy, J.R. (1989), *Cities and Automobile Dependence, A Sourcebook*, Gower, Hampshire, Technical, pp.48-9.

Newman, P.W.G. and Kenworthy, J.R. (1998), *Sustainability and Global Cities: Overcoming Automobile Dependence*, Island Press (in press).

Newman, P.W.G., Kenworthy, J.R. and Robinson, L. (1992), *Housing, Transport and Urban Form*, Background Paper 15, National Housing Strategy, Canberra.

Newman, P.W.G., Birrell, B., Holmes, D., Mathers, C., Newton, P.W., Oakley, G., O'Connor, A., Walker, B. and Soessa, A. (1996), 'Human settlements', chapter in *Australia State of the Environment*, Department of Environment, Sport and Territories, Canberra.

Newman, P.W.G., Kenworthy, J.R. and Vintila, P. (1995), 'Can we overcome automobile dependence?: physical planning in an age of urban cynicism', *Cities*, 12 (1): 53-65.

Newman, P.W.G. and Thornley, A. (1997), 'Fragmentation and centralization in the governance of London: influencing urban policy and planning agenda', *Urban Studies,* vol. 34, No. 7, pp. 967-88.

Newton P.W. (1995), 'Changing places? households, firms and urban hierarchies in the information age', in J.F. Brotchie, P.W. Newton, P. Hall, E. Blakeley, and M. Batty (eds), *Cities in Competition*, Longmans, Melbourne.

Newton, P.W. (ed.) (1997a), *Re-Shaping Cities for a More Sustainable Future*, Research Monograph 6, Australian Housing and Urban Research Institute, Melbourne.

Newton, P.W. (1997b), *Working from Home: Trends and Prospects*, AHURI, Melbourne.

Newton, P.W., Brotchie, J. F. and Gipps, P.G. (1996), 'Cities in transition: changing economic and technological processes and Australia's settlement system', Australia: State of the Environment, Technical Paper Series (Human Settlements), Environment Australia, Canberra.

Nijkamp, P., Rienstra, S. and Vleugel, J. (1995), *Long-Run Scenarios for Surface Transport*, Department of Regional Economics, Free University, Amsterdam.

Nijkamp, P., Baggen, J. and van der Knaap, B. (1996), 'Spatial sustainability and the tyranny of transport: a causal path scenario analysis', Papers in *Regional Science*, vol. 35, No. 3, pp. 13-25.

Nurske, R. (1953), *Problems of Capital Formation in Underdeveloped Countries*, Basil Blackwell.

O'Connor, K., Darby. A. and Rapson, V. (1995), 'The great mistakes consolidation policies in Melbourne and Sweden', *People and Place*, 3(3):40-5.

OECD (1993), *Partnerships: The Key to Job Creation: Experiences from OECD Countries*, Organisation for Economic Cooperation and Development, Paris.

OECD and Australian Government (1995), *Cities and the New Global Economy*, three vols., Proceedings of 1994 Conference, AGPS, Canberra.

Office of Science and Technology Policy, Executive Office of the President (1993), *Second Biennial Report: National Critical Technologies Panel*, Office of Science and Technology Policy, Washington, DC.

Ogawa, N., Jones, G.W. and Williamson, J.G. (1993), *Human Resources in Development Along the Western Pacific Rim*, Oxford University Press, Singapore and New York.

Ohmae, K. (1990), *The Borderless World*, Harper, New York.

Ohmae, K. (1990), *The End of the Nation State: The Rise of Regional Economics*, McKinsey and Company, New York.

Ohmae, K. (1993), 'The rise of the region state', *US Journal of Foreign Affairs*, Spring, pp.78-87.

Olds, K. (1995), 'Globalization and the production of new urban spaces: Pacific Rim megaprojects in the late 20th century', *Environment and Planning, A*, 27, 1713-43.

Orchard, L.(1992), 'Urban policy', in A. Parkin, and A. Patience (eds) (1992), *The Bannon Decade: The Politics of Restraint in South Australia*, Allen and Unwin, St. Leonards, NSW.

Orchard, L. (1995), 'National urban policy in the 1990s', in P. Troy (ed.), *Australian Cities*, Cambridge University Press

Park, S.O. (1995), 'Networks and competitive advantages of new industrial districts', *14th Pacific Regional Science Organisation Conference*, Taipei, pp. 39.

Parker, J. (1995), 'Turn up the lights: a survey of cities', *The Economist, Special Supplement*, 29 July.

Parkin, A. and Patience, A. (eds) (1992), *The Bannon Decade: The Politics of Restraint in South Australia*, Allen and Unwin, St.Leonards, NSW.

Parkinson, M. (1995), 'European cities towards 2000: economic and social challenges', *Cities and the New Global Economy*, an international conference presented by the OECD and the Australian Government, vol. 2, pp. 682-7, AGPS, Canberra.

Pederson, E.O. (1980), *Transportation in Cities*, Pergamon, New York.

Piore, M.J. (1979), *Birds of Passage: Migrant Labour and Industrial Societies*, Cambridge University Press, Cambridge.

Population Reference Bureau (1997), *1997 World Population Data Sheet*, Population Reference Bureau, Washington.

Porter, M. (1990), *The Competitive Advantage of Nations*, Free Press, New York.

Porter, M. and van der Linde, C. (1996), 'Green and competitive: ending the stalemate', in R. Welford and R. Starkey (eds), *Business and the Environment*, Earthscan Publications Ltd., London.

Poungsomlee, A. (1995), 'Environmental impacts on Bangkok's ecosystem', *Cities and the New Global Economy*, an international conference presented by the OECD and the Australian Government, vol. 3, pp. 709-21, AGPS, Canberra.

Powell, R., 1988, *Innovative Architecture of Singapore*, Select Books, Singapore.

Powell, R., 1993, *The Asian House: Contemporary Houses of Southeast Asia*, Select Books, Singapore.

Pressman, N. (1985), 'Forces for spatial change', in J.F. Brotchie, P. Hall, P. Nijkamp and P.W. Newton (eds), *The Future of Urban Form*, Croom Helm, London.

Prud'homme, R. (1995), 'On the economic role of cities', in *Cities and the New Global Economy: an international conference presented by the OECD and the Australian Government*, Vol.3, pp.728-24, AGPS, Canberra.

QUARG (1992), *Diesel Vehicle Emissions and Urban Air Quality*, Second Report of the Quality of Urban Air Review Group, University of Birmingham, UK. See also: http://sun1.bham.ac.uk/deacona/abstract.htm.

Radbone, I. (1992), 'Public-sector management', in A. Parkin and A. Patience (eds), *The Bannon Decade: The Politics of Restraint in South Australia*, Allen and Unwin, St.Leonards, NSW).

Rais, Tb. M. (1996), 'Development strategies of DKI Jakarta: towards an environmentally sustainable greater Jabotabek', Paper presented at the Seminar Strategies for a Sustainable Greater Jabotabek, Bappenas—Dep. PU—The World Bank, Jakarta, July 8-10.

Real Estate Research Corporation (1974), *The Cost of Sprawl*, CEQ. HUD. EPA.

REIA (1997), *Housing Prices in Australian Cities*, REIA, Melbourne.

Reich, R. (1991), *The Work of Nations. Report of the Governor's Ad Hoc Committee on High Technology*, The State of Maryland, 1982.

Reich, R. (1993), *The Work of Nations,* Simon and Schuster, New York.

Richardson, H.W. (1989), 'Urban development issues in the Pacific Rim', *Conference on Urban Development of the Pacific Rim*, Los Angeles, 7 August.

Rietveld, P. (1990), 'Infrastructure and regional development: a survey of multiregional economic models', *The Annals of Regional Science* 23:255.

Rimmer, P.J. (1986), *Rikisha to Rapid Transit: Urban Public Transport Systems and Policy in Southeast Asia*, Pergamon Press, Sydney.

Rimmer, P. (1989), 'The emerging infrastructure arena in the Pacific Rim in the early 1990s', invited paper, proceedings of the Japan Society of Engineers, *Infrastructure Planning and Management*, 13 July, No. 432(iv-15), pp. 1-17.

Rimmer, P.J. (1991), 'Exporting cities to the Western Pacific Rim: the art of the Japanese package', in J.F. Brotchie, M. Batty, P. Hall and P.W. Newton, (eds), *Cities of the 21st Century: New Technologies and Spatial Systems*, 243-61, Longman Cheshire, Melbourne.

Roach, S.S. (1988), 'Technology and the service sector: the hidden competitive challenge', *Technological Forecasting and Social Change* 34:387-404.

Roberts, J. (1989), *User Friendly Cities*, TEST, London.

Roberts, B.H. (1996), 'Cities as the engines of economic growth in the Asia Pacific region', address to the United Nations Economic and Social Committee for Asian and the Pacific Regional Forum Conference, Bangkok.

Roberts, B.H. (1997), 'Inventing a future for regions: new frameworks for regional economic development planning', *Western Regional Science Association Annual Conference*, Hawaii, 23-27 February.

Robison, R. and Goodman, D.S.G. (1996), *The New Rich in Asia: Mobile Phones, McDonalds and Middle-Class Revolution*, Routledge, London.

Rosebury, N. (1994), *Exploring the Black Box: Technology, Economics and History*, Cambridge Press, Cambridge.

Ruble, B.A., Blair, A., Tulchin, J.S. and Garland, A.M. (1996), 'Introduction: globalism and local realities—five paths to the urban future', in A. Michael and Cohen *et al.* (eds), *Preparing for the Urban Future: Global Processes and Local Forces,* TheWoodrow Wilson Center Press, Washington, DC, pp. 1-22.

Sachs, J. and Warner, A.M. (1996), 'Why competitiveness counts', *The Global Competitiveness Report 1996*, World Economic Forum, Geneva.

Sack, R.D. (1986), *Human Territoriality: Its Theories and History. Cambridge Studies in Human Geography*, Cambridge, Cambridge University Press, London, New York, New Rochelle and Sydney.

Salomon, I. (1985), 'Telecommunications and travel: substitution or modified mobility', *Journal of Transport Economics and Policy* 19:219-35.

Samuels, R. and Prasad, D.K. (1994), *Global Warming and the Built Environment*, E & FN Spon, London.

Sassen, S. (1991), *The Global City: New York, London, Tokyo*, Princeton University Press, Princeton, NJ.

Sassen, S, (1994), *Cities and the World Economy*, Pineforge Press, Thousand Oaks, Ca.

Sassen, S. (1995), 'Urban impacts on economic globalisation', in J.F. Brotchie, M. Batty, E. Blakely, P. Hall and P.W. Newton (eds), *Cities in Competition*, Longman, Melbourne.

Scott, G. McL. (1992), 'Economic policy', in A. Parkin, and A. Patience (eds), *The Bannon Decade: The Politics of Restraint in South Australia*, Allen and Unwin, St.Leonards, NSW).

Sheridan, K. (ed.) (1986), *The State as Developer: Public Enterprise in South Australia*, Royal Australian Institute of Public Administration, Wakefield Press.

Sheridan, K. (1986), Economic and social development—industrialisation with consensus', in K. Sheridan (ed.), *The State as Developer: Public Enterprise in South Australia*, Royal Australian Institute of Public Administration Wakefield Press.

Sheridan, N.R., MacPherson, R.K., Juler, P.A. and Weiss, E.G.A. (1963), *Air Conditioning: A Guide for Architects, Engineers and Prospective Purchasers*, University of Queensland Press.

Short, J., Kim, Y., Kuus, M. and Wells, H. (1996), 'The dirty little secret of world cities research: data problems in comparative analysis', *International Journal of Urban and Regional Research*, 20, 697-717.

SIAJ (1984), 'Towards a better city', *Singapore Institute of Architects Journal*, May/June: 3-17.

Silicon Valley Joint Venture Network (SVJVN) (1995), *The Joint Venture Way: Lessons for Regional Rejuvenation*, Joint Venture Silicon Valley Network.

Silicon Valley Joint Venture Network (SVJVN (1996), *Joint Venture's Index of Silicon Valley*, Joint Venture Silicon Valey Network, Palo Alto.

Si-Ming, L., Yat-Ming, S. (1994), 'Population mobility', in Y.M. Yeung, D.K.Y. Chu (eds), *Guangdong: Survey of a Province Undergoing Rapid Change*, 373-400, The Chinese University Press, Hong Kong.

Sit, V.F.S. and Yang, C. (1997), 'Foreign-investment-induced exo-urbanisation in the Pearl River Delta, China', *Urban Studies*, 34, 647-77.

Smilor, R.W. and Wakelin, M. (1990), 'Smart infrastructure and economic development: the role of technology and global networks', in G. Kozmetsky and R.W. Smilor (eds), *The Technolopolis Phenomenon*, The IC Institute, University of Texas, Austin, pp. 53-75, May.

Snickars, F. (1987), 'The transportation sector in the communications society: some analytical observations', in P. Nijkamp and S. Reichmann (eds), *Transportation Planning in a Changing World*, Gower, Aldershot, UK.

Snickars, F, (1990), 'Transport, communications and long-term environmental sustainability: a futures study of the Swedish transport and communications sector', Working Paper, Department of Infrastructure and Planning, Royal Institute of Technology, Stockholm.

Snickars, F. (1992), *Two Scenarios of Transports and the Environment in Sweden 2010*, Swedish Board for Housing and Physical Planning, Karlskrona.

Snickars, F. (1995), *Mobility Sustained*, Department of Applied Geography and Planning, University of Utrecht, Utrecht.

So, A.Y., Kwok, R.Y.-W. (1995), 'Socioeconomic center, political periphery: Hong Kong's uncertain transition toward the twenty-first century', in R.Y.-W., Kwok, A.Y. So (eds), *The Hong Kong-Guangdong Link: Partnership in Flux*, 251-7, M.E. Sharpe, London.

SOE (1996), '*Australia State of the Environment 1996*', State of the Environment Advisory Council, CSIRO Publishing, Collingwood, Australia.

Soegijoko, Budhy Tjahjati S. (1994), 'Operationalization of Indonesia's national urbanization strategy', Country paper Indonesia, Bandung, September 26-9.

Soegijko, Budhyi Tjahjati (1995), 'Evolution of urban spatial form in Jabotabek region: characteristics and its police—implications for regional development planning', Paper presented at the Seminar on Global City Regions: Their Solution and Management, Massachusetts, September 17-9.

Soegijoko, Budhy Tjahjati, S. (1997), 'Jabotabek as part of Asia Pacific intercity networks', Paper presented at Workshop on Intercity Networks in the Asia Pacific Region, Melbourne, April.

Soegijoko, Budhy Tjahjati S. and Ida Ayu Indira Dharmapatni (1994), 'Urban governance and poverty alleviation in Indonesia: a preliminary assessment', Paper presented to *Global Urban Research Initiative* in Developing World, Sub-Regional Workshop on Urban Governance and Poverty Alleviation in Southeast Asia, Manila, November 14-5.

Soedjito, B.B. and Imron Bulkin (1996), 'Country study of the national urban development policy framework in Indonesia; megacity management', vol. 2.

South Australian Government (1990), 'Adelaide. a submission to the MFP joint secretariat', May, SA Government Printer, Adelaide.

South Australian Planning Review (1992), '2020 vision: final report—a planning system', SA Government Printer, Adelaide.

Spiekermann, K. and Wegener, M. (1994), 'New space-time maps of Europe', Working Paper 132, Institute for Spatial Planning, University of Dortmund.

Stanbeck, T.M. Jr., Bearse, P.J., Noyelle, T.J. and Karasek, R.A. (1981), *Services: The New Economy*, Allanheld, Osmun, Totowa, NJ.

Standing Advisory Committee on Trunk Road Assessment (SACTRA) (1994), *Trunk Roads and the Generation of Traffic*, HMSO, London, 242pp.

Sternburg, E. (1991), 'The sectoral clusters in economic development policy: lessons from Rochester and Buffalo, New York', *Economic Development Quarterly*, vol. 4, pp. 342-56.

Stimson, R.J. (1995a), 'Processes of globalisation, economic restructuring and the emergence of a new space economy of cities and regions in Australia', in J.F. Brotchie, M. Batty, E. Blakely, P. Hall and P.W. Newton, *Cities in Competition: Productive and Sustainable Cities for the 21st Century*, Longman Australia.

Stimson, R.J. (1995b), 'Diverse multi-centered regions the future', *Urban Net*, 2 (2): 1-3.

Stimson, R.J. (1995c), 'Pacific Rim cities: trends and issues for the 21st century', *INTA19: Strategies for Cities of the 21st Century Conference*, Vienna, September.

Stimson, R.J. (1996), 'The challenges of urban development for Pacific Rim cities', *Pacific Rim Real Estate Society Conference*, Gold Coast, January.

Stimson, R.J. (1997), 'Mega-metro regions in the Pacific Rim', *Lusk Review for Real Estate Development and Urban Transformation*, vol. iii, No. 1, pp. 82-96.

Stoeckel, A, and Quirke, D, (1992), *Services: Setting the Agenda for Reform*, Centre for International Economics, Canberra.

Stoecker, W.F and Jones, J.W. (1986), *Refrigeration and Air Conditioning*, 2nd. edition, McGraw-Hill Book Company, New York.

Stoneman, P. (1983), *The Economic Analysis of Technological Change*, Oxford University Press, Oxford.

Storper, M. (1991), *Technology Districts and International Trade: The Limits to Globalisation in an Age of Flexible Production*, mimeo, School of Planning, University of California, Los Angeles.

Stough, R.R., Popina, J. and Campell, H.S. (1995), *Technology in the Greater Washington Region*, Institute for Public Policy, Centre for Regional Analysis, George Mason University, Fairfax, Virginia.

Strange, S. (1988), *States and Markets*, Frances Pinter, London.

Strange, S. (1991), 'An eclectic approach', in C.N. Murphy and R. Tooze (eds), *The New International Political Economy*, Reinner, Boulder, Colorado.

Strassmann, P.W. (I 970), 'The construction sector in the economic development', *Scottish Jr. of PE* 17 (3).

Stubbs, J. and Clarke, G. (eds) (1996), 'Megacity management in the Asian and Pacific region: policy issues and innovative approaches', vol. 1, *Proceedings of the Regional Seminar on Megacities Management in Asia and the Pacific*, Asian Development Bank and United Nations/World Bank Urban Development Programme for Asia and the Pacific, Manila, Philippines, 24-30 October (1995).

Suarez-Villa, L. and Hasnath, S.A. (1993), 'The effects of infrastructure on invention: innovative capacity and the dynamics of public construction investments', *Technological Forecasting and Social Change* 44:333-58.

Sudjic, D. (1995), 'Megalopolis now', *The Guardian Weekend*, 24 June, 27-35.

Takanashi, M., Hyodo, T. (1963), 'Kogyo (industry)', in: K. Okochi (ed.), *Keihin Kogyo Chitai no Sangyo Kozo (Industrial Structure of Keihin Industrial Belt)*, 49-116, Tokyo University Press, Tokyo.

Tan, T.H. (1994), *Tropical Architecture and Interiors: Tradition-Based Design of Indonesia, Malaysia, Singapore, Thailand*, Page One Publishing Pty Ltd., Singapore.

Taniguchi, M. and Araki, S. (1996), 'Regional competition on cognition and their affecting factors', *Infrastructure Planning Review*, vol. 13.

Taniguchi, M. and Hori, K. (1996), 'The gap between urban growth and infrastructure improvement: indices and their application', *Journal of Infrastructure planning and Management*, No. 542.

Tarr, J.A. (1984), 'The evolution of the urban infrastructure in the nineteenth and twentieth centuries', in R. Hanson (ed.), *Perspectives on Urban Infrastructure*, National Academy Press, Washington, DC.

Tatsuno, S.M. (1992), 'The multimedia city of the future', in D.V. Gibson, G. Kozmetsky and R.W. Smilor (eds), *The Technopolis Phenomenon*, Rowman and Littlefield Publishers, Lanham, pp. 197-207.

Tettoni, L.I., Warren, W. and Liu, G. (1989), *Living in Thailand: Traditional and Modern Homes and Decorations*, Thames and Hudson, London.

Thant, Myo, Tang, M. and Kakazu, H. (eds) (1994), *Growth Triangles in Asia: A New Approach to Regional Economic Cooperation*, Oxford University Press, Hong Kong.

The City Planning Institute of Japan (1992), *Tokyo Metropolitan Area* (Tokyo Daitoshi ken), Shokokusha, Tokyo, p. 117.

The Housing and Urban Development Corporation (1989), *Tsukuba Science City*, Housing and Urban Development Corporation, Tokyo.

Thurow, L. (1992), *Head to Head*, Allan and Unwin, Sydney.

Togo, H. (1991), Shaping Tokyo for the future, *Work in Progress, United Nations University, 13/3*, 7.

Troy, P.(ed.) (1995), *Australian Cities*, Cambridge University Press.

Troy, P.N. (1996), *The Perils of Urban Consolidation*, the Federation Press, Sydney.

Truman, E.M. (1996), 'The Mexican peso crisis: implications for international finance', *Federal Reserve Bulletin* March, pp. 199-207.

UN (1995a), *World Urbanization Prospects: The 1994 Revision*, United Nations, New York.

UN (1995b), The Challenge of Urbanization: The World's Largest Cities, United Nations, New York.

UNCHS (1996), *An Urbanizing World: Global Report on Human Settlements 1996*, Oxford University Press.

UNEP/WHO (1992), 'Urban Air Pollution in Megacities of the World', Earthwatch. Global Environment Monitoring System, World Health Organization and United Nations Environment Programme, Blackwell.

United Nations, Department for Economic and Social Information and Policy Analysis (1993), *World Population Prospects,* United Nations Press, New York.

United Nations (1996), *An Urbanising World: UN Global Review of Human Settlements,* UNEP, Habitat, Nairobi.

United Nations Secretariat (1997a), *World Urbanization Prospects: The 1996 Revision—Annex Tables,* UN, New York

United Nations Secretariat (1997b), *World Urbanization Prospects: The 1996 Revision,* UN, New York

United Nations, Economic and Social Commission for Asia and the Pacific (UN ESCAP) (1993), *State of Urbanization in Asia and the Pacific 1993,* United Nations, New York.

UT (1997), 'Business looking up', United Technologies (part of the Otis Group) (http://www.com/ARCHIVE/op41896.html).

Victoria's Capital City Policy (1994), *Creating Prosperity: Victoria's Capital City Policy,* Government of Victoria and Melbourne City Council.

Vining, D.R. (1986) 'Population redistribution: towards core areas of less developed countries 1950-1980, *International Regional Science Review,* vol. 10, pp. 1-45.

Virginia Department of Transportation (1989), *Northern Virginia 2010 Transportation Plan,* January, (prepared by VDOT Policy Committee, Technical Committee, and Citizens Advisory Committee).

Waits, M. (1995), *Economic Development: Building and Economic Future,* State Government News, Arizona, vol. 38.

Webber, M. (1963), 'Order in diversity: community without propinquity', in L. Wingo (ed.), *Cities and Space: the Future Use of Urban Land,* John Hopkins Press, Baltimore.

Webber, M. (1964), 'The urban place and the non-place urban realm', in *Explorations in Urban Structures,* University of Pennsylvania Press, Philadelphia.

Webber, M. (1968), 'The post city age', *Daedulu ,* 97 (4): 1093-99.

Wegener, M (1995), 'Reduction of CO_2 emissions of transport by re-organization of urban activities', in Y. Hayashi and J.R. Roy (eds), *Transport, Land-Use and the Environment,* Kluwer, Dordrecht.

Williams, P. (1985), *The Country and the City,* Hogarth Press, London.

Willoughby, K. (1994), 'The "local milieux" of knowledge based industries', in J.F. Brotchie, M. Batty, E. Blakely, P. Hall, and P.W. Newton (eds), *Cities in Competition,* Longmans, Melbourne.

Winger, A.R. (1997), 'Finally: a withering away of cities?', *Futures,* 29 (3): 251-6.

Woo, E.S.W. (1994), 'Urban development', in Y.M. Yeung, D.K.Y. Chu (eds), *Guangdong: Survey of a Province Undergoing Rapid Change*, 327-54, The Chinese University Press, Hong Kong.

World Bank (1992), *Governance and Development*, World Bank, Washington.

World Bank (1993), *The East Asia Miracle: Economic Growth and Public Policy*, Oxford University Press, Oxford.

World Bank (1994), *Governance: Development and Practice*, World Bank, Washington.

World Bank (1996), 'R&D for sustainable development—controlling pollution and strengthening institutions', A presentation by Economics of Industrial Pollution Control Research Team, World Bank, New York. See: http://www.worldbank.org/nipr/wolfpres/no_frame/sld009.htm

World Bank (1997), *World Development Report 1997*, Oxford University Press, New York.

Xu, X.-Q., Kwok, R.Y.-W., Li, L., Yan, X. (1995), 'Production change in Guangdong', in: R.Y.-W. Kwok and A.Y. So (eds), *The Hong Kong-Guangdong Link: Partnership in Flux*, 135-162, M.E. Sharpe, London.

Xu, X.-Q., Li, S.-M. (1990), 'China open door policy and urbanization in the Pearl River Delta region', *International Journal of Urban and Regional Research*, *14*, 49-69.

Yeang, K. (1987), *Tropical Urban Regionalism: Building in a South-east Asian City*, Concept Media Pty Ltd., Singapore.

Yeang, K. (1992), *The Architecture of Malaysia*, Pepin Press, Amsterdam and Kuala Lumpur.

Yeung, Y.M. (1990), *Changing Cities of Pacific Asia: A Scholarly Interpretation*, Chinese University Press, Hong Kong.

Yeung, Y.M. (1994), 'Introduction', in Y.M. Yeung and D.K.Y. Chu (eds), *Guangdong: Survey of a Province Undergoing Rapid Change*, 1-17, The Chinese University Press, Hong Kong.

Yeung, Y.M. (1996), 'An Asian perspective on the global city', *International Social Science Journal*, 147, 25-31.

Youngson, A.J. (1967), *Overhead Capital*, Edinburgh University Press, Edinburgh.

Zahavi, Y. and Ryan, J.M. (1980), 'Stability of travel components over time', *Transportation Research Record*, 750:19-26.

Zhu, J. (1994), 'Changing land policy and its impact on local growth—the experience of the Shenzhen special economic zone, China, in the 1980s', *Urban Studies*, 31, 1611-23.

Zhu, J. (1996a), 'Denationalization of urban physical development: the experiment in the Shenzhen special economic zone, China', *Cities*, 13, 187-94.

Zhu, J.M. (1996b), 'Response: Shenzhen's role and denationalization in China', *Cities*, 13, 199-201.

Index